# Data Models

# Data Models

Dionysios C. Tsichritzis

Frederick H. Lochovsky

*Department of Computer Science*
*University of Toronto*
*Toronto, Canada*

*Prentice-Hall, Inc.*
*Englewood Cliffs, New Jersey 07632*

*Library of Congress Cataloging in Publication Data*

TSICHRITZIS, DIONYSIOS C.
    Data models.

    (Prentice-Hall software series)
    Bibliography: p. 343
    Includes index.
    1. Data base management.  2. Data structures (Computer
science)  I. Lochovsky, Frederick H.  II. Title.
III. Series.
QA76.9.D3T75        001.64'2        81-8611
ISBN  0-13-196428-3            AACR2

Prentice-Hall Software Series
  Brian W. Kernighan, advisor

This book was typeset by the authors, using a Graphic Systems phototypesetter driven by a PDP-11/70 running under the UNIX operating system.

UNIX is a Trademark of Bell Laboratories.

Editorial production/supervision
  by **Aliza Greenblatt**

Cover design
  by **George Alon Jaediker**

Manufacturing buyer
  **Gordon Osbourne**

Printed in the United States of America

10  9  8  7  6  5  4  3  2  1

PRENTICE-HALL INTERNATIONAL, INC., *London*
PRENTICE-HALL OF AUSTRALIA PTY. LIMITED, *Sydney*
PRENTICE-HALL OF CANADA, LTD., *Toronto*
PRENTICE-HALL OF INDIA PRIVATE LIMITED, *New Delhi*
PRENTICE-HALL OF JAPAN, INC., *Tokyo*
PRENTICE-HALL OF SOUTHEAST ASIA PTE. LTD., *Singapore*
WHITEHALL BOOKS LIMITED, *Wellington, New Zealand*

# CONTENTS

## PART 3   DATA MODELS II

# PART 4   USING DATA MODELS

# PREFACE

The pursuit of knowledge is part of human nature. We always try to achieve some understanding of ourselves and our environment. Scientific endeavor has to do with acquiring some form of knowledge. A person may perceive or observe a phenomenon. As a result he or she acquires an incremental piece of knowledge. The increments of knowledge we will call *information* [Langefors, 1977]. The information may be valuable and may have to be recorded for purposes of communication to other people. The proper representation and communication of the information will benefit other people and will increase our collective knowledge. The representation of information is, therefore, a very important problem.

The representation of information is accomplished primarily by the use of natural language. People write papers, reports, books, etc. to communicate their ideas. Natural language, however, is not always the best tool for representing information. First, it is a general and all-encompassing tool. In certain cases, a specialized tool may be more appropriate. The use of scientific notation points to the fact that people have perceived the need for other specialized models for representing information. These models may be widely different and more appropriate for their use than natural language (e.g., maps for geographical information). Second, natural language evolved for free-style communication between human beings. As such, it did not have to be and is not a precise means for recording and transmitting information. Finally, natural language has properties that make it notoriously difficult to manipulate through computer operations.

In addition to solving complex computational problems, computers also are used to aid human intelligence by providing a tool for handling and manipulating information. This will probably continue to be the most important use of computers in the future. To utilize computers effectively for this purpose, we need to explore good ways of representing information in a manner that is amenable to computerization. As already pointed out, natural language may not be the appropriate vehicle for this role. Data models, as presented in this book, have been devised for computer-oriented representation of information. They are powerful conceptual tools for the organization and representation of information. In addition, they are translatable into structures that can be manipulated by computers. Data models provide a means for the representation and manipulation of information in a way that is amenable to computerization.

If we expect data models to fulfill such an illustrious role it is imperative that they be flexible and well understood. They should be flexible to achieve the different goals and satisfy the different tastes of their users. They should be well understood so that their properties can be rigorously defined. A general framework of data models is needed which encompasses all the different data models that have been proposed. Such a framework does not necessarily point to or propose a supermodel. It should, however, clearly identify the concepts and properties of and the similarities and differences between data models. This book is an attempt at developing such a framework, or at least recording what we know up to now in this rapidly developing area. We hope that the ideas presented will help people to organize data conceptually and to draw upon and use to advantage the information the data represent.

Social changes have created large and complex political and economic structures (e.g., large government agencies, multinational corporations, and chains of retail stores). These enterprises need to integrate the use of their data for planning and control. Data base management systems are an appropriate tool for this integration. The main issue is the effective use of the data rather than the particular system that is used for their storage. For data base technology to be introduced and used effectively, there is a need for understanding and visualizing the data and the information they represent. Data models help in achieving some understanding of the data and information needs of an organization and by extension the way in which an organization functions. They can also be used to describe any insights for both communication purposes and later use. It seems, therefore, that data modeling is an important activity for information integration regardless of the use of a data base management system. Data modeling is needed even if we use file systems.

There is a widespread misconception that data bases and data base management systems correspond to a shallow area dealing mainly with the storage and retrieval of data. Although we acknowledge that the area started out dealing with pragmatic problems, it is increasingly becoming involved with ideas that deal with the structure, organization, and effective use of data and the information they represent. This book does not deal with implementation of data models or with any properties of access paths or other access-oriented considerations. Some data models may have originated as a natural abstraction of working data base management systems. We discuss them conceptually, however, and treat only their logical properties. This is the conceptual and abstract part of data bases as opposed to the engineering part of their implementation. The richness of the logical properties should persuade readers that the area is very important, not merely fashionable.

The book is divided into four parts. The first part, consisting of the first four chapters, outlines the basic concepts used by all data models. In Chapter 1 we discuss abstractly the meaning of data and their role in an organization. The role of a data model is outlined as a conceptual tool to visualize and structure data. Data models are discussed in terms of three distinct parts: structures, constraints, and operations. Chapter 2 outlines a general framework for structuring data. Chapter 3 discusses constraints on data which provide additional semantics on the data structure. Finally, Chapter 4 discusses operations on data and relates data models to abstract data types.

The second part of the book describes the three most widely known data models in terms of the data modeling framework developed in Part 1: structures, constraints, and operations. Chapter 5 discusses relational data models, Chapter 6 network data models, and Chapter 7 hierarchical data models.

The third part of the book outlines four additional data models which, in our opinion, represent different approaches to data modeling. The order of presentation of these four data models corresponds approximately to their complexity. We start with simpler, more concrete data models and proceed to more abstract, complex, and semantically powerful data models. Entity-relationship data models are discussed in Chapter 8 as an example of simple data models which facilitates communication among users and data base designers. Binary data models are discussed in Chapter 9 as an example of data models starting out with a simple graph structure and introducing powerful operations to make them capable of modeling complex situations. Chapter 10 outlines semantic network data models as a modeling approach with a rich semantic component that can be used to move from data bases to knowledge base systems. Finally, Chapter 11 discusses infological data models which try to view information requirements in a manner most natural for people before they are mapped into data base requirements. There are many other worthwhile data models in the literature. We chose these four types not as the "best," but as representative of different approaches to data modeling. Lack of space prevents us from elaborating on other proposed models.

The last part of the book deals with the use of data models for data base design and operation. In Chapter 12 we outline the steps taken in schema design. The emphasis is mainly on capturing the application requirements in an accurate schema. Chapter 13 discusses data base theory which attempts to formalize the notion of a "good" schema. In this way a schema can be analyzed and a "better" schema can be produced. Chapter 14 concludes the book by outlining the correspondences between data models. This discussion includes schema mappings, operation mappings, and data base translation. These problems are very important to an understanding of the similarities and differences between data models. They are also relevant to important pragmatic considerations such as data base translation and data base cooperation.

This book was heavily influenced by the research conducted in the data base group at the University of Toronto over the last six years [Bernstein, 1975; Brodie, 1978; Klug, 1978; Lochovsky, 1978; Vassiliou, 1980a]. We have obviously benefited from many outside sources and had highly stimulating discussions with colleagues from many research groups. However, we have also developed our own philosophy about what data base management is and what the important problems are. In this book we try to look at data models from this perspective.

The area of data base management has attracted many researchers and ideas from widely different parts of computer science and management studies. For example, many ideas as presented in this book are drawn from other areas of computer science (e.g., artificial intelligence, operating systems, and programming languages). We hope that this intrusion into other areas and the borrowing of ideas will continue. It is not critical whether an idea started out in a different area. It is important only that it becomes useful and important in a data base context. We hope that the data base area will continue to be outward looking and serve as an umbrella for widely different ideas and people. Computer science drew from mathematics and electrical engineering. Data base management draws from computer science and management studies. Since the application of computers for management functions is one of their most important uses, we expect data base management to continue to be a focal point of much activity in the future.

The field of data base management has both practitioners who desperately need solutions and academics who would like to work on relevant problems. This book is addressed to both these widely different kinds of readers. People with practical knowledge in DBMSs may find it interesting to understand some of the more esoteric ideas of the subject. They may get some insights which may translate to useful practical techniques. In addition, they will be able to see how all the ideas in different systems fit together in a uniform conceptual framework. People with more theoretical backgrounds and little practical experience in DBMSs may also find this book useful. They hopefully will understand the different data base ideas abstractly without being hindered by all the ad hoc terminology of existing systems. Throughout the book there are many exercises, some of which can be used as a springboard for further research.

We hope that this book will provide a good framework and many ideas for research directions. Many people are becoming interested in data base problems. Their ideas are needed in the area of data models. In this way a theory can be developed. Such a theory is not only a theory of data bases. It should be the beginning of a theory of data, information, and knowledge as it can be operated on by computers. The problems associated with the development of this theory will be with us for some time even after we solve all the problems of fast data access through new hardware or software techniques.

# ACKNOWLEDGMENTS

This book could not have been written without the help, encouragement, and support of many people. Foremost among these are the members of the Data Base Group at the University of Toronto, both past and present, who by their ideas, comments, and discussions contributed greatly to the nature and content of this book. The reader will discover that the research of several former members of this group — P. A. Bernstein, M. L. Brodie, A. Klug, and Y. Vassiliou — forms the basis for several of the chapters.

We would like particularly to thank Prof. A. T. Borgida, Prof. M. L. Brodie, Prof. A. Klug, Prof. Y. Vassiliou, M. H. Graham, and L. Melli who provided us with both encouragement and many useful ideas and comments. Their criticisms and suggestions were invaluable in shaping the contents of this book.

We would like to thank I. S. Weber and R. M. Reid of the Computer Systems Research Group at the University of Toronto for typing parts of the initial draft of this book.

Facilities for preparing this book were provided by the Computer Systems Research Group and the Computing Center of the University of Toronto. Most of the research of the Data Base Group at the University of Toronto that is described in this book was funded by grants provided by the Natural Sciences and Engineering Research Council of Canada.

# *Part 1*

# BASIC CONCEPTS

For data to be useful in providing information, they need to be organized so that they can be processed effectively. Many different ways of organizing data exist, such as tables, lists, and forms. In data modeling we try to organize data so that they represent as closely as possible the real-world situation, yet are still amenable to representation by computers. These two requirements are often conflicting. To determine how best to organize data for a given application, we need to understand the characteristics of data that are important for capturing the essence of their meaning. These characteristics allow us to make general statements about how data are organized and processed. A consistent, formal set of such statements defines a data model. In Part 1 we examine those characteristics of data that comprise the definition of a data model. We also examine ways in which these characteristics can be represented so that they are amenable to computerization.

# Chapter 1

# DATA AND DATA MODELS

## 1.1 THE MEANING OF DATA

A perception of the world can be regarded as a series of distinct although sometimes related phenomena. From the dawn of time human beings have shown a natural inclination to try to describe these phenomena in some fashion whether they understand them completely or not. These descriptions of phenomena will be called *data*. Data correspond to discrete, recorded facts about phenomena from which we gain information about the world. *Information* is an increment of knowledge that can be inferred from data [Langefors, 1977].

The word "datum" comes from Latin and, literally interpreted, means a fact. Data, however, do not always correspond to concrete or actual facts. Sometimes, they are imprecise or they describe things that have never happened (e.g., an idea). For our purposes, data correspond to descriptions of any phenomenon or idea that a person considered worth formulating and recording. Data will be of interest to us if they are worth not only thinking about, but also worth recording in a somewhat precise manner.

Data are traditionally recorded using a particular communication method (e.g., pictures or language) on a particular (semi-)permanent recording medium (e.g., stone or paper). Examples of the human perpensity for recording data can be found throughout time: cave paintings of prehistoric man, ancient Greek on stone, and Egyptian on papyrus. Often, data are recorded on paper using a natural language. Usually, both the data (i.e., the facts) and their interpretation (i.e., their meaning) are recorded together, since natural languages are sufficiently flexible to do both. For example, the statement "His height is 173 cm" records both the datum "173" and its meaning "height in centimeters." In certain cases data are separated from their interpretation. For instance, an airline schedule is a table of data. Its interpretation is usually given separately at the beginning of the schedule and people are expected to know how to interpret it. However, separating data and their interpretation can lead to difficulty in using the data. Studies have shown that most people have difficulty interpreting an airline schedule. Without knowledge of its interpretation, the airline schedule is of limited use.

The use of computers for the encoding and processing of data has resulted in even more separation of the data from its interpretation. Computers deal mainly with raw data. Much of the interpretation of the data is not explicitly recorded. Consider, for instance, a numerical analysis program that solves partial differential equations. The package receives some numbers as input and produces some other numbers as output. It does not care whether the differential equation is an application in fluid mechanics or electromagnetism. The user of the package has to interpret the results in the context of the use being made of them.

There are at least two historical reasons for the separation of data and their interpretation in computers. First, computers are not very good at handling natural language, which is still the main way of encoding interpretations and meaning of data. Second, computer storage was initially rather expensive. Although there was enough storage for the actual data, their interpretation was traditionally left to the users and the manual systems outside the computer.

As the application of computers evolved, it became increasingly necessary to try to capture some of the interpretation of the data. For instance, an inventory control package interprets the data as parts and suppliers. An airline reservation package views the data as seats and flights. By interpreting the data to some extent, these systems can be useful to an inventory clerk or an airline clerk. There is no implication that the system has accurate and complete knowledge of the application. However, some understanding of the meaning of the data is present in the way that they are manipulated by the programs.

Suppose that the interpretation of data is encoded mainly in the programs that use the data. Thus, the programs are important since they interpret the world as it is portrayed by the data. The data are merely a collection of bits, on some storage device, which do not make sense unless they are first processed by a program. This approach is analogous to saying that the interpretation of the airline schedule is important, not the airline schedule itself.

In an environment where data can be shared and used by many different applications, such an approach can be followed only to a certain point. After a while, it becomes rather cumbersome to write different programs continually and provide them with similar, if not identical, interpretations of the data. At this point it is better to associate, partly, the interpretation of the data with the data themselves. In this way, the interpretation need be formulated only once instead of for each new application. This approach is analogous to the association of the explanation of an airline schedule as part of the schedule itself rather then with the use of the schedule. Thus, the schedule interpretation is not distributed repeatedly in a travel agent's manual, an airline clerk's manual, and a traveler's guide.

Following this reasoning, suppose that some of the interpretation of the data is encoded together with the data. The data now have a different role. They are no longer merely bits which, hopefully, mean something to an intelligent program. They correspond to semantically meaningful encodings of (a part of) the world. They form a *view* of the world. However, this view does not have to be exact and concrete. Indeed, it is usually rather abstract [Smith and Smith, 1977a; Lockemann et al., 1979].

Data generally are not static but correspond to a world that is evolving. Flexibility in data interpretation allows us to capture some of the evolutionary aspects of the world while still providing a fairly stable basis for the data. This flexibility can be provided in two ways. First, the system can allow the same data to be viewed in different ways. For example, different applications using the same data may want to impose their own strict and concrete interpretation. Thus, people can be viewed as employees for personnel applications, workers for manufacturing applications, and patients for medical applications. The interpretation associated with the data should be sufficiently abstract to allow all these different interpretations of the same data. Second, different data can be viewed in the same way. For instance, the interpretation should allow all managers, clerks, salespeople, and secretaries to be viewed as employees of an organization no matter what their position. The interpretation should be sufficiently abstract to allow different snapshots of the world to be viewed in a similar fashion. We discuss this notion of different abstractions of data in more detail later in the book.

## 1.2 DATA MODELING

It is apparent that an interpretation of the world is needed which is sufficiently abstract to allow minor perturbations, yet is sufficiently powerful to give some understanding concerning how data about the world are related [Rothnie and Hardgrave, 1976]. An intellectual tool that provides such an interpretation will be loosely referred to as a *data model*. It is a model about data by which a reasonable interpretation of the data can be obtained. A data model is an abstraction device that allows us to see the forest (information content of the data) as opposed to the trees (individual values of data).

Models are used extensively in many disciplines for enhancing understanding and abstracting detail [Edwards, 1967]. For instance, a mathematical model may use 5 and 3 to stand for 5 apples and 3 apples. By adding the abstract objects 5 and 3 to obtain 8, one gets the result of putting together 5 apples and 3 apples, or 5 oranges and 3 oranges. The number 8 also gives the result of putting together 5 apples and 3 oranges. The result in this case is 8 objects 5 of which are apples and 3 of which are oranges. This example illustrates that care should always be taken in the application of any model. The level of abstraction of the model can change depending on how it is being used.

There are many different models about various aspects of the world. Physical models help us understand the physical properties of the real world. Mathematical models enable us to abstract the world using notation and logic. Economic models enable us to capture economic trends and predict economic developments. Data models enable us to capture, partially, the meaning of data as related to the complete meaning of the world. This, in turn, provides us with partial knowledge of the world [Levesque, 1981].

One may argue that this is somewhat inadequate. One would really like a model that captures the complete meaning of the world. It is debatable, however, whether such a model is realizable. Complete knowledge of the world is open ended. Although we may know a great deal about some part of the real world, we, in fact, can never have complete knowledge. It is important therefore, to capture the appropriate amount of meaning as related to the desired use of the data. Although the data may have other meanings which are hidden, unknown, or even irrelevant, the meaning captured by a data model should be adequate for the purpose required.

The kind of data models that are discussed in this book are rather limited. They are essentially those models which can be encoded and manipulated easily by computers. They are those models which organize the data in ways in which computers can best handle them. There are many other models of data which are very useful to human beings. A typical example is a map. It is a model of the world which is sufficiently abstract (it does not change when a tree is felled or a house is built), yet it provides a very good and useful interpretation of land surveys. However, it is not one of the data models that will be discussed. The reason is that, so far, it has been hard to encode maps and to express operations on maps using traditional computers. Thus, we will not elaborate further on these types of data models.

It may seem strange that we are trying to interpret the world in only certain ways which fit the tools (i.e., computers) we use for our interpretations. However, this situation is not unique. Human beings have often tried to fit the world into their intellectual models. Is it true, for instance, that many physical phenomena in electromagnetism, fluid mechanics, and so on can best be understood with second-order partial differential equations, or is it that we try to explain everything with second-order partial differential equations because we have some understanding about how they behave? Whichever is the case, second-order partial differential equations provide an adequate model of the world for many physical phenomena. Similarly, the data models discussed in this book adequately model the world for their intended application (i.e., computer processing).

Before we proceed with our discussion of data modeling, it is necessary to define, even if only approximately, what the elementary objects which will be modeled are (i.e., what a datum is). Suppose that we accept as a working definition of an atomic piece of data the tuple <*object name*, *object property*, *property value*, *time*> [Langefors, 1977]. After all, a phenomenon or idea usually refers to an object (*object name*) and to some aspect of the object (*object property*) which is captured by a value (*property value*) at a certain time (*time*).

Of these four aspects of data, time is perhaps the most cumbersome aspect of data modeling. To begin with, real time implies a certain synchronization between phenomena which is usually unrealistic. Also, we are very often more interested in the relative time of phenomena (i.e., one phenomenon occurs before another phenomenon) than we are in the real time of occurrence. This aspect of data can be adequately captured by ordering phenomena rather than recording their real time. Another difficulty with time is that the information retained (at least at the surface) relates only to the last meaningful datum (phenomenon, fact, or instance) and somehow hides the datum's past history. For instance, the recording of a person's current salary does not imply knowledge of all the salaries he or she has ever received, only the last one. If there is interest in past salaries, this is encoded using a different property (e.g., salary history). Therefore, many data models completely drop the notion of time and replace it either with other kinds of explicit properties or with orderings among objects.

If time is dropped, the definition of an elementary datum becomes <*object name*, *object property*, *property value*>. There are many ways that these aspects of data can be represented and related, giving rise to many data models. A simple but very powerful manner of representing and relating elementary data is to put them in a general network where the nodes are the elementary data and the lines represent relationships among the data [Abrial, 1974; Roussopoulos, 1976]. Another very powerful way of relating data is to put them in categories [Abrial, 1974; Hawryszkiewycz, 1980]. Data in the same category are supposed to have similarities. Sometimes these similarities are stated as properties of the category. The insistence of data models for object categorization divides them into two separate classes: strictly typed and loosely typed data models.

*Strictly typed* data models are those in which each datum must belong to some category. Data that do not fall into a category have either to be subverted to fall into one, or they cannot be handled in the data model. In addition, some of these data models make the assumption that the allowable categories are predefined and cannot evolve dynamically.

*Loosely typed* data models do not make any assumptions about categories. Categories are allowed only to the extent that they are useful. Individual data can exist by themselves and they are related to some other data. Information about categories, if they exist, is treated in the same way as information about an individual datum.

Strictly typed data models put the "world" in a "straightjacket." They are sometimes rather inflexible and have difficulty protraying subtle semantic differences. Many examples of difficulties encountered using strictly typed data models can be cited [Kent, 1976, 1978, 1979]. For example, consider data about a category *EMPLOYEE*. In strictly typed data models, the category *EMPLOYEE* must be homogenous; that is, all objects in the category should have the same properties, structure, and so on. However, married and unmarried employees have different properties, as do hourly and salaried employees and temporary and permanent employees.

Despite these difficulties, strictly typed data models have a unique advantage. Properties of data can be abstracted and investigated in terms of their categories. In other words, a theory can be formulated based on categories which actually encapsulate the properties of the data themselves. Since some properties of categories are inherited by the data in them, proving anything about categories implies a proof about the data. In addition, strictly typed data models eliminate the need for repetitive naming. The names of similar objects in a category and the name of a property of that object can be abstracted out as a name for the category and the property name for the category. For instance, by naming an object category *EMPLOYEE* and the category property *Age of employee* we avoid repeating the names in each triplet < *EMPLOYEE*, *Age of employee*, *value*>.

Another advantage of strictly typed data models is that each datum fits usually into some category. Sometimes it may not fit "naturally," but at least it does not fit "naturally" under many categories. In this way, apparent inconsistencies can be avoided because data that are close semantically are at least close in the data model (i.e., in the same category). This does not necessarily happen in loosely typed data models. The flexibility which they allow enables a fact to be placed in many places in the general structure of facts. If facts are inconsistent but very remote in terms of representation, it is very difficult indeed to detect the inconsistency.

Strictly typed data models make a very clear separation between data and categories of data. Loosely typed data models mix data and categories of data in a common framework. The ultimate data modeling tool which mixes data and knowledge about the data is the predicate calculus. Using this mathematical tool we can encode data values and general properties of these values in one uniform environment. Predicate calculus can be considered as a complete, integrated, and all-encompassing framework [Kowalski, 1974, 1979; Deliyanni and Kowalski, 1979]. As a matter of fact, most data models revert to it to encode knowledge they did not anticipate handling.

If predicate calculus is such a complete data modeling tool, a natural question to ask is: Why should we bother with any other data model? Many people would argue that predicate calculus, although a complete data modeling tool, is not a nice data modeling tool notationally. They would claim that data models present facts in nice visual form and predicate calculus consists of hard-to-read one-liners. However, predicate calculus can be represented pictorially and some work in semantic network data models attests to this fact [Brachman, 1979]. Predicate calculus can also be presented, not as a terse notation, but as a reasonable programming language (e.g., PROLOG [Kowalski, 1979]). Hence, predicate calculus has been badly used or explained in the past and is not intrinsically complex, ill structured, or hard to use.

The real difference between data models as described in this book and predicate calculus is the emphasis on strict categorization of objects in data models. Strictly typed data models make some very ad hoc assumptions about what kinds of categories of objects will be allowed and what kinds of relationships between these categories can be specified. They force data to be homogenous. As a matter of fact, most data model research deals with finding good, general categories which can enforce this homogeneity requirement (e.g., the notion of a relation and a record type). In programming languages and abstract data types the emphasis is more on the types themselves and not their categories (e.g., the description and verification of a stack or a data structure). In predicate calculus the emphasis is on allowing everything to be expressed in a uniform and formal environment without artificial restrictions on typing or categorizing objects.

The main reason for imposing such a restrictive framework in strictly typed data models has to do with quantity of objects and limitations of human intelligence. We have to deal with many objects in data modeling. We need some very stringent restrictions to capture them into a limited set of ideas that we can understand. When the objects are few or the people are highly intelligent, the restrictions can be eased. Knowledge can take its natural form, rather than the arbitrary form which we impose on it.

We finish with a poor analogy to illustrate the point concerning loosely typed data models versus strictly typed data models. Let us say that general knowledge is like a jungle. To tame it we can do either one of two things. On the one hand, we can claim a small part of the jungle at a time and turn it into a Japanese garden where everything is allowed, but it is very carefully structured. On the other hand, we can claim big tracts of land, but at a cost. The development is rather unimaginative and it turns the jungle into artificial rows of trees. There is no point in arguing that the rows of trees are more or less natural or nicer than a Japanese garden. They are only a necessary means to tame the jungle (of facts) and make it productive.

## 1.3 DATA MODEL DEFINITION

Most data models used in computer data processing are strictly typed. In this book we concentrate mainly on these data models. For a particular application of a data model the names of the categories together with their properties are called a *schema*. A schema is a generic concept which identifies categories (e.g., *PERSONS*, *CARS*) their properties (e.g., *Person name*, *Car make*), and relationships between them (e.g., *OWNS*, *DRIVES*). For example, a simple data model is a "flat file" data model in which categories are called entity types and category properties are called attributes. In the application of this data model to a particular situation, for example employee data, the schema may consist of *EMPLOYEE(Name, Age, Address)*, where the name *EMPLOYEE* is the generic name of an entity type and *Name*, *Age*, and *Address* are the generic names for the attributes. All data in this application will be of the form (John Smith, 29, 190 St. George).

A data model defines the rules according to which data are structured. Structures, however, do not provide a complete interpretation about the meaning of data and the way they will be used. Operations which are permitted on the data have to be specified. For example, a list of objects can be a stack or a queue depending on the operations allowed on them. Data models also specify the general nature of the operations that are allowed on the data. The operations are normally related to the structures of the data. In other words, the operations are executed within the context provided by the structures. A data model defines general rules for the specification of the structures of the data and the operations allowed on the data.

A collection of data structured in a particular way as related to a schema is generally referred to as a *data base*. The term is used to refer both to a particular instance of a collection of data and to a series of instances which are somehow related. To illustrate, it is usually the case that an operation allowed in a data model tranforms a data base to another data base. In most cases both data bases have the same structures and relate to the same schema. It is customary to refer to the series of instances of data (data bases) as they are transformed by operations, as one data base.

Data models are not all identical and they do not have to be. They can thus provide the necessary tools for different situations and different people. However, there are some unifying concepts and definitions which relate to all data models [Falkenberg, 1976b; Rothnie and Hardgrave, 1976]. We start our discussion of data models with these basic ideas.

Let us consider a model of the world and the properties it should try to capture. These properties fall basically into two classes: static and dynamic. Static properties correspond to those that are (relatively) invariant with time. They are always true and do not change. Dynamic properties correspond to the evolving nature of the world. They allow us to capture the fact that the world is changing. Any model of data must in some way be able to capture these two classes of properties. Thus, we define a *data model* M as consisting of two parts: G, a set of generating rules, and O, a set of operations.

The set of generating rules G express the static properties of a data model and correspond to what is usually called a *data definition language* (DDL). It defines the allowable *structures* for the data within the data model M. The allowed structures are specified in two complementary ways. The allowable objects and relationships are specified using generic rules for the definition of their categories. For instance, if we define categories in terms of entity types, an entity type *EMPLOYEE* is specified in terms of its attributes and expected values for each attribute. Disallowed objects or relationships are excluded by defining restrictions, called *constraints*, on the categories. Constraints are expected to be true for any structure within the data model for which the constraint applies. For instance, we may want to guarantee that at most one employee has a given social insurance number or that no employee earns more than his or her manager. These constraints disallow the existence of certain entities.

Some data models partition the generating rules G into two parts: the structure specification $G_s$ and the constraint specification $G_c$. The generators $G_s$ generate the categories and structures of a schema and the generators $G_c$ generate the constraints associated with a schema. A schema $S$ therefore consists of two parts: a structure part $S_s$ and a constraint part $S_c$. The constraint part $S_c$ is a list of *explicit* constraints that should not be violated. For instance, in the definition of the entity type *EMPLOYEE*, a particular attribute *Employee#* may be specified as an identifier (key). That is, at any point of time a set of entities conforming to the properties of the entity type *EMPLOYEE* would not have two or more entities with the same value for *Employee#*. Such an occurrence is not disallowed by the structures, but is explicitly disallowed.

As well as explicit constraints, a data model can also provide *inherent* constraints. Inherent constraints can be associated with a data model by incorporating them in the structure part $S_s$. That is, the structure by its own definition can disallow certain objects or limit certain relationships between objects. For instance, the structure may only allow objects to be related according to a tree structure. It follows that if this constraint is enforced, objects cannot be related in a more general fashion (e.g., a network).

The generating rules **G** are generators for a set of schemas **S**. Each schema *S* defines particular structures of the data and specifies constraints on the data. There are many different data bases **D** in terms of occurrences which can correspond to the schema *S*. All of them, however, have the same generic structures and obey the constraints defined on *S*. The allowable data base occurrences **D** are obtained as a realization of the schema *S*.

The generating rules **G** of a data model **M** specify the *static* properties of a schema and its underlying data model. That is, they specify properties that must be true for all occurrences *D* of a schema *S*. These rules allow us to capture (partially) the static properties of the world. The dynamic properties of the world are expressed by the set of operations **O** which correspond to what is usually called a *data manipulation language* (DML). It defines the allowable actions that can be performed on a data base occurrence $D_i$ to arrive at another data base occurrence $D_j$.

Not all operations in **O** cause a change in data base occurrence. However, they are still dynamic in that they cause a change in the state of the data base. To capture this dynamic aspect of operations we need to consider some additional objects which are not exactly data base objects but nevertheless are associated with a data base occurrence and can change as a result of an operation. The additional objects correspond to currency indicators and other control mechanisms. Together with a particular data base occurrence *D* they define a *data base state DBS*. A data base state reflects the dynamic aspect of a data model as it changes as the result of an operation. For instance, consider sequential retrieval on a single file in a "flat file" data model and a "get next" operation. The current state of the data base is defined by the values in the file (data base occurrence *D*) and the value of a currency indicator used for retrieval. Performing a "get next" operation does not alter the data base occurrence but it alters the data base state, since it changes the value of the currency indicator. In a similar way, a DBTG Find command does not change the data base occurrence but it changes the currency indicators and thus the data base state. Each data model operation *O* maps a data base state to another data base state $O:DBS_1 \rightarrow DBS_2$. Both data base states $DBS_1$ and $DBS_2$ have data base occurrences $D_1$ and $D_2$ associated with the same schema $S$. That is, the structure of the data base is retained under any operation in $O$.

The operations $O$ are defined as partial functions on data base states. The function is partial because an operation may map a data base occurrence into another occurrence which has structures as defined in $S$ but violates some constraints associated with $S$. Some data models allow explicit constraints to be violated as a result of an operation in $O$. The operations $O$ are defined in general for any schema without any particular provision for preserving explicit constraints. When these operations are applied to data base occurrences associated with a particular schema, constraints can be violated. The operation maps into another data base occurrence retaining the structures as defined in $S$. However, the operation is undefined when a constraint is violated. For example, a relational update can violate an explicit constraint, so it is sometimes undefined.

Although a data model may allow explicit constraints to be violated, it usually does not allow the operations to violate the inherent constraints of the data model. As a matter of fact, if the data model does not allow the specification of explicit constraints, it is usual for all operations to be totally defined and to retain automatically the inherent constraints. A hierarchical insert command is always defined because it cannot violate any inherent constraint, although there are many of them.

In the following chapters the structure part $G_s$ and constraint part $G_c$ are discussed separately. Many data models mix structures and constraints, but it will be simpler (hopefully) to discuss them separately. In addition, different types of operations will be discussed as they apply to different structures of data.

A *data base management system* (DBMS) is a system that "manages" data bases. That is, it is a system that provides facilities to define data base schemas and provides operations that can be used to transform one data base to another one, usually of the same schema. It should be apparent that a data base management system has an inherent data model. Some data base management systems are based completely on a data model (e.g., System R [Astrahan et al., 1976]). Others are loosely based on a data model (e.g., IMS [McGee, 1977]). The latter data models evolved historically and incorporate many diverse ideas, some of which are implementation dependent.

The understanding obtained from the descriptions of the data is important irrespective of the particular system used for the storage of data. DBMSs may have started by being a better access method for increasing programmer's productivity. They have pointed the way, however, to all the advantages provided by data integration. This integration provides a framework for the operation of an organization. It needs as a prerequisite, however, a good understanding of the data. Data models provide a tool for obtaining such understanding. As such, they may be more important than DBMSs per se. DBMSs may be very general or border on being a file system. In any case, proper integration is important. Proper integration needs understanding. Understanding is obtained partially through data models.

In this book, although data models are discussed abstractly, many of the abstract ideas have concrete realizations in existing systems. Therefore, examples relating the abstract ideas to the concrete realizations will be given wherever possible. However, the emphasis is on the ideas and how they can be perceived clearly and naturally, not on how they relate to a particular system.

## EXERCISES

**1.1** Data models usually imply that all knowledge in the world has to fit within allowable structures. To what degree is this a limiting factor? Can you think of examples of data or information that are impossible to structure?

**1.2** Some epic poems, for instance Homer's, have a very strict type in terms of syllables or words used. Outline some examples of structural constraints used in poems as opposed to prose writing. Do these restrictions affect in any way the expressive quality of the poems? Is it harder for the reader to understand the meaning of the poem? Was it harder for the poet to abide by the rules?

**1.3** Data base technology is a partial solution to some of the organizational problems that appear in large organizations. To what degree is it responsible for some of the dubious benefits that society reaps from such large organizations [Weizenbaum, 1976]? For instance, if data base integration were impossible, maybe large organizations would operate with more decentralized and fragmented control. Would this situation be good or bad for the organization in particular and society in general?

**1.4** Introducing computers in an organization involves a learning curve which takes from six to eight years to level out. Does the introduction of data base technology imply another learning curve? Would this continual upheaval be beneficial? Is it inevitable?

**1.5** Outline a single-function computer application that will not be affected seriously by the introduction of data base technology.

**1.6** Computer fraud is a risk associated with any data processing operation. Do DBMSs increase or decrease the risk of unauthorized access and manipulation of an organization's data base?

**1.7** In what ways do DBMSs help or hinder the auditing of a data base? Outline an auditing facility to be used in connection with a data base.

**1.8** The introduction of a programming package (e.g., a new compiler or operating system) implies some conversion effort and affects the programming effort in an organization. It does not, however, generally affect the organization's procedures for doing business. What is so different about a DBMS that its introduction may affect business procedures and entire organizations?

**1.9** Consider a developing country with limited resources and technology and an inadequate bureaucracy. On the one hand, the introduction of data base technology is very difficult and perhaps questionable because of the lack of expertise. On the other hand, maybe it is easier to circumvent an inefficient bureaucracy with a good DBMS rather than organize an efficient and successful manual system. Argue the case and the trade-offs.

**1.10** Large multinational corporations have some advantages in terms of capital mobilization and market diversification. In addition, they have a much more complex operation and may require better decision support systems and DBMSs. Will the integration and control provided by these systems eliminate some of their most pressing needs? Will they give them an unfair advantage? Argue the case.

**1.11** Consider a cartel such as the Organization of Petroleum Exporting Countries (OPEC). Without an integrated information system there can be only limited cooperation because of the communication problems between different levels of the organization. With an integrated information system the cooperation can be much more effective. Is an integrated information system a good idea in this context? What about interference, security, and national goals? Argue the case.

**1.12** An army is traditionally organized hierarchically. Communications between units are effected according to the hierarchy. With an integrated information system there is a possibility for direct communication and exchange of information among all levels of the hierarchy. Argue the advantages and disadvantages of this type of operation. What are the pitfalls, if any?

# Chapter 2

# STRUCTURES

## 2.1 ABSTRACTIONS

One of the main ways of structuring and visualizing data is through the use of abstraction. *Abstraction* is the ability to hide detail and concentrate on general, common properties of a set of objects. In data modeling, abstraction is used to obtain categories of data. In addition, abstraction can be used to combine categories into more general categories [Smith and Smith, 1977a,b; Lockemann et al., 1979].

Abstraction has been used extensively in computer science to reduce complexity and aid understanding [Dijkstra, 1972; Hoare, 1972; Brodie and Zilles, 1981]. An elementary form of abstraction distinguishes between the token level and the type level. A *token* is an actual value or a particular instance of an object. Abstraction is used to define a *type* from a class of similar tokens. For instance, abstraction is applied to a set of tables to form the generic concept *TABLE*. One can have many levels of abstraction. That is, an abstraction at one level may be a constituent object at another level, and so on. Thus, abstraction can be used to form a type from other types. For example, the types *TABLE*, *CHAIR*, and *BED* can be combined into one type, *FURNITURE*.

The types generated by using abstraction can be quite complex. For example, the type *HOUSEHOLD* is a very complex type which incorporates many objects: *UTENSILS*, *FURNITURE*, *RUGS*, and so on. *FURNITURE* in turn can be composed of the objects *TABLE*, *CHAIR*, *BED*, and so on. The advantage of generating a type using abstraction comes from the descriptive power of the hierarchy of types and their relationships. The generated type is easier to understand and to visualize through this hierarchy. For instance, by understanding the properties of furniture one

16

can better understand the relationships and common usage of tables, chairs, beds, and so on.

In terms of data base objects, abstraction is used in two ways: *generalization* and *aggregation* [Smith and Smith, 1977a,b; Brodie, 1978]. *Generalization* views a set of tokens or a set of types as one generic type. Token-type generalization is usually differentiated from type-type generalization. The former process is referred to as *classification*, while the latter process is called *generalization*. For instance, viewing a set of individual employee tokens as one generic type *EMPLOYEE* is considered classification. Viewing the types *EMPLOYEE* and *STUDENT* as one generic type *PERSON* is considered generalization. *Instantiation* is the opposite process to classification, and *specialization* is the opposite process to generalization. Thus, an employee token is an instantiation of the type *EMPLOYEE*, and the type *EMPLOYEE* is a specialization of the type *PERSON*. In what follows we generally do not distinguish between classification abstraction and generalization abstraction unless explicitly stated otherwise.

Generalization enhances understanding by allowing individual tokens to be classified into types. Types can be further classified into other, more general types. By using generalization, emphasis is placed on the similarities of objects while abstracting away their differences. Figure 2.1—1 illustrates a generalization hierarchy for a university data base [Brodie, 1978]. The arrows indicate the direction of generalization.

In general, a generalized type can have all the common properties of each constituent token or type. That is, *all* properties of the generalized type can be inherited downward to the constituent types. However, the inheritance of specific properties can be explicitly disallowed. In addition, properties can be specified that are specific to a type and are not inherited. The concept that an employee has a salary is inherited from the type *EMPLOYEE* by each individual instance of an employee. In addition, the concept that a person has a name, address, and age is inherited by each participating type of *PERSON* (e.g., *EMPLOYEE* and *STUDENT*). The concept of an average salary for the type *EMPLOYEE* is an example of a property that can be specific to the type *EMPLOYEE* and is not inherited. A generalization at the type level implies a set of generalizations at the token level of the participating types. For instance, the fact that *PERSON* is a generalization of *EMPLOYEE* implies that each (token) employee can be regarded as a person.

*Aggregation* is the abstraction by which an object is constructed from its constituent objects. For instance, a person can be characterized by his or her name, address, and age. Aggregation can be used at either the token or the type level. For instance, the type *EMPLOYEE* can be constructed from the types *NAME*, *AGE*, and *ADDRESS* (Figure 2.1—2). The properties, such as *NAME*, *AGE*, and *ADDRESS*, of a type are

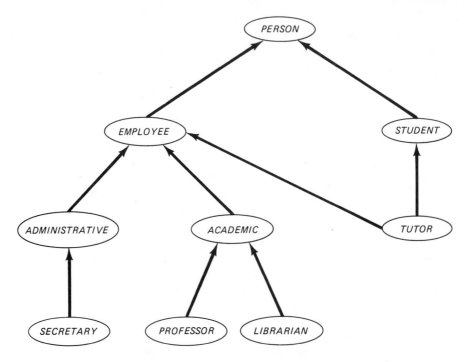

**Fig. 2.1—1** Generalization hierarchy.

*definitional* and will be referred to as *intensional* properties [Mylopoulos et al., 1980]. The instance of John Smith as a person is constructed by the tokens "John Smith" as a name, "29" as an age, and "190 St. George" as an address. The properties of a token, such as John Smith as a person, are *factual* and will be referred to as *extensional* properties [Mylopoulos et al., 1980]. This distinction between intensional and extensional properties is very important in data modeling and will be discussed in more detail later in this chapter.

An aggregation at the type level portrays a set of aggregations at the token level of the constituent types. Figure 2.1—2 illustrates aggregation hierarchies for types *PERSON*, *EMPLOYEE*, and *STUDENT*. Since *PERSON* is a generalization of the latter types (Figure 2.1—1), they inherit the properties *NAME*, *AGE*, and *ADDRESS* from *PERSON* unless the inheritance is explicitly disallowed. Aggregation implies that the aggregated object has as part of its structure its constituent objects. The properties of each constituent object are inherited by, respectively, each constituent object of the aggregate object. For example, the constituent objects of the type *EMPLOYEE* will inherit, respectively, all the properties of the types *NAME*, *AGE*, and *ADDRESS* as viewed separately. Aggregation, as a form of abstraction, is very helpful because it gradually makes visible the structure of an object and how the individual components of the object relate to it

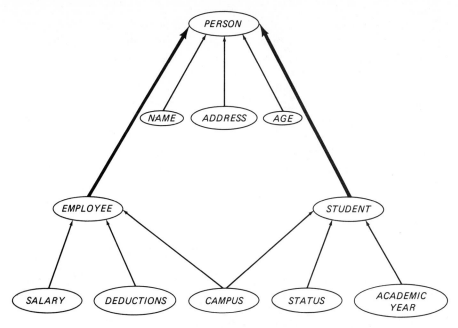

**Fig. 2.1—2** Some aggregation hierarchies.

and to each other. Aggregation can be used repeatedly. The inverse process, called *stepwise refinement*, has been used extensively as an aid in programming [Dijkstra, 1972; Hoare, 1972; Mills, 1973].

Generalization and aggregation are related to the concepts of PART_OF and IS_A in artificial intelligence [Roussopoulos, 1976; Wong and Mylopoulos, 1977]. The concept PART_OF expresses the fact that an object type is an aggregate of another object type (e.g., a *NAME* is PART_OF an *EMPLOYEE*). The concept IS_A expresses the fact that an object type is a generalization of another object type (e.g., an *EMPLOYEE* IS_A *PERSON*). Both of these concepts are defined as relationships between types. They imply a relationship between their tokens. However, traditionally the terms IS_A and PART_OF are not defined at the token level.

Abstractions have been used informally in data management for a long time. Aggregation is used during file design to group fields in a common file. Generalization is used by introducing the notion of a file as a generic object type representing the properties of many records. Generalization is also used in the opposite direction as the specialization of a selected subset of records during file record selection. Treating generalization and aggregation in their own right allows us to define them individually and to deal with them explicitly as semantically meaningful relationships. The objects related by them then also have semantic meaning and are no longer only uninterpreted subsets of objects. For instance, there is a differentiation between the employees with skill equal to secretary and the generic type *SECRETARY*, which is related by generalization to the type *EMPLOYEE*. In the second case the object has an associated semantic interpretation and is a generic object in its own right.

Aggregation and generalization can be used in a complementary fashion to express both the structure and classification of types. The structure of a generic type may be expressed as an aggregate of constituent types, and aggregates can be classified under a generic type. The classification of a type can be expressed in a generalization hierarchy. The structure of a type can be expressed in an aggregation hierarchy. The two hierarchies can be thought of as independent (or represented orthogonally) in that one can be considered independently of the other. Figure 2.1—3 illustrates an abstraction of person [Smith and Smith, 1977a,b].

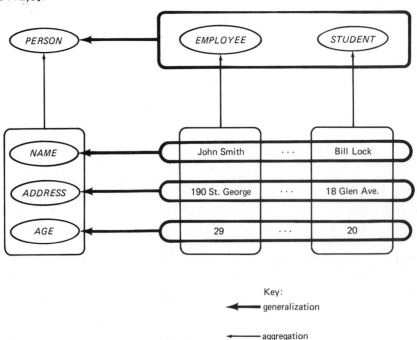

**Fig. 2.1—3** Abstraction of person.

Using a bottom-up approach, abstraction can be viewed as a synthesis of simple objects that enables us to understand a complex object. We start with observations, the tokens, to which we apply classification to produce types. Generalization and aggregation can then be used to classify and structure types into new generic and aggregate types. Alternatively, an analytical, top-down method may be used to decompose complex types.

We start with a complex type and we decompose it into its components, through specialization and instantiation, to the token level. Typically, the bottom-up approach is used to understand a complex phenomenon and the top-down approach is used to design a complex object. Both methods can also be used together.

The two abstraction techniques — generalization and aggregation — are generally present in most data models. Some data models first define the tokens of information and then give structuring principles to combine and categorize them [Langefors, 1974]. These data models usually allow many different types. Sometimes they do not make a great distinction between type information and token information. Other data models enable the user to specify complex types which are associated with constituent types and eventually with tokens of information [CODASYL, 1971]. All tokens conform to the predefined types. The latter kind of strictly typed data model is rigid, expecting all facts about the real world to be structured only in certain prespecified ways. The former kind of loosely typed data model allows complete modeling flexibility but at the same time requires a very careful specification of the structure.

Abstractions are used in data modeling to give meaning to sets of objects. In the next section, sets are discussed first as uninterpreted objects and then abstraction is used to give them additional interpretation.

## 2.2 SETS — DOMAINS AND ATTRIBUTES

A *set* is any collection of objects that is properly identified and is characterized by a membership condition. The membership condition qualifies an object for membership in the set. For example, a membership condition might be all positive, even integers (i.e., $\{2,4,6,...\}$) or all decimal digits (i.e., $\{0,1,2,...,9\}$). A set can be infinite or finite. In the preceding example, the first set is infinite and the second is finite. Sets can themselves be members of sets (e.g., $\{\{0\}, \{1,3,5,7\}, \{2,4,6,8\}\}$). The null (empty) set, denoted $\{\}$ or $\phi$, is always a member of a set of sets.

In classical set theory the membership condition does not imply any order, duplicates do not make sense, and the membership condition is independent of the representation of the elements of the set. For example, the set $\{1,2,3\}$ is equivalent to the set $\{3,2,3,1,3\}$. Similarly, the sets $\{a \,|\, a = 0 \text{ or } a = 1\}$ and $\{b \,|\, b \text{ is a binary digit}\}$ are equivalent; both define the set $\{0,1\}$. Classical set theory encompasses a vast body of theoretical work, including different axiomatizations [Fraenkel et al., 1973]. This book uses set theory only informally and in such a way as to not need much of its theoretical results.

A set does not have any order associated with its members. Order in classical set theory is obtained in terms of two-tuples (e.g., [Childs,

1977]). For instance, the ordered set $\{a, b, c\}$ is the set $\{<1, a>, <2, b>, <3, c>\}$. Two-tuples themselves are defined using nesting of sets (e.g., $\{\{1\}, \{1, a\}\}$ defines the tuple $<1, a>$) [Kuratowski and Mostowski, 1975]. This representation of order is rather arbitrary and can lead to ambiguities if it is not properly specified. The problem is compounded when dealing with ordered $n$-tuples. In this case, exact assumptions are needed about the way the nesting is specified.

Information systems need to deal with ordered $n$-tuples for several reasons. The first is that, eventually, data must be stored in computer memory, which because of its nature, is an ordered set of cells. Hence, at some point all data have to be mapped into an ordered set of words, bytes, and so on. Another very important reason to deal with order is that order is often used to represent a deeper semantic property, such as time. Although time is a part of the real world and may be present in a computer system as time stamps, it usually is not incorporated explicitly in most data models because it is too complicated to handle properly. Order within the computer system is then used to signify time differences of transactions or occurrences of phenomena. Order, in this case, is an integral, although implicit, part of the descriptive power of the data model and must be handled correctly.

An extension to set theory, in the context of data modeling, which formally introduces order, has been proposed [Childs, 1974]. This extended set theory can also be used as a notation or metamodel to define other data models and mappings between them [Sibley and Hardgrave, 1977; Hardgrave, 1981]. The salient features of the formalism of extended set theory are presented below. An axiomatic development of extended set theory can be found in the work of Childs [Childs, 1974, 1977].

The basic object of the formalism is the *complex*. The basic relation defined by a complex is that of $i$-membership. (Here both $n$ and $i$ range over the natural numbers.) If $x$ is an $i$th member of $y$, then $x$ is at position $i$ in the set $y$ (written $x \in i\, y$). For any $i$, a complex may have any number of values $(0, 1, 2, ...)$ at position $i$ ($i$-members) in the complex. The positions of the elements in complexes are written as superscripts. For example, the complex $\{b^1, c^1, d^3\}$ has members $b$ and $c$ at position 1, $d$ at position 3, and no others. Sets and $n$-tuples are special cases of complexes. A set has all members at position 1 (1-members), since no order is defined for sets. An $n$-tuple has exactly one value at each position $i$ for each $i$ from 1 to $n$. For example, a three-tuple $<a, b, c>$ may be written as the complex $\{a^1, b^2, c^3\}$, and a set $\{a, b, c\}$ is the complex $\{a^1, b^1, c^1\}$.

Extended sets provide a very powerful and general data modeling capability. A complex can model any structure, including some structures that are seldom, if ever, used in data modeling. For example, a complex of complexes can be used to model a repeating group. In what follows we use mainly complexes that represent ordered sets of $n$-tuples. These complexes appear in many data models.

As well as introducing order, extended sets also allow us to capture content duplication. That is, the same extended set may have the same value at different positions in the set. These two identical values are thus distinct set values. For example, the extended set $\{a^1, b^2, a^3\}$ has value $a$ at both positions 1 and 3. However, these are distinct $a$ values because of the order associated with them.

Both sets and extended sets are characterized by two important properties. The first property is *definitional* in nature and is called the *intension* of the set or extended set. For example, the set definition $\{a \mid a$ is an even, positive integer$\}$ gives the intension of the set. It defines the *permissible* occurrences of the set by specifying the membership condition. The second property of a set is *representational* in nature and is called the *extension* of the set or extended set. For example, the set representation $\{2, 4, 6, 8, ...\}$ gives one possible extension of the set. It specifies an *actual* occurrence of the set by explicitly giving its members.

An intension is sometimes used to specify not only exactly one set, but rather a collection of sets all of which have some common properties defined in the intension. This way of using intensions is used a great deal to define a collection of data objects as they evolve over time. For instance, the definition of the structure of a file does not exactly define a set of records. It defines allowable records from which different extensions can be constructed. Intensions and extensions of sets correspond roughly to the types and token level, respectively, of abstraction. The intension is a generalization of a collection of extensions. It defines all the common properties of the extensions.

Sets and extended sets allow us to formally define collections of objects by specifying their membership condition and introducing ordering. However, these collections are completely uninterpreted in that they have not been related to real-world objects. Explicit rules for associating meaning with sets are required. In the remainder of this section and in the next section we discuss only classical sets, sets in which order (and content duplication) is not important. However, it should be apparent that the discussion can be applied equally well to extended sets. In Section 2.4 we again discuss, explicitly, the role of extended sets in data modeling.

There are some sets whose members are more or less homogenous: for example, the set of integers between 10 and 20, the alphabetic strings of length up to 20, and so forth. These homogenous sets are called *domains* in data modeling. Domains are used as sets of values from which certain semantically meaningful objects and their properties can take values over time. For instance, six-digit numbers form a domain from which salaries can take values. The use of the word "domain" does not imply the usual mathematical definition of a function argument. In data modeling domains can be used as both arguments and results (ranges) of mappings.

A named domain that represents a semantically meaningful object is called an *attribute* and represents the intension of the domain (e.g., *Salary*). The extension of the domain corresponds to (*attribute*) *values* (e.g., salary values). Attributes and their values are interpretations of real-world objects and their properties. By introducing attributes as named domains, abstract concepts such as numbers and strings are given interpretation and are restricted both operationally and conceptually.

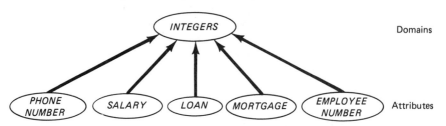

Fig. 2.2—1 Abstraction of attributes and domains.

In terms of abstractions, a domain is a generalization of attributes. Attributes sharing a common domain inherit the properties of the domain. Conversely, a domain has all the properties that are common to the attributes that share the domain. For instance, salary, loan, and mortgage share a common domain of values (i.e., integers) (Figure 2.2—1). Generalization abstraction, when applied to attributes, allows us to determine the structure of the data with respect to domains. It also lets us see how different attributes are similar and how they are related to each other.

Attributes are not seen in isolation, but as part of other objects. They are also associated with other attributes by means of aggregation. For instance, name, address, and age may form the aggregate person. The manner by which attributes are viewed and related defines aggregates which correspond to objects in the real world. Before these more complex objects can be discussed, however, it is necessary to discuss their underlying structure. This structure can be represented by sets which themselves have some internal structure.

## 2.3 RELATIONS — ENTITIES AND RELATIONSHIPS

Consider a number of sets, each representing a particular type of object. Sets can have interpretations related to domains, roles, and attributes.

These sets can be combined through aggregation to establish more complicated types. This aggregation on types of objects can be viewed abstractly. That is, the interpretation of the aggregation is temporarily overlooked to study the common properties of the aggregates. An aggregation of sets is naturally expressed as a relation.

A *mathematical relation* is a set that expresses a correspondence between (aggregation of) two or more sets. The correspondence between two sets $S_1$ and $S_2$, called a binary relation, is a subset of the cross product of $S_1$ and $S_2$ ($S_1 \times S_2 = \{<s_1, s_2> | s_1 \in S_1 \text{ and } s_2 \in S_2\}$). A binary relation defines a set of ordered pairs $<s_1, s_2>$ that conform to some correspondence criterion. The order (i.e., first $S_1$ elements then $S_2$ elements) in each tuple is important, as the following example illustrates. Consider two sets $S_1 = \{1, 3, 8, 9\}$, $S_2 = \{2, 3\}$, and the relation $S_1 < S_2$. The cross product of these two sets is $S_1 \times S_2 = \{<1, 2>, <3, 2>, <8, 2>, <9, 2>, <1, 3>, <3, 3>, <8, 3>, <9, 3>\}$. The relation $S_1 < S_2$ is the subset of tuples $\{<1, 2>, <1, 3>\}$ of $S_1 \times S_2$. Note that whereas $<1, 2>$ belongs to the relation, $<2, 1>$ does not. Thus, the order is important. Relations can be generalized to be ternary (an ordered triple) or, more generally, $n$-ary (an ordered $n$-tuple). An $n$-ary relation $R$ is simply a subset of the Cartesian product of its domains ($R \subseteq S_1 \times S_2 \times ... \times S_n$).

Just as for sets, a relation can be described in terms of its *intension* and *extension.* Consider, for example, the relation defined by $R \subseteq S_1 \times S_2$ where $S_1 = \{s | s \text{ is a letter of the alphabet}\}$ and $S_2 = \{s | s \text{ is a binary digit}\}$. The preceding statement defines the intensional properties of the relation, namely, that it consists of 2-tuples with one alphabetic letter and one binary digit. The set $T = \{<a, 1>, <a, 0>, <c, 1>, <b, 0>\}$ specifies an extension of the relation $R$ consisting of exactly four tuples that conform to the intensional properties of $R$. In terms of abstractions, the intension of the relation is a generalization of the set of extensions. That is, the extensions are the tokens and the intension is the type. The tokens obviously inherit properties from the type.

A relation as defined in mathematics is simply a set. It is a completely uninterpreted object without any particular semantic meaning. However, in data modeling the same term "relation" is used to define a relation as a type. A relation $R$ is considered an object type which defines a set of token tuples. All of these tuples are defined over the same domains and have similar properties. Because of the dynamic aspect of data modeling, these relations of data evolve over time. However, at any point in time, an instance of a generic relation as used in data modeling is a mathematical relation. Different interpretations can be applied to these relations to impart some meaning to them.

One semantic interpretation that can be applied to a relation is to make each tuple correspond to a particular *entity.* Although it is difficult to give a rigorous definition of an entity, it is fairly easy to convey the general idea of what constitutes an entity. It is something with objective reality which exists or can be thought of [Hall et al., 1976]. For example, house, employee, and sale can all be considered entities. Abstraction can be applied to entities to obtain a generic entity type (e.g., the category of *HOUSE, EMPLOYEE,* or *SALE*). An entity type is a data model representation that corresponds to a categorization of real-world objects.

Like relations, entities have intensions and extensions. The intension of an entity is called an *entity type.* It corresponds to a definition of the entity in terms of its attributes. For example, the entity type *EMPLOYEE* can have attributes *Employee#, Name, Address, Age, Department, Skill,* and *Salary.* When a relation represents an entity type, the domains of the relation correspond to the attributes of the entity type. The extension of an entity type is called an *entity set.* It corresponds to all actual values currently associated with each attribute of the entity type. In terms of a relation, an entity set corresponds to a relation extension (subset of the Cartesian product of the underlying domains). A particular set of values for the attributes of an entity type is called an *entity (instance)* and corresponds to a tuple of a relation.

There is no absolute distinction between entity types and attributes. Sometimes an attribute can exist only as related to an entity type. In a different context, it can be an entity type in its own right [Schmid and Swenson, 1975]. For example, to a car manufacturer, a color is merely an attribute of one of its products; to the company that made the paint, a color may well be an entity type [Hall et al., 1976].

In terms of abstractions, an entity type corresponds to an aggregation of attributes. For example, an *EMPLOYEE* entity type is an aggregation of the attributes *Employee#, Name, Address, Age, Department, Skill,* and *Salary* (Figure 2.3—1). Different attributes of an entity type can share the same domain.

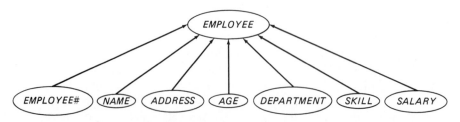

**Fig. 2.3—1** Entity type as an aggregation of attributes.

An entity type may correspond to a generalization of one or more entity types. For example, the entity type *PERSON* can be represented as a generalization of the entity types *EMPLOYEE, STUDENT,* and *SALESPERSON* (Figure 2.3—2). The entity type *PERSON* is composed of all the attributes common to *EMPLOYEE, STUDENT,* and *SALESPERSON.*

These entity types in turn inherit these attributes from the more general type *PERSON*. This inheritance has certain implications for the attributes and attribute values associated with the entity types. For instance, when the entity type *PERSON* changes age, its realization as an *EMPLOYEE* also changes age, since the properties of a person are inherited by their role as an employee.

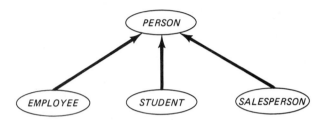

**Fig. 2.3—2** Generalization hierarchy of entity types.

Generalization can be used to represent fairly complex categorizations of entity types that are not necessarily tree structured. For example, a person can be an employer or an employee, and an employer can be a person or a company [Bachman and Daya, 1977]. This situation can be handled through generalization by distinguishing five entity types: *EMPLOYER PERSON*, *EMPLOYER COMPANY*, *EMPLOYEE PERSON*, *PERSON*, and *EMPLOYER*. *PERSON* is obtained through generalization of *EMPLOYER PERSON* and *EMPLOYEE PERSON*. *EMPLOYER* is obtained through generalization of *EMPLOYER PERSON* and *EMPLOYER COMPANY* (Figure 2.3—3). Generalization hierarchies such as those in Figures 2.3—2 and 2.3—3 relate to the concept of *roles* of entity types [Bachman and Daya, 1977].

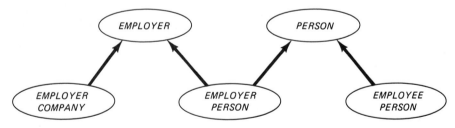

**Fig. 2.3—3** Nontree generalization hierarchy of entity types.

Entity types are one interpretation that can be applied to relations. We can, however, also apply a different interpretation. Rather than interpreting a relation as being between attributes of the same entity type, we can interpret a relation as being between separate entity types. For example, the relation *MARRIED TO* can be interpreted as a relationship between the entity types *MEN* and *WOMEN*. Since relationships are also relations, they, too, have intensions (relationship types) and extensions (relationship sets and instances).

As for entity types and attributes, there is similarly no clear distinction between an entity type and a relationship type. In the preceding example, we interpreted *MARRIED TO* as a relationship type between entity types. It could also be represented as a relation between the attributes *Name* and *Spouse* of the entity type *PERSON*. One distinction that can be used to separate entity types and relationship types is whether the existence of one entity type depends on the presence of another [Codd, 1979]. If instances of relations cannot stand on their own, the relation does not represent an entity type. For instance, persons can be entity types but marriages cannot; they cannot exist without the associated persons.

In terms of abstractions, a relationship type corresponds to an aggregation of two or more entity types. For example, *MARRIED TO* can be represented as an aggregation of the entity types *MEN* and *WOMEN*. A relationship type can be binary, when only two entity types are aggregated, or of higher order (e.g., *n*-ary). However, most data models handle only binary relationship types.

A relationship type may correspond to a generalization of one or more relationship types. For example, *PARTNERSHIP* can be viewed as a generalization of the relationship types *BUSINESS PARTNERSHIP* and *SOCIAL PARTNERSHIP*.

Much discussion has centered around the concepts of attributes, entity types, and relationship types and their representation and materialization [Kent, 1976, 1978]. For example, one can accept the concept entity type together with associated attributes and try to fit it to particular data models. Another approach is to start from attributes and interpret them using abstraction techniques to arrive by synthesis at the entity types. One may actually reject the concept outright and not use it at all in the data model. There is disagreement on whether entity types are semantic objects, or whether they are an abstraction of the record idea which is so predominant in data base management. It may be that the record concept is a representation of a not advertised, but subconciously assumed, entity type concept. It is hard to settle whether entity types are useful conceptual objects in every data modeling situation. It depends on what objects they are trying to model and the bias of the person who is doing the modeling.

## 2.4 REPRESENTATION – TABLES AND GRAPHS

In the preceding sections we have shown how sets, and by implication extended sets, can be used to capture data modeling concepts. However, sets and extended sets are abstract concepts and have no implied representation. In data modeling we have to be able to represent the modeling concepts in some way. This representation capability is necessary because, first, we need to store data in computers and, second, we need to present to the user a representation of the data that he or she can interpret and understand.

Perhaps one of the simplest ways to represent data is in table form. Tables of data are used by people every day (e.g., sports team standings, stock market listings, and menus). Data processing uses tables implicitly in the form of files, records, and fields. Most data models use some form of table to represent data modeling concepts. All tables, however, are not exactly alike structurally. By distinguishing tables according to their structure, different data models are realized.

Consider an attribute, such as *Employee#*, corresponding to a domain (e.g., three-digit integers). The properties of this attribute can be captured by a set in which order is not important and duplication is irrelevant. These properties can be represented by a table as shown in Figure 2.4—1. The table contains a single column headed by the attribute name. The attribute name corresponds to the intension (definition) of the table. The collection of values currently associated with the table corresponds to the extension of the table. All values are at position 1 in the complex (i.e., a classical set).

| *Employee#* |
|---|
| 123 |
| 862 |
| 781 |
| 523 |
| 324 |

**Fig. 2.4—1** Table representation of an attribute.

Consider now an attribute such as *Salary*. For this attribute order and content duplication might be important. In this case the properties of the attribute can be captured by an extended set, restricted as discussed in Section 2.2. This extended set can still be represented as a table of data. Now, however, the order and content duplication are important. Such a table representation is shown in Figure 2.4—2. The numbers beside the table indicate the ordering. The attribute name at the head of the column again corresponds to the intension of the table and the collection of values corresponds to the current table extension. The values are at the indicated positions in the complex.

With tables as a basis for attribute intension and extension representation, we can now build on this representation method to devise

|      | Salary |
|------|--------|
| (1)  | 10000  |
| (2)  | 12500  |
| (3)  | 22500  |
| (4)  | 18600  |
| (5)  | 14200  |
| (6)  | 30300  |
| (7)  | 25000  |
| (8)  | 12500  |

**Fig. 2.4—2** Ordered table representing an attribute.

representations for entity types and relationship types. Both of these data modeling concepts correspond to aggregations of, respectively, attributes and entity types (i.e., aggregations of complexes). Aggregations between attributes represented as tables can be represented in two equivalent ways. In one, the aggregation is also represented as a table. In the other, it is represented by drawing lines among the aggregates and, in essence, representing it as a graph.

If we represent the aggregation of attributes into entity types as a table and duplicate rows are not allowed and order is not important, the table corresponds to a mathematical relation. Such a table is commonly called a *(data base) relation* and corresponds to the representation of the intension and extension of an entity type [Codd, 1970]. A column of the table represents the extension of an attribute and is called an *attribute*. A row of the table, called a *tuple*, represents an entity (instance). The entire table represents an entity set. Such a table corresponds to a complex with all the tuples at position 1 in the complex (i.e., a classical set).

If duplicate rows are permitted and order is important, the table represents an extended set. Such a table can also represent the extension of an entity type, but its properties are different from that of a relation table. Such a table is commonly called a *record type*. A column of the table represents the extension of an attribute and is called a *data item*. A row of the table, called a *record (instance)*, represents an entity (instance). The entire table represents an ordered collection of records which corresponds to an entity set. Such a table corresponds to a complex with at most one record at each position in the complex.

These two types of tables are used very often in data modeling to represent structure. The relation table representation allows us to apply the mathematical theory of relations to this representation. For example, set operations are well defined for these types of tables. On the other hand, record-type tables may be required for operational purposes. For example, order may be required for representing time.

Figure 2.4—3 presents an example data base consisting of employees

RECORD TYPES

EMPLOYEE

| Employee# | Name | Address | Sex |
|---|---|---|---|

COMPANY

| Firmname | Location |
|---|---|

RECORDS

EMPLOYEE

| | Employee # | Name | Address | Sex |
|---|---|---|---|---|
| (1) | 123 | Smith J. | 19 Evelyn | Female |
| (2) | 781 | Barr T. | 16 Queen | Male |
| (3) | 324 | Piitz W. | 22 Lundy | Female |
| (4) | 523 | Jones S. | 3 George | Female |
| (5) | 862 | Lock P. | 85 Shuter | Male |

COMPANY

| | Firmname | Location |
|---|---|---|
| (1) | AES | Toronto |
| (2) | IBM | New York |
| (3) | AES | Toronto |

(a)

RELATIONS

EMPLOYEE(Employee#, Name, Address, Sex)
COMPANY(Firmname, Location)

TUPLES

EMPLOYEE

| Employee # | Name | Address | Sex |
|---|---|---|---|
| 123 | Smith J. | 19 Evelyn | Female |
| 862 | Lock P. | 85 Shuter | Male |
| 781 | Barr T. | 16 Queen | Male |
| 523 | Jones S. | 3 George | Female |
| 324 | Piitz W. | 22 Lundy | Female |

COMPANY

| Firmname | Location |
|---|---|
| AES | Toronto |
| IBM | New York |

(b)

**Fig. 2.4—3** Tables representing entity types: (a) intension; (b) extension.

31

and companies. The example demonstrates the difference between tables viewed as relations and as record types. Both types (intensions) and instances (extensions) are depicted. The types correspond to the schema. The instances are data base structures corresponding to the generic types defined by the schema. The instances of the record types are ordered as indicated by the numbers to the left of the table. The instances of the relations have no order. The record-type table for *COMPANY* shows two record instances of (AES, Toronto). This duplication can be used to indicate, for instance, that AES has two offices located in Toronto. No duplicate tuples are shown for the relation tables since duplication is not allowed. The presence of several offices in one city would have to be represented by means other than duplication. For example, an additional attribute could be added to the *COMPANY* relation that indicates the number of offices in one location.

The preceding example illustrates an important aspect of data model structure representation: implicit versus explicit representation. Duplication is an example of implicit representation. Duplication requires interpretation of the duplicates either by the user or in the schema. No duplication implies an explicit representation of the meaning of the data. The choice of structure representation determines whether information will be represented implicitly or explicitly in the structure.

### EMPLOYER

| Employee# | Name | Address | Sex | Firmname | Location |
|-----------|------|---------|-----|----------|----------|
| 123 | Smith J. | 19 Evelyn | Female | AES | Toronto |
| 862 | Lock P. | 85 Shuter | Male | AES | Toronto |
| 781 | Barr T. | 16 Queen | Male | AES | Toronto |
| 523 | Jones S. | 3 George | Female | IBM | New York |
| 324 | Piitz W. | 22 Lundy | Female | IBM | New York |

**Fig. 2.4—4** Table representing a relationship type.

The aggregation of entity types to form relationship types can also be represented by our two types of tables. Again, both intensions and extensions can be represented. For example, consider tables (relation or record type) representing entity sets. A relationship type may exist between two different tables. The extension of this relationship type can be represented as a separate table. The extension of the relationship type can be represented either symbolically or by actual tuples of the entity sets that participate in the relationship type[1]. Figure 2.4—4 shows the intension and extension of a relationship type *EMPLOYER* between the two

---

[1] In Chapter 3 we see that the relationship-type extension can also be represented by unique identifiers for the entity sets.

entity types *EMPLOYEE* and *COMPANY* as a relation table. Each row of the table corresponds to some tuple of the Cartesian product of the entity sets *EMPLOYEE* and *COMPANY* (relationship instance). The entire table represents a relationship set.

The aggregation of attributes to form entity types can also be represented by a graph of nodes and arcs. The nodes and arcs can represent either intensions or extensions of attributes and their aggregation. In terms of intensions, a node represents an attribute and an arc represents a generic aggregation of two attributes. The aggregations can be named so that there can be more than one aggregation between the same two nodes. The names provide some interpretation of the aggregations. The combination of many aggregations, obtained by following a path in the graph, produces an aggregation that can represent an entity type. In terms of extensions, a node represents attribute values. The extension can be either in terms of a set or an extended set. A path of arcs can represent an aggregation of attribute values to form entity instances.

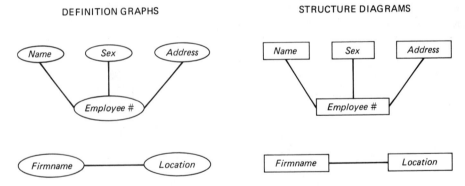

Fig. 2.4—5 Intension graphs representing entity types.

Figures 2.4—5 and 2.4—6 present the example of Figure 2.4—3 as a graph structure. Graphs are used both for the definition of the types, or schema (intension) as in Figure 2.4—5, and for the instance description (extension) as in Figure 2.4—6. The example depicts both a graph representation with sets in the nodes and a graph representation with extended sets in the nodes. The arcs between the types represent generic aggregations between the nodes. The generic aggregations are realized as a set of instance connections between instances of the nodes.

A graph of nodes and arcs can also represent aggregations of entity types and entity sets into, respectively, relationship types and relationship sets. In this case, each node represents an entity type (intension) or entity set (extension). An arc between two nodes represents a

34

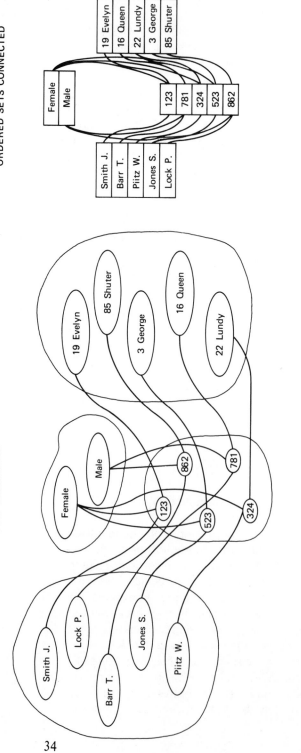

ORDERED SETS CONNECTED

SETS CONNECTED

**Fig. 2.4—6** Extension graphs representing entity types.

relationship type among entity types (intension) or a relationship instance among entity instances (extension). The relationship type can be binary, involving only two entity types, or of higher degree (*n*-ary). In most graph data models the relationship types are binary.

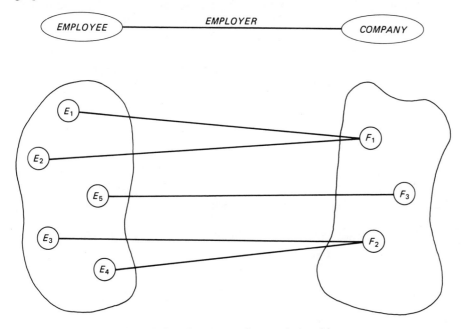

**Fig. 2.4—7** Graph representing a relationship type.

We can represent a relationship type between *EMPLOYEE* and *COMPANY* in Figure 2.4—5 by drawing an arc between the *Employee#* and *Firmname* attribute nodes in the definition graphs or structure diagrams. We can then make the appropriate connections between sets or extended sets in the extension of Figure 2.4—6. In this way, a relationship-type arc is structurally the same as an entity-type arc. However, semantically the two arcs are different. To distinguish between them, we call a relationship-type arc a *link* [Tsichritzis, 1975a,b]. A link is normally named and depicted as being between two nodes labeled with the entity-type names as in Figure 2.4—7. In this way we make no assumption about how the entity types are represented. They can be tables, as in Figure 2.4—3, or graphs as in Figure 2.4—4. The extension of the relationship type between *EMPLOYEE* and *COMPANY* is shown as a series of connections between entities as in Figure 2.4—7. The entities here are identified by symbolic labels $E_1$, $E_2$, ..., $F_3$. In this case the symbolic labels refer to the ordered sets *Employee#* and *Firmname* in Figure 2.4—6 according to the ordering implied.

As far as description is concerned, both table and graph

representations have the same capabilities. A graph representation can represent a table by specifying a path which connects the appropriate attributes that form the table. A table representation, on the other hand, can represent all the nodes and arcs of a binary graph as binary tables.

In many data models, table and graph capabilities are combined. The most widely used combination is to have a graph with tables as nodes. Relationship types are represented either within the tables or as links between the tables. This redundancy of representation capability can be used to distinguish between relationship types. For instance, relationship types between attributes of the same entity type can be represented within tables (i.e., tables represent entity sets). Relationship types among entity types can be represented as links between the tables.

## EXERCISES

**2.1** Explain Russell's paradox and determine whether it arises in data base management systems [Church, 1956].

**2.2** Consider the political and functional organization of your local municipal or state government. Construct a generalization hierarchy that describes the government organization.

**2.3** Generally, properties of types are inherited downward in a generalization hierarchy. However, some properties of types should not be inherited downward. For example, the type *EMPLOYEE* might have as a property average salary. This property should not be inherited by the individual tokens of *EMPLOYEE*. Distinguish, formally, between those properties of types that should normally be inherited and those that should not [Mylopoulos et al., 1976, 1980].

**2.4** Consider an existing application in your organization. Construct generalization and aggregation hierarchies for this application. What insights, regarding the application, did you gain from this exercise?

**2.5** Consider two relations $R_1 = \{<a, b, c>\}$ and $R_2 = \{<a, b, d>\}$ each consisting of one tuple. Suppose we take the intersection $R_1 \cap R_2$. The result of the intersection can be taken to be $\{<a, b, ->\}$ or $\{\}$. Use extended set theory to differentiate between the two cases.

**2.6** It is often difficult to distinguish between entities and attributes on the one hand, and relationships and entities on the other. If possible, provide some guidelines that can be used to resolve these two issues or explain why such guidelines cannot be provided.

**2.7** What are the advantages and disadvantages of the table and graph representations for each of the following: attributes, entities, and relationships? Is one representation better than the other overall?

**2.8** Design a procedure that transforms a graph representation of a schema into an equivalent table representation [Borkin, 1980].

**2.9** Design a procedure that transforms a table representation of a schema into an equivalent graph representation [Borkin, 1980].

# Chapter 3

# CONSTRAINTS

## 3.1 INTRODUCTION

Attributes, entity types and relationship types, based on sets and relations, can be used to represent the structures of data. The structure specification captures some of the properties of the data. For example, an attribute, based on a set, specifies that the values of the attribute conform to the underlying set membership condition. Thus, employee salaries in a particular organization, expressed in dollars as numbers, may take their values from an underlying set of integer numbers that range from 0 to 100,000.

Structures, based on sets and relations, cannot capture all the properties of attributes, entity types, and relationship types. There are usually additional properties of data that we would like to capture in a data model. These properties can be expressed as additional restrictions on the values of the data and/or how the data may be related (structured). For example, it may be company policy that a manager's salary is always higher than the salary of any of his or her subordinates. Such a restriction cannot be expressed in terms of structures, but must be captured by some additional mechanism. Note that both of the preceding examples express restrictions on the data values. The difference between them is that the range of salary values can be captured by the structure specification, whereas the manager's salary being higher than his or her subordinates cannot.

Logical restrictions on data are called *constraints*. A constraint is a property which, for a set or a relation, is either true or false. Moreover, the intention is that if the data values actually conform to the existing knowledge about an object, the constraints are expected to be true always.

Namely, they are true for every possible extension of the object as represented by the values that the object may take. For instance, the expectation that a manager's salary is always higher than any employee's salary is useful only if it is true continuously over time, not just at some point of time, and if it is true irrespective of changes in individual salaries.

In data modeling, constraints are especially useful when they are generic. That is, when they can be defined and applied to a set of objects and not just on a particular instance of an object. For instance, it is much more useful to express a constraint as "All managers' salaries are higher than those of their employees" than having to state, for example, that "Bills's salary is higher than Harry's."

Constraints are required in a data model for semantic and integrity reasons. In terms of semantics, they permit schemas to more accurately reflect the real-world situation. In terms of integrity, they permit the DBMS to restrict the possible data base states that can be generated from a given schema to those that meet the constraints. Thus, if in the real world no employee is allowed to earn more than his or her manager, then by means of suitable constraints we are able to express this requirement in the schema. Furthermore, the DBMS is able to translate this requirement into suitable mechanisms that guarantee that any data base state derivable from the schema obeys the constraints.

Recall from Chapter 1 that we can identify two basic types of constraints. The first type is an integral part of the structures of a data model. These constraints are called *inherent constraints* [Brodie, 1978]. For example, a hierarchical definition tree has an inherent constraint which specifies that all relationships in the hierarchical data base are structured as trees [Tsichritzis and Lochovsky, 1977]. Sets and relations also impose inherent constraints on attributes, entity types and relationship types (e.g., no duplication and no ordering).

Inherent constraints provide a very limited and restricted constraint specification facility. In some cases, they may even force a data base structure that does not correspond to a completely faithful semantic description of the real-world situation. The structure is neccessitated by the presence of the inherent constraints. For example, not all relationship types are functional or tree structured; yet the hierarchical data model requires that these constraints be enforced for all schemas.

To overcome the disadvantages and limited constraint specification facility provided by inherent constraints alone, some data models allow the specification of *explicit constraints*[1] [Brodie, 1978]. Explicit constraints provide a flexible mechanism for augmenting the structure specification of data bases.

---

[1] Explicit constraints have also been called *semantic integrity constraints* or *assertions* in the literature [Eswaran and Chamberlin, 1975; Hammer and McLeod, 1975; Stonebraker, 1975].

There is a third type of constraint that can be derived from stated inherent or explicit constraints. This type of constraint is called an *implicit constraint* [Brodie, 1978]. For example, in a hierarchical data base (e.g., IMS) each segment has at most one parent segment [IBM, 1975]. It follows from this that each segment has only one ancestor segment of any type. The first constraint is inherent. The second can be considered implicit.

Inherent and explicit constraints lie on a continuum. Whether a constraint is inherent or explicit depends very much on the structures provided by a data model. Consider, as an example, the functionality of relationship types. In some data models (e.g., DBTG-network and hierarchical) functionality is an inherent constraint. The data model permits only functional relationship types. In other data models (e.g., relational) functionality of relationship types has to be explicitly defined. Thus, the more restrictive a data model is in terms of structures, the greater the number of inherent constraints it incorporates, and the fewer explicit constraints that need to be, or can be, specified.

To examine the nature of constraints, we examine them as explicit constraints. Explicit constraints are specified separately from the structure specification via a constraint specification facility. Such a facility consists of a constraint specification language for defining constraints, a verification mechanism for ensuring that the set of constraints is consistent, and enforcement algorithms for guaranteeing that the constraints are adhered to for a given data base.

Explicit constraints can be specified in two ways [Hammer and McLeod, 1975]. A *static specification* expresses rules that specify which data base states are permissible (valid). Such a specification is usually expressed, using predicate calculus [Enderton, 1972; Mendelson, 1979], as predicates on data base states. It is widely accepted that any constraint can be expressed with formulas of the second-order predicate calculus. The first-order predicate calculus is, however, adequate in most cases for data modeling.

A second way to specify explicit constraints is by a *dynamic specification*. This type of specification is operation oriented in that it specifies what state transitions are allowed. The operations on a data base are defined so that only legal data base states result as a consequence of an operation or set of operations. Since this type of specification is operation oriented, we will postpone its discussion until Chapter 4. Note, however, that usually both types of specification are necessary to specify all applicable constraints.

Constraint verification requires that the set of constraints is consistent, is satisfiable, and corresponds to the existing knowledge of the real world. Consider the verification of constraints for a schema $S$ and a data base state $DBS_k$. An explicit constraint $C_i$ expressed in a schema $S$ is said to be [Brodie, 1978]:

1. *Well formed* if it obeys the syntactic rules for specifying constraints in the schema.
2. *Satisfied* by a data base state $DBS_k$ if it is true for $DBS_k$.
3. *Satisfiable* if there is some data base state $DBS_k$ that satisfies $C_i$.
4. *Invalid* if no data base state satisfies $C_i$.
5. A *logical consequence* of $C_1, ..., C_n$ (and therefore redundant) if $C_i$ is satisfied whenever $C_1, ..., C_n$ are satisfied.
6. *Equivalent* to $C_j$ if $C_i$ and $C_j$ are logical consequences of each other.

A schema $S$ is *satisfied* by a data base state if all its constraints are satisfied by the data base state. A schema $S$ is *satisfiable* if some data base states exist which satisfy it. A schema $S$ is *inconsistent* if no data base state satisfies it. A data base state $DBS_k$ is said to be *consistent* if all constraints are satisfied.

A good schema should be satisfiable. In addition, it may be important to substitute some constraints with other equivalent constraints which are more understandable or easier to validate. To meet these requirements, the constraints should be expressed in a form that is amenable to precise specification and verification.

Enforcement of explicit constraints is an extremely difficult implementation problem [Badal and Popek, 1979; Furtado et al., 1981]. In fact, most data models used in commercial systems have mainly inherent constraints. Since inherent constraints usually relate to the structures of the data base and not its contents, they are easy to implement. When coupled with carefully chosen operations in the data manipulation language, they can be enforced automatically. If an inherent constraint is violated, it amounts to a data structuring error. An explicit constraint, on the other hand, has to be enforced independent of the schema specification and operations on the data base. It usually requires checking of many data values to ensure its enforcement.

In the next two sections we consider the types of constraints that are used most frequently in data modeling. All constraints will be considered as explicit constraints even though many of them are inherent constraints in several data models. In Section 3.4 we consider the representation of constraints, both explicitly and inherently, in tables and graphs.

## 3.2 SETS — DOMAINS AND ATTRIBUTES

Attributes take their values from underlying domains which can be defined in terms of sets. Attributes inherit some constraints from sets as a consequence of the set membership condition. Thus, a set can be defined so as to restrict the values that an attribute may have. For example, we can define a set of integers from 16 to 65. This set can be used as the basis for a domain from which an attribute *Age* takes its values. This attribute may be part of an entity type *EMPLOYEE*. Such a domain can represent the real-world constraint that employees of a company be between the ages of 16 and 65 inclusive.

As constraints, set membership conditions are often not sufficient for data modeling. We usually require that additional semantics be associated with a domain. Consider, for example, the set of integers from 1 to 60. Such a domain could be the basis for an attribute *Age* as well as for an attribute *Speed*. With only the set membership condition as a constraint, we are unable to determine that it is not meaningful to compare *Age* and *Speed* or to associate a speed as the value of someone's age. In data modeling and data base management, it is necessary to be able to differentiate domains based on the same underlying set. We need to be able to associate some interpretation or semantics with a domain that enables us to distinguish two domains based on the same underlying set.

Some semantics is provided by the attribute name. For example, we, as human beings, have implicit knowledge that an attribute named *Age* and one named *Speed* are not comparable. However, because it has no implicit knowledge about attribute names, such a semantic distinction is at too high a level for a computer. We need to specify more precisely the semantic distinction between attributes such as *Age* and *Speed*. Attribute names alone are not sufficient since attributes may be named differently, yet still be the same semantically (e.g., *Speed* and *Velocity*).

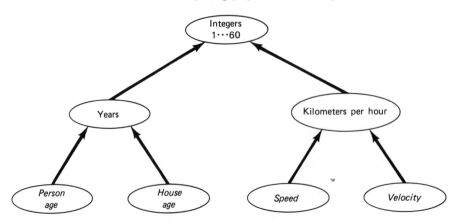

**Fig. 3.2—1** Example of interpreted domain.

The usual way of associating semantics with attributes is by abstraction techniques such as those discussed in Chapter 2. Consider, for example, the attributes *Age* and *Speed*. We would like both of these attributes to be based on the same set of values, yet to have a different semantic. Suppose that we add a level of abstraction between an attribute and a domain as in Figure 3.2-1. We call this intermediate abstraction level an *interpreted domain*[1]. Its purpose is to allow us to distinguish the possible different uses of the same underlying domain. Thus, the interpreted domain upon which *Age* is based is not the same as that for *Speed*. Hence, any comparison between them is not meaningful.

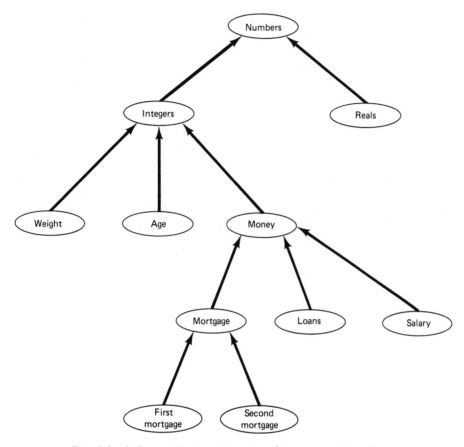

**Fig. 3.2—2** Generalization hierarchy of interpreted domains.

One way of looking at an interpreted domain is that it associates some *units* with the domain. Thus, the units years may be associated with *Age* and kilometers per hour with *Speed*. Two attributes are not comparable unless the units of the attributes are the same or can be converted to a common unit. The concept of an interpreted domain is much more general than merely associating units with an attribute. In addition, because it is an abstraction, it is possible to have several levels of interpretation (e.g., Figure 3.2—2). The number of levels in the

---

[1] Interpreted domains have been called roles in some data models [Codd, 1970].

generalization hierarchy depends on how fine a distinction is required between the semantics of different domains.

Interpreted domains can also be constrained according to the operations allowed on them. For example, one may be able only to add to *Age* but to add or subtract from *Speed.* In Section 3.4 we examine ways of representing the interpreted domain concept.

An interpreted domain allows us to specify *value constraints* on the individual values that an attribute can have. It provides the ability to specify a membership condition and to associate a semantic with a domain. We may also want to specify constraints on some aggregation of the values of an attribute. *Aggregate constraints* are of the form "The total of all salaries cannot exceed $1,000,000" or "The average of all ages is less than 50." These types of constraints on attributes need to be specified by predicates.

Aggregate constraints are usually much more difficult to enforce than are value constraints. Value constraints can normally be checked in the schema. That is, it is possible to check a new value for the attribute without access to the data base. For example, one can check whether a value belongs to a certain set without accessing values stored in the data base. Aggregate constraints may need to be checked by accessing values in the data base. For instance, to check whether the insertion of a new employee would violate an aggregate constraint on average salaries, it may be necessary to compute the average. The checking of some aggregate constraints can be simplified if aggregate data are maintained by the system [Bernstein et al., 1980].

## 3.3 RELATIONS — ENTITIES AND RELATIONSHIPS

When attributes are aggregated to form entity types and relationship types, we may want to impose constraints on the aggregation. For example, we may want to restrict the number of employee numbers that an employee may have or the number of employees that work in a certain department. These types of constraints specify restrictions on the mappings between attributes and/or between entity types. Although not the only types of constraints that can be specified for entity types and relationship types, they represent a very important and commonly occurring class of constraints.

Recall that a relation specifies a mapping among two or more sets. Specifically, a relation is defined as the subset of the cross product of two or more sets. In the absence of constraints, all possible subsets of the cross product are valid extensions of a relation. When sets represent attributes and relations represent entity types or relationship types, we may want to restrict the possible extensions of a relation to correspond to some real-world semantics. We will consider the properties of relations defined by the mappings between sets and see how these properties provide us with some data modeling semantics.

Without loss of generality, consider a binary relation $R$ between two sets $S_1$ and $S_2$. The binary relation $R$ defines two mappings, $R:S_1 \rightarrow S_2$ and $R^{-1}:S_2 \rightarrow S_1$, one the inverse of the other. The property of these mappings that is important for data modeling and that will be investigated is that of *cardinality* [Abrial, 1974; El-Masri and Wiederhold, 1979]. Cardinality of the mapping refers to the number of objects of $S_1$ that can be related to $S_2$ objects, and vice versa. For each mapping of a binary relation $R$ we can specify a minimum cardinality and a maximum cardinality.

Consider the relation $R$ defined previously consisting of the two mappings $R:S_1 \rightarrow S_2$ and $R^{-1}:S_2 \rightarrow S_1$. If we do not place any constraints on these mappings, any number of objects (0 or more) of $S_1$ can be related to $S_2$ objects, and vice versa. Thus, there are no minimum and maximum cardinalities for either of the two mappings. We use the notation $R(S_1(0,\infty):S_2(0,\infty))$ to denote a relation with these types of mappings. Here $S_1(0,\infty)$ indicates that the minimum and maximum cardinality of the mapping from $S_2$ to $S_1$ is 0 and $\infty$, respectively. That is, consider any object in $S_2$. This object must be related to at least 0 objects and at most $\infty$ objects in $S_1$. Similar remarks apply for $S_2(0,\infty)$. In data modeling, such a mapping in both directions is often referred to as a many-to-many $(N:M)$ mapping when specified for a relationship type.

By placing specific restrictions on the minimum and maximum cardinalities of a mapping, we obtain different types of mappings. For example, consider two entity types *COURSE* and *STUDENT* and an *ENROLLMENT* relationship type between them. It may be the case that every student must be enrolled in between four and six courses. This can be specified as $ENROLLMENT(STUDENT(0,\infty):COURSE(4,6))$[1]. If we also want to impose enrollment restrictions, say 10 to 100, this could be specified as $ENROLLMENT(STUDENT(10,100):COURSE(4,6))$.

A mapping $S_1 \rightarrow S_2$ where the minimum cardinality is at least one (e.g., $R(S_1(0,\infty):S_2(1,\infty))$) requires that every object of $S_1$ be mapped to at least one object of $S_2$. In mathematical terms the mapping is *total* with respect to $S_1$. The mapping constraint says that for an $S_1$ object to exist, it must be related to an $S_2$ object (i.e., $S_2$ maps onto $S_1$). This type of mapping constraint is called an *existency constraint* in data modeling [Brodie, 1978]. Existency constraints usually refer to relationship types and specify the mapping requirements that must exist between entities for one or both of the entities to exist. In the case of our first enrollment

---

[1] Read as: Consider any object in *STUDENT*. This object must be related to at least 4 and at most 6 objects in *COURSE*.

constraint it says that a student cannot exist unless he or she is related to at least four courses. Existency constraints are also referred to as *existence dependency constraints* or simply *dependency constraints*[1] in the literature [Chen, 1976; El-Masri and Wiederhold, 1979].

When the maximum cardinality of a mapping is one, the mapping is a function (in the mathematical meaning of the word). Thus, $R(S_1(0,1):S_2(0,\infty))$ defines a functional mapping from $S_2$ to $S_1$. It says that any $S_2$ object is mapped to at most one $S_1$ object (although not all $S_2$ objects need be mapped and not all $S_1$ objects need be mapped). An example of a functional mapping is shown in Figure 3.3−1.

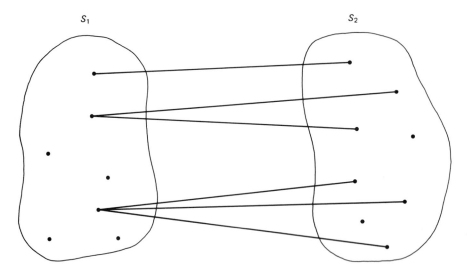

**Fig. 3.3−1** Functional mapping from $S_2$ to $S_1$.

Functional mappings appear often in data modeling. For relations representing entity types, we sometimes want to restrict the mapping between attributes so that it is functional. As an example, consider a simple entity type *EMPLOYEE* with two attributes *Employee#* and *Name*. Valid extensions of this entity type consist of any subset of the cross product of the underlying domains of *Employee#* and *Name*. Suppose that the domain for *Employee#* is {100,115,111} and for *Name* it is {Smith J.,Jones S.,Hall T.,Lock P.}. An extension of *EMPLOYEE* according to these domains is shown in Figure 3.3−2. Suppose further that there is a (plausible) real world constraint that no two employees can have the same employee number. Then the extension of *EMPLOYEE* in Figure 3.3−2 is not a valid extension in light of this additional constraint since there are

---

[1.] Dependency constraints as they refer to existence are not to be confused with dependency constraints as they refer to functionality.

*EMPLOYEE*

| Employee# | Name |
|-----------|----------|
| 100 | Jones S. |
| 115 | Smith J. |
| 100 | Lock P. |
| 111 | Hall T. |

**Fig. 3.3−2** *EMPLOYEE* entity set.

two employees with *Employee#* 100.

A functional mapping between two attributes such as *Name* and *Employee#* (written *Employee#* → *Name*) is normally called a *functional dependency* in data modeling. A functional dependency is nothing more than a statement about a real-world constraint that can be expressed very precisely in terms of relations and sets. The concept of functionality between attributes is very important in data modeling and is considered in more detail in Chapter 13.

For relations representing relationship types, functional mappings are also very important. Such mappings are called one-to-many $(1:N)$ relationship types. For example, in an organization there may be a functional mapping between employees and the departments in which they work. That is, every employee works in at most one department. This constraint could be expressed as a functional relationship type between entity types *EMPLOYEE* and *DEPARTMENT*. Several data models, including the DBTG-network and hierarchical data models, are based on functional relationship types.

Additional restrictions can be placed on functional mappings. A *partial functional mapping* from $S_2$ to $S_1$, also called an *into mapping* from $S_1$

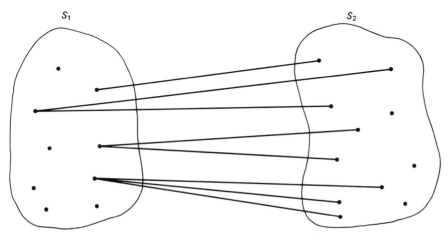

**Fig. 3.3−3** Partial functional mapping from $S_2$ to $S_1$.

to $S_2$, is one where an $S_1$ object is mapped to zero or more $S_2$ objects. An $S_2$ object is mapped to at most one $S_1$ object, but not all $S_2$ objects need be mapped (Figure 3.3—3). This is specified as $R(S_1(0,1):S_2(0,\infty))$. In our employees and departments example this would mean that every employee works in at most one department. However, not all employees need be assigned to a department and not all departments need have employees assigned to them.

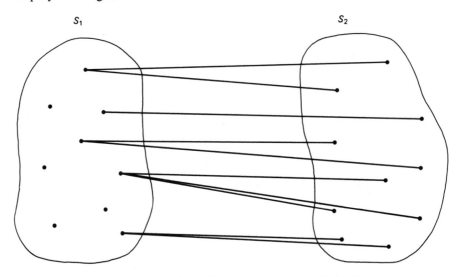

**Fig. 3.3—4** Total functional mapping from $S_2$ to $S_1$.

A *total functional mapping* from $S_2$ to $S_1$, also called an *onto mapping* from $S_1$ to $S_2$, is one where every $S_2$ object is mapped to exactly one $S_1$ object. In addition, an $S_1$ object is mapped to zero or more $S_2$ objects (Figure 3.3—4). This is specified as $R(S_1(1,1):S_2(0,\infty))$. This type of functional mapping expresses an existency constraint. In our employees and departments example it can take the form that every employee must belong to a department. This requirement can have several real-world semantics. For instance, it may be expected that once employees are hired, they immediately report to a department and they cannot change departments. Alternatively, it may be expected that they can change departments, but at any point in time they are associated with some department. The latter properties of an existency constraint cannot be specified as mapping properties but require predicates to specify them.

Both mappings in a binary relation can be functions. In data modeling, such a mapping is called a one-to-one (1:1) mapping. One-to-one mappings can again be partial (into) and total (onto). A partial one-to-one mapping from $S_2$ to $S_1$ ($S_1$ maps into $S_2$) is written as $R(S_1(0,1):S_2(0,1))$. A total one-to-one mapping from $S_2$ to $S_1$ ($S_1$ maps onto $S_2$) is written as $R(S_1(1,1):S_2(0,1))$.

These mappings for binary relations can be extended in a natural way for *n*-ary relations. They can then be used to specify constraints for entity types and relationship types represented by *n*-ary relations.

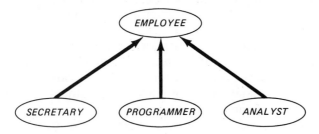

**Fig. 3.3—5** Generalization hierarchy.

Mappings so far have been used to represent aggregations of objects (e.g., attributes and entity types). They can also specify constraints for generalizations. Consider the generalization hierarchy shown in Figure 3.3—5, where *EMPLOYEE* is a generalization of *SECRETARY*, *PROGRAMMER*, and *ANALYST*. We can specify this generalization as a series of one-to-one mappings between each of *SECRETARY*, *PROGRAMMER*, *ANALYST*, and *EMPLOYEE*. In addition, the mapping must be total. Thus *ISA (EMPLOYEE* (1, 1) *:SECRETARY* (0, 1)) specifies the mapping between *EMPLOYEE* and *SECRETARY*. We use the special term *ISA* to indicate the fact that this mapping represents a generalization. Such a mapping also relates to the concept of roles of entity types as discussed in Section 2.3 [Bachman and Daya, 1977].

Another property of a relation that can be used to specify constraints is whether the mapping it represents can be described in a closed form. Consider, for instance, the two sets $S_1$ and $S_2$ of the relation $R$. Suppose that there is a closed-form formula $m(S_1, S_2)$ which describes the mapping of $S_1$ and $S_2$ as it manifests itself in the relation $R$. That is, in every extension of the relation the sets $S_1$ and $S_2$ are related exactly by $m(S_1, S_2)$. In this case the fact that the extension contains a certain tuple does not convey any additional information. The mapping between $S_1$ and $S_2$ is represented by $m$ in any extension of $R$. This type of mapping between $S_1$ and $S_2$ is called *non-information bearing*. A mapping that cannot be expressed in a closed form but must be expressed by a relation extension is called *information bearing* [Metaxides, 1975].

The simplest case of a non-information-bearing relation occurs when $S_1$ and $S_2$ are aggregates of attributes (e.g., $S_1(A_1, ..., A_n)$ and $S_2(B_1, ..., B_n)$). Suppose that the mapping between $S_1$ and $S_2$ is specified by saying that $A_1 = B_1$ for the corresponding objects of $S_1$ and $S_2$. In this case it is obvious that if we have the two sets $S_1$ and $S_2$, the mapping is completely defined by the closed-form formula $A_1 = B_1$. There is no need for any additional encoding of the mapping since we add no information by specifying it separately. On the other hand, if there is no such formula that characterizes the mapping between $S_1$ and $S_2$, the mapping is represented solely by the relation extension. In this case the relation is information bearing.

In addition to mapping constraints, we may also wish to express other, more general, constraints on relations. For example, a constraint such as "a manager must earn more than any of his subordinates" cannot be expressed as a mapping constraint. Such a constraint is similar to an aggregate constraint on attributes since an aggregate is involved (maximum salary of all subordinates must be less than the manager's salary). However, other atttributes are involved in this constraint (i.e., *Manager name* or *Employee#*). This type of constraint needs to be expressed by an explicit predicate.

## 3.4 REPRESENTATION — TABLES AND GRAPHS

Many of the constraints we have discussed can be specified as either inherent or explicit constraints. In this section we consider the specification of constraints for attributes, entity types, and relationship types both inherently and explicitly in terms of tables and graphs.

We consider first the specification of constraints on attributes. These constraints are either value or aggregate constraints. Value constraints relate to set membership conditions and semantics of domains (i.e., interpreted domains). Each of these different aspects of value constraints can be specified explicitly for each attribute in terms of types, ranges, units, and comparability of domain values. Thus, for an attribute *Salary* one may have statements such as

*Salary*   **TYPE INTEGER**
           **RANGE 0 TO** 100000
           **UNITS DOLLARS**

Another approach to specifying value constraints, used in programming languages, is to use abstraction to encapsulate the properties of an attribute as a data type. We start with specific primitive types such as integer, character, Boolean, and so on. These types provide the basic semantics of a domain. Additional semantics can be added by further specializing and aggregating types. Such a type has been called an *interpreted type* in both programming languages [Wegbreit, 1974] and data base management [Brodie, 1978, 1980], and corresponds to the concept of an interpreted domain. The advantage of this approach is that it is possible, first, to use a data type specification as the basis for an

**INTERPRETED TYPE** *Social security number* =
   **SUBRANGE** (550000000..850000000)
**INTERPRETED TYPE** *Course number type* = **STRING**[1..6] **OF CHARACTER**
**INTERPRETED TYPE** *Postal code type* = **STRING** [1..6] **OF CHARACTER**
**INTERPRETED TYPE** *Money* = **SUBRANGE**(0..100000) **OF INTEGER**
**INTERPRETED TYPE** *Grade* =
   (incomplete, F, pass, C-, C, C+, B-, B, B+, A-, A, A+)

**Fig. 3.4−1** Example of interpreted types.

interpreted domain and, second, to use the data type repeatedly for different attributes. The data type encodes all the relevant constraints for the attributes specified on the data type.

Using a modified form of the constraint language Beta, some examples of interpreted type specifications are shown in Figure 3.4−1 [Brodie, 1978, 1980]. Both *Course number type* and *Postal code type* are defined on the same underlying type, but are incompatible. We see that the value sets of an interpreted type can be defined in terms of other types (e.g., *Course number type*), be enumerated (e.g., *Grade*), or be specified as subranges (e.g., *Social security number*). The domain of an attribute can then be specified as corresponding to an interpreted type. For example, a *Salary* attribute can now be specified as

*Salary* : *Money*

More general constraints on attributes, such as aggregate constraints, are specified by predicates. Consider, for example, an *EMPLOYEE* entity type with attributes *Employee#*, *Name*, *Address*, *Sex*, and *Salary*. We may have a constraint on the *Sex* attribute that at least 40% of employees must be females. In Beta this would be expressed as

**ASSERT**
   **COUNT**[EACH e **IN** *EMPLOYEE*] * .4 ≤
   **COUNT**[EACH e **IN** *EMPLOYEE* **WHERE** e. *Sex* = Female]

A constraint such as "The average of all ages cannot exceed 50" would be expressed as

**ASSERT**
   **AVERAGE**[EACH e. *Age* **FOR** e **IN** *EMPLOYEE*] < 50

These types of constraints make use of aggregate functions such as **COUNT, AVERAGE, SUM, MAXIMUM, MINIMUM**, and so on. They are specified nonprocedurally in a constraint specification language such as Beta. However, their enforcement usually requires a procedure specification in terms of operations in the data model.

Consider now entity types and relationship types represented by tables and/or graphs. The mapping property of the underlying relation can be specified explicitly as constraints on rows of the tables or arcs of the graph, or inherently in the kinds of rows or arcs allowed. For some of the mapping properties, it may be important to distinguish between tables representing (data base) relations and tables representing record types. We will distinguish between these two cases when necessary.

We consider first the specification of functional mappings (functional dependencies) between attributes of an entity type. Functional dependencies apply equally well to tables which are either relations or record types, since they concern only the values of the attributes. In general, a functional dependency constraint has to be specified as an explicit constraint on an entity type. There are, however, certain functional dependencies that can be considered as inherent constraints on tables.

Consider the entity type *EMPLOYEE* specified previously. If there exists a functional dependency from *Employee#* to every other attribute in *EMPLOYEE*, we call *Employee#* a *candidate key* of the entity type *EMPLOYEE*. We call it a candidate key because there may be other attributes (or sets of attributes) with this property. For example, *Name* and *Address* taken together may also be a candidate key of *EMPLOYEE*. Usually, one of the candidate keys of an entity type is designated as the *(primary) key*. A (primary) key can be considered an inherent constraint in a data model because there is an implied understanding that this constraint will be enforced automatically by the DBMS.

By definition, a key uniquely identifies the contents of a row as well as the row in a table. In tables that represent record types, duplicate records may exist which have the same contents, but are different record occurrences. If we want to allow duplicate contents yet uniquely identify record occurrences, we need a different definition of a key. An *external key* is an attribute whose value identifies uniquely a record occurrence, but not necessarily its contents. An external key cannot be operated on or accessed the same way as the other attributes in a record type.

The notions of key and external key should not be considered as part of accessing a table, although they are sometimes used for accessing. Neither should they carry any connotations of physical placement, although they may be used for physically placing or clustering the table instances. They are constraints, and these properties should be considered independent of any use of a key or external key for accessing a table.

Functional dependencies appear naturally in graph data models as restrictions on the connections allowed between nodes. For instance, the functional dependency *Employee#* $\rightarrow$ *Name* signifies that the arc between *Employee#* and *Name* is functional or represents a function in the direction *Name* to *Employee#*. In a graph, we can show functionality by means of

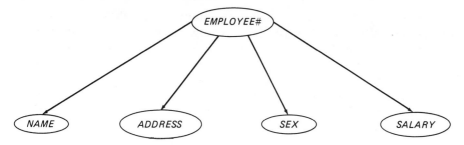

**Fig. 3.4—2** Representing functional dependencies in graphs.

directed arcs as in Figure 3.4—2. Note that the arcs point in the direction opposite that of the functionality. Such a graph can be used to define an entity type as discussed in Section 2.4.

If we have functional dependencies which have more than one attribute on their left side, it is awkward to express them in a graph data model. For instance, *Name, Address → Salary* cannot be expressed as a property of one arc in the graph. In the case of a graph data model that has tables as nodes, these functional dependencies can be expressed within the tables. In the case of a graph data model with simple attributes, there may be a need to form artificial nodes (Figure 3.4—3). These nodes, which are called *internal nodes*, are not a radical departure for a graph data model. Their presence does not necessarily affect the data base structures or operations on them. They are there to encode constraints. Internal nodes can also be used for defining an entity type by grouping together many interdependent simple attributes.

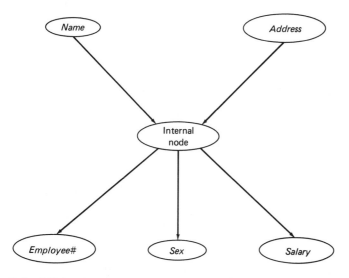

**Fig. 3.4—3** Using internal nodes to represent functional dependencies.

Consider now a mapping among entity types that represents a relationship type. In table data models, this mapping can be represented by a table. Normally, a table representation of such a mapping implies that all the attributes of the entity types appear in the table. However, we can capture the same information if we only place the keys of the entity types involved in the table. We will consider the constraints we need to place on such a table in order to represent a binary relationship type between two entity types.

EMPLOYEE

| Employee# | Name | Address | Sex |
|---|---|---|---|
| 123 | Smith J. | 19 Evelyn | Female |
| 862 | Lock P. | 85 Shuter | Male |
| 781 | Barr T. | 16 Queen | Male |
| 523 | Jones S. | 3 George | Female |
| 324 | Piitz W. | 22 Lundy | Female |

SKILL

| Title | Pay rate |
|---|---|
| Typist | 12.50 |
| Stenographer | 14.25 |
| Clerk | 13.00 |
| Receptionist | 13.50 |

SKILLPOOL

| Employee# | Title |
|---|---|
| 123 | Typist |
| 862 | Typist |
| 781 | Stenographer |
| 523 | Clerk |
| 862 | Stenographer |
| 123 | Stenographer |
| 781 | Clerk |
| 324 | Receptionist |
| 523 | Receptionist |
| 862 | Clerk |

**Fig. 3.4—4** Table representing a many-to-many relationship type.

A many-to-many relationship type, such as *SKILLPOOL* between *EMPLOYEE* and *SKILL*, can be represented by a table whose attributes correspond to the key of *EMPLOYEE* and of *SKILL* (Figure 3.4—4). Such a table represents an unrestricted many-to-many relationship type (e.g., $SKILLPOOL(EMPLOYEE(0,\infty):SKILL(0,\infty))$). To ensure that the

EMPLOYEE

| Employee# | Name | Address | Sex |
|-----------|------|---------|-----|
| 123 | Smith J. | 19 Evelyn | Female |
| 862 | Lock P. | 85 Shuter | Male |
| 781 | Barr T. | 16 Queen | Male |
| 523 | Jones S. | 3 George | Female |
| 324 | Piitz W. | 22 Lundy | Female |

COMPANY

| Firmname | Location |
|----------|----------|
| AES | Toronto |
| IBM | New York |

EMPLOYER

| Firmname | Employee# |
|----------|-----------|
| AES | 123 |
| AES | 862 |
| AES | 781 |
| IBM | 523 |
| IBM | 324 |

**Fig. 3.4—5** Representing a functional relationship type.

SKILLPOOL table represents only valid relationships between EMPLOYEE and SKILL, subset constraints need to be imposed on the Employee# and Title attribute values in SKILLPOOL. In Beta these would be specified as

```
ASSERT
      SKILLPOOL. Employee# IN EMPLOYEE. Employee#
      SKILLPOOL. Title IN SKILL. Title
```

Subset constraints are required in general for relationship types represented as separate tables. In what follows we assume such constraints unless noted otherwise.

We can specify cardinality constraints for the relationship type by explicit predicates on the table. For example, the requirement that each employee must have at least two skills is stated in Beta as

```
MAP
      FROM e IN EMPLOYEE
      TO[2..*] sp IN SKILLPOOL
      WHERE e. Employee# = sp. Employee#
```

where * means no maximum number. Note that this is also an existency constraint since for an EMPLOYEE tuple to exist, it must map to at least two tuples in SKILLPOOL.

Consider now the two entity types *EMPLOYEE* and *COMPANY* shown in Figure 3.4−5 and a functional relationship type from *EMPLOYEE* to *COMPANY*. This relationship type can be represented by the table *EMPLOYER*. To guarantee functionality, we need to specify that there is at most one *Firmname* associated with each unique value of *Employee#* in *EMPLOYER*. In Beta this would be stated as

**MAP**
    **FROM** e **IN** *EMPLOYEE*
    **TO** [0..1] ep **IN** *EMPLOYER*
    **WHERE** e.*Employee#* = ep.*Employee#*

If we wanted a total functional relationship type, the minimum cardinality would be one rather than zero.

A one-to-one relationship type can also be represented by a separate table. In this case explicit constraints such as the one between *EMPLOYEE* and *EMPLOYER* are required for both directions of the mapping.

It is possible to represent some of the explicit constraints on tables representing relationship types inherently in the table structure. We will illustrate the procedure for functional relationship types.

*EMPLOYER*

| Employee# | Name | Address | Sex | Firmname |
|-----------|----------|-----------|--------|----------|
| 123 | Smith J. | 19 Evelyn | Female | AES |
| 862 | Lock P. | 85 Shuter | Male | AES |
| 781 | Barr T. | 16 Queen | Male | AES |
| 523 | Jones S. | 3 George | Female | IBM |
| 324 | Piitz W. | 22 Lundy | Female | IBM |

*COMPANY*

| Firmname | Location |
|----------|----------|
| AES | Toronto |
| IBM | New York |

**Fig. 3.4−6** Representing a functional relationship type inherently.

Consider the functional relationship type *EMPLOYER* between *EMPLOYEE* and *COMPANY* shown in Figure 3.4−5. We can represent the functionality of the relationship type by adding the attribute *Firmname* to the *EMPLOYEE* table as shown in Figure 3.4−6. We call this procedure *key propagation* since we in effect place the key of *COMPANY* in the *EMPLOYEE* table. *Firmname* in *EMPLOYEE* is called a *foreign key* of *COMPANY* in *EMPLOYEE*. This representation inherently preserves the functional nature of the relationship type from *EMPLOYEE* to *COMPANY* since the *Firmname* attribute in *EMPLOYEE* can have at most one value in each row of the *EMPLOYEE* table. If *Firmname* in *EMPLOYEE* is required to have a value (i.e., cannot be null), the relationship type from *EMPLOYEE* to *COMPANY* is total.

*COMPANY*

| | | EMPLOYEE | | | |
|---|---|---|---|---|---|
| *Firmname* | *Location* | *Employee#* | *Name* | *Address* | *Sex* |
| AES | Toronto | 123 | Smith J. | 19 Evelyn | Female |
| | | 862 | Lock P. | 85 Shuter | Male |
| | | 781 | Barr T. | 16 Queen | Male |
| IBM | New York | 523 | Jones S. | 3 George | Female |
| | | 324 | Piitz W. | 22 Lundy | Female |

**Fig. 3.4—7** Representing a functional relationship type inherently.

A functional relationship type can also be represented inherently in the structure of a table if we allow *composite attributes.* Composite attributes are attributes which are themselves tables (Figure 3.4—7). Their presence results in either *attribute relations,* in the case of relations, or *repeating groups,* in the case of record types. Both of these representations correspond to a complex of complexes (i.e., *EMPLOYEE* is a complex within the complex *COMPANY*). Composite attributes can be nested in arbitrary ways. Note that composite attributes enforce a total mapping from *EMPLOYEE* to *COMPANY* (i.e., every employee is related to a company). Historically, composite attributes and especially repeating groups are introduced for performance considerations. A repeating group is assumed to be close, physically, to the rest of the record occurrence.

In graph data models, mappings among entity types are represented by links between nodes which represent entity types. The link, in effect, serves the purpose of the extra table in table data models. The links are usually labeled to indicate the relationship type and its meaning. Figure 3.4—8 shows the intension and extension of the many-to-many relationship type *SKILLPOOL* between *EMPLOYEE* and *SKILL* entity types in terms of a graph. For identification purposes, we use the key of *EMPLOYEE* and *SKILL* to identify the entities. The relationships are indicated by the arcs connecting *EMPLOYEE* and *SKILL* entities. The entity types can also be represented by tables in graph data models. In this case the relationship type is represented as in Figure 3.4—9.

Cardinality constraints on relationship types for graphs can be specified in a manner similar to that for tables. To specify that every employee must have at least two skills we could use the Beta predicate

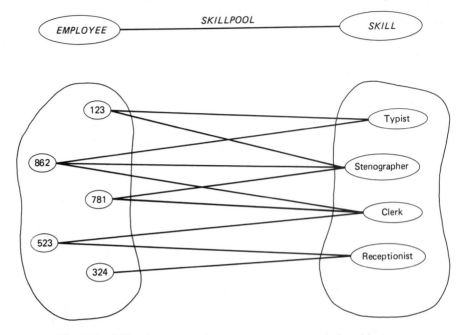

**Fig. 3.4—8** Graph representing a many-to-many relationship type.

**MAP**
> **FROM** e **IN** *EMPLOYEE*
> **TO** [2..*] s **IN** *SKILL*

Some graph data models require that cardinality constraints (sometimes only maximums) be specified on the graph directly for each link.

Functional and one-to-one mappings can be represented and specified in the same way as many-to-many mappings. However, many graph data models permit only functional relationship types, and special notation has

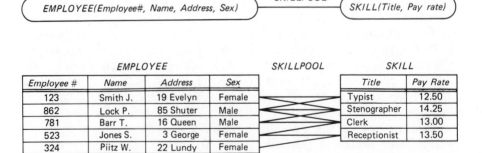

**Fig. 3.4—9** Graph and tables representing a many-to-many relationship type.

been established for such graphs. In these graphs, functionality of relationship types is indicated by a directed link between two entity types.

Figure 3.4—10 shows the graph representation of the functional relationship type *EMPLOYER* between *EMPLOYEE* and *COMPANY*. Usually, there is no maximum cardinality restriction on functional relationship types in these graph data models. Minimum cardinality constraints (partial or total) can be either inherent in some graph data models (e.g., as in the IMS hierarchical data model) or specified explicitly (e.g., as in the DBTG-network data model). Sometimes further inherent constraints are also imposed on how entity types can be related (e.g., in hierarchical data models). When functionality is inherent in the data model, it is enforced automatically by the DBMS.

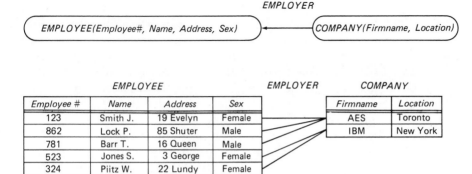

**Fig. 3.4—10** Graph representing a functional relationship type.

Some graph data models name a link in both directions to represent the two mappings implied by a relationship type (Figure 3.4—11) [Abrial, 1974]. Such a representation makes explicit the nature of the mapping. We examine this representation for graph data models in more detail in Chapter 10.

*ISA* relationship types (i.e., generalization hierarchies) can be represented in both tables and graphs as one-to-one relationship types. They can also be specified as subsets of an entity set and explicitly named. In Beta, for example, we can specify typists as a separate entity type by the statements

*TYPIST* = **OBJECT** [**EACH** e **IN** *EMPLOYEE* **WHERE** e. *Title* = Typist]
*Typing speed*: **SUBRANGE** (0..150) **OF INTEGER**

We can associate additional attributes with such an entity type (e.g., *Typing speed* with *Typist* as specified above).

In table data models, information-bearing relationship types are represented by additional tables. The tables explicitly specify the

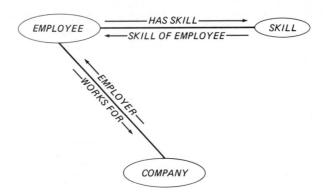

**Fig. 3.4—11** Graph representing relationship types.

relationships between entities (e.g., Figure 3.4—4). Non-information bearing relationship types are represented within tables that represent entity types. The relationships are given by closed-form formulas between tables (e.g., *EMPLOYEE.Firmname = COMPANY.Firmname* in Figure 3.4—6).

In a graph data model, both information-bearing and non-information-bearing relationship types are represented by links. In Figure 3.4—10 the *EMPLOYER* relationship type is information bearing; the connections between the entities determine the relationships. The *EMPLOYER* relationship type can be made non-information bearing if we add the attribute *Firmname* to the *EMPLOYEE* entity type. The relationships are then determined by the same closed-form formula as for the table given above.

Information-bearing relationship types are important in graph data models since it is very restrictive to have all the connections in a graph established with closed-form formulas of values. In fact, if each node contains only a single attribute, only trivial non-information-bearing relationship types based only on the order of the attribute values can be specified. If the nodes contain at least binary tables, it is not as restrictive to have only non-information-bearing relationship types.

Other constraints can be defined in both tables and graphs. These constraints are usually expressed as predicate calculus expressions. In table data models the predicate calculus expressions involve the attribute names of the tables. In a graph data model they involve the attribute nodes and they are expressed as general restrictions on a single link, or a path through the graph. Although they can be quite easy to specify in terms of a constraint specification language such as Beta, their enforcement is a difficult implementation problem in general.

## EXERCISES

**3.1** What types of constraints require second order predicate calculus for their specification? Can you give some realistic examples of constraints that require second order predicate calculus expressions?

**3.2** Give some examples of realistic partial and total one-to-one mappings. Specify these mappings in terms of the notation introduced in Section 3.3.

**3.3** Investigate the data types provided in a high-level programming language such as Euclid [Lampson et al., 1977]. Are the facilities provided adequate for data modeling? What extensions, if any, would you propose for the language to make it suitable for data modeling (e.g., PLAIN [Wasserman, 1979] or PASCAL [Schmidt, 1977])?

**3.4** Using the constraint language Beta, specify the predicates necessary to define a partial and total one-to-one mapping between two tables.

**3.5** How would you represent a many-to-many relationship type inherently in the structure of a table data model?

**3.6** How would you represent an *ISA* relationship type inherently in the structure of a table data model?

**3.7** How would you represent an *ISA* relationship type inherently in the structure of a graph data model?

**3.8** What storage mechanisms would you use to enforce a key as a constraint? How would you enforce a functional dependency?

**3.9** Consider an *ENROLLMENT* relationship type with cardinality *ENROLLMENT(STUDENT(10,100):COURSE(4,6))*. How would you describe this cardinality constraint in terms of predicate calculus? How would you enforce this constraint?

**3.10** In our discussion of complexes in Chapter 2, we used integers to indicate the position of an object within a complex. Alternatively, we can use symbolic position indicators as in [Hardgrave, 1981]. What is the correspondence between such a representation for entity and relationship types and the table and graph representations discussed in this chapter?

# Chapter 4

# OPERATIONS

## 4.1 SELECTION

As defined in Chapter 1, the operations of a data model, called a *data language*, transform a data base state $DBS_i$ to another data base state $DBS_k$ (or undefined). The operations can change the data base state by either changing the data base occurrence or related control mechanisms (e.g., currency indicators). These data base states relate to a particular schema defined according to the data model. It is implied therefore that the operations preserve the properties of a schema and, of course, of the data model. We discuss these kinds of operations in this chapter. There are also operations which transform schemas and/or data models. These operations are discussed in Chapter 14.

When we perform operations on a data base, it is a natural restriction to focus them in one small part of the data base. This focusing is important both for user convenience and for the ability to concentrate on a few narrowly defined tasks at one time. Focusing on a certain part of the data base implies a *selection* [Earnest, 1975]. Regardless of the operation that is to be performed, this selection needs to be specified. For example, the selected data base part may be retrieved or updated, new data may be inserted into it or old data deleted from it.

Traditionally, most data models discuss data selection in terms of accessing the data. The reason for equating selection with access is that under current computer architectures selected data needs to be brought into main memory before it can be operated on. However, future architectures may allow in-place processing of data by local processors. Thus, selection is important by itself since it may not always be an integral part of accessing.

62

In data modeling we need to define the operations in a way that a user can understand them. Since the structures available to a user are usually either tables, graphs, or both, we concentrate on operations for these structures. The operations usually follow a pattern of specifying an action and a selection. The *action* specifies what is to be done. The *selection* selects the part of the data base to which the action is to be applied.

Traditionally, an action on tables or graphs is one of, or a combination of, five generic operations:

1. Set currency — establish one or more logical positions, with respect to the structure representation, in the data base.
2. Retrieve — access or make available to the user data in the data base.
3. Insert — add new data to the data base.
4. Delete — remove data from the data base.
5. Update — change existing data in the data base.

These actions apply equally well to attributes, entity types, or relationships types. Depending on the structures and constraints on the structures, an action is not always defined for all data base states. This is because the action may violate the structures or constraints if allowed to proceed. In this case the action is usually not allowed and an indication of failure of the operation is returned to the user. This indication can be in terms of an explicit error message or through flags that indicate the status of an operation (success, failure, etc.). Such information is part of the data base state.

A selection of a part of the data base can be specified by:

1. Logical position.
2. Value of the contents of the data.
3. Relationships among the data.

We can select data based on their *logical position* in a table or a node in a graph. Although the data may not have an order according to the data model, it certainly has an order according to an implementation in a computer. This order can be exploited to provide selection by logical position in a table or node in a graph. Thus, we may be able to select the first, last, next, prior, or $n$th row in a table or value in a node. We call this type of selection *thru currency*. It implies that we can establish a logical position (i.e., currency indicator) in the data base and then use this currency indicator to perform some actions.

The sequence of logical positions may be fixed or it may be arbitrary if no explicit ordering is defined for rows in a table or values in a node. For example, the order could be chronological according to insertion or determined by operational properties (e.g., last updated [Smith and Smith, 1977c]). In these cases the ordering is not controlled by the user but by the DBMS. That is, there is no guarantee that a row $x$ is before a row $y$ or will remain in any fixed position with respect to row *y*. On the other hand, the data model may allow an ordering to be defined according to an attribute's values and this ordering to be used to establish currency (i.e., next according to the value ordering).

In a data language, selection thru currency takes the form of currency manipulation operations. The manipulation of the currency indicators can be explicit. For example, we can

**SET CURRENCY TO NEXT**

Alternatively, the manipulation can be implicit in other actions, such as

**GET NEXT**

which is a retrieve action that implies a set currency.

We can select data according to the *values* in a row of a table or a node in a graph. A row or rows in a table can be selected based on the value of a column of the row. Similarly, we can select one or more values in a node. For example, we can select one or all rows with value less than $20,000 in a *Salary* column or one or all values less than $20,000 in a *Salary* node. This type of selection is called *content addressibility*. It implies that given a certain value we can select one or all rows in a table or instances in a node which bear a direct relationship to that value.

For tables, the implication is that when we select a row by content addressibility we, in effect, select an entity (or perhaps a relationship). We thus have available, via the selection, the values for all attributes of the entity. If the nodes in a graph correspond to tables, the same remarks apply. However, if the nodes correspond to attributes, content addressibility selects only the value(s) for that attribute. The values for other attributes of the entity have to be obtained by selection based on relationships between nodes.

In a data language, content addressibility usually takes the form of a *qualification* on attribute values which specifies the criterion of selection. A qualification can specify the selection according to a simple condition or a Boolean condition. A *simple condition* specifies a selection criterion on one attribute and one attribute value, usually of the form

attribute-name conditional-operator value

The conditional operator is traditionally one of the logical operators $<$, $\leqslant$, $>$, $\geqslant$, $=$, or $\neq$, or equivalent mnemonic or English words (e.g., EQ or EQUALS). Thus, a simple condition might be

*Salary* = 20000

Simple conditions provide a limited selection specification facility. To allow more flexible selection one is usually able to construct more complex criterion by the use of Boolean operators such as AND, OR, and NOT. Simple conditions are connected by these Boolean operators to form more complex selections.

*EMPLOYEE*(*Employee#*, *Name, Address, Salary, Sex, Firmname*)
*COMPANY*(*Firmname, Location*)

**Fig. 4.1—1** Example table schema.

In a graph with attributes as nodes, all simple conditions are specified on one attribute only. In a table, several attributes may participate in the selection. Thus, in the table of Figure 4.1—1, the qualification to select all female employees who earn more than $20,000 is

*Sex* = Female **AND** *Salary* > 20000

As in some programming languages, precedence rules usually apply to the Boolean operators (e.g., NOT, AND, and OR, in decreasing order). Precedence can also be specified by the use of parentheses to indicate the order of evaluation. Thus,

*Sex* = Female **AND** *Salary* > 20000 **OR** *Name* = Robins

selects all female employees who earn more than $20,000 *plus* all employees named Robins. On the other hand,

*Sex* = Female **AND** (*Salary* > 20000 **OR** *Name* = Robins)

selects female employees only if they earn more than $20,000 or their name is Robins.

In addition to logical position and value, we can select data according to logical relationships with other data. For example, if there is a relationship type *OWNERSHIP* between two entity types *PERSON* and *CAR*, we can select all people who own cars or all cars owned by people. This type of selection is called *data relatability*. It implies that if we know the relationships between data, we can select data that participate in the relationships.

In a data language, data relatability can take the form of a closed-form formula to specify the selection if the relationship type is non-information bearing. For example, for the table specifications in Figure 4.1—1, we can specify data relatability selection according to the *EMPLOYEE* and *COMPANY* tables by

*EMPLOYEE. Firmname = COMPANY. Firmname*

The selection is the same regardless of whether we are selecting employees or companies.

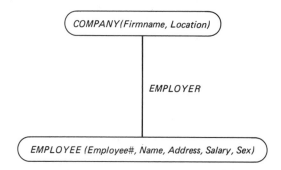

**Fig. 4.1—2** Example graph.

In a graph data model, data relatability can also take the form of following connections according to the links between nodes. Thus, to obtain all attribute values for an entity, one follows the connections among all the nodes that comprise the entity; similarly for entities connected via relationships. For example, in the graph of Figure 4.1—2, we can specify the selection of companies that employees work for according to the *EMPLOYER* relationship type by following the connections

*EMPLOYEE* **TO** *COMPANY* **VIA** *EMPLOYER*

Selection thru currency, content addressibility, and data relatability can be combined to provide different types of data languages and different data models. For example, selection thru currency and content addressibility can be combined to

**SET CURRENCY TO NEXT** *EMPLOYEE* **WHERE** *Salary* = 20000

Many different combinations are possible. It is also possible to provide the data selection capabilities in different ways in data languages.
Data languages can be distinguished according to whether they select many (sets of) objects (values, entities, relationships) at a time or only a single object at a time. If they select the data one object at a time by following a logical path (i.e., *navigating*) through the data base structure, the associated operations are called *navigation operations*. Alternatively, they can specify a new data base structure which is defined on an existing data base structure and which potentially describes many data objects. The system fills the new structure according to the data present in the

original data base structure. The associated operations are called *specification operations.* Navigation operations always use selection thru currency. Specification operations may or may not use currency in the data language. If currency is used, a set of objects are indicated rather than a single object as in navigation operations.

In the following two sections we discuss navigation and specification operations for tables and graphs. The objective is to characterize the types of operations needed to manipulate data represented according to these structures. To illustrate the concepts, examples will be presented using pseudo-languages which are a composite of several data languages. The reader should keep in mind that no syntax or implementation is advocated by use of these examples.

There are operations on a data base that do not follow the pattern of navigation and specification operations (i.e., selection of a small part of the data base followed by manipulation of it). These more general operations, called *data base procedures*, are discussed in Section 4.4. Finally, in Section 4.5 we discuss the relationship between abstract data types and data models.

## 4.2 NAVIGATION

In this section we consider navigation operations on tables and graphs. The operations on tables and graphs are discussed separately, although in a data model one may get a combination of both (i.e., if the nodes in a graph are tables).

The notion of currency is central to the concept of navigation. Currency can be manipulated either explicitly or implicitly, as pointed out in the preceding section. In our discussion here we assume that currency is manipulated explicitly (i.e., currency is set and data are retrieved in separate operations). It is also necessary to know how currency is affected as the result of operations which do not manipulate currency directly (e.g., a delete operation). Because several possibilities usually exist, it is important that a consistent set of rules be specified so that operations in the language are well defined.

If we consider only selection thru currency in tables, we can distinguish different types of tables according to the manner in which the currency can be manipulated. Central to the concept of establishing a logical position in a table is the notion of an ordering on the rows of the table. The ordering may not have any semantics for the user. Operationally, the table can be thought to be augmented with an extra column of consecutive integers 1 to $n$ which specify the ordering. The user cannot operate on this column. It is used only for setting the currency. Such a table is called a *sequential table.*

In a sequential table each row has a next row, except possibly the last row, and a previous row, except possibly the first row. In addition, the table also has a first and last row and an *n*th row, where *n* is an integer that is less than or equal to the number of rows in the table. At any point in time there is one current row in the table. For the *EMPLOYEE* table in Figure 4.2−1 the currency can be set to the next row according to the order by

**SET CURRENCY TO NEXT** *EMPLOYEE*

Sequential tables can be used to represent relations or record types since duplication does not pose problems operationally.

A table can be ordered explicitly according to the values of one of its columns. Such a table is called an *ordered table*. In this case the ordering according to the column values is used explicitly to set the currency in the table.

If we select rows by content addressibility, we specify a specific value for a column. This implies a mechanism for selecting rows by the value of their contents. We call a table that allows content addressibility an *indexed table*. We call the column according to which we select rows an *index*. The operations on this table allow currency to be set to a row with a specific value for a column. Thus, if the *EMPLOYEE* table in Figure 4.2−1 is indexed, we can, for example,

**SET CURRENCY TO NEXT** *EMPLOYEE* **WHERE** *Sex* = Female

If we can select according to several columns, the table is a *partially/totally indexed table*.

The index for an indexed table can correspond to a key of the entity type represented by the table. In this case the values of the index are unique if we enforce the functional dependencies. We call such a table a *keyed table*. If many attributes participate in the key, we have a *multikey table*. The key in this case is used both as a constraint and for accessing the table. If we suppose that *Employee#* is a key for *EMPLOYEE* in Figure 4.2−1, we can

**SET CURRENCY TO** *EMPLOYEE* **WHERE** *Employee#* = 781

and be guaranteed to get a unique row in the table (if the value 781 exists in the table as a value for *Employee#* ).

The key of a keyed table can be an external key. Operationally, the external key can be used in the same way as any other column of the table. The distinction is that the user is not allowed to change the value of the external key. A value is assigned for the external key of a row

EMPLOYEE

| Employee# | Name | Address | Sex | Firmname |
|---|---|---|---|---|
| 123 | Smith J. | 19 Evelyn | Female | AES |
| 862 | Lock P. | 85 Shuter | Male | AES |
| 781 | Barr T. | 16 Queen | Male | AES |
| 523 | Jones S. | 3 George | Female | IBM |
| 324 | Piitz W. | 22 Lundy | Female | IBM |

COMPANY

| Firmname | Location |
|---|---|
| AES | Toronto |
| IBM | New York |

SKILL

| Title | Pay rate |
|---|---|
| Typist | 12.50 |
| Stenographer | 14.25 |
| Clerk | 13.00 |
| Receptionist | 13.50 |

SKILLPOOL

| Employee# | Title |
|---|---|
| 123 | Typist |
| 862 | Typist |
| 781 | Stenographer |
| 523 | Clerk |
| 862 | Stenographer |
| 123 | Stenographer |
| 781 | Clerk |
| 324 | Receptionist |
| 523 | Receptionist |
| 862 | Clerk |

**Fig. 4.2—1** Example tables.

when the row is added to the table. This value may or may not be available directly to the user. In any case, it can only be used for setting currency.

In a table that is both keyed and ordered, we can select according to both value and order. Thus, if the current row has *Employee#* equal to 324 and the table is ordered on *Employee#*,

**SET CURRENCY TO NEXT** *EMPLOYEE*

will select the row with minimum value for *Employee#* greater than 324. Such tables are called *indexed sequential tables.*

Data relatability requires the ability to go between tables according to relationship types. Since we navigate one row at a time, the usual way to obtain data relatability is to take a value from a row in one table and match it with a value in a row in another table. For example, in Figure 4.2−1, to relate employees to their companies, we can select a row in the *EMPLOYEE* table. Then using the value of *Firmname* we can select a row in the *COMPANY* table. To relate employees to their skills we need to go through the *SKILLPOOL* table. Thus, we would go from *EMPLOYEE* to *SKILLPOOL* via *Employee#* and from *SKILLPOOL* to *SKILL* via *Title.* At each stage we select at most one row in each table. If many rows are related (i.e., if an employee has several skills) we need to iterate for all applicable rows.

Retrieval is always with respect to a currency indicator. Since there is only one row current at a time in a table, the retrieval operation is very simple. For example, to retrieve the current row in the *EMPLOYEE* table we could say

**RETRIEVE CURRENT OF** *EMPLOYEE*

For insertion, we need to specify the semantics carefully. They depend somewhat on the type of table. For sequential and indexed tables, insertion can be immediately before or after the current or *n*th row or at the start or end of the table. One semantic can be defined or the insert operation can explicitly specify which semantic to use. For ordered tables we want to maintain the ordering. Thus, insertion would be according to the ordering. If the system maintains the ordering, the user does not need to worry about setting currency. Otherwise, it is necessary first to correctly set the currency before insertion. For indexed and keyed tables the currency can be established separately or in the insert operation using a combined set currency and insert operation. For keyed tables we select at most one row, and insertion can be before or after this row. Insertion should be disallowed if a duplicate key value is inserted. For indexed tables we select only one row, but several rows may have the same index value. Insertion can be before or after the first, last or *n*th row with the given value. In general, currency manipulation is required to distinguish between rows with the same value.

We also need to specify what happens to the currency indicator after the insert operation. Possible semantics are:

1. It remains unchanged; that is, it points at the row it pointed at before the insert operation.
2. It points at the inserted row.
3. It is undefined; that is, it cannot be referred to and needs to be set again explicitly.

Deletion semantics are somewhat simpler since the delete operation refers to the current row. The semantics are the same for all types of tables. For keyed and indexed tables currency can be established via the delete operation or separately via currency operations.

After a delete operation the currency indicator can have one of the following semantics:

1. It remains unchanged.
2. It points at the previous row (if any).
3. It points at the next row (if any).
4. It is undefined.

In the first case operations on the current row are undefined. However, unlike the last case, there is still a next and previous row defined.

An update operation applies to the current row. In an ordered table the rows may need to be reordered after the update. In a keyed table, the update may not be allowed if the key is changed or if it is changed to an already existing value. After the update operation the currency indicator can continue to point at the row. However, for an ordered table, the position of this row in relation to other rows may have changed. In this case the currency indicator may be undefined after the operation.

In a graph data model, the nodes can be internal nodes, represent simple attributes, or represent tables. If a node represents a table, the navigation operations discussed for tables apply. Even if the node represents an internal node or simple attribute, we can consider the node as a one-column table. Table navigation operations thus apply for selection thru currency and content addressibility.

The difference in graph navigation operations is in the way they provide data relatability. They make use of the connections between nodes to navigate in the data base. We consider the operations that can be defined to exploit connections between nodes. The graph of Figure 4.2—2 will be used to illustrate the operations.

We can navigate in a graph data model by selecting an object in one node connected to an object in another node. We set the currency in one node via the connections defined by a link and the currency within another node. For example, in Figure 4.2—2 we can set the currency in the *COMPANY* table via the connections defined by the *EMPLOYER* link and a current row in the *EMPLOYEE* table with a statement such as

**SET CURRENCY TO** *COMPANY*
**VIA** *EMPLOYER* **AND CURRENT OF** *EMPLOYEE*

In general, there will be many objects connected to many other objects via a link in a graph. If we are to select only one object at a time via a

**Fig. 4.2–2** Example graph.

72

connection, we need to be able to specify which object we want. The connections from an object in a node $N_1$ to objects in a node $N_2$ can be thought of as a table connecting $N_1$ to $N_2$. Thus, we can navigate the connections in a manner similar to navigating a table. For example, in Figure 4.2−2 there may be, in general, many connections from a row in the *EMPLOYEE* table to rows in the *SKILL* table. For a particular employee we can iteratively navigate all of their associated connections to the *SKILL* table with a statement such as

**SET CURRENCY TO NEXT** *SKILL*
**VIA** *SKILLPOOL* **AND CURRENT OF** *EMPLOYEE*

Just as for table navigation we can set the currency to the first, last, next, previous, or *n*th such connection. It may also be desirable to select only certain connections based on what they are connected to. If a node is keyed or indexed, we can select specific connections between nodes by a qualification. For example, we might want to select connections to the *SKILL* table only if the *Pay rate* is less than some amount, such as

**SET CURRENCY TO NEXT** *SKILL* **WHERE** *Pay rate* < 14.00
**VIA** *SKILLPOOL* **AND CURRENT OF** *EMPLOYEE*

The currency indicator manipulated by the selection can be the currency indicator for the target node (i.e., *SKILL*) or a separate currency indicator associated with the link (i.e., *SKILLPOOL*). The latter method may allow more flexibility in navigating. The retrieval in the first case would be specified as

**RETRIEVE CURRENT OF** *SKILL*

whereas in the latter case we would need to specify which object connected by the link is desired:

**RETRIEVE** *SKILL*
**VIA CURRENT OF** *EMPLOYER*

Insertion, deletion, and update of objects in nodes can be specified in a manner similar to tables. We need to define what happens to the connections after these operations are performed. In the absence of constraints, the objects in a node are independent and connections are not affected by insertion or update operations. For a deletion operation the connections from the deleted object to all other objects must be removed. Semantics for currency indicators under these operations need to be specified.

In a graph data model, we need operations for connecting and disconnecting objects according to a link. These operations can use currency indicators implicitly to establish the connection. We first set the currency indicators to appropriate objects in the nodes and then establish the connections according to a link. To remove a connection we again establish currency of the objects in the nodes and then disconnect them via a link. To disconnect objects, currency may also be established according to a connection rather than the objects in a node. In general, we need to specify the link, since several links can exist between two nodes. If the link is unique, it does not need to be named. If the link between the two tables is functional, it is necessary to establish currency in only one node since there will be at most one connection between any two objects of the nodes.

We have discussed the navigation operations on tables and graphs generically. As we pointed out in several instances, it is possible to combine separate operations into one operation (e.g., currency manipulation and retrieval). In fact, most data languages do combine some of the operations. However, by discussing them separately, the reader should be able to determine more easily the characteristics of any one navigation data language and to compare different navigation data languages from a common basis.

## 4.3 SPECIFICATION

In this section we consider specification operations on tables and graphs. We again discuss the operations on tables and graphs separately, although in a data model they may be combined. Currency in specification operations is not visible at the user level. Usually, a set of rows in a table or objects in a node are current at any one time. The operations are specified in such a way that they define a new structure according to the data model. This structure then contains the objects that are current according to the selection.

If we consider a table data model, the tables can represent either a data base relation or a record type. We discuss specification operations as they apply to tables that represent data base relations. Later we indicate how these operations can be extended to apply also to tables that represent record types.

A data base relation corresponds to a mathematical relation which is a set. Thus, set operations are applicable to tables that represent data base relations. The only restriction is that set operations are performed on *compatible tables*. That is, the tables have the same number of columns and there is a correspondence between columns according to the type of data they contain (i.e., similar domains).

The basic set operations are union, intersection, and relative complement. The union (set sum) of two tables $T_1$ and $T_2$ is the table

$T_1 \bigcup T_2 = \{t | t \in T_1 \text{ or } t \in T_2\}$

The union contains those rows in either $T_1$ or $T_2$ or both. The intersection (set product) of two tables $T_1$ and $T_2$ is the table

$T_1 \bigcap T_2 = \{t | t \in T_1 \text{ and } t \in T_2\}$

The intersection contains only those rows in both $T_1$ and $T_2$. Finally, the relative complement (set difference) of two tables $T_1$ and $T_2$ is the table

$T_1 - T_2 = \{t | t \in T_1 \text{ and } t \notin T_2\}$

The relative complement contains those rows in $T_1$ that are not also in $T_2$. The operations relative complement and either one of union or intersection form a complete set of mathematical operations for tables representing relations.

Set operations alone provide a somewhat limited data manipulation facility for tables. Other operations are usually defined that provide content addressibility and data relatability. For tables representing relations, data manipulation operations have been defined in terms of relational algebra and relational calculus [Codd, 1971b, 1972b]. We will consider those relational algebra operations that are generally found in data languages. Other relational algebra operations have also been defined [Codd, 1972b].

The relational algebra operation *projection* allows columns in a table to be masked. A projection on a table $T$ is the table

$\pi_X(T) = \{\pi_X(t) | t \in T\}$

That is, the projection $(\pi)$ of a table $T$ on columns $X$ is defined as the projection of each row $t$ in $T$ on the columns $X$. The masking resulting from a projection is specified by explicitly naming those columns that are to appear in the result table. For example, the specification

**SELECT** *Employee#, Name, Sex* **FROM** *EMPLOYEE*

for the *EMPLOYEE* table in Figure 4.3—1 results in the table shown in Figure 4.3—2.

Content addressibility is provided by an operation called *selection*. A selection on a table $T$ is the table

$\sigma_Q(T) = \{t | t \in T \wedge Q\}$

where $Q$ is a qualification. A selection operation on a table $T$ defines a

EMPLOYEE

| Employee# | Name | Address | Sex | Firmname |
|-----------|------|---------|-----|----------|
| 123 | Smith J. | 19 Evelyn | Female | AES |
| 862 | Lock P. | 85 Shuter | Male | AES |
| 781 | Barr T. | 16 Queen | Male | AES |
| 523 | Jones S. | 3 George | Female | IBM |
| 324 | Piitz W. | 22 Lundy | Female | IBM |

COMPANY

| Firmname | Location |
|----------|----------|
| AES | Toronto |
| IBM | New York |

SKILL

| Title | Pay rate |
|-------|----------|
| Typist | 12.50 |
| Stenographer | 14.25 |
| Clerk | 13.00 |
| Receptionist | 13.50 |

SKILLPOOL

| Employee# | Title |
|-----------|-------|
| 123 | Typist |
| 862 | Typist |
| 781 | Stenographer |
| 523 | Clerk |
| 862 | Stenographer |
| 123 | Stenographer |
| 781 | Clerk |
| 324 | Receptionist |
| 523 | Receptionist |
| 862 | Clerk |

**Fig. 4.3—1** Example tables.

new table which contains all the rows of $T$ that satisfy the qualification $Q$. In general, the qualification involves a Boolean combination of simple conditions on the columns of the table. For example, in Figure 4.3—1 we can select all female employees with a statement like

**SELECT FROM** *EMPLOYEE* **WHERE** *Sex* = Female

The result is the table shown in Figure 4.3—3.
Data relatability is provided by an operation called *join*. A join of two

$$\pi_{\text{Employee\#, Name, Sex}}(EMPLOYEE)$$

| Employee# | Name | Sex |
|-----------|----------|--------|
| 123 | Smith J. | Female |
| 862 | Lock P. | Male |
| 781 | Barr T. | Male |
| 523 | Jones S. | Female |
| 324 | Piitz W. | Female |

**Fig. 4.3—2** Projection on *EMPLOYEE*.

tables $T_1$ and $T_2$ is the table

$$T_1 \underset{X \Theta Y}{*} T_2 = \{(t_1 \cap t_2) | t_1 \in T_1 \wedge t_2 \in T_2 \wedge (\pi_X(t_1) \Theta \pi_Y(t_2))\}$$

where $X$ and $Y$ are compatible sets of columns from $T_1$ and $T_2$, respectively, and $\Theta$ is one of the conditional operators $<$, $\leqslant$, $>$, $\geqslant$, $=$, or $\neq$. The notation $(t_1 \cap t_2)$ denotes the concatenation of a row of $T_1$ with a row of $T_2$. A concatenation of a row $t_1$ of $T_1$ with a row $t_2$ of $T_2$ consists of all column values in $t_1$ followed by all column values in $t_2$. A join operation between two tables $T_1$ and $T_2$ defines a new table which contains the concatenated rows from $T_1$ and $T_2$ that satisfy the join condition $X \Theta Y$.

$$\sigma_{\text{Sex} =\text{Female}}(EMPLOYEE)$$

| Employee# | Name | Address | Sex | Firmname |
|-----------|----------|-----------|--------|----------|
| 123 | Smith J. | 19 Evelyn | Female | AES |
| 523 | Jones S. | 3 George | Female | IBM |
| 324 | Piitz W. | 22 Lundy | Female | IBM |

**Fig. 4.3—3** Selection on *EMPLOYEE*.

A join can be specified as an explicit construct in a data language, or the join condition can appear as part of the qualification. For example, in Figure 4.3—1 a join between *EMPLOYEE* and *COMPANY* on *Firmname* can be specified as

**SELECT FROM** *EMPLOYEE, COMPANY*
**WHERE** *EMPLOYEE.Firmname* = *COMPANY.Firmname*

The result is the table shown in Figure 4.3—4.

There are several types of join operations. The difference between them relates to what columns appear in the result table. If all columns from both tables appear in the result, the join is said to be a *generalized join*. Figure 4.3—4 is an example of a generalized join. A join where $\Theta$ is equality and the join column is not duplicated in the result is called a

$$EMPLOYEE \underset{Firmname = Firmname}{*} COMPANY$$

| Employee# | Name | Address | Sex | Firmname | Firmname | Location |
|-----------|------|---------|-----|----------|----------|----------|
| 123 | Smith J. | 19 Evelyn | Female | AES | AES | Toronto |
| 862 | Lock P. | 85 Shuter | Male | AES | AES | Toronto |
| 781 | Barr T. | 16 Queen | Male | AES | AES | Toronto |
| 523 | Jones S. | 3 George | Female | IBM | IBM | New York |
| 324 | Piitz W. | 22 Lundy | Female | IBM | IBM | New York |

**Fig. 4.3—4** Join of *EMPLOYEE* and *COMPANY*.

*natural join* (specified simply as $T_1 * T_2$). Finally, a *composition join* is a natural join where neither of the columns in the join condition appear in the result table.

A join can be specified for any number of columns in a table. As long as the join columns in both tables are compatible, appropriate rules can be applied to perform the matching. Depending on the data type of the columns, not all conditional operators may be applicable. The join of more than two tables can be specified in any order since a join operation is associative and commutative. A join of the *EMPLOYEE, SKILLPOOL,* and *SKILL* tables can be specified as

**SELECT FROM** *EMPLOYEE, SKILLPOOL, SKILL*
**WHERE** *EMPLOYEE.Employee# = SKILLPOOL.Employee#*
**AND** *SKILL.Title = SKILLPOOL.Title*

The operations projection, selection, and join can be combined into a uniform data language statement such as specified here, or they can be separate operations that create new tables that can be operated on.

In a specification data language it is necessary to be able to name new tables that result from the operations and to use the tables in other operations. There is also a problem of uniquely identifying columns in a table that is the result of a join operation. The data language can allow the user to rename columns in the result table, or they can be renamed automatically if ambiguity arises. The usual way of renaming columns automatically is to qualify them with the table name as in *EMPLOYEE.Firmname*.

For tables representing record types, we can use set operations as defined in extended set theory which are generalizations of the usual set operations. For example, intersection is defined as $T = T_1 \cap T_2$ such that for all $t$ and $i$, $t \in i \; T$ if and only if $t \in i \; T_1$ and $t \in i \; T_2$. That is, $t$ must be at position $i$ in both $T_1$ and $T_2$ to be included in the intersection. Other table operations can be extended in a similar manner for record types [Childs, 1968].

Insertion, deletion, and update operations on tables consider sets of rows at a time, but in only one table at a time. An insertion operation can insert one or more rows into a table. Usually, the insertion is done at the end of the table unless the table is ordered. If the table is keyed, insertion of duplicate rows should not be allowed.

Deletion requires a selection of the rows to be deleted. This selection can be done in a separate operation or it can be part of the deletion operation. If it is part of the deletion operation, all rows selected according to the qualification are deleted. A qualification on a key would select at most one row in the table.

Update also requires a selection of the rows to be changed. A selection followed by an update allows manipulation of the selected data prior to update. A combined select and update operation requires that the operation also specify the changes to be made to the data. Semantics for update need to be specified, such as what happens if the number of rows to be updated is larger than the number of values supplied.

For graph data models, selection within a node can be specified by operations similar to table specification. For selection between nodes we can use a matching operation similar to a join if the link is non-information bearing. However, not all links are non-information bearing. As a matter of fact, only information-bearing links can be specified in graphs with only simple attributes in the nodes. In these situations we need to be able to navigate among nodes selecting objects according to the connections. Such a navigation can proceed by specifying a subgraph of the entire graph according to the links between nodes. At any point in the navigation we can select objects from a node using table specification operations such as selection and projection.

Consider the graph of Figure 4.3—5. Suppose that we have selected some employees via a selection and now wish to associate the employees' skills with the selected employees. We can specify this selection by following the connections between the *EMPLOYEE* and *SKILL* nodes. For example, to specify a subgraph of all female employees and their skills we could use a sequence of statements like

**SELECT FROM** *EMPLOYEE* **WHERE** *Sex* = Female
**LINK TO** *SKILL* **VIA** *SKILLPOOL*

Such a specification facility allows the specification of a path in a graph. For example, we can go from companies to employees to skills with a series of statements like

**Fig. 4.3—5** Example graph.

80

```
SELECT FROM COMPANY WHERE Firmname = IBM
LINK TO EMPLOYEE VIA EMPLOYER
    SELECT Name, Address, Sex FROM EMPLOYEE
    WHERE Sex = Female
    LINK TO SKILL VIA SKILLPOOL
        SELECT Title FROM SKILL
```

In general, we would like to be able to specify general graph structures. Such a capability requires that we be able to "remember" previous selections in the graph. For example, suppose that we want to specify a treelike structure in Figure 4.3−5, with *EMPLOYEE* as the root and *SKILL* and *COMPANY* as the leaves. We first select employees, then link to skills, and then link to companies. The second linking requires that we remember which employees were selected originally. In a specification of such a construct it may be necessary to name intermediate selection structures so that it is possible to refer back to them explicitly. For the example outlined above we might use statements like

```
WOMEN EMPLOYEES ←
    SELECT FROM EMPLOYEE WHERE Sex = Female
LINK WOMEN EMPLOYEES TO SKILL VIA SKILLPOOL
LINK WOMEN EMPLOYEES TO COMPANY VIA EMPLOYER
```

As well as being able to use links to specify subgraphs of a graph, they can also be used to select objects in a node. In this case data relatability is used somewhat like content addressibility except that the content here is the presence or absence of connections to other nodes. This type of selection requires quantifiers. As an example, we may want to select all employees who have at least two skills. This can be specified by a statement such as

```
SELECT FROM EMPLOYEE WHERE
LINK VIA SKILLPOOL HAS AT LEAST 2 SKILL
```

Other useful quantifiers are **SOME, ALL, NO, AT MOST** $n$, and **EXACTLY** $n$, where $n$ is a positive integer [Deheneffe and Hennebert, 1976].

Insertion, deletion, and update for objects in nodes can be specified as for tables. Again, for deletion it is necessary to remove connections to objects in other nodes. For insertion and update of objects in nodes it may be necessary to establish or change connections.

If the link is non-information bearing, the connections that need to be established can be specified as a closed-form formula. In this case, whenever new objects are inserted or values changed, it is possible to apply the closed-form formula to the objects in the nodes and establish or change connections. For example, if we had a *Firmname* attribute in the

*EMPLOYEE* table of Figure 4.3—5, we could define the connections between *COMPANY* and *EMPLOYEE* by the closed-form formula *COMPANY.Firmname* = *EMPLOYEE.Firmname.* When we insert a new row in the *EMPLOYEE* table we can establish the connection to the *COMPANY* table using this formula. We can use the same procedure if we change the *Firmname* value for an employee.

Some links in a graph data model will be information bearing. In this case it is necessary to establish a current set of objects in all nodes to which the inserted objects are to be connected. The operation here is somewhat akin to navigation operations for establishing a connection except that many objects may be current at one time. Since information-bearing links between nodes are not based on values in the nodes, altering values cannot affect the connections. Separate operations for connecting and disconnecting objects as in navigation are required. The use of keys is one possible way to uniquely select objects to connect and disconnect.

We have discussed specification operations on tables and graphs according to the types of operations required for data manipulation. Many of these operations have been defined precisely in terms of sets and data base relations [Codd, 1972b]. These operations can take many forms in a data language. The emphasis here was to describe operations that are oriented to manipulating a set of objects at a time and that define what the result should look like rather than how to obtain it.

## 4.4 DATA BASE PROCEDURES

The operations discussed in previous sections are limited in that they conform to a strict pattern of selection followed by a set currency, retrieve, update, insert, or delete action. Other operations are also possible which have a more global scope or a different pattern. For instance, consider an integrity mechanism which is triggered when particular data are selected. The integrity mechanism can potentially check many data objects to verify a constraint. As such, it does not fit the pattern selection followed by a local action. It is, however, within the definition of an operation which maps a data base state to another data base state within the same schema and data model.

More general data base operations are encapsulated by the definition of *data base procedures* [CODASYL, 1971]. A data base procedure consists of a series of operations which are effected upon the satisfaction of certain conditions. Since the conditions can be very general, the procedures may be triggered automatically without user intervention. The actions of data base procedures can be very general in scope without necessarily being restricted to one part of the data base. The data base procedures notify the system and the user of success or failure upon completion. This is effected by setting up appropriate status information which is part of the data base state.

Data base procedures are different from programming language procedures. They correspond more closely to automatic procedures as defined in artificial intelligence (e.g., actors [Hewitt, 1973] or TAXIS transactions [Mylopoulos and Wong, 1980]). Data base procedures are specified in the schema and consist generally of a condition part, an action part, and a notification part. The condition part is used to check the validity of certain prerequisites before the actions are performed. The action part specifies the things to be done in the procedure. The notification part specifies what and/or where the procedure should return.

Data base procedures can be considered as a general, monolithic mechanism for altering a data base state. However, such a view makes it very difficult to specify precisely the effects of a procedure on a data base state. Instead, different uses of data base procedures can be distinguished and specific constructs identified for each use. In this way there is some indication in the schema about the main action of a data base procedure and its side effects.

One important use of a data base procedure is to calculate a value which is not stored explicitly in the data base. For instance, statistical operations such as sum, average, maximum, minimum, and count can be defined as data base procedures. We call these data base procedures *aggregate functions*. In many data models aggregate functions are an integral part of the data language.

A related use of a data base procedure is to calculate a value for an attribute. For instance, a data base procedure may calculate a person's age given the current date and birthdate of the person and set the value of age for retrieval upon request. It may also obtain the value from another part of the data base. For example, in the two tables

*EMPLOYEE*(*Employee#*, *Name, Address, Sex, Firmname*)
*COMPANY*(*Firmname, Location*)

the value for *Firmname* in *EMPLOYEE* may be obtained via a data base procedure from the *COMPANY* table. Any data base procedure that results in the calculation of a value for an attribute is called a *virtual attribute*. A virtual attribute has the same properties as any other attribute except that its storage may have different side effects and error conditions.

A third use of a data base procedure is for checking the integrity of the data base. In Chapter 3 the specification of constraints was discussed in great length. The verification of these constraints on the data base can be done automatically by the system as a result of specific data base procedures which are given control either explicitly by the user or are triggered by specific conditions or operations. Data base procedures used to check and/or enforce constraints are called *integrity triggers* [Astrahan et al., 1976; Eswaran, 1976]. Integrity triggers do not produce a value. They either notify the system of their success or failure, or produce side effects that force the data base to comply with certain constraints.

A fourth use of data base procedures is to provide access control. The access control is usually not simple like yes/no, depending on a password. It can be data dependent as well as user dependent. The data base procedure can perform a very complicated computation on which to base its decision and it can provide an equally complicated action. For example, the data base procedure may take the user, the time, the date, and the action as input and may produce output to the user, to logs, and to security officers. A data base procedure used for access control is called a *security trigger*.

A further use of a data base procedure is to extend the data language with an operation that was not there before. For instance, a sorting operation can be defined as a data base procedure that is executed before output of the result of a specification operation. Duplicates or nulls can be eliminated using such a data base procedure. In this way, a specification operation can be defined for either relations or record types. Such a data base procedure is called an *access operator*. Access operators are restricted to access only the data base.

Data base procedures can be defined which, as a side effect, change the data base as a result of another operation. According to the type of action performed they are called either *triggered insert, triggered delete*, or *triggered update*. These data base procedures are activated on certain conditions and perform one or more inserts, deletes, or updates. For instance, if a relationship type is total, the deletion of an entity can trigger the deletion of other entities according to the relationship type (e.g., in a hierarchical data model).

Another use of data base procedures is to initiate monitoring, gather statistics of the data base, or perform other data base administration functions. Such a data base procedure is called a *DBA procedure*. Although DBA procedures do not change the data base occurrence, they modify the data base state in the general sense of the term.

It is often necessary to define several operations on a data base as one indivisible operation as far as the DBMS is concerned. For example, an access procedure may initiate several actions on a data base, such as retrieving and updating data. We call such a data base procedure a *transaction*. Once the transaction has started it should not be preempted. Indivisibility of action is one of the principal ways in which data base procedures differ from similar types of actions performed in procedures defined by the user within a programming language.

A data base procedure can be defined for schema transformations. For instance, on certain conditions such as the specification of a new input form, a new attribute may be defined and used to store values. Such data base procedures do not conform to our strict definition of data base procedures. They are, rather, schema operations and are discussed in Chapter 14.

Data base procedures are different in the following ways from the data base operations discussed in the first part of this chapter. First, they do not follow the very stringent pattern of selection followed by an action. Second, their scope of operation can be global. Third, they incorporate many data-dependent side effects. Fourth, their invocation is usually not user initiated. Fifth, they can have many very general actions. Finally, they are usually encoded in the schema, unlike other operations which are incorporated into users' programs.

Data base procedures can be a very powerful tool for defining operations in a data model. They can be very general and be defined in terms of other data base procedures. We have detailed some uses of data base procedures because it is important to be careful about their use. Since they are very general mechanisms, care is required to ensure that the procedures operate in the correct environment and produce a correct result without undesirable side effects. Data base procedures are like goto's or pointers in a programming language. They can do almost anything, which means they can also do much harm if not used in a structured way.

## 4.5 DATA TYPES AND DATA MODELS

In previous chapters and sections, structures, constraints, and operations in data models were discussed separately. However, it should be obvious that structures, constraints, and operations are very interrelated. That is, in a data model we can trade structures for constraints, constraints for operations, and vice versa. For example, a functional mapping can be specified as an explicit constraint in a data model or it can be encoded in the structures and/or the operations. It seems, therefore, that a common specification technique would be appropriate to define these three aspects of a data model.

Such a specification technique has been developed in the area of programming languages and is referred to as a data type. A *data type* is a definition of data objects together with their invariant properties (constraints) and the operations allowed on them [Hoare, 1972; Liskov and Zilles, 1974, 1975; Guttag, 1975; Smith and Smith, 1977a,b]. A data type is the result of applying classification generalization to a particular collection of data values (tokens). For example, a record type *EMPLOYEE* with its structures, constraints, and associated operations constitutes a data type. A *data type category* results from the application of generalization to a collection of similar data types. For instance, the concept record type, with its structuring of attributes, types of constraints, and allowed operations, is a data type category. Data types can also be obtained from other data types by using generalization and aggregation.

A data type is either structured or unstructured. A structured type is defined as an aggregate of constituent types. The way in which the constituents are aggregated is defined by a structuring rule. Ultimately, the constituent types are unstructured. The lowest-level unstructured data types are *primitive data types* (e.g., integer, real, character, Boolean, and pointer). The most primitive data types are assumed to be provided by the hardware. An unstructured data type is ultimately based on one primitive type.

The stages of the abstraction process may be used to summarize the essential parts of a data-type definition [Hoare, 1972]. In the first stage, we use *abstraction* to obtain a data type from certain tokens or perhaps via other data types. Next, we choose a *representation* (set of symbols) to stand for the abstraction. Then, we specify the *manipulations* (i.e., the operations) which are used for transforming representations. Finally, we use *axiomatization* to rigorously specify those properties (i.e., constraints) that have been abstracted from tokens.

The development of programming languages has profited greatly by considering the data-type concept as fundamental. In their development from data files, data bases have not typically used the data-type concept. However, in recent years the concepts of data type and data value, developed for programming languages, have been applied directly to data modeling [Hammer, 1976; Brodie, 1978; Schmidt, 1978; Lockemann et al., 1979]. Some data model concepts have been defined in terms of data types.

A schema can be viewed as a collection of data types and a schema specification as a collection of data-type specifications. The schema constraints can be used to verify that types are specified consistently and to validate the type and manipulation of data values. A data base can be viewed as a collection of data values stored as instances of the types defined in the schema. In terms of programming languages, a schema comprises the type level and the corresponding data base comprises the token level.

A data model can be viewed as a collection of data-type categories. The data types corresponding to those categories are used to represent attributes, entity types, and relationship types of the real world. The data-type categories of the data model can be defined by specifying the properties shared by all data types represented by the category. Each data-type category is defined in terms of constituent data-type categories.

Despite efforts to marry ideas in programming languages and data models, there are several differences between the two areas which make it difficult to apply data types to data bases [Hammer, 1976; Brodie, 1978]. We consider these differences independently; however, they are closely related.

A fundamental difference between programming languages and data models is the relative importance placed on algorithms versus data. This has been a matter of the approach taken to the subject. The stepwise refinement technique for developing programs advocates postponing the decision on the structure of data until after the algorithm is designed [Wirth, 1971]. In data modeling, however, data structures must be designed without knowing exactly what algorithms will be applied. Data independence requires that new or modified programs, as well as the original programs, be able to access the data base. Logical data independence implies a certain insulation of programs from changes in the logical data representation and in the schema. These requirements imply that the data types specified in the schema have a general applicability for many different programs and a certain insensitivity to changes in these programs. To meet these requirements, the binding relationship between programs operating on the types and the specification of types in the schema should be flexible.

In data modeling there are generally several programs accessing a very large interrelated collection of data. As a result, data bases tend to have more data types and data values than do programs. In addition, programming languages use heavily the concept of context to make the number of objects under consideration intellectually manageable. In data models, there is usually no clear notion of context. The concepts of subschema [CODASYL, 1971] and multileveled schemas [Tsichritzis and Klug, 1978] have been proposed to overcome these difficulties, but problems remain [Pelagatti et al., 1978].

A third difference between the two areas is the strength of type checking. Although programming languages, generally, provide fairly extensive type checking, it is usually not as stringent as in data modeling.

Another difference between programming languages and data modeling is the emphasis on data sharing. In programming languages, few instances or variables are shared and they are usually treated specially. Typically, when the scope of a variable is exited, the related instance is lost. On the other hand, the sharing of interrelated data is fundamental to data models. Different programs view the same data in logically different ways. Successive or concurrent invocations of the same or different programs access the same data base instances. Hence, the data base must be viewed in such a way that instances exist independently of the variables used to access them. Some extensions have been proposed to the programming language concepts of data type, variable and instance to accommodate the differences noted above [Schmidt, 1978].

Finally, the most important difference between data types and data models is the relative emphasis they place on problems. In abstract data types there is much emphasis on general specification tools for data types and techniques for their verification. In data models the emphasis is mainly on defining appropriate data-type categories which can be used in many general situations.

In spite of these differences, data types can still be useful in data modeling. They can be used for abstracting and relating data values via generalization and aggregation. They can be used for binding values to variables and instances of a type. Finally, data types provide a uniform framework for viewing both programming languages and data models.

## 4.6 CONCLUDING REMARKS

In this chapter we considered operations on data models in terms of operations on tables and graphs. For both tables and graphs these operations usually consist of an action and a selection of a part of the data base to which the action applies. This action and selection can be effected by either navigation or specification operations.

Navigation operations are traditionally associated with host programming languages such as COBOL or PL/1. The programming language provides the control mechanisms necessary for controlling navigation through a data base. The navigation operations provide at most one object at a time for the programming language to manipulate. This simplifies greatly the interface between the DBMS and the host programming language.

Specification operations are traditionally associated with query languages. The query language provides both the DBMS operations and the control mechanisms in a self-contained manner. The two types of operations are not mutually exclusive but form a continuum of operations that have been characterized as procedural (navigation) and nonprocedural (specification) [Olle, 1974]. It is usually the case that navigation operations are required, if not at the user level then at the system level, to implement specification operations.

In this part of the book we have presented a framework for data models. The framework consists of three basic components: structures, constraints, and operations. In terms of our discussion we have at least the following possibilities for these components.

1. For structures a data model can have tables, graphs, or both.
2. For instances within the structures a data model can allow sets, ordered sets, or both.
3. For constraints it can have inherent constraints, explicit constraints, both, or none.
4. For operations it can have navigation operations, specification operations, or some combination.

Each combination of structures, instance type, constraints, and operations yields a different data model. We can have, therefore, according to the different combinations of the factors listed above at least 108 different data models. Obviously some of them are better than others. At the same time we did not distinguish different features within each component. For instance, according to this classification hierarchical and DBTG-network data models are counted as one. There is also a wide variety in methods of handling currency indicators. No wonder there are so many data models proposed.

## EXERCISES

**4.1** Given a relation $R(A, B, C)$ and the two projections $R_1(A, B)$ and $R_2(B, C)$, prove that the join of $R_1$ and $R_2$ is not always equal to $R$. Under what conditions is it equal to $R$?

**4.2** Specification operations for a graph data model can be restricted to specify always only a path through the graph, or they can be more general and specify a tree of the graph. Discuss the advantages and disadvantages of each approach.

**4.3** Do graph data models inherently have complex data languages, or is this a result of other factors?

**4.4** Define an algebra of operations such as union, intersection, and join on tables that allow duplication. Specify the properties of your algebra.

**4.5** A data model can be obtained by defining first a structures, constraints, and an operations framework. The implicit assumption is that all information about an application can be structured in the way specified by the data model. Alternatively, a data model can define the elementary structures for representing a datum and then provide ways of organizing these elementary pieces into structures and data types. Comment on the relative advantages of these two essentially dual ways of defining a data model.

**4.6** Prove or disprove that there are some requests for which navigation operations in either a table or a graph data model will require an unbounded number of currency indicators. You will have to assume that the storage outside the data base is bounded. Are your example requests expressible with the relational algebra?

**4.7** Outline a framework which allows you to prove that a specification language for a graph data model is "equivalent" to the relational algebra.

**4.8** Are navigation operations natural for graphs, or equally natural for graphs and tables? Argue your case.

**4.9** Are specification operations natural for tables, or equally natural for tables and graphs? Argue your case.

**4.10** What are the main criteria for choosing specification or navigation operations? Can they coexist in the same data model? Give an example.

**4.11** Consider a graph of record types containing *PERSON*, *CAR*, and *HOUSE* which are related by non-information-bearing links according to house owner and car owner. Suppose that we go from cars to persons to houses by following the links using a specification data language. In what way is this type of specification like and/or unlike a join?

# Part 2

# DATA MODELS I

As pointed out at the conclusion of Part 1, there are potentially many data models that could be specified. However, not all of these would be practical and useful. In fact, very few data models have received wide acceptance and use. In this part we examine three of the most widely accepted and used types of data models: hierarchical, DBTG-network, and relational data models. For historical and pedagogical reasons these three types of data models are the "basic" data models discussed in most introductory DBMS texts [Everest, 1977; Haseman and Whinston, 1977; Kroenke, 1977; Tsichritzis and Lochovsky, 1977; Ross, 1978; Cardenas, 1979; Ullman, 1980; Date, 1981]. In addition, they are the data models to which most other data models are compared. Not surprisingly, the hierarchical and DBTG-network data models evolved from early file processing and report generation systems [Fry and Sibley, 1976]. Relational data models, on the other hand, are based more on theoretical foundations than on practical experience. They draw from the mathematical theory of relations for their basis [Codd, 1970].

# Chapter 5

# RELATIONAL DATA MODELS

## 5.1 INTRODUCTION

The properties of relations as mathematical sets, their representation as tables, and the properties of table data models were discussed in Chapters 2 to 4. A data model based on relations and their representation as tables was first proposed by Codd [Codd, 1970]. In the formulation of relational data models, the mathematical theory of relations is extended logically where required to meet data management objectives. The mathematical foundation of relational data models permits elegant and concise definition and deduction of their properties [Chamberlin, 1976]. In this chapter we discuss this type of data model and its implementation in various prototype and commercial DBMSs [Czarnik et al., 1975; Todd, 1975; Zloof, 1975a; Astrahan et al., 1976; Stonebraker et al., 1976; Kornatowski, 1979; RSI, 1980]. Our examples of possible implementations will be drawn mainly from the System R prototype DBMS [Astrahan et al., 1976; Blasgen et al., 1981].

The discussion of relational data models will be based mainly on the relational data model defined by Codd in a series of papers [Codd, 1970, 1971a,b, 1972a,b]. This data model is quite simple in terms of structures and constraints. Research on data models since the relational data model was defined has pointed out the inadequacy of the basic relational data model in these areas. Accordingly, an extended relational data model has been defined which addresses these inadequacies [Codd, 1979]. These extensions are outlined in Section 5.6.

## 5.2 STRUCTURES

The only data structuring tool used by relational data models is a relation. The definition of a relation in relational data models is identical to the mathematical definition except that data base relations are time varying. That is, tuples are inserted, deleted, and modified in data base relations.

In Chapter 2, a relation was defined as a subset of the cross product of its underlying domains. A less mathematical, but equivalent definition is: given sets $D_1, D_2, ..., D_n$ (not necessarily distinct), $R$ is a *relation* on these $n$ sets if it is a set of *n-tuples* or simply *tuples* each of which has its first element from $D_1$, second element from $D_2$, and so on [Codd, 1970]. The sets $D_i$ are called the *domains* of $R$. The number $n$ is the *degree* of $R$, and the number of tuples in $R$ is called its *cardinality*.

*HOSPITAL(Hospital code, Name, Address, Phone#, # of beds)*

*WARD(Hospital code, Ward code, Name, # of beds)*

*STAFF(Hospital code, Ward code, Employee#, Name, Duty, Shift, Salary)*

*DOCTOR(Hospital code, Doctor#, Name, Specialty)*

*PATIENT(Registration#, Name, Address, Birthdate, Sex, SSN)*

*DIAGNOSIS(Registration#, Diagnosis code, Diagnosis type, Complications, Precautionary info)*

*LAB(Lab#, Name, Address, Phone#)*

*TEST(Registration#, Lab#, Test code, Type, Date ordered, Time ordered, Specimen/order#, Status)*

*HOSPITAL LAB(Hospital code, Lab#)*

*ATTENDING DOCTOR(Doctor#, Registration#)*

*OCCUPANCY(Hospital code, Ward code, Registration#, Bed#)*

**Fig. 5.2—1** Relational schema for medical data base.

The intension of a relational data base is specified by a *relational schema* which consists of one or more *relation schemes*. A relation scheme is a listing of a relation name and its corresponding domain names. Figure 5.2—1 represents a relational schema for the example medical data base outlined in the Appendix. The specification

*HOSPITAL (Hospital code, Name, Address, Phone#, # of beds)*

is an example of a relation scheme. A relation scheme can be used to represent an entity type in relational data models.

Since relational data models are table data models, a relational schema does not reflect, explicitly, all the relationship types between relations in the data base. Some relationship types are contained only implicitly in the schema. As discussed in Chapter 3, these relationship types are represented by key propagation from one relation scheme to another. For example, *Hospital code* has been added to the *WARD* relation scheme to represent the functional relationship type between *HOSPITAL* and *WARD*. Alternatively, the relationship type can be represented explicitly via a separate relation scheme. For example, the *ATTENDING DOCTOR* relation scheme represents the many-to-many relationship type between the *DOCTOR* and *PATIENT* relations. Thus, a relation scheme can represent either an entity type or a relationship type in relational data models.

A relationship type can be represented by either key propagation or a relation scheme in a relational schema. However, because of the semantics of the relationship types, it is usually the case that one-to-one and functional relationship types are represented by key propagation, whereas many-to-many relationship types are represented by separate "relationship" relations. A consequence of using the second method is that the relational schema for the medical data base contains more relation schemes than there are entity types in the application (see the Appendix).

The case of the OCCUPANCY relation scheme in Figure 5.2−1 is an example of an exception to the preceding generalization. It represents the functional relationship type between *WARD* and *PATIENT*. Key propagation is not used mainly because of the presence of the *Bed#* domain. *Bed#* is really a characteristic of both *WARD* and *PATIENT*. That is, the assignment of a bed number depends on the occupancy of the bed in a ward by a patient. It should not be assigned to a patient independent of a ward. By the same token, it should not be associated only with a ward (except in the case of an empty bed, which cannot be modeled by the given representation). Thus, to effect a "cleaner" semantic interpretation of the data base, *Bed#* has been placed in the "relationship" relation OCCUPANCY.

An extension of a relational data base is represented as tables. An extension of part of the medical data base is presented in Figure 5.2−2. Each table represents some relation scheme of the relational schema. A column of a table is called an *attribute*. For example, *Hospital code*, *Name*, *Address*, *Phone#*, and *# of beds* are attributes of the *HOSPITAL* relation. Two or more attributes of a table may be based on the same underlying domain. To distinguish between such attributes, each one is given a distinctive *role name*. For example, the domain *positive integer* underlies the distinctive roles of *Hospital code* and *Ward code* as attributes of the *WARD* relation. Each row of a table corresponds to a tuple of the relation represented by the table. For example, in the *DOCTOR* relation, each row represents a unique doctor.

All relational data models use the concept of a relation as defined above. While the syntax may vary, the structure definition of a relation using a DDL consists of specifying at least the relation name, all of its attribute's names, and the underlying domain of each attribute.

HOSPITAL

| Hospital code | Name | Address | Phone# | # of beds |
|---|---|---|---|---|
| 22 | Doctors | 45 Brunswick | 923-5411 | 412 |
| 13 | Central | 333 Sherbourne | 964-4264 | 502 |
| 45 | Childrens | 555 University | 597-1500 | 845 |
| 18 | General | 101 College | 595-3111 | 987 |

WARD

| Hospital code | Ward code | Name | # of beds |
|---|---|---|---|
| 22 | 1 | Recovery | 10 |
| 13 | 3 | Intensive Care | 21 |
| 22 | 6 | Psychiatric | 118 |
| 45 | 4 | Cardiac | 55 |
| 22 | 2 | Maternity | 34 |
| 13 | 6 | Psychiatric | 67 |
| 18 | 3 | Intensive Care | 10 |
| 45 | 1 | Recovery | 13 |
| 18 | 4 | Cardiac | 53 |
| 45 | 2 | Maternity | 24 |

STAFF

| Hospital code | Ward code | Employee# | Name | Duty | Shift | Salary |
|---|---|---|---|---|---|---|
| 22 | 6 | 1009 | Holmes D. | Nurse | M | 18500 |
| 13 | 6 | 3754 | Delagi B. | Nurse | A | 17400 |
| 22 | 6 | 8422 | Bell G. | Orderly | M | 12600 |
| 22 | 2 | 9901 | Newport C. | Intern | M | 17000 |
| 45 | 4 | 1280 | Anderson R. | Intern | E | 17000 |
| 22 | 1 | 6065 | Ritchie G. | Nurse | E | 20200 |
| 13 | 6 | 3106 | Hughes J. | Orderly | A | 13500 |
| 45 | 1 | 8526 | Frank H. | Nurse | A | 19400 |
| 18 | 4 | 6357 | Karplus W. | Intern | M | 18300 |
| 22 | 1 | 7379 | Colony R. | Nurse | M | 16300 |

DOCTOR

| Hospital code | Doctor# | Name | Specialty |
|---|---|---|---|
| 45 | 607 | Ashby W. | Pediatrics |
| 18 | 585 | Miller G. | Gynecology |
| 22 | 453 | Glass D. | Pediatrics |
| 13 | 435 | Lee A. | Cardiology |
| 45 | 522 | Adams C. | Neurology |
| 22 | 398 | Best K. | Urology |
| 18 | 982 | Russ J. | Cardiology |
| 22 | 386 | Stone C. | Psychiatry |

**Fig. 5.2—2** Partial extension of relational schema for medical data base.

PATIENT

| Registration# | Name | Address | Birthdate | Sex | SSN |
|---|---|---|---|---|---|
| 63827 | Rasky P. | 60 Bathurst | Jun 1 1945 | M | 100973253 |
| 36658 | Domb B. | 55 Patina | Apr 8 1954 | M | 660657471 |
| 64823 | Fraser A. | 11 Massey | May 3 1960 | F | 985201776 |
| 74835 | Bower E. | 15 Ontario | Oct 16 1933 | M | 654811767 |
| 18004 | Shiu W. | 14 Ivy | Jan 22 1916 | F | 914991452 |
| 59076 | Miller G. | 80 Lawton | Jun 4 1971 | F | 611969044 |
| 24024 | Fourie M. | 40 Donora | Jul 9 1966 | F | 321790059 |
| 10995 | Lista M. | 58 Olsen | Nov 7 1963 | M | 980862482 |
| 39217 | Birze H. | 51 Dallas | Aug 20 1958 | M | 740294390 |
| 38702 | Neal R. | 65 Halsey | Nov 3 1949 | F | 380010217 |

LAB

| Lab# | Name | Address | Phone# |
|---|---|---|---|
| 56 | Alpha | 18 Kipling | 929-9611 |
| 84 | Nucro | 62 Lyons | 368-9703 |
| 16 | Atcon | 14 Main | 532-4453 |
| 42 | Clini | 55 King | 447-6448 |

HOSPITAL LAB

| Hospital code | Lab# |
|---|---|
| 22 | 56 |
| 22 | 84 |
| 13 | 16 |
| 18 | 56 |
| 45 | 16 |
| 18 | 84 |
| 18 | 16 |
| 13 | 42 |
| 18 | 42 |

**Fig. 5.2—2** Partial extension of relational schema for medical data base (cont'd).

As an illustration, the definition of the relational schema for the medical data base is expressed in a DDL based on the SEQUEL DDF as implemented for System R [Astrahan et al., 1976].

**CREATE TABLE** *HOSPITAL*:
    *Hospital code* **(INTEGER, NONULL)**,
    *Name* **(CHAR(15))**,
    *Address* **(CHAR(20))**,
    *Phone#* **(CHAR(7))**,
    *# of beds* **(SMALLINT)**

**CREATE TABLE** *WARD*:
    *Hospital code* **(INTEGER, NONULL)**,
    *Ward code* **(INTEGER, NONULL)**,
    *Name* **(CHAR(15))**,
    *# of beds* **(SMALLINT)**

**CREATE TABLE** *STAFF*:
    *Hospital code* **(INTEGER, NONULL)**,
    *Ward code* **(INTEGER, NONULL)**,
    *Employee#* **(INTEGER, NONULL)**,
    *Name* **(CHAR(20))**,
    *Duty* **(CHAR(\*))**,
    *Shift* **(CHAR(10))**,
    *Salary* **(DECIMAL(7,2))**

**CREATE TABLE** *DOCTOR*:
    *Hospital code* **(INTEGER, NONULL)**,
    *Doctor#* **(INTEGER, NONULL)**,
    *Name* **(CHAR(20))**,
    *Specialty* **(CHAR(\*))**

**CREATE TABLE** *PATIENT*:
    *Registration#* **(INTEGER, NONULL)**,
    *Name* **(CHAR(20))**,
    *Address* **(CHAR(20))**,
    *Birthdate* **(CHAR(8))**,
    *Sex* **(CHAR(1))**,
    *SSN* **(INTEGER, NONULL)**

**CREATE TABLE** *DIAGNOSIS*:
    *Registration#* **(INTEGER, NONULL)**,
    *Diagnosis code* **(INTEGER, NONULL)**,
    *Diagnosis type* **(CHAR(\*))**,
    *Complications* **(CHAR(\*))**,
    *Precautionary info* **(CHAR(\*))**

**CREATE TABLE** *LAB*:
    *Lab#* **(INTEGER, NONULL)**,
    *Name* **(CHAR(20))**,
    *Address* **(CHAR(20))**,
    *Phone#* **(CHAR(7))**,

**CREATE TABLE** *TEST*:
    *Registration#* **(INTEGER, NONULL)**,
    *Lab#* **(INTEGER, NONULL)**,
    *Test code* **(INTEGER, NONULL)**,
    *Type* **(CHAR(20))**,
    *Date ordered* **(CHAR(8))**,
    *Time ordered* **(CHAR(4))**,
    *Specimen/order#* **(INTEGER)**,
    *Status* **(CHAR(\*))**

CREATE TABLE *HOSPITAL LAB*:
    *Hospital code* (INTEGER, NONULL),
    *Lab#* (INTEGER, NONULL)

CREATE TABLE *ATTENDING DOCTOR*:
    *Doctor#* (INTEGER, NONULL),
    *Registration#* (INTEGER, NONULL)

CREATE TABLE *OCCUPANCY*:
    *Hospital code* (INTEGER, NONULL),
    *Ward code* (INTEGER, NONULL),
    *Registration#* (INTEGER, NONULL),
    *Bed#* (INTEGER, NONULL)

The specification NONULL means that a row in the corresponding table must have a value specified for this attribute. Usually, if an attribute participates in identifying the contents of a relation's tuples uniquely (see Section 5.3), it must have the NONULL specification.

## 5.3 CONSTRAINTS

Since a data base relation is basically a mathematical relation, it inherits the properties of a set. The first of these is that, for the table representation of a data base relation, no duplicate rows are permitted. This constraint naturally leads to the notion of a key for a relation. Informally, a *key* in the relational data model is any subset of the attributes of a relation the values of which uniquely identify a tuple in the relation. The fact that duplicate rows are not permitted means that every relation has at least one key (the combination of all the attributes of the relation). However, a relation may have several keys (termed *candidate keys* since they are possible keys). To eliminate the trivial (and nonuseful) keys, a key of a relation must satisfy the following two properties [Codd, 1972a]:

### P1. Unique Identification

In each tuple of the relation the value of the key uniquely identifies that tuple; that is, no two rows have the same values for the attributes in the key taken as a whole.

### P2. Nonredundancy

No attribute that is part of the key can be removed without destroying property P1; that is, the key is minimal.

The key property of data base relations can also be expressed in terms of functional dependencies. That is, if a set of attributes $X$ is a key of a relation $R$, the value of $X$ determines the value of every other attribute in a tuple of *R*. This property, and its enforcement, is the basis of schema analysis, which is discussed in Chapter 13.

In a given relation scheme, one of the candidate keys is selected as the *primary key*. Primary keys differ from other keys in the operations allowed on them [Codd, 1979] (i.e., they cannot be updated). In addition, no primary key value of a relation is allowed to be null or to have a null component.

The second property of a set inherited by a data base relation is that the ordering of the rows in the table is not significant since a set has no order defined for its members. Normally, the ordering of the columns (or sets in a tuple) is significant in a relation (see Section 2.2). However, because each column has a distinctive role name by which it can be identified, the ordering of the columns is *not* significant in a data base relation.

Relational data models contain very few inherent constraints. The lack of inherent constraints provides a great deal of freedom to the data modeler in terms of representing entity types and relationship types. However, it also presents difficulties to the user in terms of exploiting meaningful relationships between relations. To provide some explicit semantic interpretation of a relational schema, most relational data models augment the relations by providing a facility for specifying explicit constraints on the relations. In the following discussion, we describe mainly the constraint facilities provided by System R [Astrahan et al., 1976].

In System R it is possible to place different kinds of constraints on attributes. For example, one can specify a *scope* for an attribute [Boyce and Chamberlin, 1973]. The scope limits the possible values that an attribute may have (e.g., integer, real, or character). One can also construct new scopes from existing scopes, for example,

$$POSINT = \textbf{FROM } INTEGER \textbf{ WHERE } INTEGER > 0.$$

One can also specify a *comparability domain* for an attribute in System R. The comparability domain is used to determine if it is semantically meaningful to compare two values. If two attributes do not have the same comparability domain, they cannot be compared or used in a join operation. This facility reduces the possibility of forming meaningless relationships in the data base such as that between *Hospital code* and *Ward code* in our example.

System R permits *units* to be specified for an attribute. A unit is a standard of measurement such as inches, miles, or dollars. Some arithmetic operations may be disallowed if the two values do not have the same units (e.g., adding miles to dollars). All these different types of constraints for attributes provide the ability to define interpreted domains in the data model.

More general types of constraints are specified by an assertion facility in System R [Boyce and Chamberlin, 1973; Eswaran and Chamberlin, 1975; Chamberlin et al., 1976]. Assertions are predicates that specify conditions that must be satisfied by the data base. The assertion can describe permissible states of the data base as well as permissible transitions (changes of state). We will illustrate the assertion facility of System R by expressing some of the constraints on the medical data base (see the Appendix). The assertion facility uses the System R query language SQL [Denny, 1977], which is described in Section 5.5.

The first constraint **C1** expresses a restriction on the values that the *Time ordered* attribute may assume. It is expressed as

**ASSERT** *C*1 **ON** *TEST*:
    *Time ordered* > 0 **AND**
    *Time ordered* ⩽ 2400

The second constraint **C2** requires the use of an SQL built-in function **SUM**. The *HOSPITAL* relation is labeled with the letter *H* so that it can subsequently be referenced using only this label and not the entire relation name.

**ASSERT** *C*2:
    (**SELECT** # *of beds*
    **FROM** *HOSPITAL H*)

    =

    (**SELECT SUM** (# *of beds*)
    **FROM** *WARD*
    **WHERE** *WARD.Hospital code* = *H.Hospital code*)

Constraint **C3** restricts the value of the *Sex* attribute of *PATIENT* to be one of two specific values.

**ASSERT** *C*3 **ON** *PATIENT*:
    *Sex* **IS IN** 'F', 'M'

Constraint **C4** is similar to the specification of a key for a relation.

**ASSERT** *C*4 **ON** *PATIENT*:
    **COUNT** (*) = **COUNT** (**UNIQUE** *SSN*)

This assertion states that the number of tuples in *PATIENT* (**COUNT** (*)) must equal the number of unique values of *SSN*.

To ensure that a bed number is assigned to only one patient in a ward, constraint **C5** is stated as

**ASSERT** *C5* **ON INSERTION OF** *OCCUPANCY* (*Bed#*),
    **UPDATE OF** *OCCUPANCY* (*Bed#*) :
    **NOT NEW** *Bed#* **IS IN**
    (**SELECT** *Bed#*
    **FROM** *OCCUPANCY*
    **WHERE** *Ward code* = **NEW** *Ward code*)

**NEW** is a keyword of the assertion language. Along with the keyword
**OLD**, it allows one to reference values in a tuple before and after a change
and to use them as arguments in the assertion. In this case, the
qualification ensures that we only select bed numbers from the ward into
which we would like to place the patient. This example also illustrates
that one can specify when an assertion is to be invoked (i.e., on update,
insertion, deletion, or any change to the data base).

Constraint **C6** is similar to **C2** except that here we count tuples in a
relation rather than summing the values of an attribute.

**ASSERT** *C6*:
    (**SELECT** # *of beds*
    **FROM** *WARD W*)

    $\geqslant$

    (**SELECT COUNT** (*)
    **FROM** *OCCUPANCY*
    **WHERE** *Ward code* = *W. Ward code*)

Constraint **C7** is expressed in a manner analogous to **C4** with
appropriate substitution of relation and attribute names.

Besides specifying static properties of the data base, assertions can also
specify conditions that must be true after a change has occurred to the
data base. For example, one could specify that when an employee's salary
is updated, it is never decreased. This would be stated as

**ASSERT ON UPDATE OF** *STAFF*(*Salary*) :
    **NEW** *Salary* $\geqslant$ **OLD** *Salary*

Invocation of assertions can be immediate after each change or they
can be delayed until after a transaction. A transaction is one or more data
language statements. For example, an immediate invocation may be
desired for the constraint that the value of the *Sex* attribute is always
either 'M' or 'F'. A delayed invocation may be desired for assertion **C2**
when adding or removing beds in a ward. The assertion may not be true
during the transaction, but it should be true after all the changes have
occurred.

Assertions are a mechanism for imposing constraints that ensure the
validity of the data in the data base. The invocation of an assertion results
in either a true or a false result. Sometimes it may be necessary to

perform data base operations to guarantee the integrity of the data base. In the example medical data base, constraint **C8** requires that every *DIAGNOSIS* tuple corresponds to a *PATIENT* tuple. Thus, it is necessary to delete a patient's *DIAGNOSIS* tuples when the *PATIENT* tuple is deleted from the data base.

System R allows the specification of a form of data base procedure, called a *trigger*, to perform this type of constraint maintenance [Eswaran, 1976]. A trigger defines an action or set of actions that are to be performed on the data base. It is invoked automatically when the invocation condition arises. A trigger can be used to express the existence constraint of a *DIAGNOSIS* tuple(s) on a *PATIENT* tuple as follows:

> **DEFINE TRIGGER** *DELETE DIAGNOSIS* **ON DELETION OF** *PATIENT*:
>     (**DELETE** *DIAGNOSIS*
>     **WHERE** *Registration#* = **OLD** *PATIENT.Registration#* )

To guarantee that a *DIAGNOSIS* tuple corresponds to some *PATIENT* tuple, we can use the assertion

> **ASSERT** *PATIENT DIAGNOSIS DEPENDENCY*:
>     (**SELECT** *Registration#*
>     **FROM** *DIAGNOSIS*)
>     **IS IN**
>     (**SELECT** *Registration#*
>     **FROM** *PATIENT*)

The combination of the trigger and the assertion enforce the existence constraint.

Assertions and triggers in System R are specified using data language statements, but are really schema-oriented facilities. By allowing arbitrary data language statements in assertions and triggers, System R provides a very flexible and powerful constraint specification facility.

## 5.4 NAVIGATION OPERATIONS

The navigation operations required for relational data models are similar to those required for tables. After all, relations can be represented as tables. However, in this section we present the operations with a view to embedding them in a host programming language. The operations are based on the facilities available in GAMMA-0 [Bjørner et al., 1973] and SCAN [Zahle, 1978].

In order to navigate through tables we needed two basic concepts: currency in the table and order of retrieval. Relational data models have no notion of ordering as pointed out in the preceding section. However, relations eventually have to be implemented on physical hardware devices. So even though, logically, relations have no ordering on their tuples, physically, they will be stored in some sequence. We can utilize this physical ordering to obtain an ordered reading of a relation and to maintain currency.

To initiate navigation in a relation the statement

**CREATE SCAN** *scan name* **ON** *relation name*

signals the user's intention to perform an ordered reading (or *scan*) of a relation. There may be several scans of any one relation active at the same time by the same user. Associated with every scan is a currency indicator which marks the current position of the scan in a relation. To set or reset the currency indicator of a scan to the start of a relation one uses the statement

**SET SCAN** *scan name*

Finally, a scan is erased by the statement

**DROP SCAN** *scan name*

The position of the currency indicator within a relation is controlled by the statement

**GET NEXT** *scan name* **[WHERE** *qualification***]**

where [ ] indicates that the enclosed construct is optional. This statement sets the currency indicator for scan name to the next tuple that either satisfies the qualification, if a qualification is present, or simply to the next tuple, if there is no qualification. The order of retrieval is system defined. No data are actually retrieved by this statement. An indication of success or failure of the retrieval is returned via a predefined variable which can be examined by the user.

To retrieve data from the current tuple of a scan one uses the statement

**SELECT FROM** *scan name* ... **[:***attribute name* ... **]**

where ... indicates repeat the immediately preceding, nonkeyword construct one or more times separated by commas. Thus, one can select attribute values from several scans at one time. The output is concatenated in the order indicated by the list of attribute names, if present, or by the list of scan names. An attribute name may be qualified with a scan name to resolve ambiguity. Omission of a list of attribute names results in the selection of all attribute values from the indicated scans. The result of a selection can be assigned to a host programming language variable for later use. The preceding statements will be illustrated by several queries.

The first query illustrates the relational operations selection and projection.

**Q1.** Find the names of all doctors whose specialty is gynecology.

```
CREATE SCAN GYNECOLOGISTS ON DOCTOR
SET SCAN GYNECOLOGISTS
loop until end of scan
    GET NEXT GYNECOLOGISTS
    WHERE Specialty = 'GYNECOLOGY'
    exit loop if status – check
    output SELECT FROM GYNECOLOGISTS: Name
end loop
```

Besides the statements of the data language, we also need the notion of looping in the host programming language. This permits us to step through the tuples of the relation one at a time. The procedure *status – check* is used to check for error conditions and exceptional processing conditions (e.g., end of relation or no more tuples satisfy the qualification).

The next example involves a slightly more complex qualification.

**Q2.** Find the names and salaries of all interns working the evening shift.

```
CREATE SCAN E Shift ON STAFF
SET SCAN E Shift
loop until end of scan
    GET NEXT E Shift WHERE Duty = 'INTERN' AND Shift = 'E'
    exit loop if status – check
    output SELECT FROM E Shift: Name, Salary
end loop
```

A projection operation is performed by stepping through a relation and selecting the appropriate attribute value(s). This operation is not strict projection since duplicates may appear in the result. If duplicates are not desired, they must be removed using host programming language facilities.

**Q3.** List the different specialties of doctors.

```
CREATE SCAN SPECIALTIES ON DOCTOR
SET SCAN SPECIALTIES
loop until end of scan
    GET NEXT SPECIALTIES
    exit loop if status — check
    output SELECT FROM SPECIALTIES: Specialty
end loop
```

To express a join, it is necessary to retrieve data from two relations at the same time. This can be accomplished by using two nested loops, as the next query illustrates.

**Q4**. List the name, registration number, and bed number of all patients in ward 2.

```
CREATE SCAN P ON PATIENT
CREATE SCAN O ON OCCUPANCY
SET SCAN P
loop1 until end of scan P
    GET NEXT P
    exit loop1 if status — check
    registration# ←SELECT FROM P: Registration#
    SET SCAN O
    loop2 until end of scan O
        GET NEXT O WHERE Registration# = registration#
        AND Ward code = '2'
        exit loop2 if status — check
        SELECT FROM P :Name, O :Registration#, Bed#
    end loop2
end loop1
```

This query illustrates the necessity of the **SET SCAN** statement. It is used here inside the first loop to reset the currency indicator for the scan on the *OCCUPANCY* relation to the start of the relation. The query also illustrates the use of multiple scans. Like the procedure that implements the projection operation, the preceding join procedure preserves duplicates in the final result.

In the preceding query to do the join operation we can choose from at least two different strategies. First, we can step through the *PATIENT* relation one tuple at a time. Each time we select a tuple, we use the value of *Registration#* to access the *OCCUPANCY* relation and retrieve the appropriate tuple. This is the strategy employed above. Alternatively, we could first step through the *OCCUPANCY* relation retrieving all tuples where *Ward code* is equal to 2. Each time we select a tuple, we use the value of *Registration#* to access the *PATIENT* relation and retrieve the appropriate tuple.

Modification of relations is accomplished using three statements: **INSERT, UPDATE** and **DELETE**. The **INSERT** statement is

**INSERT INTO** *scan name* (*attribute name = value ...*)

The indicated values are inserted as a tuple, logically, at the end of the relation indicated by *scan name*. The inserted tuple becomes the current tuple of the scan. For example, to insert a new tuple into the *STAFF* relation, we would

**CREATE SCAN** *S* **ON** *STAFF*
**SET SCAN** *S*
**INSERT INTO** *S*
    *Hospital code* = '45',
    *Ward code* = '1',
    *Employee#* = '3637',
    *Name* = 'SMITH J.',
    *Salary* = '15500',
    *Duty* = 'NURSE'

Attributes which are not specified, such as *Shift* in the preceding example, are set to null.

To change the value of an attribute in a tuple, the tuple must first be selected via a retrieval operation using **CREATE SCAN**, **SET SCAN** and **GET NEXT**. The tuple may then be altered with the statement

**UPDATE** *scan name* (*attribute name = value*)

The updated tuple remains the current tuple of the scan. Several attribute values can be changed in a tuple by one **UPDATE** statement. The value argument can be a literal value or a valid arithmetic expression in the host programming language. The arithmetic expression may reference attribute values in any current tuple of an active scan. To change the value of the *Salary* attribute in a tuple of the scan *S* on relation *STAFF*, we use

**UPDATE** *S* (*Salary* = '20000')

To raise the salary by 10% we use

**UPDATE** *S* (*Salary* = $1.1 \times$ **SELECT** *S: Salary*)

Deletion of a tuple in a relation is accomplished by the statement

**DELETE** *scan name*

The tuple to be deleted is first selected by a retrieval operation as for **UPDATE**. **DELETE** then works on the current tuple of the scan. After the deletion, the previous tuple becomes the current tuple of the scan.

In this section we presented navigation operations for navigating through relational tables. The operations required the concept of an ordered reading of a table, currency in the table, and looping in the host programming language. The operations may seem rather tedious to program, especially for complex queries. This is no doubt the case. However, these or similar operations are required in any relational data model. Although they may not be visible to the enduser, they are needed to interface with current file systems which have navigation operations. As such, they form the basis for any implementation of specification operations [Bjørner et al., 1973]. In fact, the operations proposed here can be used to implement the specification operations discussed in the next section [Astrahan et al., 1976].

## 5.5 SPECIFICATION OPERATIONS

Since relational data models are based on a set oriented concept (i.e., relations) they naturally lend themselves to specification operations. It should come as no surprise, therefore, that most relational data languages use specification operations [Codd, 1971b; Held et al., 1975; Chamberlin et al., 1976]. The main feature of all these languages is the ability to define a new relation based on the existing relations using relational algebra or similar types of operations. The new relation is usually made available to the user as a *snapshot* of the current extensions of the relations on which it is defined. That is, the resulting relation is a "picture" (snapshot) of the data base state at the time the relation was defined. A snapshot can be considered equivalent to the creation of an output file into which the result of an operation is placed.

There is another, quite different, way of making the definition of a new relation available to the user. It can be made available as a *view* of the relation(s) on which it is defined [Chamberlin et al., 1975]. A view is an extension of the schema and, as such, the new relation remains as a new type in the schema even after execution of the statement that defines it. The result of an operation on the new relation at any point after it has been defined is equivalent to a macro-expansion of its definition into its constituent parts. That is, the operation on the new relation is mapped, whenever possible, into operations on the relations on which it is defined. We discuss views on relations when we discuss mappings and transforms in Chapter 14.

It is sometimes confusing that relational operations can be used for both specification operations in a data language (i.e., snapshots) and DDL operations that define new relations (i.e., views). In the mathematical definition of relational data models the operations are discussed uniformly regardless of their use. In the definition of a data model and data language, however, specification operations and views should be clearly distinguished. They differ not only in terms of implementation, but there is a deep distinction between them as data types. For instance, consider the join of two relations $R_1$ and $R_2$. If considered as a snapshot, all update, insertion, and deletion operations are well defined. If considered as a view, however, some of the update operations may be undefined [Chamberlin et al., 1975]. The two definitions are identical in terms of relation operations. The two data types, however, are different since they allow different operations.

Most relational specification languages provide a high degree of integration between data language and DDL statements. For example, snapshots and views can be specified by the same specification operations [Chamberlin et al., 1975]. However, a view is more DDL oriented since it "creates" a new relation in the schema. Constraint specification, a DDL function, usually involves some data language statements (see Section 5.3).

There is a close relationship between the amount of information specified in the DDL and the data language. In relational data models the DDL usually specifies a minimal amount of information. This provides the data language with a great deal of flexibility in specifying relationship types between relations (e.g., via joins). In this section we are concerned primarily with data language specification operations.

Relational specification data languages can be classified as to one of three types. The first type is based on the relational calculus. Examples of these types of languages are the INGRES data language QUEL [Held et al., 1975] and the ALPHA data language [Codd, 1971b]. Although specification languages, they are highly mathematical, requiring quantification. The second type of specification language is a display-oriented language. Typically the user is required to make choices or fill in blanks on a CRT display to formulate a query. Two such languages are Query by Example [Zloof, 1975a,b] and CUPID [McDonald and Stonebraker, 1975], which runs on INGRES. The third type of specification language is a mapping-oriented language. This type of language maps a known attribute or set of attributes into a desired attribute or set of attributes via some relation. SQL [Denny, 1977] is the prime example of this type of language and its facilities will be presented as an example of relational specification operations.

SQL (*S*tructured *Q*uery *L*anguage), formerly called SEQUEL (*S*tructured *E*nglish *QUE*ry *L*anguage), is an English-keyword, set-oriented relational data language that is part of the System R DBMS [Chamberlin and Boyce, 1974; Astrahan et al., 1976; Chamberlin et al., 1976; Blasgen et al., 1981]. SQL is based on the concept of a *mapping* operation. For retrieval, the effect is as if one scanned the column(s) of a relation looking for a value or set of values. The tuples in which the value(s) is found is returned as the result.

A mapping is specified in SQL by the statement

**SELECT [UNIQUE]** *attribute name* ...
**FROM** *relation name* [*label*] ...
**[WHERE** *qualification*]
**[GROUP BY** *attribute name*
**[HAVING** *qualification*]]
**[ORDER BY** *attribute name* [ASC | DESC] ...]

where [ ] indicates optional constructs and ... indicates repeat the last, nonkeyword construct one or more times separated by commas. The values of the attributes to be retrieved can be specified explicitly following the **SELECT** keyword, or the symbol * can be used to indicate that the values of all attributes are to be returned. The relation(s) from which values are to be selected is specified after the **FROM** keyword. The relations may be assigned labels in the **FROM** clause. The labels are used to resolve ambiguities and to qualify references in the rest of the mapping (e.g., when a relation is joined with itself). The qualification in the **WHERE** and **HAVING** clauses is used to specify the criterion for selecting or grouping tuples. The **GROUP BY** clause is used to treat specified subsets of a relation as a single unit (e.g., to express a membership criterion). Finally, the **ORDER BY** clause is used to order the result according to the attribute specified. The facilities of the **SELECT** statement will be illustrated by examples.

**Q1.** Find the names of all doctors whose specialty is gynecology.

**SELECT** *Name*
**FROM** *DOCTOR*
**WHERE** *Specialty* = 'GYNECOLOGY'

This query illustrates selection and projection on a table. The value of the *Name* column is retrieved where the value of the *Specialty* column is equal to gynecology.
Data from several or all columns can be retrieved, as Query 2 illustrates.

**Q2.** Find the names and salaries of all interns working the evening shift.

**SELECT** *Name, Salary*
**FROM** *STAFF*
**WHERE** *Duty* = 'INTERN'
**AND** *Shift* = 'E'

This query also shows that a complex Boolean qualification may be used in the **WHERE** clause.

If the **WHERE** clause is omitted as in Query 3, then all the values in a column can be retrieved (simple projection).

**Q3.** List the different specialties of doctors.

> **SELECT UNIQUE** *Specialty*
> **FROM** *DOCTOR*

The use of the keyword **UNIQUE** removes duplicate values from the result.

SQL provides several built-in arithmetic functions to aid data manipulation. The built-in functions provided are **MAX** (select the maximum of a set of values), **MIN** (select the minimum of a set of values), **COUNT** (count the number of values), **SUM** (sum a list of values), and **AVG** (calculate the average for a list of values). The use of the **COUNT** function is illustrated by Query 4.

**Q4.** How many employees are there in ward 6?

> **SELECT COUNT** (*Employee#*)
> **FROM** *STAFF*
> **WHERE** *Ward code* = '6'

The data retrieved from one table may be used to select data from another table by means of nested **SELECT** statements. Although this facility is similar to a join operation, it is unlike a join in that ultimately data from only one table is returned. Query 5 expresses a nested selection.

**Q5.** List the names of those patients whose diagnosis is cardiac arrest.

> **SELECT** *Name*
> **FROM** *PATIENT*
> **WHERE** *Registration#* =
>     **SELECT** *Registration#*
>     **FROM** *DIAGNOSIS*
>     **WHERE** *Diagnosis type* = 'CARDIAC ARREST'

Nesting of **SELECT** statements can be done to any number of levels, not just two as in the example.

The results of several mappings can be combined by means of set operations. Three set operations — **UNION**, **INTERSECT**, and **MINUS** — are provided.

**Q6**. List the names of those doctors on the staff whose specialty is cardiology, who are female, and who are also patients.

**SELECT** *Name*
**FROM** *DOCTOR*
**WHERE** *Specialty* = 'CARDIOLOGY'
**INTERSECT**
**SELECT** *Name*
**FROM** *PATIENT*
**WHERE** *Sex* = 'F'

It is sometimes necessary to partition a table into groups (e.g., to find the average salary by ward). The SQL **GROUP BY** clause provides this facility. It is always used with one of the built-in functions. The **SELECT** statement using a **GROUP BY** clause only specifies attributes that are a unique property of a group rather than an individual row of a table. The presence of a built-in function helps enforce this requirement, since it specifies a property of a group (e.g., **AVG**, **SUM**, etc.).

**Q7**. Find the average salary for each ward.

**SELECT** *Ward code*, **AVG** (*Salary*)
**FROM** *STAFF*
**GROUP BY** *Ward code*

The **HAVING** clause option of the **GROUP BY** clause is used to select certain groupings that meet the qualification in the **HAVING** clause.

**Q8**. Find the average salary for those occupations where the minimum salary is greater than $15,000.

**SELECT** *Duty*, **AVG** (*Salary*)
**FROM** *STAFF*
**GROUP BY** *Duty*
**HAVING MIN** (*Salary*) > '15000'

Query 9 illustrates the combination of most of the preceding language constructs.

**Q9**. Find those hospitals that have more than five pediatricians.

```
    SELECT Name
    FROM HOSPITAL
    WHERE Hospital code =
        SELECT Hospital code
        FROM DOCTOR
        WHERE Specialty = 'PEDIATRICS'
        GROUP BY Hospital code
        HAVING COUNT (*) > '5'
```

To return values from more than one table at a time, it is necessary to do a join. SQL has a specific syntax for expressing a join, as shown in Query 10.

**Q10**. List the name, registration number, and bed number of all patients in ward 2.

```
    SELECT PATIENT.Name, PATIENT.Registration#, OCCUPANCY.Bed#
    FROM PATIENT, OCCUPANCY
    WHERE PATIENT.Registration# = OCCUPANCY.Registration#
    AND OCCUPANCY.Ward code = '2'
```

In addition to the mapping operation, SQL provides facilities for inserting, updating, and deleting tuples of a relation. The statement for inserting new tuples into a relation is

**INSERT INTO** *relation name* (*attribute name* ...) : < *value* ... >

There must be a one-to-one correspondence between values and attributes. Any attributes that are omitted are set to null. The value may be either a literal value or the result of a **SELECT** statement.

The statement for updating tuples in a relation needs to perform two functions: selecting the appropriate tuples and changing the specified values. The update statement is

**UPDATE** *relation name* [*label*]
**SET** *attribute name* = *update − value* ...
[**WHERE** *qualification*]

The update value can be either a literal value or it can be the result of a **SELECT** statement.

The statement

**DELETE** *relation name* [*label*]
[**WHERE** *qualification*]

deletes tuples from a relation. It can delete either selected tuples or all tuples in a relation. Omission of the **WHERE** clause results in deletion of all tuples.

The form of SQL as presented here is for a stand-alone data language. SQL also provides facilities for interfacing with a host programming language [Chamberlin et al., 1976].

## 5.6 THE RM/T DATA MODEL

The properties of relational data models discussed in this chapter are those originally defined by Codd [Codd, 1970, 1971a,b, 1972a,b]. Since that time, much research has been done on data models in general and on relational data models in particular. The salient results of this research were discussed in Part 1. The most obvious concepts missing from relational data models deal with the specification and representation of constraints on and among relations (i.e., the specification of "semantics"). Accordingly, Codd has defined an extended relational data model, called RM/T, which incorporates the specification and representation of several types of constraints directly in the data model [Codd, 1979].

In RM/T, it is recognized that existence constraints are required between some relations. Thus, the following constraint applies to primary keys.

### Referential Integrity

Suppose that $A$ is a simple (single attribute) primary key of a relation $R_1$ and that attribute $B$ of a composite (multiattribute) primary key of a relation $R_2$ is defined on the same domain as $A$. Then, at all times, for each value of $B$ in $R_2$ there must exist a value of $A$ in $R_1$ equal to the value of $B$.

This constraint, together with the constraint that prohibits null values for primary keys, constitute the insert-update-delete rules for relational data models [Codd, 1979].

Perhaps the most important extension in RM/T, and the one that is the basis for the other extensions, is the introduction of external keys (called *permanent surrogates*). External keys are created and deleted by the system as a result of user operations on the data base and can be used in operations such as joins. However, they are not controlled or seen by the user. External keys take their values from a special domain (E-domain). An external key uniquely identifies an entity (as opposed to a tuple) within the entire data base. Relations can still have user-controlled and -defined keys, but this is no longer required.

In RM/T, it is recognized that not all relations are the same in terms of what they represent. Basically, relations can represent both entity types and relationship types. In addition, entity types and relationship types are distinguished according to their "independence" of existence. If an instance of an entity type can exist on its own without being related to any other entities, the entity type is called a *kernel entity type*. If an instance of an entity type depends on other entities for its existence (i.e., the mapping is total in one direction), the entity type is called a *characteristic entity type*. If an instance of a relationship type can exist on its own without the corresponding entities existing, the relationship type is called an *associative entity type*. Otherwise, it is called a *nonentity association*. Both types of relationships can have their own attributes describing them. However, nonentity associations are not allowed to have characteristic entity types related to them. Kernel, characteristic, and associative entity types may also have subtypes.

The preceding classification of entity types and relationship types determines the properties of the relations used to represent them. Each kernel, characteristic, or associative entity type[1] has a corresponding E-relation. An E-relation is a unary relation that stores the external keys for all RM/T entities of that type that exist in the data base. The properties (attributes) of RM/T entity types are represented by one or more P-relations. Each P-relation has as its primary key an external key of some E-relation. Existence constraints are also defined on the primary keys of P-relations and E-relations that represent characteristic entity types. RM/T entities and their properties are related by joins (outer natural joins to be exact) on the external key values among E-relations and P-relations. Note that this representation scheme can accommodate anything from a binary relation to an *n*-ary relation representation of a data base.

Unlike the basic relational data model, RM/T entity types cannot be related in arbitrary ways based solely on values of attributes. The way in which RM/T entity types are related to each other is specified by means of several relations, called *graph relations*. These relations also have existence constraints specified on them to ensure that only valid relationships can be obtained using relational operations. The graph relations, in effect, provide the ability to specify, in the schema, the meaningful relationship types that exist between entity types, generalization hierarchies, timing of events, and other semantics.

The *property graph relation* (PG-relation) specifies which P-relations go with which E-relations (i.e., the attributes of an RM/T entity type). The *association graph relation* (AG-relation) specifies which RM/T entity types participate in which relationship types. The *characteristic graph relation* (CG-relation) specifies which RM/T entity types are characteristic entity types and the RM/T entity types they are related to. All three graph relations are binary relations containing P-relation and/or E-relation names.

Aggregation of attributes, entity types, and relationship types is

---

[1]. We will refer to these entity types as collectively RM/T entity types in the sequel.

specified using the P-, PG-, CG-, and AG-relations. E-relations represent generalization from the token to the type level. Generalization hierarchies at the type level are described by two graph relations. The *unconditional gen inclusion relation* (UGI-relation), a ternary relation, specifies an RM/T entity type, its generalization RM/T entity type, and the category to which the generalization belongs. If an RM/T entity type can be generalized to more than one RM/T entity type, this is specified in the *alternate gen inclusion relation* (AGI-relation), also a ternary relation.

Sometimes we would like to specify an RM/T entity type that is a collection of, possibly several RM/T entity types, but it is not an aggregation as defined previously. For example, a convoy of ships may include several types of ships. This kind of aggregation is called *cover aggregation* and the RM/T entity type representing the aggregation is called a *cover aggregation type*. The *cover membership relation* (KG-relation) specifies, for every cover aggregation type, the allowed RM/T entity types that may become members of the cover type.

Entities of type event are distinguished in RM/T. These are entities that have as part of their description a time of occurrence or a start and/or stop time. Four binary graph relations — *unconditional successor relation* (US-relation), *alternate successor relation* (AS-relation), *unconditional predecessor relation* (UP-relation), and *alternate predecessor relation* (AP-relation) — are used to record timing of events. These four relations indicate, respectively, which events must succeed a certain event (US-relation), which events may succeed a certain event (AS-relation), which events must precede a certain event (UP-relation), and which events may precede a certain event (AP-relation).

The relational algebra operations are extended in RM/T to the case where null values are present in the relations. The usual relational operations are redefined where necessary to handle null values. In addition, two more operations — outer union and outer join — are defined which insert null values into the result in a controlled manner. Outer union is defined for non-union-compatible relations and inserts null values where necessary in the union. The outer join joins a tuple with a null tuple if the join condition cannot be satisfied.

RM/T also defines operations for manipulating the schema and graph relations. Schema operations allow one to obtain the name of a relation given its extension and vice versa, and to manipulate schema names. Graph operations allow one to manipulate the graph relations to determine such things as adjacency, transitive closure, and so on. Finally, additional set operations are introduced that enable one to apply an operation to an arbitrary number of relations, to partition a relation according to attribute value or tuple value, and to manipulate sets of relation names.

The RM/T data model was prompted by a lack of inherent constraints in basic relational data models. The extensions, in effect, allow the specification of certain constraints on the structure of the relations in a schema. As such, the extensions are aimed more at data base designers and sophisticated users than at the majority of users. Most of the details of the extended relational data model can be hidden from the users, resulting in the simple data model outlined in Sections 5.2 and 5.3.

The basic relational data model has had a tremendous impact on data base management in general, and on data models in particular. It is a simple, concise data model which was nicely outlined in Codd's original papers [Codd, 1970, 1971a,b, 1972a,b]. For the first time, many people could understand a data model by reading a few key papers. This led to a great deal of research by many people throughout the world. As a matter of fact, that the significant results of data base theory, as outlined in Chapter 13, would never have been attained without the basic relational data model. Many claims have been made about relational data models being better or simpler or nicer. Most of these arguments are subjective. However, even if relational data models are not superior to any other data model, they have achieved a great goal. They have brought together the practitioners who implement systems and the researchers who conceptualize about them.

## EXERCISES

**5.1** Propose a mechanism for specifying relationship types between relations similar to the specification of links in graph data models. Incorporate the mechanism into the DDL of System R.

**5.2** How would you express a total, one-to-one constraint on a relationship type using the facilities of System R? Give an example.

**5.3** What are the implications for a relational data language if a relational data base is implemented via a data base machine [Hsiao and Kannan, 1977]?

**5.4** Express the example queries of SQL (Section 5.5) in both the relational algebra and the relational calculus. Discuss the advantages and disadvantages of each of the three languages.

**5.5** The main properties of relational data models are not related to the basic structure (i.e., the relation) but to the relational operations. As a result, some commercial systems that claim to be "relational" may not really be relational at all because they do not adequately support the relational operations. Survey some commercial "relational" systems and decide whether they are, in fact, relational.

**5.6** Is a view facility a necessary feature for a relational system? Would you consider this facility as part of the data model?

**5.7** Translate each of the statements of SQL as specified in Section 5.5 into a corresponding program in the relational navigation language specified in Section 5.4.

**5.8** For some time, relational systems were assumed to lead to a less efficient implementation. Is there anything in a relational data model that would support this viewpoint? Justify your answer.

**5.9** The theory of relational data models implies an automatic elimination of duplicates after every operation. Prove that elimination of duplicates is equivalent, in terms of order of complexity, to sorting.

**5.10** Consider the natural join of two relations $R_1 \underset{A=B}{*} R_2$ according to two compatible attributes $A$ and $B$. Suppose that we isolate the values of $B = \{b_1, ..., b_n\}$ in $R_2$. We then obtain only the tuples of $R_1$ where the values of $A$ are equal to one of the elements among $\{b_1, ..., b_n\}$. This is called the *semi-join* of $R_1$ in terms of $R_2$. Suppose that we are given the two semi-joins of $R_1$ and $R_2$. Is the join operation simpler to implement? How would you obtain the semi-joins of $R_1$ and $R_2$ if $A$ and $B$ are indexed? Is there a reason why we may want to perform join operations using semi-joins [Bernstein and Goodman, 1979; Bernstein and Chiu, 1981]?

**5.11** Consider the E-relations and P-relations, and the graph relations (PG, AG, and CG) in RM/T. What constraints are required for these relations to ensure that the tuples represent only valid entities and relationships in the data base?

# Chapter 6

# NETWORK DATA MODELS

## 6.1 INTRODUCTION

Network data models are based on tables and graphs. The nodes of a graph usually correspond to the entity types, which are represented as tables. The arcs of a graph correspond to relationship types, which are represented as connections between tables. Network data models are embodied in many diverse forms in different commercial systems [Sperry Univac, 1973; Cincom, 1974; Philips, 1974; Burroughs, 1975; Cullinane, 1975; Honeywell, 1975].

The most comprehensive specification of a network data model (the DBTG-network data model) is in the April 1971 report published by the Data Base Task Group (DBTG) of the Conference on Data Systems Languages (CODASYL) [CODASYL, 1971; Taylor and Frank, 1976]. The original report has gone through several iterations [CODASYL, 1973, 1976, 1977b, 1978; Manola, 1977, 1978]. The objective of the original report was, in general, to specify facilities of a DBMS and, in particular, to propose such a facility for embedding into COBOL. The specifications draw a great deal from two early network DBMSs, Integrated Data Store (IDS) [Bachman and Williams, 1964] and Associative PL/1 (APL) [Dodd, 1966]. These two systems evolved from the early report generation systems (Mark I, Mark II and 9PAC) [Fry and Sibley, 1976]. The need to cross-link different files to obtain a single report resulted in the network structure of IDS and APL.

The DBTG proposal is a fairly detailed specification of a data base management facility. Not all of the proposal relates to the specification of a network data model. In the following sections we present those aspects of the DBTG proposal related to data modeling. In addition, we present only those features outlined in the most recent specification of the modeling capabilities of a DBTG-based network system [ANSI, 1981]. For details on other facilities and earlier features, the interested reader can consult the appropriate reports [CODASYL, 1971, 1973, 1978].

## 6.2 STRUCTURES

The DBTG-network data model uses two data structuring tools: the record type and the link. Record types are used to represent entity types and to specify the generic structure of the tables. Links are used to represent the relationship types and to specify the generic connections between record types. Links between record types in a graph must be functional[1]. A graph representing record types and links which abides by this restriction is called a *data structure diagram* [Bachman, 1969]. Figure 6.2–1 shows a data structure diagram for the medical data base outlined in the Appendix. A data structure diagram conveys the intension of a DBTG-network data base.

A node in a data structure diagram, called a *record type*, is labeled and usually represents an entity type. For example, *HOSPITAL*, *WARD*, *STAFF*, and so on, are record types in Figure 6.2–1 which represent the corresponding entity types of the medical data base. Some record types, such as the *HOSPITAL LAB* record type, do not represent entity types. The nature of these record types is discussed in Section 6.3.

A record type is composed of zero or more *data items*. In Figure 6.2–1 the *STAFF* record type is composed of the data items *Employee#*, *Name*, *Duty*, *Shift*, and *Salary*. In its simplest form, a data item represents a simple domain as an attribute does in relational data models. However, it can also represent a named collection of data (composite attribute) called an *array*. An array consists of one or more occurrences of a single data item within a record. It may be multidimensional. In effect, an array corresponds to the repeating group concept discussed in Chapter 3.

An arc in a data structure diagram, called a *set type*, is labeled and represents a functional link. The set type concept in the DBTG-network data model is not, however, the same as a mathematical set. To avoid confusion with mathematical sets, the term *DBTG-set type*[2] will be used to refer to the set-type concept of the DBTG-network data model.

If all the links are functional, as in a data structure diagram, the roles of the two record types connected by the functional link can be distinguished. For example, in Figure 6.2–1 the *HOSPITAL* and *WARD* record types are related by the functional link *HOSPITAL WARDS*. In this

---

[1.] One-to-one links are allowed, of course, since they are a special case of functional links.

[2.] Equivalent terminology which the reader may find in the literature is coset, CODASYL set, owner-coupled set, and fan set [Nijssen, 1975].

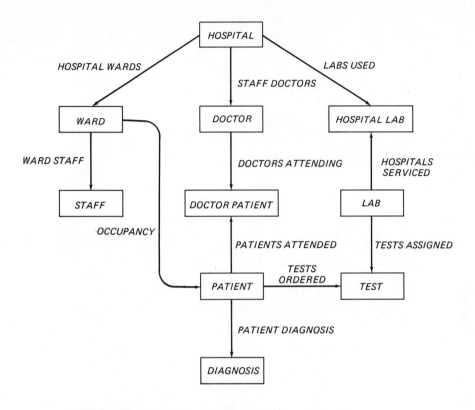

HOSPITAL(Hospital code, Name, Address, Phone#, # of beds)
WARD(Ward code, Name, # of beds)
STAFF(Employee#, Name, Duty, Shift, Salary)
DOCTOR(Doctor#, Name, Specialty)
DOCTOR PATIENT(Doctor#, Registration#)
PATIENT(Registration#, Bed#, Name, Address, Birthdate, Sex, SSN)
DIAGNOSIS(Diagnosis code, Diagnosis type, Complications, Precautionary info)
HOSPITAL LAB(Hospital code, Lab#)
LAB(Lab#, Name, Address, Phone#)
TEST(Test code, Type, Date ordered, Time ordered, Specimen/order#, Status)

**Fig. 6.2—1** Data structure diagram for medical data base.

DBTG-set type, *HOSPITAL* is said to be the *owner record type* and *WARD* the *member record type*. In general, in any DBTG-set type the record type at the tail of the arc is the owner and the one at the head of the arc is the member. The direction of the arc is opposite the direction of functionality. A DBTG-set type may contain more than one member record type. Only one owner record type is allowed, although there have been proposals to permit alternate owner record types [Bachman, 1977; Manola, 1977].

The extension of a data structure diagram consists of occurrences of record types and DBTG-set types. The extension of a record type can be

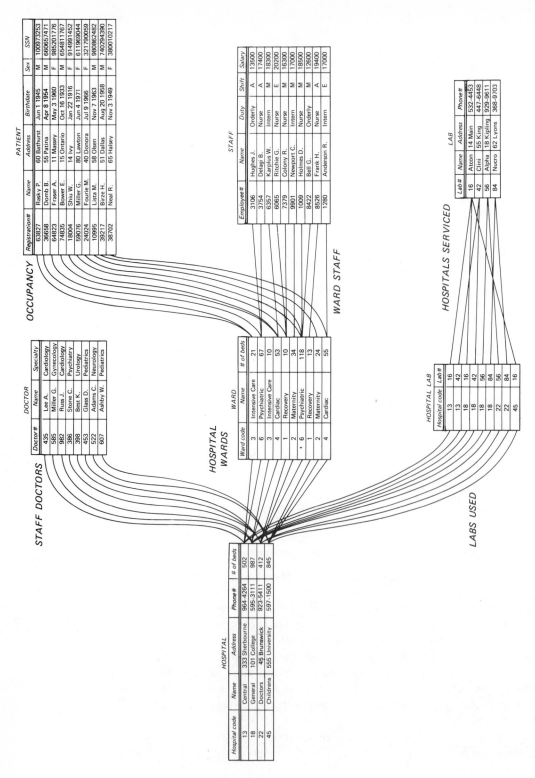

**PATIENT**

| Registration# | Name | Address | Birthdate | Sex | SSN |
|---|---|---|---|---|---|
| 63827 | Rasky P. | 60 Bathurst | Jun 1 1945 | M | 100973253 |
| 36658 | Domb B. | 55 Patina | Apr 8 1954 | M | 660657471 |
| 64823 | Fraser A. | 11 Massey | May 3 1960 | F | 985201776 |
| 74835 | Bower E. | 15 Ontario | Oct 16 1933 | M | 654811767 |
| 18004 | Shiu W. | 14 Ivy | Jan 22 1916 | F | 914991452 |
| 59076 | Miller G. | 80 Lawton | Jun 4 1971 | F | 611969044 |
| 24024 | Fourie M. | 40 Donora | Jul 9 1966 | F | 321790059 |
| 10995 | Lista M. | 58 Olsen | Nov 7 1963 | M | 980862482 |
| 39217 | Birze H. | 51 Dallas | Aug 20 1958 | M | 740294390 |
| 38702 | Neal R. | 65 Halsey | Nov 3 1949 | F | 380010217 |

**STAFF**

| Employee# | Name | Duty | Shift | Salary |
|---|---|---|---|---|
| 3106 | Hughes J. | Orderly | A | 13500 |
| 3754 | Delagi B. | Nurse | A | 17400 |
| 6357 | Karplus W. | Intern | M | 18300 |
| 6065 | Ritchie G. | Nurse | E | 20200 |
| 7379 | Colony R. | Nurse | M | 16300 |
| 9901 | Newport C. | Intern | M | 17000 |
| 1009 | Holmes D. | Nurse | M | 18500 |
| 8422 | Bell G. | Orderly | M | 12600 |
| 8526 | Frank H. | Nurse | A | 19400 |
| 1280 | Anderson R. | Intern | E | 17000 |

**LAB**

| Lab# | Name | Address | Phone# |
|---|---|---|---|
| 16 | Atcon | 14 Main | 532-4453 |
| 42 | Clini | 55 King | 447-6448 |
| 56 | Alpha | 18 Kipling | 929-9611 |
| 84 | Nucro | 62 Lyons | 368-9703 |

**DOCTOR**

| Doctor# | Name | Specialty |
|---|---|---|
| 435 | Lee A. | Cardiology |
| 585 | Miller G. | Gynecology |
| 982 | Russ J. | Cardiology |
| 386 | Stone C. | Psychiatry |
| 398 | Best K. | Urology |
| 453 | Glass D. | Pediatrics |
| 522 | Adams C. | Neurology |
| 607 | Ashby W. | Pediatrics |

**WARD**

| Ward code | Name | # of beds |
|---|---|---|
| 3 | Intensive Care | 21 |
| 6 | Psychiatric | 67 |
| 3 | Intensive Care | 10 |
| 4 | Cardiac | 53 |
| 1 | Recovery | 10 |
| 2 | Maternity | 34 |
| * 6 | Psychiatric | 118 |
| 1 | Recovery | 13 |
| 2 | Maternity | 24 |
| 4 | Cardiac | 55 |

**HOSPITAL LAB**

| Hospital code | Lab# |
|---|---|
| 13 | 16 |
| 13 | 42 |
| 18 | 16 |
| 18 | 42 |
| 18 | 56 |
| 18 | 84 |
| 22 | 56 |
| 22 | 84 |
| 45 | 16 |

**HOSPITAL**

| Hospital code | Name | Address | Phone# | # of beds |
|---|---|---|---|---|
| 13 | Central | 333 Sherbourne | 964-4264 | 502 |
| 18 | General | 101 College | 595-3111 | 987 |
| 22 | Doctors | 45 Brunswick | 923-5411 | 412 |
| 45 | Childrens | 555 University | 597-1500 | 845 |

OCCUPANCY

STAFF DOCTORS

HOSPITAL WARDS

WARD STAFF

HOSPITALS SERVICED

LABS USED

**Fig. 6.2−2** Extension of data structure diagram for medical data base.

122

represented as a table. Unlike the relational data model where the tables are sets, the tables in a DBTG-network data base can be considered extended sets. That is, duplicates are allowed and an ordering can be specified on the rows of the table. Each row of the table is called a *record* and corresponds to an occurrence of the generic record type. Figure 6.2−2 shows part of the extension of the data structure diagram of Figure 6.2−1.

The extension of a DBTG-set type can be represented as a collection of arcs between the tables representing the owner and member record types. The collection of arcs connecting one *owner record* and zero or more *member records* is called a *DBTG-set occurrence* or simply *DBTG-set.* Figure 6.2−2 shows four, four, and ten DBTG-sets of the *HOSPITAL WARDS, STAFF DOCTORS* and *WARD STAFF* DBTG-set types, respectively. For the four occurrences of the *HOSPITAL WARDS* DBTG-set type, the first (owner record *Hospital code* 13) has two member records, the second (owner record *Hospital code* 18) has two member records, the third (owner record *Hospital code* 22) has three member records, and the fourth (owner record *Hospital code* 45) has three member records. A DBTG-set need not have any member records, as illustrated by the first, third, and ninth *WARD STAFF* DBTG-sets (owner records *Ward code* 3, 3, and 2).

A DBTG-set type may consist of exactly one occurrence whose owner is the DBMS (i.e., it has no owner). Such a DBTG-set type is called a *singular set type.* A singular DBTG-set type is a mechanism for logically grouping records of one or more type.

The definition of the medical data base according to the DBTG-network data model follows. The definition uses the proposed ANSI DDL [ANSI, 1981] and specifies only the structure of the data base. A complete definition would also specify certain constraints on the record types and DBTG-set types. The nature of these constraints and their specification are discussed in the next section.

RECORD NAME IS *HOSPITAL.*
    *Hospital code* TYPE IS FIXED 6
    *Name* TYPE IS CHARACTER 15
    *Address* TYPE IS CHARACTER 20
    *Phone#* TYPE IS CHARACTER 7
    *# of beds* TYPE IS FIXED 4

RECORD NAME IS *WARD.*
    *Ward code* TYPE IS FIXED 6
    *Name* TYPE IS CHARACTER 15
    *# of beds* TYPE IS FIXED 4

**RECORD NAME IS** *STAFF.*
    *Employee#* **TYPE IS FIXED** 6
    *Name* **TYPE IS CHARACTER** 20
    *Duty* **TYPE IS CHARACTER** 15
    *Shift* **TYPE IS CHARACTER** 10
    *Salary* **TYPE IS FIXED** 5 2

**RECORD NAME IS** *DOCTOR.*
    *Doctor#* **TYPE IS FIXED** 6
    *Name* **TYPE IS CHARACTER** 20
    *Specialty* **TYPE IS CHARACTER** 20

**RECORD NAME IS** *DOCTOR PATIENT.*
    *Doctor#* **TYPE IS FIXED** 6
    *Registration#* **TYPE IS FIXED** 6

**RECORD NAME IS** *PATIENT.*
    *Registration#* **TYPE IS FIXED** 6
    *Bed#* **TYPE IS FIXED** 4
    *Name* **TYPE IS CHARACTER** 20
    *Address* **TYPE IS CHARACTER** 20
    *Birthdate* **TYPE IS CHARACTER** 8
    *Sex* **TYPE IS CHARACTER** 1
    *SSN* **TYPE IS FIXED** 6

**RECORD NAME IS** *DIAGNOSIS.*
    *Diagnosis code* **TYPE IS FIXED** 6
    *Diagnosis type* **TYPE IS CHARACTER** 25
    *Complications* **TYPE IS CHARACTER** 25
    *Precautionary info* **TYPE IS CHARACTER** 40

**RECORD NAME IS** *HOSPITAL LAB.*
    *Hospital code* **TYPE IS FIXED** 6
    *Lab#* **TYPE IS FIXED** 6

**RECORD NAME IS** *LAB.*
    *Lab#* **TYPE IS FIXED** 6
    *Name* **TYPE IS CHARACTER** 20
    *Address* **TYPE IS CHARACTER** 20
    *Phone#* **TYPE IS CHARACTER** 7

**RECORD NAME IS** *TEST.*
    *Test code* **TYPE IS FIXED** 6
    *Type* **TYPE IS CHARACTER** 20
    *Date ordered* **TYPE IS CHARACTER** 8
    *Time ordered* **TYPE IS CHARACTER** 4
    *Specimen/order#* **TYPE IS FIXED** 6
    *Status* **TYPE IS FIXED** 15

**SET NAME IS** *HOSPITAL WARDS.*
    **OWNER IS** *HOSPITAL.*
    **MEMBER IS** *WARD.*

**SET NAME IS** *WARD STAFF.*
    **OWNER IS** *WARD.*
    **MEMBER IS** *STAFF.*

**SET NAME IS** *OCCUPANCY.*
    **OWNER IS** *WARD.*
    **MEMBER IS** *PATIENT.*

**SET NAME IS** *STAFF DOCTORS.*
    **OWNER IS** *HOSPITAL.*
    **MEMBER IS** *DOCTOR.*

**SET NAME IS** *DOCTORS ATTENDING.*
    **OWNER IS** *DOCTOR.*
    **MEMBER IS** *DOCTOR PATIENT.*

**SET NAME IS** *PATIENTS ATTENDED.*
    **OWNER IS** *PATIENT.*
    **MEMBER IS** *DOCTOR PATIENT.*

**SET NAME IS** *PATIENT DIAGNOSIS.*
    **OWNER IS** *PATIENT.*
    **MEMBER IS** *DIAGNOSIS.*

**SET NAME IS** *TESTS ORDERED.*
    **OWNER IS** *PATIENT.*
    **MEMBER IS** *TEST.*

**SET NAME IS** *TESTS ASSIGNED.*
    **OWNER IS** *LAB.*
    **MEMBER IS** *TEST.*

**SET NAME IS** *LABS USED.*
    **OWNER IS** *HOSPITAL.*
    **MEMBER IS** *HOSPITAL LAB.*

**SET NAME IS** *HOSPITALS SERVICED.*
    **OWNER IS** *LAB.*
    **MEMBER IS** *HOSPITAL LAB.*

## 6.3 CONSTRAINTS

The functionality of links in the DBTG-network data model is an inherent constraint. It means that any member record in a DBTG-set can have at most one owner record. However, it is not necessary that every record be a member of a DBTG-set. For example, a record of a member record type for a DBTG-set type need not be a member (have an owner) in a corresponding DBTG-set. This latter property can be expressed as a requirement by the use of an explicit constraint on a link (as discussed below).

The owner record in a DBTG-set can be connected to zero or more member records. Thus, when a DBTG-set is empty, it still has one member (the owner record). This is one of the reasons that a DBTG-set is not a mathematical set.

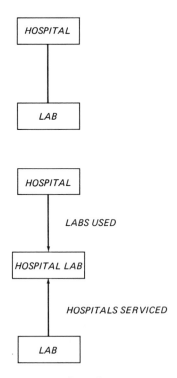

**Fig. 6.3−1** Intension representation of a many-to-many relationship type.

The functional restriction on a link makes it impossible to represent directly many-to-many relationship types in the DBTG-network data model. However, an intermediate record type and two functional links can be used to represent such a relationship type. Figure 6.3−1 demonstrates the technique for the many-to-many relationship type between *HOSPITAL* and *LAB* in the example medical data base. This technique is used twice in the data structure diagram of Figure 6.2−1.

For the extension of the technique used in Figure 6.3−1, one record of the intermediate record type is introduced for each connection between

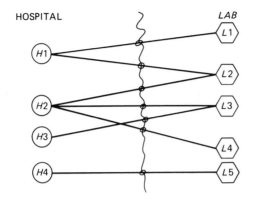

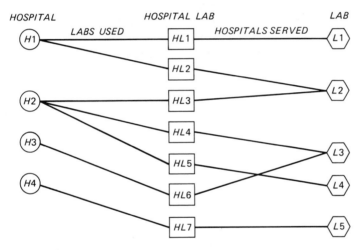

Fig. 6.3—2 Extension representation of a many-to-many relationship type.

the records. Figure 6.3—2 illustrates the method. Each *HOSPITAL LAB* record has at most one *HOSPITAL* and one *LAB* owner record in each *LABS USED* and *HOSPITALS SERVED* DBTG-set, respectively. The introduction of the intermediate record type to represent the many-to-many relationship type is not always artificial. The intermediate records can be used to contain data that belong with the relationship type or are common to the two original record types.

As a result of functional links, there is an implicit constraint in the DBTG-network data model that the same record cannot be a member in more than one DBTG-set of the same type. Thus, in the example medical data base, the situation depicted in Figure 6.3—3 would not be allowed.

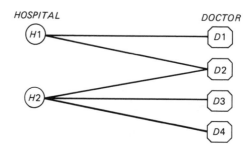

**Fig. 6.3—3** Illegal relationship in a DBTG-network data base.

The *DOCTOR* record *D2* has two *HOSPITAL* owner records (*H1* and *H2*). This situation destroys the functionality of the link.

Another situation disallowed in the DBTG-network data model is that of recursive links. A recursive link is one in which both owner and member record types are the same. Figure 6.3—4 illustrates the nature of a recursive link where a manager is also considered an employee. Such a link does not cause difficulties with respect to functionality. However, it can cause "context" difficulties in a navigation data language. That is, suppose that we navigate the *MANAGES* link among *EMPLOYEE* records with a data language statement such as

**GET NEXT** *MANAGES* **SET**

If we are currently at *EMPLOYEE* record *E2*, it is not clear whether the "next" record is *E3* or *E5*. Unless more context is supplied, the ambiguity cannot be resolved. Since the COBOL DML, which was defined together with the DBTG-network data model, provides navigation operations such as this, recursive links were prohibited.

A record type can have one or more keys declared for it. A key consists of one or more data items that identifies a record uniquely. This feature can be used to specify constraints **C4** and **C7** for the medical data base. Constraint **C4** would be specified as

**DUPLICATES ARE NOT ALLOWED FOR** *SSN*

This specification would be part of the record specification for the *PATIENT* record type. Constraint **C7** is expressed in a similar manner for each data item.

One can specify simple value constraints on and among data items of a record type by a **CHECK** clause. A (record) **CHECK** clause specifies a value constraint on or among data items of a record type. Consider a record type *ITEM* with data items *Item#*, *Cost*, and *Price*. We could specify a constraint that *Price* must always exceed *Cost* as

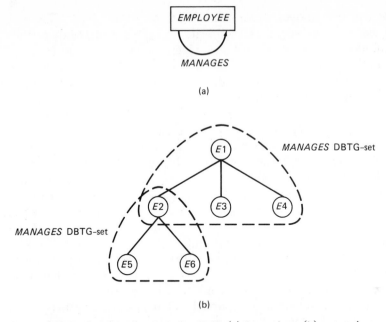

Fig. 6.3—4 Example of a recursive link: (a) intension; (b) extension.

**CHECK IS** *Cost> Price*

Such a value constraint can only be specified among data items of the same record type. More general value constraints and aggregate constraints are specified by data base procedures.

Value constraints can also be specified on individual data items. A (data) **CHECK** clause is used for this purpose. As examples, constraint **C1** and **C3** would be specified, respectively, as

**CHECK IS VALUE** 0 **THRU** 2400
**CHECK IS VALUE** 'F', 'M'

The **CHECK** clause is associated, in the record specification, with the data item to which the constraint applies.

Explicit constraints can be placed on the functional link between record types. The constraints specify the time-independent and the time-dependent properties of the link [Date, 1981]. The collection of properties is termed *set membership*. The time-independent set membership property relates to the nature of a connection in a DBTG-set. That is, it specifies the permanence of the connection between owner and member records. The options available, called *set retention* options, are fixed, mandatory, and optional membership.

*Fixed* set membership means that once a record has become a member of a DBTG-set (been connected according to the link), it cannot be disconnected or moved to another DBTG-set of any type. The only way to disconnect a record is to delete it. This constraint permits the specification and enforcement of certain semantic properties of a link. Consider, for example, the *HOSPITAL WARDS* DBTG-set type in Figure 6.2−1. Logically, a ward cannot exist without being part of a hospital. Additionally, a ward cannot be moved from one hospital to another (physically at least). Fixed set membership for the *HOSPITAL WARDS* DBTG-set type enforces this semantic constraint.

*Mandatory* set membership is similar to fixed set membership. The only difference is that a member record in a DBTG-set can be moved to another DBTG-set of the same type. For example, consider the *WARD STAFF* DBTG-set type in Figure 6.2−1. A staff member should be associated with some ward in the hospital. However, staff can be moved from ward to ward. Mandatory set membership for the *WARD STAFF* DBTG-set type enforces this constraint.

*Optional* set membership implies that a record can be connected or disconnected from a DBTG-set at any time. As an example, the membership of the *PATIENT* record type in the *OCCUPANCY* DBTG-set type (Figure 6.2−1) can be optional. Semantically, this may reflect the fact, for example, that patients do not need to be assigned to a ward to be treated by the hospital (e.g., outpatients).

The time-dependent property of set membership relates to how and when a member record is connected in a DBTG-set. That is, it specifies the mechanism for establishing a connection in a DBTG-set. This specification is used to determine the action to be taken at the time that a record of the member record type is created. The options, called *set insertion* options, are automatic or manual membership.

*Automatic* set membership means that, at the time that a record of the member record type is created, it is immediately made a member of some DBTG-set for all DBTG-set types in which its membership is automatic. This implies that the correct DBTG-set for each DBTG-set type can be selected by the DBMS or the DBMS can assume that this selection has occurred previously. Semantically, it means that the record cannot have an existence (at least initially) independent of its membership in all DBTG-set types for which its insertion option is automatic. If, in addition, its retention option is fixed or mandatory, this condition is enforced as long as the record exists in the data base. Thus, the insertion option for the *PATIENT DIAGNOSIS* DBTG-set type would be automatic since every *DIAGNOSIS* record is associated with some *PATIENT* record.

*Manual* set membership means that no action is taken by the DBMS concerning connection in a DBTG-set when the record is created. Thereafter, a record is connected in a DBTG-set explicitly by the user via data language operations. This means that the record can have an existence independent of the DBTG-set types for which its insertion option is manual. In addition, if its retention option is optional, this freedom can be exercised throughout the record's existence. If, on the other hand, its retention option is fixed or mandatory, the restrictions associated with those options come into force whenever the record is initially connected in the affected DBTG-set type. Since a patient can be an outpatient, the insertion option for the *OCCUPANCY* DBTG-set type would be specified as manual.

Set membership is always specified as one insertion option and one retention option. Thus, there are six possible set membership types. Constraint **C8** can be specified as the set membership type automatic fixed. Automatic fixed set membership would enforce the constraint that every *DIAGNOSIS* record be associated with the same *PATIENT* record throughout its existence.

Set membership can be controlled using *structural constraints* [CODASYL, 1978]. A structural constraint is specified in the schema and states that the value of a data item in the member records must be equal to the value of a data item in the owner record of a DBTG-set. For example, in Figure 6.2−1 a structural constraint could specify that the *Doctor#* in a *DOCTOR PATIENT* record must be equal to the *Doctor#* of the *DOCTOR* record to which it is connected. At the time that the connection between a *DOCTOR PATIENT* record and a *DOCTOR* record is made, the DBMS checks the validity of the constraint. If it is not satisfied, the connection is not allowed.

A structural constraint can be used to specify how the connection is to be made for automatic set membership. That is, the structural constraint can be used to select the owner record to which a member record is to be connected. For the data item specified in the structural constraint, its value is taken from the member record and matched with the corresponding data item in the owner record. In this case, the corresponding data item in the owner record type must be a key to permit selection of a unique owner record and consequently unique DBTG-set (functional link restriction).

Set membership defines the nature of the connection between owner and member records in a DBTG-set. It specifies how a connection is to be established and under what conditions it can be broken. The insertion options specify what action is to be taken concerning formation of any connections when a record is first created. The retention options specify how the connection is to be maintained during a record's existence. These options also have implications for the data language operations concerning the action taken when a record is inserted into and deleted from the data base.

When a record is inserted into the data base and its membership is automatic in some DBTG-set type, it must be connected to an appropriate owner record in a DBTG-set of the correct type by the DBMS. This implies that the DBMS is able to select the correct DBTG-set (i.e., the correct owner record). The way in which the DBMS selects the DBTG-set is defined in the schema by a **SET SELECTION** clause. A **SET SELECTION** clause defines the default rules for selecting an occurrence of a DBTG-set type for inserting or accessing a member record.

Set selection can be one of system, application, key, or structural constraint. Selection by structural constraint was discussed above. Selection by key means that the user supplies the value of a key of the owner record of the DBTG-set to the DBMS, which then uses this value to select the DBTG-set. Selection by application means that the user has previously established currency of the correct owner record (and thus the correct DBTG-set) and the DBMS can make use of this currency to establish the connection. Finally, selection by system is allowed only for singular DBTG-set types. Set selection by structural constraint and by key are both defined in the schema by the **SET SELECTION** clause. Set selection by system and by application are not defined in the schema.

When a record is deleted from the data base and it is still connected to some other records, these connections must be broken. Breaking a connection may cause additional actions to be taken by the DBMS, depending on the nature of the connection. If the owner of a DBTG-set, whose membership is fixed, is deleted, it seems logical also to delete the member records since their existence depends on that of the owner (according to the semantics of fixed membership). If the owner of a DBTG-set with optional membership is deleted, disconnection of the member records, only, seems logical, since their existence does not depend solely on the owner record. The action required for mandatory membership is not clear. Disconnection is not possible, but transfer to another DBTG-set of the same type is. Current DBTG specifications provide for the deletion of mandatory members. In addition, deletion of all members regardless of their membership option is possible. It is also necessary to consider the consequences of the deletion of a member on any records of which it is an owner. Recursive application of the preceding actions is one possibility.

The members of a DBTG-set must have an ordering specified for them in the schema. The ordering determines where a new member is placed, in relation to existing members in a DBTG-set, when it is connected to an owner record. The possible orderings are first, last, next, prior, system default, and sorted. First and last refer to the relative ordering with respect to the owner record. Next and prior refer to the relative ordering with respect to currency. System default specifies that no particular ordering is to be enforced. The sorted ordering can be with respect to record types within a DBTG-set type or with respect to data item values within a member record type.  The manner in which duplicate values are to be handled can also be specified.

The medical data base example can now be specified more completely, incorporating various constraints.

**RECORD NAME IS** *HOSPITAL*
    **DUPLICATES ARE NOT ALLOWED FOR** *Hospital code.*
       *Hospital code* **TYPE IS FIXED** 6
       *Name* **TYPE IS CHARACTER** 15
       *Address* **TYPE IS CHARACTER** 20
       *Phone#* **TYPE IS CHARACTER** 7
       *# of beds* **TYPE IS FIXED** 4

**RECORD NAME IS** *WARD*
    **DUPLICATES ARE NOT ALLOWED FOR** *Ward code.*
       *Ward code* **TYPE IS FIXED** 6
       *Name* **TYPE IS CHARACTER** 15
       *# of beds* **TYPE IS FIXED** 4

**RECORD NAME IS** *STAFF*
    **DUPLICATES ARE NOT ALLOWED FOR** *Employee#.*
       *Employee#* **TYPE IS FIXED** 6
       *Name* **TYPE IS CHARACTER** 20
       *Duty* **TYPE IS CHARACTER** 15
       *Shift* **TYPE IS CHARACTER** 10
       *Salary* **TYPE IS FIXED** 5 2

**RECORD NAME IS** *DOCTOR*
    **DUPLICATES ARE NOT ALLOWED FOR** *Doctor#.*
       *Doctor#* **TYPE IS FIXED** 6
       *Name* **TYPE IS CHARACTER** 20
       *Specialty* **TYPE IS CHARACTER** 20

**RECORD NAME IS** *DOCTOR PATIENT*
    **DUPLICATES ARE NOT ALLOWED FOR** *Doctor# Registration#.*
       *Doctor#* **TYPE IS FIXED** 6
       *Registration#* **TYPE IS FIXED** 6

**RECORD NAME IS** *PATIENT*
    **DUPLICATES ARE NOT ALLOWED FOR** *Registration#*
    **DUPLICATES ARE NOT ALLOWED FOR** *SSN.*
       *Registration#* **TYPE IS FIXED** 6
       *Bed#* **TYPE IS FIXED** 4
       *Name* **TYPE IS CHARACTER** 20
       *Address* **TYPE IS CHARACTER** 20
       *Birthdate* **TYPE IS CHARACTER** 8
       *Sex* **TYPE IS CHARACTER** 1
          **CHECK IS VALUE** 'F', 'M'.
       *SSN* **TYPE IS FIXED** 6

RECORD NAME IS *DIAGNOSIS.*
    *Diagnosis code* **TYPE IS FIXED** 6
    *Diagnosis type* **TYPE IS CHARACTER** 25
    *Complications* **TYPE IS CHARACTER** 25
    *Precautionary info* **TYPE IS CHARACTER** 40

RECORD NAME IS *HOSPITAL LAB*
   **DUPLICATES ARE NOT ALLOWED FOR** *Hospital code Lab#.*
    *Hospital code* **TYPE IS FIXED** 6
    *Lab#* **TYPE IS FIXED** 6

RECORD NAME IS *LAB*
   **DUPLICATES ARE NOT ALLOWED FOR** *Lab#.*
    *Lab#* **TYPE IS FIXED** 6
    *Name* **TYPE IS CHARACTER** 20
    *Address* **TYPE IS CHARACTER** 20
    *Phone#* **TYPE IS CHARACTER** 7

RECORD NAME IS *TEST.*
    *Test code* **TYPE IS FIXED** 6
    *Type* **TYPE IS CHARACTER** 20
    *Date ordered* **TYPE IS CHARACTER** 8
    *Time ordered* **TYPE IS CHARACTER** 4
       **CHECK IS VALUE** 0 **THRU** 2400.
    *Specimen/order#* **TYPE IS FIXED** 6
    *Status* **TYPE IS FIXED** 15

**SET NAME IS** *HOSPITAL WARDS.*
   **OWNER IS** *HOSPITAL*
    **ORDER IS SORTED BY DEFINED KEYS**
    **DUPLICATES ARE NOT ALLOWED.**
   **MEMBER IS** *WARD*
    **INSERTION IS AUTOMATIC RETENTION IS FIXED**
    **SET SELECTION IS BY VALUE OF** *Hospital code.*

**SET NAME IS** *WARD STAFF.*
   **OWNER IS** *WARD*
    **ORDER IS SORTED BY DEFINED KEYS**
    **DUPLICATES ARE NOT ALLOWED.**
   **MEMBER IS** *STAFF*
    **INSERTION IS AUTOMATIC RETENTION IS MANDATORY**
    **SET SELECTION IS BY VALUE OF** *Ward code.*

**SET NAME IS** *OCCUPANCY.*
   **OWNER IS** *WARD*
    **ORDER IS SYSTEM DEFAULT.**
   **MEMBER IS** *PATIENT*
    **INSERTION IS MANUAL RETENTION IS OPTIONAL**
    **SET SELECTION IS BY VALUE OF** *Ward code.*

**SET NAME IS** *STAFF DOCTORS.*
  **OWNER IS** *HOSPITAL*
    **ORDER IS SORTED BY DEFINED KEYS**
    **DUPLICATES ARE NOT ALLOWED.**
  **MEMBER IS** *DOCTOR*
    **INSERTION IS MANUAL RETENTION IS OPTIONAL**
    **SET SELECTION IS BY VALUE OF** *Hospital code.*

**SET NAME IS** *DOCTORS ATTENDING.*
  **OWNER IS** *DOCTOR*
    **ORDER IS NEXT.**
  **MEMBER IS** *DOCTOR PATIENT*
    **INSERTION IS AUTOMATIC RETENTION IS FIXED**
    **SET SELECTION IS BY STRUCTURAL** *Doctor# = Doctor#.*

**SET NAME IS** *PATIENTS ATTENDED.*
  **OWNER IS** *PATIENT*
    **ORDER IS NEXT.**
  **MEMBER IS** *DOCTOR PATIENT*
    **INSERTION IS AUTOMATIC RETENTION IS FIXED**
    **SET SELECTION IS BY**
      **STRUCTURAL** *Registration# = Registration#.*

**SET NAME IS** *PATIENT DIAGNOSIS.*
  **OWNER IS** *PATIENT*
    **ORDER IS LAST.**
  **MEMBER IS** *DIAGNOSIS*
    **INSERTION IS AUTOMATIC RETENTION IS FIXED**
    **SET SELECTION IS BY VALUE OF** *Registration#.*

**SET NAME IS** *TESTS ORDERED.*
  **OWNER IS** *PATIENT*
    **ORDER IS FIRST.**
  **MEMBER IS** *TEST*
    **INSERTION IS AUTOMATIC RETENTION IS FIXED.**

**SET NAME IS** *TEST ASSIGNED.*
  **OWNER IS** *LAB*
    **ORDER IS LAST.**
  **MEMBER IS** *TEST*
    **INSERTION IS AUTOMATIC RETENTION IS FIXED.**

**SET NAME IS** *LABS USED.*
  **OWNER IS** *HOSPITAL*
    **ORDER IS NEXT.**
  **MEMBER IS** *HOSPITAL LAB*
    **INSERTION IS AUTOMATIC RETENTION IS FIXED**
    **SET SELECTION IS BY**
      **STRUCTURAL** *Hospital code = Hospital code.*

**SET NAME IS** *HOSPITALS SERVICED.*
    **OWNER IS** *LAB*
       **ORDER IS NEXT.**
    **MEMBER IS** *HOSPITAL LAB*
       **INSERTION IS AUTOMATIC RETENTION IS FIXED**
       **SET SELECTION IS BY STRUCTURAL** *Lab# = Lab#*.

The DBTG proposal provides facilities for specifying constraints via data base procedures. Data base procedures in the DBTG-network data model can be very general. User-defined procedures can be called before or after a specified data language operation or if an error occurs during an operation. There are no restrictions on the form of a user-defined procedure or on the operations it may perform. Constraints **C2**, **C5** and **C6** need to be specified via data base procedures.

## 6.4 NAVIGATION OPERATIONS

As discussed in Chapter 3, navigation operations for a graph data model need to:

1. Establish a position in the data base independent of the relationships between records.
2. Permit navigation among records, via connections, according to the links.

These are the basic ways of setting currency in the data base. Usually, in commercial data languages, there are several data language statements in each category to provide a flexible navigation language. As an example of a navigation data language for a DBTG-network data model, a pseudo-language based on the IDMS COBOL DML will be presented [Cullinane, 1975]. The IDMS operations are based in turn on the DBTG COBOL DML first proposed in the DBTG report [CODASYL, 1971].

To navigate by setting currency, currency indicators are required to mark the progress of the navigation (current position(s)) in the data base. IDMS provides one currency indicator for each record type and DBTG-set type. In addition, there is one currency indicator which indicates which record is most current. All relevant currency indicators are updated implicitly on the successful completion of a data language statement. That is, if a record is selected via a navigation operation and that record is a member of DBTG-set type $S$, the currency indicator for DBTG-set type $S$ is adjusted to point at the selected record. The DBTG-set type currency indicator for $S$ is updated even though the navigation operation contains no explicit reference to $S$. These currency indicator updates result in the implicit nature of currency manipulation.

In IDMS, a *data-base-key* is assigned to each record stored in the data base.  A data-base-key is an external key used by the DBMS to identify uniquely a record within the data base.  The concept of a data-base-key was included in the original DBTG report on which IDMS is based.  Since then, the concept, as originally proposed, has been removed from the DBTG-network data model [CODASYL, 1978].  A data-base-key is still allowed, but it is now recognized as an access convenience.  As such, its use is as a unique record reference within the invocation of a program only and no longer as a data model concept.

There are two data language statements which set currency independent of links.  The statement

**FIND** *record name* **RECORD USING** *identifier*

locates a record based on the value of its data-base-key.  *Identifier* is a variable containing the data-base-key value.

The statement

**FIND [NEXT DUPLICATE]** *record name* **RECORD [WHERE** *qualification*]

locates a record based on the value of a data item.  The **WHERE** *qualification* is not part of the IDMS data language.  Only qualifications that use the equality conditional operator are permitted in the IDMS data language.  Query 1 illustrates this latter use of the **FIND** statement in a program.

**Q1**.  Find the names of all doctors whose specialty is gynecology.

```
FIND DOCTOR RECORD WHERE Specialty = 'GYNECOLOGY'
exit if status − check
GET DOCTOR RECORD
output Name of DOCTOR
loop until no more records
    FIND NEXT DUPLICATE DOCTOR RECORD
    exit loop if status − check
    GET DOCTOR RECORD
    output Name of DOCTOR
end loop
```

The purpose of the **GET** statement is to transfer the selected record from the data base into a buffer.  IDMS provides a shorthand form of the **FIND/GET** combination via the **OBTAIN** statement.

There are three navigation operations in IDMS which set currency based on links between record types.  The statement

$$\text{FIND} \begin{Bmatrix} \text{NEXT} \\ \text{PRIOR} \\ \text{FIRST} \\ \text{LAST} \\ n \end{Bmatrix} \; [\textit{record name}] \; \textbf{RECORD OF} \; \textit{set name} \; \textbf{SET}$$

permits a specified member of a DBTG-set to be located. The ordering of the DBTG-set type, as specified in the schema, is used to determine the next, prior, first, last, or *n*th record of the DBTG-set. This form of the FIND statement can be used to answer the following query.

**Q2.** List the doctors on staff at the hospital with hospital code 22.

> **FIND** *HOSPITAL* **RECORD WHERE** *Hospital code* = 22
> *exit if status* − *check*
> *loop until end of set*
>     **OBTAIN NEXT** *DOCTOR* **RECORD OF** *STAFF DOCTORS* **SET**
>     *exit loop if status* − *check*
>     *output Name of DOCTOR*
> *end loop*

The statement

**FIND OWNER RECORD OF** *set name* **SET**

locates the owner of a DBTG-set. As for the preceding statement, it is assumed that the currency indicator for the DBTG-set has been initialized previously. The OWNER form of the FIND statement is used in Query 3.

**Q3.** List the names of those patients whose diagnosis is cardiac arrest.

> **FIND** *DIAGNOSIS* **RECORD**
> **WHERE** *Diagnosis type* = 'CARDIAC ARREST'
> *exit if status* − *check*
> *loop until no more records*
>     **OBTAIN OWNER RECORD OF** *PATIENT DIAGNOSIS* **SET**
>     *exit loop if status* − *check*
>     *output Name of PATIENT*
>     **FIND NEXT DUPLICATE** *DIAGNOSIS* **RECORD**
>     *exit loop if status* − *check*
> *end loop*

The FIND statement

**FIND** *record name* **RECORD**
**VIA [CURRENT OF]** *set name* **SET WHERE** *qualification*

locates a record based on its membership in a DBTG-set and on the value of a data item. In IDMS this statement can only be used if the members of the DBTG set are ordered according to the data item specified in the *qualification.* If the **CURRENT OF** option is omitted, the search begins at the owner record. If the **CURRENT OF** option is included, the search begins at the current record of the DBTG-set as specified by the DBTG-set currency indicator. Query 4 illustrates the use of this statement.

**Q4.** How many employees are there in ward 6 of Doctors hospital?

> **FIND** *HOSPITAL* **RECORD WHERE** *Name* = 'DOCTORS'
> *exit if status* − *check*
> **FIND** *WARD* **RECORD**
> **VIA** *HOSPITAL WARDS* **SET WHERE** *Ward code* = 6
> *exit if status* − *check*
> *set COUNT to* 0
> *loop until no more records*
>     **FIND NEXT RECORD OF** *WARD STAFF* **SET**
>     *exit loop if status* − *check*
>     *increment COUNT by* 1
> *end loop*

One data language statement is provided for currency indicator manipulation. The statement

$$\textbf{FIND CURRENT OF} \left\{ \begin{array}{c} record\ name\ \textbf{RECORD} \\ set\ name\ \textbf{SET} \\ \textbf{RUN}-\textbf{UNIT} \end{array} \right\}$$

makes most current the specified currency indicator. Some data language operations, such as **GET** and **DELETE**, apply only to the record that is most current and use this currency indicator implicitly. Thus, it may be necessary to make most current a previously established currency indicator.

As in a relational data language, a DBTG-network data language requires facilities to insert new records, update existing records, and delete records from the data base. Additionally, we need operations that connect and disconnect records from DBTG-sets (e.g., for manual and optional set membership options).

The statement

    **STORE** *record name* **RECORD**

inserts a new record of type *record name* into the data base. As discussed in Section 6.3, the new record is connected to some DBTG-set for all DBTG-set types in which its set membership is automatic. The DBMS uses the set selection specified for each DBTG-set type to select the correct DBTG-set into which to connect the record. The record becomes the current record of the *record name* record type, the current record of all DBTG-sets into which it is connected and the most current record.

The statement

**MODIFY** *record name* **RECORD**

updates the most current record, which must be of type *record name*. The record must have been previouly located by a **FIND** or **STORE** statement. Values for the data item of the record are taken from a buffer area that is set up and maintained by the host programming language. The record remains the current record of *record name* record type.

The statement

$$\textbf{DELETE } record\ name\ \textbf{RECORD} \begin{bmatrix} \textbf{ONLY} \\ \textbf{SELECTIVE} \\ \textbf{ALL} \end{bmatrix}$$

deletes a record from the data base. The IDMS **DELETE** provides several procedures for handling member records when an owner record is deleted. The first procedure allows deletion of an owner only if it has no member records connected to it (no option specified). In this case the user must first make certain that this condition is met. A second procedure deletes mandatory members and disconnects optional members (**ONLY** option). A third procedure deletes all member records but only if they are not also members in some other DBTG-set (**SELECTIVE** option). Finally, all member records are deleted regardless of their membership option or membership in other DBTG-sets (**ALL** option). In all cases where member records are deleted, the **DELETE** statement propagates to the member records as if the original **DELETE** statement had been specified for the member record. This propagation continues until a member record is encountered that is not also the owner record of a DBTG-set. All the currency indicators for which the deleted record was the current record are set to null. However, it is still possible to locate the next, prior, first, last, and owner records using these currency indicators.

To connect a record into a DBTG-set the statement

**INSERT** *record name* **RECORD INTO** *set name* **SET**

is used. Conversely, to disconnect a record from a DBTG-set the statement

**REMOVE** *record name* **RECORD FROM** *set name* **SET**

is used. An **INSERT** operation can be used only if set membership is manual or optional. A **REMOVE** operation can be used only if set membership is optional. The current record of *record name* record type is inserted or remove from *set name*. For an **INSERT** operation, the inserted record becomes the current record of the *set name* DBTG-set type and the most current record. For a **REMOVE** operation, the currency indicator for *set name* DBTG-set type becomes null. However, next and prior members in *set name* can still be located. In both cases, the user must first establish currency of the correct record of *record name* record type. In addition, for an **INSERT** operation the currency of the correct occurrence of *set name* DBTG-set type must also be established.

## 6.5 SPECIFICATION OPERATIONS

Specification operations in a network data model can be very similar to those in a relational data model. However, network specification operations are constrained to follow the links between the record types in a network schema where no such constraint need exist for relational specification operations. Just as relational specification operations define a subset of the schema and the data base, similarly network specification operations can specify a subgraph of the schema and of the data base.

As for network navigation operations, network specification operations must be able to select records independent of links between them as well as according to links. In addition, the operations should be able to specify hierarchies and paths in the schema so as to allow specification of general subgraphs. A network specification data language based on the operations available in NUL will be outlined [Deheneffe and Hennebert, 1976].

NUL is a nonprocedural, hierarchically structured, English-keyword specification data language. The operations allow one to specify a subgraph of the schema, called a *data context*, and then to manipulate this subgraph. A data context is specified by a set of labeled statements. Each labeled statement denotes a set of occurrences of records of one type. Records can be selected in one of two ways. First, they can be selected according to a Boolean expression of criteria on the attributes of a record type and on the existence of connected records meeting other criteria. Second, a record can be selected according to its relationship with a previously selected record via a link.

The NUL language is applicable to a general network data model in which there are no cardinality restrictions on the links. Obviously, however, it is also applicable to the DBTG-network data model. The only additional requirement for the NUL language is that every record type have a key. As we will see, this requirement simplifies somewhat the establishment and removal of connections between records.

A data context is specified by one or more statements of the form[1]

---

[1] We depart slightly from the original notation of NUL, but the essence of the language is the same.

*statement label* ←
    [**FOR** *statement label*
    [**BY** *link name*]]
    *record name*
    {[**WHERE** *qualification*]
    [[**AND**] [*link name*] *has op*
    [*quantifier*] *record name*]}

Any construct enclosed in [ ] is optional, whereas { } means that the enclosed construct can be repeated zero or more times. As NUL is an interactive language, the *statement label* to the left of the ←, as well as the ←, are generated automatically by the system. The result of such an assignment can be used in a subsequent statement. We illustrate the nature of the language by examples.

The setting of currency to records of one type with a qualification is illustrated by Query 1.

**Q1**. Find those doctors whose specialty is gynecology.

    *S*1←*DOCTOR*
      **WHERE** *Specialty* = 'GYNECOLOGY'

An existence test can be performed by use of the *has op* and *quantifier*.

**Q2**. Find all wards that have staff.

    *S*1←*WARD*
      **WHERE**
      **HAS** *STAFF*

This statement selects a *WARD* record only if it is connected to some *STAFF* record. The default quantifier is **SOME** if no quantifier is stated explicitly. Other quantifiers that may be used are **ALL**, **NO**, **AT LEAST** *n*, **AT MOST** *n*, and **EXACTLY** *n*, where *n* is some number. To allow better phrasing of a query, the keyword **HAS** can be substituted with any one of the following keywords: **HAVE**, **IS**, **ARE**, **IN**, **BY**, **OF**, or **WITH**.

Both the record type that is to be selected and the connected record type(s) may be further qualified as illustrated by Query 3.

**Q3**. Find all recovery wards that have orderlies as employees.

    *S*1←*WARD*
      **WHERE** *Name* = 'RECOVERY'
      **AND** *WARD STAFF* **HAS** *STAFF*
      **WHERE** *Duty* = 'ORDERLY'

If there is more than one link between two record types, the link to be used can be stated explicitly, as illustrated in Query 3. However, if there is only one link between the two record types, the link name can be omitted.

Query 4 illustrates that existence testing can be carried out to an arbitrary number of levels.

**Q4.** Find all hospitals that have two psychiatric wards in which a nurse earns less than $16,000.

```
S1←HOSPITAL
    WHERE
    HOSPITAL WARDS HAS EXACTLY 2 WARD
    WHERE Name='PSYCHIATRIC'
    AND HAS STAFF
    WHERE Duty='NURSE'
    AND Salary<'16000'
```

So far, existence testing has been in the owner-to-member direction. We can also test whether a record is connected to any or to a particular owner record.

**Q5.** Find all employees in the recovery ward of hospital 22.

```
S1←STAFF
    WHERE IN WARD
    WHERE Name='RECOVERY'
    AND IN HOSPITAL
    WHERE Hospital code='22'
```

The language constructs that we have introduced allow us to select records of only one type. However, we can use the result of such a selection to select other records related to these records. If such a selection is done in one data context, we can specify a subgraph of the schema and the data base. This subgraph will consist of a path or a tree of the schema. For example, we can specify a path subgraph consisting of *WARD* and *STAFF* records with the following query.

**Q6.** Find all psychiatric wards and any orderlies who work in these wards.

```
S1←WARD
    WHERE Name='PSYCHIATRIC'

S2←FOR S1
    BY WARD STAFF
    STAFF
    WHERE Duty='ORDERLY'
```

In *S*1, we select all psychiatric wards. In *S*2, for each psychiatric ward selected by *S*1, we follow the connections to *STAFF* records via the *WARD STAFF* link and select those *STAFF* records where the *Duty* data item has the value Orderly.

In general, within a data context we can refer to a *statement label* any number of times. Thus, we can specify a tree subgraph, as Query 7 illustrates.

**Q7.** Find all hospitals named Doctors and any psychiatrists and psychiatric wards with nurses on staff and any patients in these wards who have psychiatrists as doctors.

```
S1←HOSPITAL
    WHERE Name='DOCTORS'

S2←FOR S1
    BY HOSPITAL WARDS
    WARD
    WHERE Name='PSYCHIATRIC'
    AND HAS STAFF
    WHERE Duty='NURSE'

S3←FOR S2
    PATIENT
    WHERE
    HAS DOCTOR PATIENT
    WHERE
    IN DOCTOR
    WHERE Specialty='PSYCHIATRIC'

S4←FOR S1
    DOCTOR
    WHERE Specialty='PSYCHIATRY'
```

This query specifies a tree subgraph whose structure and contents follow the graph shown in Figure 6.5—1.

The statements identified by *statement labels* within a data context establish the currency of a set of records of a given type. Thereafter, these records can be manipulated by other data language statements.

The statement

**PRINT** *statement label* [.*data item name*] ...

is used to retrieve and display the records in a data context. One or more hierarchies of the data context can be retrieved in one **PRINT** statement. To retrieve and display the hospital names, ward records, and patient names for Query 7, we would use the statement

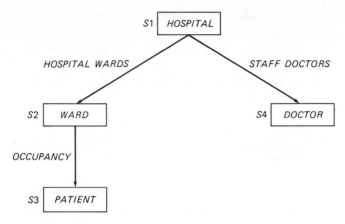

**Fig. 6.5—1** Subgraph specified by Query 7.

**PRINT** *S*1.*Name,* (*S*2, (*S*3.*Name*))

The parentheses indicate the structure (indentation) for the output. In our example it would look as follows

*S*1.*HOSPITAL*
    *Name*=DOCTORS

       *S*2.*WARD*
          *Ward code*=6
          *Name*=PSYCHIATRIC
          # *of beds*=118

             *S*3.*PATIENT*
                *Name*=FOURIE M.
                *Name*=LISTA M.

To update records in the data base, the appropriate records are first selected via a data context. The statement

    **UPDATE [ALL]** *statement label.data item name ...*

is then used to specify the update. The update is guided by NUL interactively. For every data item specified in the **UPDATE** statement, the current value is displayed and a new value can be entered. If the **ALL** option is used, all values for the specified data item(s) are changed to the new value.

The statement

    **INSERT** *record name*

will add a new record to the data base. It is not necessary to establish a data context first. The insertion of data item values is done interactively one data item at a time. If the *record name* record type is an automatic member in some DBTG-set types, it needs to be connected to the correct owners in each of these DBTG-set types. The correct owner is selected according to its key value, which is supplied by the user (i.e., set selection by key).

The statement

$$\textbf{DELETE} \left\{ \begin{array}{l} \textit{record name} \\ \textbf{ALL } \textit{statement label} \end{array} \right\}$$

deletes one record at a time according to its key value (*record name* option) or all records selected by a statement label (**ALL** *statement label* option). All fixed and mandatory members are also deleted. As for navigation operations, this deletion rule propagates down the path or hierarchy.

For links with manual or optional set membership the statement

**ATTACH** *member name* **TO** *owner name* **BY** *link name*

is used to establish a connection between an owner and member record. The owner and member records to connect are selected by their key values.

For links with optional set membership a connection can be broken with the statement

**DETACH** *member name* **FROM** *owner name* **BY** *link name*

Again the correct owner and member records are selected by their key value.

Finally, for links with mandatory or optional set membership, the owner of a member record can be changed with the statement

**TRANSFER** *member name* **TO** *owner name* **BY** *link name*

The new owner record and the correct member record to transfer are selected by their key value.

## EXERCISES

**6.1** Recursive links are not allowed in the DBTG-network data model. Why?

**6.2** The DBTG-network data model does not support many-to-many links directly. Why? Are they needed?

**6.3** Set membership constraints can be used to express existence constraints. Give examples to illustrate the procedure.

**6.4** Explain the semantics of each of the six types of set membership.

**6.5** Express each of the six set membership types in terms of the cardinality notation introduced in Chapter 3. Does this notation capture all the semantics of set membership? Explain.

**6.6** Propose a DBTG-network navigation language based on the explicit manipulation of currency indicators. Outline the syntax and semantics of each operation.

**6.7** Translate the features of the NUL data language into specific programs using the IDMS data language outlined in Section 6.4. Comment on the nature of the translation problem in this case.

**6.8** Discuss the possibility of implementing a DBTG-network navigation data language on set-oriented hardware (e.g., on a data base machine such as RAP [Ozkarahan et al., 1975]).

**6.9** Codd's relational data model was initially proposed as a model and later implemented, while the DBTG-network data model was initially defined through a system. Discuss the relative merits of each approach. Point out some features of the DBTG-network data model which are either obscure or difficult to understand. Point out some realistic considerations that relational data models abstract away although they have to be dealt with in an implementation of the data models.

*Chapter 7*

# HIERARCHICAL DATA MODELS

## 7.1 INTRODUCTION

A DBTG-network data model is a restricted case of a graph data model with tables at the nodes. The restriction arises mainly because many-to-many relationship types are not permitted between nodes. In this chapter we look at hierarchical data models which are an even more restricted case of a graph data model with tables at the nodes.

Hierarchical data models are embodied mainly in the form of IBM's Information Management System (IMS) [IBM, 1975; McGee, 1977] and MRI's System 2000 (S2K) [MRI, 1974]. IMS is an outgrowth of the Apollo moon-landing program. The hierarchical data model employed in IMS can no doubt be traced to the sequential access method (SAM) and indexed sequential access method (ISAM) used in its implementation [Martin, 1975]. S2K is a direct descendant of TDMS [Vorhaus and Mills, 1967] and RFMS [Everett et al., 1971] developed at System Development Corporation and the University of Texas at Austin, respectively. It is based on an inverted file implementation of hierarchical data structures.

## 7.2 STRUCTURES

The structure of a data base according to a DBTG-network data model is represented by a data structure diagram. The nodes in a data structure diagram usually correspond to entity types which are represented as tables of data. The arcs between the nodes correspond to functional relationship types between the tables. Both nodes and arcs are labeled. The main restriction on the relationship types between tables is the functional link restriction.

A hierarchical data model imposes a further restriction on the relationship types. The arcs in a data structure diagram representing a hierarchical data base must form an ordered tree. An *ordered tree* is a tree where the relative order of the subtrees is important [Knuth, 1968]. That is, the placement of the nodes in the tree (to the right or left of each other) is significant. In addition, because the data structure diagram must form a tree, the direction of the functional arcs is always toward the leaves of the tree and away from the root. Such a restricted data structure diagram is called a *hierarchical definition tree* or simply *definition tree* [Tsichritzis and Lochovsky, 1976, 1977]. Figure 7.2−1 represents one definition tree for the medical data base.

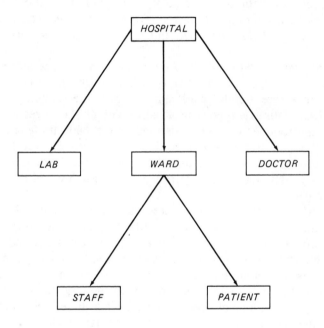

HOSPITAL(Hospital code, Name, Address, Phone#, # of beds)
LAB(Lab#, Name, Address, Phone#)
WARD(Ward code, Name, # of beds)
STAFF(Employee#, Name, Duty, Shift, Salary)
PATIENT(Registration#, Bed#, Name, Address, Birthdate, Sex, SSN)
DOCTOR(Doctor#, Name, Specialty)

**Fig. 7.2−1** One definition tree for the medical data base.

A definition tree represents the intension of a hierarchical data base just as a data structure diagram and a relational schema represent the intension of a DBTG-network and relational data base, respectively. A node in a definition tree corresponds to an entity type. It is called a *record type*, is labeled, and is composed of one or more *data items*. Unlike a

DBTG-network data model, a data item in a hierarchical data model represents only a simple domain.

An arc is a functional link called a *parent-child relationship* and is not labeled since, due to the tree structure, there can be at most one parent-child relationship between any two record types. The *parent record type* in the relationship type is the record type from which the arc emanates. The *child record type* is the record type which the arc enters. Considering a sequence of parent-child relationships, it is possible to identify *ancestor record types* and *descendant record types* of a record type in a natural way.

There is one specially designated node in a definition tree called the *root record type*. This node has no arcs entering it and is normally the topmost node in a definition tree (e.g., *HOSPITAL* in Figure 7.2−1). All other nodes in a definition tree are termed *dependent record types*. For example, *WARD, STAFF, DOCTOR,* and *LAB* are dependent record types in Figure 7.2−1.

A *hierarchical path* or *path* in a definition tree is a sequence of record types, starting at the root record type, in which the record types are alternately in a parent-child relationship. Thus, the sequence *HOSPITAL, WARD, STAFF* defines a hierarchical path. The *level* of a record type with respect to the root record type is defined as the path arc length from the root record type. If the root record type *HOSPITAL* is at level 0, the *WARD* record type is at level 1 and the *STAFF* record type is at level 2 in Figure 7.2−1. The length of a path is equal to the level of the last record type in the path.

The extension of a definition tree can be represented in a manner similar to the extension of a data structure diagram. Each record type has an extension as a table (with ordering and duplicates allowed) and each parent-child relationship has an extension as a set of connections between the tables, as shown in Figure 7.2−2. Each row of a table is called a *record* and corresponds to an occurrence of the generic record type.

This representation of a hierarchical data base does not convey, naturally, the hierarchical structure. An alternative view is to represent the extension of a definition tree as a collection, or *forest*, of disjoint trees. Each disjoint tree is called a *data base tree* and consists of one root record and all its dependent records [Tsichritzis and Lochovsky, 1976, 1977]. All data base trees are constructed according to the definition tree. Figure 7.2−3 presents this alternative view of a hierarchical data base for two data base trees in Figure 7.2−2.

In our discussion of a hierarchical data model we have assumed that the placement of the data in a data base tree determines the hierarchical structure. That is, in Figure 7.2−1 every node represents a record type and in Figure 7.2−3 every node represents a record. This representation is valid for the IMS hierarchical data model [IBM, 1975]. However, there is an alternative representation, used by S2K, that separates the data and

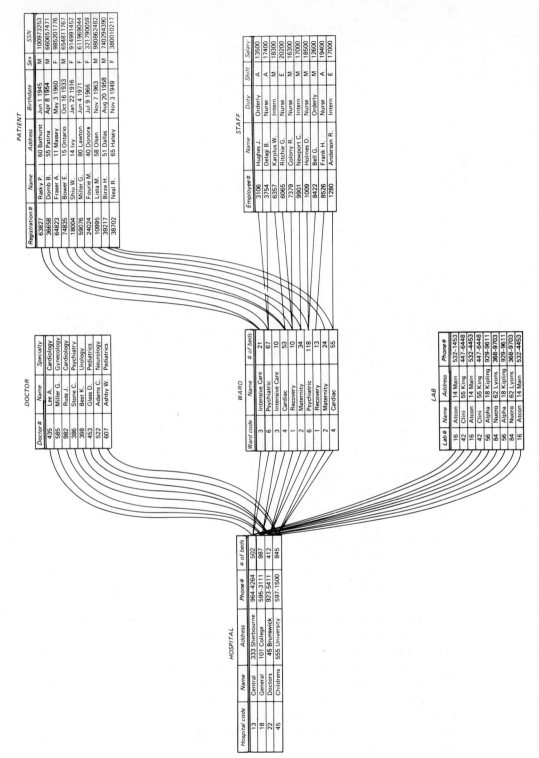

Fig. 7-2. Extension of definition tree for medical data base.

151

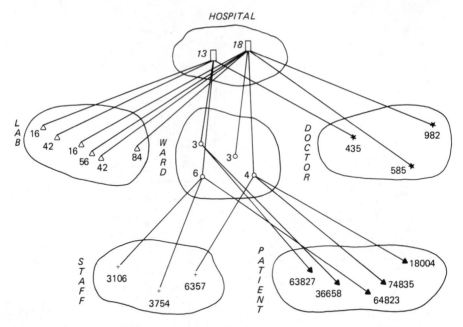

**Fig. 7.2—3** Partial extension of definition tree as data base trees.

the hierarchical structure [Bleier, 1967; MRI, 1974].

Figure 7.2—4 represents a definition tree and a hierarchical data base in the alternative notation. The structure nodes (marked ◉) serve only to maintain the hierarchical structure. Data nodes are associated only with structure nodes, never with other data nodes. This notation has advantages in instances where some data nodes may be missing or their value unknown. For example, consider the path *HOSPITAL*, *WARD*, *STAFF*. In the first notation, if an employee's ward is not known, it is not possible to associate the *STAFF* record with a *HOSPITAL* record except by using an empty *WARD* record. Such an association is not semantically "clean." In the second notation this association is possible without resort to any representation "tricks."

In terms of describing the structure of a hierarchical data base, both notations are equivalent. For clarity and uniformity, the first notation will be used throughout this chapter. The second notation does have advantages in terms of eliminating side effects of certain operations on a hierarchical data base. These advantages are discussed in Section 7.5 in the context of S2K specification operations.

As an example of the definition of a hierarchical data base, the medical data base of Figure 7.2—1 is defined in a DDL based on the S2K DDL. The S2K DDL closely resembles that of COBOL file definition. A schema consists of entries called *components*. A component consists of a component number, a name, and some description of the component.

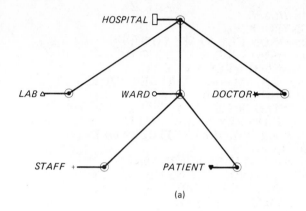

(a)

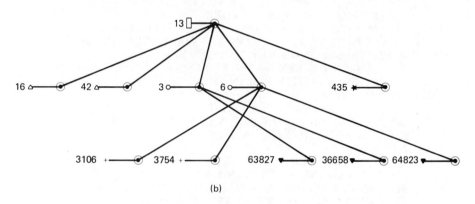

(b)

**Fig. 7.2−4** Separation of hierarchical structure and data.

For structure definition, a component may define either a *data element* or *repeating group*. Data element is the S2K term for data item while repeating group is the term for record type.

The definition of a data element consists of specifying a unique name for the data element within the definition tree, a data type, the repeating group of which it is a part, and a key option. The term key as used in S2K does not mean a key as defined in Chapter 3. Instead, it is used to define an index for the data element. The hierarchical structure in an S2K schema definition is displayed by indentation. The S2K schema definition for the medical data base of Figure 7.2−1 is shown in Figure 7.2−5. Nonunique data-item names are preceded by their corresponding record-type names.

**DATABASE NAME IS** *HOSPITAL*:
   **1\*** *Hospital code* **(INTEGER** 9(6)):
   **2\*** *HOSPITAL Name* **(NON-KEY NAME X**(15)):
   **3\*** *HOSPITAL Address* **(NON-KEY NAME X**(20)):
   **4\*** *HOSPITAL Phone#* **(NON-KEY NAME X**(7)):
   **5\*** *HOSPITAL # of beds* **(NON-KEY INTEGER** 9(4)):
   **6\*** *WARD* **(REPEATING GROUP)**:
      **7\*** *Ward code* **(INTEGER** 9(6) **IN** 6):
      **8\*** *WARD Name* **(NON-KEY NAME X**(15) **IN** 6):
      **9\*** *WARD # of beds* **(NON-KEY INTEGER** 9(4) **IN** 6):
      **10\*** *STAFF* **(RG IN** 6):
         **11\*** *Employee#* **(INTEGER** 9(6) **IN** 10):
         **12\*** *STAFF Name* **(NON-KEY NAME X**(20) **IN** 10):
         **13\*** *Duty* **(NAME X**(15) **IN** 10):
         **14\*** *Shift* **(NAME X**(10) **IN** 10):
         **15\*** *Salary* **(MONEY IN** 10):
      **16\*** *PATIENT* **(RG IN** 6):
         **17\*** *Registration#* **(INTEGER** 9(6) **IN** 16):
         **18\*** *Bed#* **(NON-KEY INTEGER** 9(4) **IN** 16):
         **19\*** *PATIENT Name* **(NON-KEY NAME X**(20) **IN** 16):
         **20\*** *PATIENT Address* **(NON-KEY NAME X**(20) **IN** 16):
         **21\*** *Birthdate* **(NON-KEY DATE IN** 16):
         **22\*** *Sex* **(NON-KEY NAME X**(1) **IN** 16):
         **23\*** *SSN* **(INTEGER** 9(6) **IN** 16):
   **24\*** *DOCTOR* **(RG)**:
      **25\*** *Doctor#* **(INTEGER** 9(6) **IN** 24):
      **26\*** *DOCTOR Name* **(NON-KEY NAME X**(20) **IN** 24):
      **27\*** *Specialty* **(NAME X**(20) **IN** 24):
   **28\*** *LAB* **(RG)**:
      **29\*** *Lab#* **(INTEGER** 9(6) **IN** 28):
      **30\*** *LAB Name* **(NON-KEY NAME X**(20) **IN** 28):
      **31\*** *LAB Address* **(NON-KEY NAME X**(20) **IN** 28):
      **32\*** *LAB Phone#* **(NON-KEY NAME X**(7) **IN** 28):

**Fig. 7.2—5** Hierarchical schema definition for medical data base.

## 7.3 CONSTRAINTS

The hierarchical data model incorporates two important inherent constraints. The first is that all relationship types must be functional[1]. The second is that the relationship types must be structured according to a tree. These constraints have several implications for structuring data.

The constraint that all relationship types be functional means that a record can have at most one parent of any record type. This is true in the IMS as well as the S2K hierarchical data models. However, in the S2K hierarchical data model the parent record may not exist, whereas in the IMS hierarchical data model it must exist for the child record to exist.

---
[1] One-to-one is, of course, allowed as a subcase of a functional relationship type.

The only exception to this rule is that a root record does not require a parent record in either IMS or S2K.

A parent record can have any number of children records connected to it. That is, a *HOSPITAL* record can have any number of *WARD* records connected to it (Figures 7.2–3 and 7.2–4). Conversely, a child record can have only one parent record. That is, each *WARD* record must be connected to one and only one *HOSPITAL* record (Figure 7.2–3) or, for S2K, to a structure node that is connected to a structure node for a *HOSPITAL* record (Figure 7.2–4).

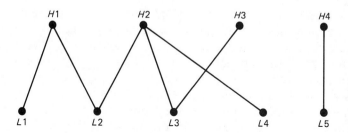

**Fig. 7.3–1** Many-to-many relationship type.

Because of the functional restriction on relationship types, it is not possible to represent many-to-many relationship types directly in a hierarchical data model. Two methods are available to get around this restriction. Consider the many-to-many relationship type between *HOSPITAL* and *LAB* in Figure 7.3–1. Figure 7.3–2 illustrates one method of representing this many-to-many relationship type. One of the record types, in this case *LAB*, is made a subordinate of the other record type (*HOSPITAL*). Duplication of *LAB* records is used to represent the many-to-many relationship type.

An alternative method of modeling many-to-many relationship types is illustrated in Figure 7.3–3. In this case, two definition trees are used.

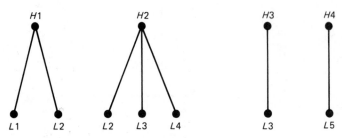

**Fig. 7.3—2** Using duplication to represent a many-to-many relationship type.

One has *HOSPITAL* as the parent record type and *LAB* as the child record type. The other has *LAB* as the parent record type and *HOSPITAL* as the child record type. Even though this representation implies more data duplication than the previous representation, it may be desirable for effective data access. That is, in Figure 7.3—2, queries that access *LAB* records via *HOSPITAL* records (e.g., "Find all labs used by hospital H") are fairly simple to answer. However, the symmetric query "Find all hospitals using lab L" is more complex. In Figure 7.3—3, both queries are of equal complexity when both definition trees are employed.

It should be noted that the definition trees shown in Figure 7.3—3 need not correspond to actual physical storage structures. Hierarchical DBMSs provide mechanisms whereby it is possible to define different logical views on one physical storage structure [IBM, 1975]. Thus, the duplication of data implied by Figure 7.3—3 may be only logical and need not correspond to physical duplication.

The second inherent hierarchical data model constraint is that the data be structured according to a tree. This restriction presents no problems if the data are naturally hierarchical. However, if the structure of the data is as for the medical data base (see the Appendix), difficulties arise. The problems arise because of many-to-many relationship types and because some record types (i.e., *PATIENT* and *TEST*) logically have more than one

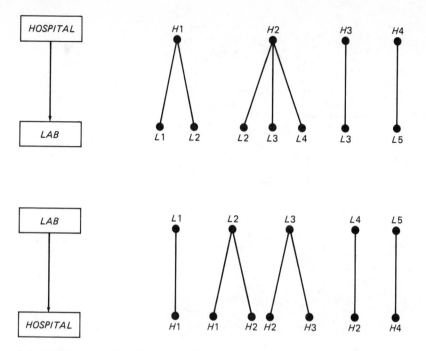

**Fig. 7.3—3** Using two functional relationship types to represent a many-to-many relationship type.

parent record type. In this case, it is necessary to define *spanning trees* [Harary, 1969] of the general graph structure that capture all of the "information" but abide by the tree restriction. Figure 7.3—4 depicts the spanning trees required for the medical data base.

The difficulty with this technique is that there are now several definition trees which are unconnected. Applications that require data from several trees simultaneously may find it very difficult to obtain these data. Hierarchical systems do not provide any, or provide hard to use, facilities for accessing several hierarchical data bases simultaneously.

The preceding inherent constraints have as their consequence the implicit constraint that every record has a unique set of ancestors in a data base. That is, in Figure 7.2—3 each *STAFF* record has at most one parent record *WARD*, which, in turn, has at most one parent record *HOSPITAL*. However, in general, a record may have several descendant records of each descendant record type. That is, a *HOSPITAL* record may have several *WARD*, *DOCTOR*, and *LAB* children records, which, in the case of *WARD* records, may have several *STAFF* and *PATIENT* children records.

Most hierarchical data models do not provide any explicit constraints. An indirect explicit constraint mechanism is provided in IMS via the definition of logical relationships [IBM, 1975]. By means of logical

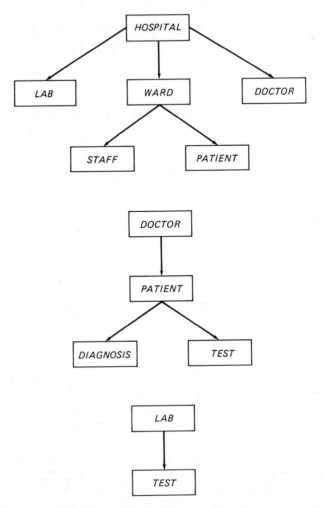

Fig. 7.3—4 Spanning trees for medical data base.

relationships it is possible to assure the consistency of certain data by constraining the data to be identical in two different definition trees.

As an example, the three spanning trees shown in Figure 7.3—4 need not exist as actual, physical hierarchical data bases. If they did, there would be a great deal of data duplication — for *PATIENT*, *DOCTOR*, *LAB*, and *TEST* record types — and data consistency would be difficult to maintain. Instead, in IMS, one can define nonredundant, interrelated physical data bases. One can then use logical relationships to define definition trees over the interconnected physical data bases. These "logical" data bases provide the view of the data as seen by the user.

Figure 7.3—5 depicts Figure 7.3—4, but with the logical relationships

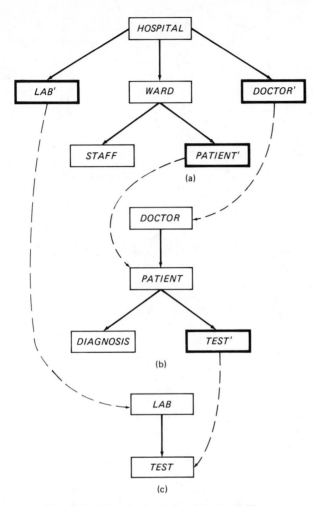

**Fig. 7.3—5** Logical relationships in IMS.

indicated. Three physical data bases are shown. The thin line rectangles indicate physical occurrences of the named record types in the data base extensions. The record types shown as bold rectangles are logical children of their respective parent record types. That is, they do not imply a physical existence of instances of the named child record type connected to the parent. Instead, they indicate that a record containing a pointer (actual or symbolic) exists to the occurrence of the child record elsewhere in the same or a different physical data base.

The consequence is, for example, that *DOCTOR* records are not stored twice — once as a child of a *HOSPITAL* record and once as a root record in physical data base Figure 7.3—5(b). Instead, the *DOCTOR* records

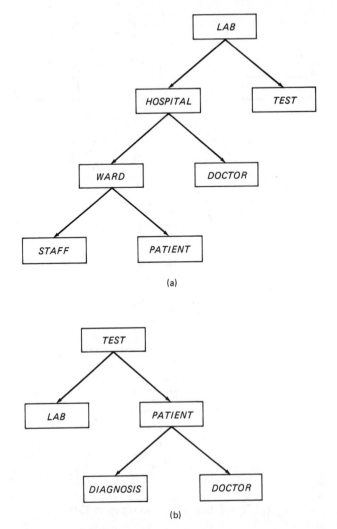

Fig. 7.3—6 Definition trees according to bidirectional logical relationships.

connected as children to a *HOSPITAL* record can merely contain a pointer to the actual physical *DOCTOR* records[1]. Thus, the *DOCTOR* records are not duplicated and modification of a *DOCTOR* record implies that only one *DOCTOR* record need be modified.

Obviously, rules need to be specified concerning the action taken when a logical record or a physical one that participates in a logical relationship is updated, inserted, or deleted [IBM, 1975]. For example, does deletion of a *DOCTOR* record as a child of a *HOSPITAL* record imply

---
[1]. They may also contain additional data.

deletion of the corresponding *DOCTOR* record as the root of a data base tree in physical data base Figure 7.3—5(b)? This problem is similar to the deletion problem in a DBTG-network data model.

As discussed so far, the logical relationships shown in Figure 7.3—5 are all unidirectional. That is, the parent-child relationship is in the direction specified by the dashed arc. However, the logical relationships can be specified as bidirectional. For example, suppose that the logical relationship involving the *LAB* record type is bidirectional. In this case, we can define the definition tree shown in Figure 7.3—6(a). The parent-child relationship between *HOSPITAL* and *LAB* is now reversed. Figure 7.3—6(b) shows the definition tree that can result if the logical relationship involving the *TEST* record type is bidirectional. In both cases, the definition tree does not correspond to a physical data base. Thus, no data duplication is involved. The IMS logical relationship facility provides a very flexible view definition mechanism. However, the specification of the access rules for the view, especially modification rules, can be quite complex.

Most of the constraints specified in the Appendix need to be implemented via host programming language procedures in both IMS and S2K. Constraint **C8** is enforced directly by the structure of a hierarchical data model. Constraints **C4** and **C7** can be enforced directly in IMS. To do this, the data item is declared as a hierarchical key (unique sequence field) of the record type. A *hierarchical key* is a data item whose values are unique only with respect to the hierarchical path in which it occurs and not with respect to the entire data base. For example, *Ward code* can be a hierarchical key. This means that for a given *HOSPITAL* parent record, every *WARD* child record must have a unique *Ward code* value. However, the same *Ward code* value can appear in a *WARD* record that is a child of another *HOSPITAL* record. Obviously, for root records a hierarchical key is exactly a key as defined in Chapter 3.

## 7.4 NAVIGATION OPERATIONS

Hierarchical navigation is similar to relational and DBTG-network navigation in that order of retrieval needs to be defined and currency needs to be maintained. In addition, we can make use of the tree structure to guide the navigation. Several tree traversal orders have been defined for binary trees [Knuth, 1968] and these can be extended to *n*-ary trees. If one of these orders is used, it is sufficient to maintain only one currency indicator for the extension of a definition tree. Disjoint data base trees can be handled by defining an ordering on them and then traversing them in turn according to the traversal order. It is always possible to determine the next record in a data base tree without explicit knowledge of the context of the retrieval. This is because the path to any record in a data base tree is unique due to the hierarchical structure.

Although a single currency indicator is adequate for hierarchical navigation, it may not provide sufficient flexibility for all queries. For example, one may want to retrieve children only within a certain parent or to retrieve records simultaneously along two distinct paths from a given parent. Thus, several currency indicators may be desirable. However, the complexity of processing increases as the number of currency indicators allowed increases.

Hierarchical navigation operations will be discussed in the context of the tree traversal language of IMS [IBM, 1975]. This language uses a preorder tree traversal of a data base tree. This order is defined as [Knuth, 1968]:

1. Visit the record if it has not already been visited.
2. Else, visit the leftmost child not previously visited.
3. Else, if no children, grandchildren, and so on, remain to be visited, go back to the parent record.

These steps are applied to each record of the data base tree whenever it is reached. It is assumed that the children of each parent are ordered according to the appearance of the child record type in the definition tree. That is, for the extension of the definition tree of Figure 7.2−1, under a given *HOSPITAL* record all *WARD* records come before all *DOCTOR* records, which in turn come before any *LAB* records.

The traversal begins at a root or any dependent record and visits all remaining records in the data base tree in a top-to-bottom, left-to-right order. As an example, the first data base tree in Figure 7.2−3 would be

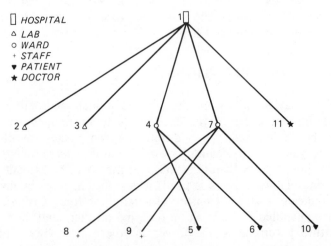

**Fig. 7.4−1** Preorder traversal of a data base tree.

traversed in the order indicated in Figure 7.4—1. If one imagines all the disjoint data base trees in a hierarchical data base as being connected to an imaginary head node, a single data base tree is formed. It is then possible to apply the preceding procedure to this single data base tree and to visit all records in a hierarchical data base.

In IMS, requests to access the data base are specified as procedure calls to Data Language/1 (DL/1) from application programs written in a host language. The calls to DL/1 require several parameters and prior definition of communication and I/O buffers. These aspects of DL/1 are not relevant to the nature of the tree navigation operations. Therefore, for pedagogical purposes, a simplified syntax for DL/1 statements will be presented. This syntax will convey the semantics of the statements and facilitate understanding while relieving the reader of coping with many of the intricacies of DL/1.

The data access statements of IMS combine the set currency action and retrieve action in one operation. They are designed to facilitate a preorder traversal of the data base trees. Such a traversal is essentially sequential in nature and retrieves one record at a time. To mark the user's current logical position ("current" record) in the data base, a currency indicator, called the *position pointer*, is maintained. The position pointer marks a program's progress through the data base according to a preorder traversal of the data base trees. For sequential processing it is used to mark the boundary between previous records (those that have been or could have been visited already) and next records (those that still can be visited).

The DL/1 statement

**GET UNIQUE** *record name* **WHERE** *qualification*

allows direct access of a record. Its main function is to set or reset the position pointer to a specific record of a specific type for subsequent sequential processing. It can also be used for nonsequential processing of the data base. In general, the *leftmost* record in the data base trees, which satisfies the qualification, is selected. This record is guaranteed to be unique only if the qualification involves an equality condition on the (hierarchical) key of the root record type. Query 1 illustrates the use of the **GET UNIQUE** statement. We assume that *Hospital code* is the hierarchical key of the *HOSPITAL* record type.

**Q1.** Find the hospital record with hospital code 22.

**GET UNIQUE** *HOSPITAL* **WHERE** *Hospital code* = 22

The **GET UNIQUE** statement can be used to select any record in the data base, not just a root record. The qualification need not necessarily qualify on a hierarchical key, as Query 2 demonstrates.

**Q2.** Find the names of all doctors whose specialty is gynecology.

> **GET UNIQUE** *DOCTOR* **WHERE** *Specialty* = 'GYNECOLOGY'

This statement is sufficient to establish a starting position for processing Query 2. However, as explained earlier, it only selects the leftmost record satisfying the qualification. In addition, repetition of the statement would result in selection of the same record. What is required now is a statement that can sequentially select all the other doctor records with specialty gynecology.

The statement

> **GET NEXT** [*record name* [**WHERE** *qualification*]]

is used for sequential processing. It processes in a forward direction (to the right) from the current position in the data base according to a preorder traversal. If no option is specified (i.e., the statement is unqualified), the next record in the data base, according to a preorder traversal, is retrieved. If only the *record name* option is specified, only next records of *record name* record type are considered for retrieval. Intervening records of other types are skipped. Using this option it is possible to retrieve sequentially all records of a certain type within the data base. Finally, if the *qualification* option is also specified, the records considered for retrieval are further restricted to those next records of *record name* record type that satisfy *qualification.* Processing begins at the "current" record and all records that come "before" the current record are automatically disqualified from consideration.

Using the **GET UNIQUE** and **GET NEXT** statements Query 2 is now expressed as

> **GET UNIQUE** *DOCTOR* **WHERE** *Specialty* = 'GYNECOLOGY'
> *exit if status* − *check*
> *output Name of DOCTOR*
> *loop until no record qualifies*
>      **GET NEXT** *DOCTOR* **WHERE** *Specialty* = 'GYNECOLOGY'
>      *exit loop if status* − *check*
>      *output Name of DOCTOR*
> *end loop*

This form of the **GET NEXT** statement processes sequentially *across* data base trees. Tree structure or preorder traversal is not considered when selecting a record.

To retrieve records in the preorder sequence, the unqualified form of the **GET NEXT** statement is used. For example, to retrieve all the records in the data base of Figure 7.2−2 in preorder, the following program can be used.

```
GET UNIQUE HOSPITAL WHERE Hospital code > 0
exit if status − check
output record
loop until end of data base
    GET NEXT
    exit loop if status − check
    output record
end loop
```

In this program, the **GET UNIQUE** statement establishes a start position for sequential processing. The **GET NEXT** statement within the loop sequentially retrieves each record in the data base in preorder. The preceding program can also be used to sequentially retrieve all records of one type. For example, to retrieve only all *HOSPITAL* records, we substitute the statement **GET NEXT** *HOSPITAL* for **GET NEXT** in the program above.

A **GET NEXT** statement selects records from the data base independent of their parentage (i.e., membership in a data base tree or subtree). Sometimes it is useful to restrict the selection to be from within one data base tree or part of a data base tree (subtree). The **GET NEXT WITHIN PARENT** statement performs this function. It is similar in effect to a **GET NEXT** statement. However, it is used to select only those records that are descendants of a previously specified record. That is, it operates only within a subtree of a data base tree. The "root" of the subtree, or parent record, is established by the last **GET UNIQUE** or **GET NEXT** statement. When all records within the subtree have been exhausted, an "end of parent" condition is raised to signal that all records have been processed. Query 3 requires use of this type of statement.

**Q3.** How many employees are there in ward 6 of Doctors hospital?

```
GET UNIQUE WARD
WHERE HOSPITAL Name = 'DOCTORS' AND Ward code = '6'
exit if status − check
set COUNT to 0
loop until no more children
    GET NEXT WITHIN PARENT STAFF
    exit loop if status − check
    increment COUNT by 1
end loop
```

This query also illustrates the use of a path qualification in the **GET UNIQUE** statement. That is, a *WARD* record is selected based on a path to it from a *HOSPITAL* record. Path qualification can be used with any IMS statement. We assume in the query that hospital names are unique, else an additional loop that would select all Doctors hospitals would be required. The **GET NEXT WITHIN PARENT** statement selects only those *STAFF* records that are children of the *WARD* record selected by the **GET UNIQUE** statement. One of the qualified forms of the **GET NEXT WITHIN PARENT** statement is used here. It may also be unqualified and qualified with a qualification as for the **GET NEXT** statement. However, its range of selection is limited to be within the subtree specified by the previously selected (via a **GET UNIQUE** or **GET NEXT** statement) parent record.

An insert operation in the IMS hierarchical data model requires that one must first select uniquely the parent-to-be of the new record. The record is then stored and connected to the parent record in one operation. Thus, the parent-child connection in the IMS hierarchical data model corresponds to a total functional relationship type[1] (*IMS PARENT−CHILD RELATIONSHIP*($PARENT(1,1):CHILD(0, \infty)$)). The new record becomes the current record in the data base following an insert operation.

Because of the nature of a parent-child relationship in the IMS hierarchical data model, the deletion of a record causes the deletion of all its descendant records from the data base. In this sense, the delete operation is a triggered delete since the record selected and all its descendants are deleted. The triggered delete can be implemented via a data base procedure associated with the delete operation. Following the delete operation the current record can be thought of as being the record immediately preceding, according to a preorder traversal, the deleted record.

The update operation requires that the record to be updated first be selected by a retrieval statement. The record can then be changed via host programming language statements and subsequently replaced in the data base. The updated record remains the current record in the data base following the update operation.

## 7.5 SPECIFICATION OPERATIONS

The restrictions on the connections between records in a hierarchical data model permits the selection of a set of records according to hierarchical paths. Consider, for example, the selection of a *WARD* record in Figure 7.2−3 according to some qualification. The selection of a record in a hierarchical data base determines a unique set of ancestors for the record according to the tree structure. In our example selection, a unique *HOSPITAL* record is determined since a *WARD* record must have only one

------

[1] This corresponds to fixed, automatic set membership in a DBTG-network data model.

parent of type *HOSPITAL*. The selection of ancestor records according to the tree structure is called *upward hierarchical normalization* [Lowenthal, 1971].

The selection of a record in a hierarchical data base also determines a possible set of descendants. In our example the selection of a *WARD* record determines a set of *STAFF* records and a set of *PATIENT* records (i.e., those connected to the *WARD* record). The selection of descendant records according to the tree structure is called *downward hierarchical normalization* [Lowenthal, 1971]. Downward hierarchical normalization is usually confined to a single hierarchical path because of quantification problems associated with the negation (NOT) Boolean operator [Hardgrave, 1972].

Specification operations for a hierarchical data model, based on upward and downward hierarchical normalization, select sets of records based on the tree structure. In addition, simple conditions specified on data items in the tree can further restrict the retrieval. For example, a record can be selected based on a simple condition in a descendant record, an ancestor record, itself, or any combination of these. Thereafter, other records may be selected based on an upward and/or downward hierarchical normalization.

Hierarchical specification operations will be discussed in the context of the Immediate Access feature of S2K [MRI, 1974]. Immediate Access provides an English-like, keyword hierarchical specification language. The S2K retrieval statement

**PRINT** *print clause* [**WHERE** *qualification*]

heavily utilizes the concept of hierarchical normalization. The *print clause* specifies printing options, formatting of output, retrieval of disjoint records in data base trees, and data items to be retrieved and output.

The **PRINT** statement without a **WHERE** clause retrieves records in preorder. For example, to list all the records in the data base trees of Figure 7.2−3, one uses the statement

**PRINT** *HOSPITAL*

The records are output in preorder. This statement performs the same function as the program in Section 7.4 using the unqualified **GET NEXT** statement of IMS. Other record types can be specified, but in all cases all descendants of the specified record type(s) are also output. If two record types lie in a hierarchical path, the higher-level record type naturally includes the lower-level record type as a descendant. Thus, in effect, the highest level record type in the *print clause* determines which descendant records appear in the output.

One can specify that only certain data items, of the record type to be output, be printed. For example,

**PRINT** *HOSPITAL*, *Ward code*, *STAFF Name*

outputs all the data base trees, but only *Ward code* and *Name*, of, the *WARD* and *STAFF* record types, respectively. The statement

**PRINT** *DOCTOR*, *LAB*

ouputs only the *DOCTOR* and *LAB* records since they have no descendants.

To print only the records of one record type, there is a **GROUP** option that can be specified in the *print clause*. The statement

**PRINT / GROUP /** *HOSPITAL*

outputs only *HOSPITAL* records.

The presence of a **WHERE** clause implies a **GROUP** option in the *print clause*. Thus, a **WHERE** clause restricts selection of records to those specified in the *print clause* that satisfy the qualification. The qualification consists of a Boolean combination of simple conditions or S2K conditions. S2K conditions allow the specification of such things as quantifiers on links. The definition trees of Figure 7.2−2 are used in the following example queries.

Query 1 shows simple selection.

**Q1**. Find the names of all doctors whose specialty is gynecology.

**PRINT** *DOCTOR Name*
**WHERE** *Specialty* **EQ** GYNECOLOGY

All doctor records satisfying the qualification are selected and their names output.

Upward and downward hierarchical normalization are specified by the **PRINT** statement using the **WHERE** clause. The *print clause* selects the records to be retrieved, and the **WHERE** clause selects the level from which hierarchical normalization is to begin.

Upward hierarchical normalization is usually used to process a query whenever the *print clause* specifies record types at a higher level than those specified in the **WHERE** clause. Upward hierarchical normalization is illustrated by Query 2.

**Q2**. List the names of those patients whose diagnosis is cardiac arrest.

> **PRINT** *PATIENT* Name
> **WHERE** *Diagnosis type* **EQ** CARDIAC ARREST

In this query, *DIAGNOSIS* records are first selected by the **WHERE** clause. This defines the level at which hierarchical normalization is to be initiated. Since the *print clause* specifies that *PATIENT* records are to be selected, an upward hierarchical normalization from *DIAGNOSIS* records is performed.

In general, for upward hierarchical normalization, if the **WHERE** clause specifies a qualification on several record types, the lowest level in the tree (largest level number) is the point from which hierarchical normalization is initiated. The remaining conditions in the **WHERE** clause are then used to "screen out" ancestor records that do not satisfy the qualification. Query 3 illustrates these points.

**Q3**. List the names of the hospitals where interns in the cardiac ward earn more than $17,000.

> **PRINT** *HOSPITAL* Name
> **WHERE** *WARD Name* **EQ** CARDIAC
> **AND** *Duty* **EQ** INTERN
> **AND** *Salary* **GT** 17000

The record type at the lowest level in this query is *STAFF*. Those parts of the **WHERE** clause that apply to the *STAFF* record type (i.e., *Duty* **EQ** INTERN and *Salary* **GT** 17000, are used to select *STAFF* records. An upward hierarchical normalization is then performed to select *WARD* records using that part of the **WHERE** clause that applies to *WARD* records (i.e., *WARD Name* **EQ** CARDIAC). Note that if the **WHERE** clause did not contain a qualification on *WARD* records, *HOSPITAL* records could be selected directly from the *STAFF* records. Finally, an upward hierarchical normalization is performed to select *HOSPITAL* records. By this process, only those *HOSPITAL* records that have descendants that satisfy the **WHERE** clause are selected.

Downward hierarchical normalization is usually used to process a query whenever the *print clause* specifies record types at a lower level than those specified in the **WHERE** clause. Downward hierarchical normalization is illustrated by Query 4.

**Q4**. List the name, registration number, and bed number of all patients in ward 2 of hospital 22.

**PRINT** *PATIENT Name, Registration#, Bed#*
**WHERE** *Hospital code* **EQ** 22
**AND** *Ward code* **EQ** 2

First *HOSPITAL* records satisfying the **WHERE** clause are selected. Then a downward normalization is performed to select all *WARD* records satisfying the **WHERE** clause. Finally, all *PATIENT* records connected to the *WARD* records are selected via downward normalization.

In general for downward hierarchical normalization, if the **WHERE** clause specifies a qualification on several record types, the highest level in the tree (smallest level number) is the point from which hierarchical normalization is initiated. The remaining conditions in the **WHERE** clause are then used to "screen out" descendant records that do not satisfy the qualification.

In query 4, several records may be selected at each level. If *Hospital code* and *Ward code* are hierarchical keys, only one record will be selected at these levels. It should be noted that there is an alternative method for processing this query. Namely, one can first select *WARD* records satisfying the **WHERE** clause, perform an upward normalization to select *HOSPITAL* records, and then perform a downward normalization to select *PATIENT* records. In either case a downward normalization would have to be performed to select *PATIENT* records. The exact method used would depend on considerations of efficiency of implementation.

An existence constraint can be tested by determining whether some decendants satisfying a qualification exist. This existence test is expressed in S2K by a **HAS** clause.

**Q5**. List those hospitals that use lab 84 and 56.

**PRINT** *HOSPITAL Name, Hospital code*
**WHERE** *HOSPITAL* **HAS** *Lab#* **EQ** 84
**AND** *HOSPITAL* **HAS** *Lab#* **EQ** 56

If a *HOSPITAL* record has *LAB* descendants that satisfy the **WHERE** clause, it is selected.

Note that this query cannot be expressed as

**PRINT** *HOSPITAL Name, Hospital code*
**WHERE** *Lab#* **EQ** 84
**AND** *Lab#* **EQ** 56

In order to perform upward hierarchical normalization, some *LAB* record would have to be selected. However, no *LAB* record can satisfy the **WHERE** clause such that its *Lab#* is simultaneously equal to 84 *and* 56. Thus, no *HOSPITAL* record can be selected. By use of the **HAS** clause the level at which hierarchical normalization is initiated is raised to the record type specified after the **HAS** keyword. Since a *HOSPITAL* record can have descendants where the *Lab#* is equal to 84 and 56, some *LAB* record can be selected.

The **HAS** clause is also used to express a selection of disjoint records (i.e., records not in the same path). In this case the record type following the keyword **HAS** is a common ancestor[1] of the disjoint records. This allows hierarchical normalization to be performed via the common ancestor record type. For example, *WARD* records can be selected based on the selection of *LAB* records via the *HOSPITAL* records.

**Q6**. List the wards of those hospitals that use lab 84.

> **PRINT** *Ward code*, *WARD Name*
> **WHERE** *HOSPITAL* **HAS** *Lab#* **EQ** 84

It should be clear how upward hierarchical normalization (from *LAB* records to *HOSPITAL* records) and downward hierarchical normalization (from *HOSPITAL* records to *WARD* records) are used to answer this query.

Although S2K has many other nice query features, the operations outlined above form the basis of the specification language. They use tree operations to select sets of records. Movement up, down, and across trees can be specified concisely in a single statement.

Insertion, update, and deletion of records require appropriate selection of the parent-to-be, record-to-be-changed, or record-to-be-deleted, respectively. An insert operation can insert either one new record or a subtree of records under one or several parent records. The parent(s)-to-be of the record or subtree is selected by a **WHERE** clause. An update operation can change values in one or several records. Again, the records in which values are to be changed are selected by a **WHERE** clause.

Because S2K separates the structure of a data base tree from the data, a delete operation does not necessarily trigger the deletion of all descendants connected to the deleted record(s). The data part can merely be deleted (updated to *null*), leaving the structure part intact. Subsequently, null data (values or records) can be assigned new values via an update operation. Alternatively, both the data part and the structure part can be deleted, which results in a triggered delete operation.

## EXERCISES

**7.1** Why is the tree order of record types in a definition tree important?

---

[1] Note that all record types have at least one common ancestor — the root record type.

**7.2** What explicit constraint specification facilities are required for a hierarchical data model? Give examples to illustrate your arguments.

**7.3** Consider a unidirectional logical relationship in IMS as defined in Section 7.3. Specify appropriate insert, delete, and update rules for this type of relationship. Are more than one set of rules appropriate? Explain.

**7.4** Define a tree navigation language that does not use a preorder tree traversal.

**7.5** Discuss the implication of a NOT Boolean operator on tree operations [Hardgrave, 1972].

**7.6** In terms of DBTG-set membership, what type of membership is an S2K parent-child relationship?

**7.7** Translate each of the statements of the Immediate Access feature of S2K into a corresponding program using IMS DL/1 statements.

**7.8** Both DBTG-network and hierarchical data models were initially proposed as DBMSs and not data models. The data models as described in this part of the book are the result of an abstraction of the DBMSs. Outline the data model inherent in other commercial DBMSs (e.g., ADABAS [Software AG, 1971]).

# Part 3

# DATA MODELS II

At one time, there was a "great debate" concerning the relative merits of relational and network data models [Rustin, 1974]. However, just as it was eventually recognized in programming languages that there is no one "best" programming language, so it is also now generally conceded that there is no one "best" data model. Different data models may be appropriate for different users, different tasks, and so on. According to some surveys [Kerschberg et al., 1976; Senko, 1977], over thirty different data models have been defined and more are constantly being proposed. In this part we examine four additional types of data models. These data models can be characterized as being "higher-level" data models than those discussed in Part 2, in that they provide very flexible structuring capabilities and usually incorporate explicit constraint specification capabilities. In addition, the four types of data models are representative of the different approaches to data modeling found in the literature.

# Chapter 8

# ENTITY-RELATIONSHIP
# DATA MODELS

## 8.1 INTRODUCTION

Entity-relationship data models are a type of data model based on tables and graphs [Chen, 1976; Pirotte, 1977]. They are an outgrowth of the practice of designing data bases using available commercial DBMSs [Olle, 1979]. As such, they have a great deal in common with network and hierarchical data models. However, because they are intended primarily for the data base design process, they are generalizations of network and hierarchical data models. The generalization is usually in terms of allowing the representation of explicit constraints and many-to-many relationship types directly in the data model.

In this chapter we discuss perhaps the best known data model of this type, Chen's entity-relationship (ER) data model [Chen, 1976]. The ER data model was conceived to facilitate data base design by allowing the specification of an *enterprise schema* [Chen, 1977]. An enterprise schema represents the entire enterprise's view of data and is independent of storage or efficiency considerations. The enterprise schema is mapped into an appropriate data base schema which is realized by some DBMS. The stability of the enterprise schema allows it, hopefully, to survive through changes in user views of the data and even changes in the DBMS.

The enterprise schema of the ER data model and the ANSI/X3/SPARC conceptual schema [Tsichritzis and Klug, 1978] are very similar. Their main difference is that the conceptual schema serves as an interface for the mapping between the external schema and the internal schema. As such, it is always directly accessible by the DBMS. The ER data model enterprise schema is basically a documentation of the logical properties of a data base. This description may or may not be directly accessible by the DBMS [Benneworth et al., 1981].

## 8.2 STRUCTURES

The ER data model uses the concepts of entity type and relationship type, as defined in Part 1, as its basic structures. In the ER data model, an entity type is called an *entity set* and represents the generic structure of an entity in an enterprise's realm of interest. A relationship type is called a *relationship set.* It' represents the generic structure of the relationships among entity sets.

The structure of a data base organized according to the ER data model can be depicted by a diagrammatic technique called an entity-relationship diagram (ERD) [Chen, 1976]. Figure 8.2−1 shows an ERD for the medical data base described in the Appendix. An ERD conveys the intension of a data base according to the ER data model.

An entity set is represented by a rectangular, labeled box in an ERD. For example, in Figure 8.2−1, *HOSPITAL*, *WARD*, *STAFF*, and so on, are entity sets. Entity sets correspond to different, generic classifications of entities. The membership of an entity set is determined by a predicate. That is, the properties of a particular instance of an entity can be tested to determine whether or not the entity belongs to an entity set. Membership of entities in entity sets need not be mutually disjoint. That is, a particular entity may belong to more than one entity set. For example, a doctor may also be a patient.

A relationship set is represented by a diamond, labeled box in an ERD. In Figure 8.2−1, *HOSPITAL WARDS*, *WARD STAFF*, *OCCUPANCY*, and so on, are relationship sets. The entity sets that participate in a relationship set are indicated by arcs which connect the entity sets to a relationship set. Thus, in Figure 8.2−1, the *WARD* and *PATIENT* entity sets participate in the *OCCUPANCY* relationship set. In network and hierarchical data models, only binary, functional links are allowed. In the ER data model, links can represent *n*-ary relationships among the entity sets and be one to one, functional, or many to many. Also, recursive links are allowed.

The mapping property of a relationship set is given explicitly in an ERD. However, only the maximum cardinality permitted for an entity set in a relationship set is indicated by a label on the connecting arc. In Figure 8.2−1 the 1 label on the arc between *WARD* and *OCCUPANCY* indicates that at most one *WARD* entity may participate in a given *OCCUPANCY* relationship. A letter label indicates that there is no maximum limit on the cardinality (i.e., maximum is $\infty$).

A relationship set in the ER data model can be defined as a

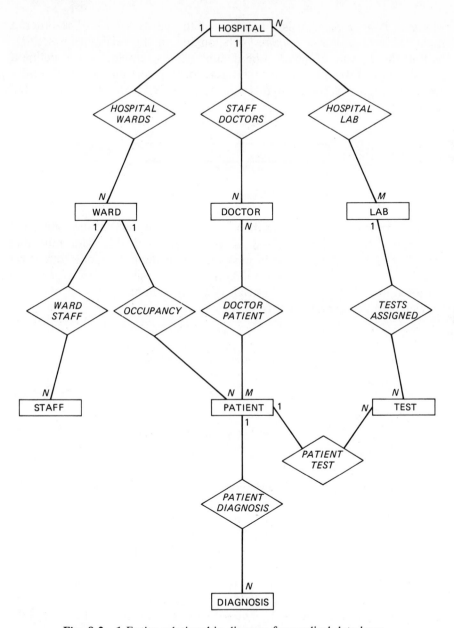

**Fig. 8.2—1** Entity-relationship diagram for medical data base.

mathematical relation among $n$ entity sets. Thus, if $RT$ is a relationship set, it can be defined as

$$RT = \{[e_1, e_2, ..., e_n] | e_1 \in E_1, e_2 \in E_2, ..., e_n \in E_n\}$$

where $e_i$ is an *entity* that is a member of the entity set $E_i$. The ordered tuple $[e_1, e_2, ..., e_n]$ is a *relationship* belonging to the relationship set $RT$. Not all the $E_i$'s in $RT$ need to be distinct. For example, we can define a relationship set *MANAGES* (recursive relationship set) on the *STAFF* entity set as in Figure 8.2−2. In this case, all the $E_i$'s would be the *STAFF* entity set.

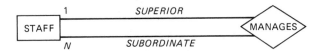

Fig. 8.2−2 Recursive relationship set.

It is possible to have more than one relationship set between the same two entity sets. Figure 8.2−3 is an example of this data modeling capability. The diagram indicates that a patient has one attending physician, but may have several consulting physicians. Conversely, a doctor can be the primary physician of many patients. As well, a doctor may consult on several patients.

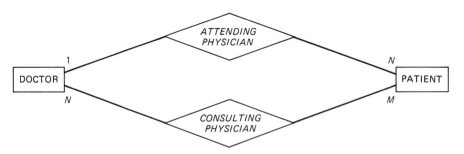

Fig. 8.2−3 Two relationship sets between the same entity sets.

A relationship set may be *n*-ary (i.e., among *n* entity sets). Figure 8.2−4 shows the representation of a ternary relationship set in the ER data model. The diagram represents a relationship among *DOCTOR*, *PATIENT*, and *TEST* entity sets. The relationship indicates that a doctor can prescribe several tests for several patients, a test can be prescribed by several doctors for several patients, and a patient can have several tests prescribed by several doctors. The semantics of ternary and higher-order relationship sets can become quite complex to comprehend.

An entity set in a relationship set may have a *role* (i.e., the function that it plays in the relationship). For example, *SUPERIOR* and *SUBORDINATE* are roles played by the (*STAFF*) manager and the (*STAFF*) person in the relationship set *MANAGES* (Figure 8.2−2). These roles can be explicitly defined in the ERD by labeling the arcs as in Figure 8.2−2.

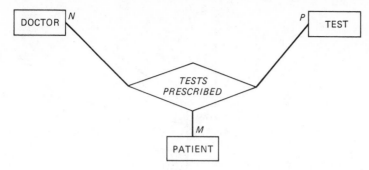

**Fig. 8.2—4** Ternary relationship set.

Since a relationship set is a mathematical relation, ordinarily the ordering of the entities in the relationship is important. However, if roles are used, the relationship can be stated as follows:

$$(r_1/e_1, r_2/e_2, ..., r_n/e_n)$$

where $r_i$ is the role of $e_i$ in the relationship. In this case, the ordering of the entities is not important.

In the ER data model, a domain is called a *value set*. A value set may be associated with either an entity set or a relationship set. A *value* is a particular instance of some value set. Membership of a value in a value set can be specified by a predicate in a manner analogous to entity membership in an entity set. Examples of value sets are INTEGER, PHONE#, and DATE. Corresponding values are '3', '788-7654', and 'May 1, 1980'. Membership of values in value sets need not be disjoint. For example, '3' may be a member of the value set DAY OF MONTH as well as the value set NUMBER OF YEARS. Diagrammatically, a value set is represented as a circle in an ERD (Figure 8.2—5).

An *attribute* is a mapping between an entity set or relationship set and a value set. It associates an entity set or relationship set with a value set and provides an interpretation of a value set in the context of an entity set or relationship set. For example, in Figure 8.2—5, the attribute *Birthdate* gives the interpretation (semantics) of the value set DATE in the context of the *PATIENT* entity set. Attributes may have the same name as their associated value set. The attribute mapping is represented in an ERD by a directed arc from the entity set or relationship set to the value set(s).

Formally, an attribute is defined as the mapping

$$f: E_i \text{ or } RT_i \rightarrow V_i \text{ or } V_{i_1} \times V_{i_2} \times ... \times V_{i_n} \quad 1 \leqslant i \leqslant n$$

where the $V_i$'s are value sets, $E_i$ is an entity set, and $RT_i$ is a relationship set. The mapping can be to a single value set or to the Cartesian product

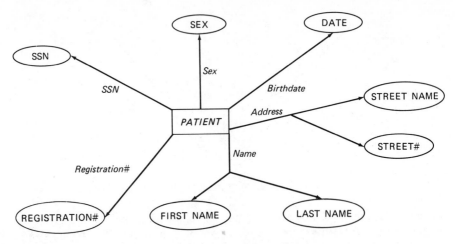

**Fig. 8.2—5** Attributes and value sets.

of several value sets. An example of this latter type of mapping is that of *Name* in Figure 8.2—5. *Name* maps into two value sets FIRST NAME and LAST NAME.

Some attributes are multivalued. For example, the *Phone#* of a lab could have more than one value. In this case, the arc is labeled 1:*N* as in Figure 8.2—6. Multivalued attributes correspond to the composite attribute concept. Different attributes may also map into the same value set. For example, *Birthdate* and *Date ordered* map into the same value set DATE.

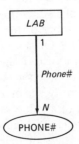

**Fig. 8.2—6** Multivalued attribute.

An attribute can be associated with a relationship set as well as an entity set in the ER data model. For example, it is possible to associate the attribute *Bed#* directly with the relationship set *OCCUPANCY* in our example data base (Figure 8.2—7). Such a direct association was not possible in hierarchical or network data models and required an additional "relationship" relation in relational data models.

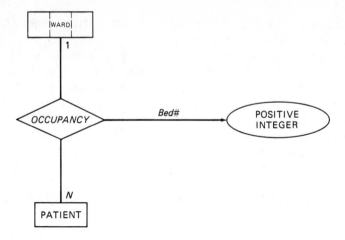

Fig. 8.2—7 Attribute of relationship set.

## 8.3 CONSTRAINTS

Most constraints in the ER data model are explicit. A possible inherent constraint is the requirement that entity set and value set membership be specifiable via a predicate. However, even in this case the predicate can be explicitly given as a procedure for determining membership eligibility.

Several explicit constraints can be specified for attributes. The first of these is the value set (domain) of an attribute. For example, *Bed#* and *# of beds* could both have value set POSITIVE INTEGER. Thus, values like 1.5 and -6 would not be allowed for *Bed#* and *# of beds*. These value sets may be further restricted by specifying a range for the permitted values. For example, we can specify the range for *Bed#* as from 1 to 100 and for *# of beds* as from 1 to 100 for the *WARD* entity set and from 1 to 1000 for the *HOSPITAL* entity set. Finally, the ER data model can express constraints on existing values in the data base. These constraints can be between sets of values or between particular values. An example of the former occurs if we have a separate entity set for those doctors that are also patients, say *ILL DOCTORS*. In this case, we want the entities of *ILL DOCTORS* to be a subset of those of the entity set *DOCTOR*. This can be expressed as

$$\{Name\,(e)\,|e\in ILL\ DOCTORS\} \subseteq \{Name\,(e)\,|e\in DOCTOR\}$$

The latter type of constraint occurs in example constraint **C2** for the medical data base, where the sum of the beds in all wards must equal the total number of beds in the hospital. This can be expressed as

$$\#\ of\ beds\,(e_1) = \sum \#\ of\ beds\,(e_2)$$

where $e_1 \in HOSPITAL$, $e_2 \in WARD$, and $[e_1, e_2] \in HOSPITAL\ WARDS$.

To uniquely identify an entity within an entity set, an *entity key* (i.e., a key) can be specified for the entity set. An entity key is a group of attributes (one or more) such that the mapping from the entities to the group of values is one-to-one. The entity key can be formed from existing attributes of the entity set or an artificial attribute may be added to the entity set to serve this purpose (i.e., an external key). However, every entity set need not have an entity key.

Relationship types also have keys. In this case the key, called a *relationship key*, is composed of the entity keys of the entity sets involved in the relationship set. For example, in Figure 8.3−1, the relationship key of the *HOSPITAL WARDS* relationship set would be the entity keys of the *HOSPITAL* entity set (*Hospital code*) and the *WARD* entity set (*Ward code*).

**Fig. 8.3−1** Existence constraint.

The ER data model can explicitly represent an existence constraint (called an *existence dependency* in the ER data model). This constraint specifies that, for example, the existence of a *WARD* entity depends on the existence of an associated *HOSPITAL* entity. Thus, if a *HOSPITAL* entity is deleted, its associated *WARD* entities are also deleted. An existence constraint is represented in an ERD by a double-rectangle, labeled box, the label E in the associated relationship set box, and an arrow pointing at the dependent entity (Figure 8.3−1). The dependent entity set (e.g., *WARD*) is termed a *weak entity set*, and the associated relationship set (e.g., *HOSPITAL WARDS*) is called a *weak relationship set*. Single-rectangle box entity sets are called *regular entity sets*. Relationship types not involving weak entity sets are called *regular relationship sets*. A weak relationship set can be one-to-one, functional, or many-to-many. In the latter case, the deletion of a regular entity does not necessarily imply the deletion of the associated weak entities if more than one regular entity is associated with the weak entities.

Another kind of constraint arises when an entity cannot be identified by the value of its own attributes, but has to be identified by its relationship(s) with other entities. Such a constraint is called an *ID dependency* in the ER data model. For example, constraint **C8** for the medical data base can be represented as an ID dependency since the *DIAGNOSIS* entity set could possibly have entities which are indistinguishable. However, they can be uniquely identified by their relationship with a *PATIENT* entity. *DIAGNOSIS* is said to have an ID dependency with *PATIENT*. An ID dependency is represented in an ERD in a manner similar to an existence constraint except that the label ID is placed in the associated relationship set box (Figure 8.3−2).

**Fig. 8.3−2** ID dependency.

An ID dependency is automatically an existence constraint, but an existence constraint is not necessarily an ID dependency. For example, suppose that there is an existence constraint between *WARD* and *STAFF* entity sets. This would mean that all *STAFF* entities have to be related to some *WARD* entity. However, this is not an ID dependency since *STAFF* entities can still be uniquely identified (by *Employee#*) independent of their relationship to *WARD* entities. In Figure 8.3−3 the ERD for the medical data base showing various constraints is presented.

The extension of an ERD can be represented as a series of tables [Chen, 1976]. The extension of an entity set can be represented as a table called an *entity relation*. In general, the table does not represent a data base relation but a record type because of the possibility of weak entity sets and no requirement for an entity key. However, if the entity set has

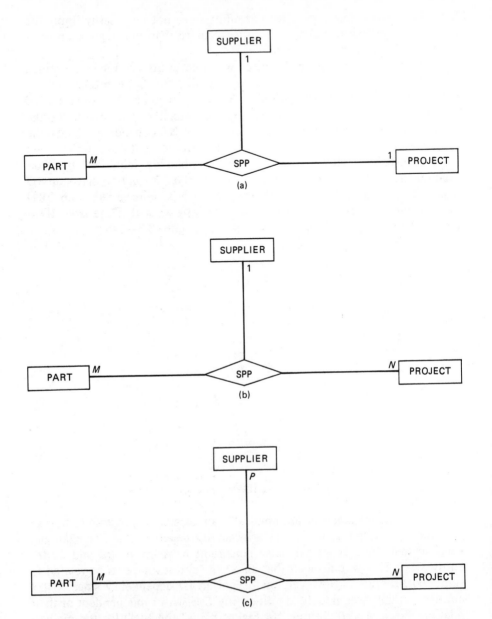

**Fig. 8.3—3** Entity-relationship diagram for medical data base.

an entity key, the table can be viewed as a data base relation. Each row of the table corresponds to an occurrence of the generic entity set and is called an *entity tuple*. Each column corresponds to the values of the underlying value set of the attribute.

The extension of a regular entity set corresponds naturally to the definition of the entity set. That is, there is one column for each attribute associated with the entity set. The extension of a weak entity set, called a *weak entity relation*, consists of the attributes of the weak entity set plus the entity key of the regular entity set(s) with which it is associated. Such a representation corresponds to key propagation as discussed in Chapter 3. For example, the extension of the *DIAGNOSIS* entity set would consist of the attributes of the *DIAGNOSIS* entity set plus the *Registration#* attribute (entity key) of the *PATIENT* entity set.

The extension of a regular relationship set can be represented as a table called a *relationship relation*. In this case the attributes of the relationship relation consist of the entity keys of the entity sets associated with the relationship set plus the attributes, if any, of the relationship set. Each row of the table corresponds to an occurrence of the generic relationship set and is called a *relationship tuple*. The columns correspond to the associated entity keys plus the attributes of the relationship set. The role names for the entity sets provide the semantic meaning of the corresponding entity keys. A weak relationship set can also be represented as a table called a *weak relationship relation*. In this case, since the weak entity set(s) do not have entity keys, they need to be identified by their relationship with other entity sets.

## 8.4 OPERATIONS

At the time that the ER data model was defined, no data language was specified specifically for the data model. It was merely indicated that information requests could be expressed using set notions and set operations [Chen, 1976]. Subsequently, a specification data language was defined for the data model called CABLE (ChAin-Based LanguagE) [Shoshani, 1978]. The language specification concentrates on output and selection and is based on the concepts of chains, or paths, through the entities and relationships of the data base. The language makes use of the fact that usually not all elements of a chain need to be specified, but can be inferred from the schema. In this way, the complexity of a retrieval specification is greatly reduced.

A chain or path in the data base is composed of elements called *beads*. Each bead is an elementary selection criterion on either an entity set or a relationship set. The syntax of a bead is

$$\left\{ \begin{array}{l} \textit{entity set name} \\ \textit{relationship set name} \end{array} \right\} .\textit{qualification}$$

Since relationship sets may have attributes, they can be qualified in a retrieval.  Both the *qualification* and the *entity set name* or *relationship set name* can be optional in a bead.  If the attribute names are unique in a schema, the *entity set name* or *relationship set name* can be omitted.  If the bead is not qualified, the *entity set name* or *relationship set name* serves merely to specify the path in the data base.  Beads in a path can be omitted if no ambiguity arises.  An example of a qualified bead is given in Query 1.

**Q1.**  List the names of all doctors whose specialty is gynecology.

>   **SELECT** *DOCTOR. Specialty*='GYNECOLOGY'

Since *Specialty* is unique within the data base, the *DOCTOR.* qualifier could have been omitted.

Another example of a qualified bead is given in Query 2.

**Q2.**  List the names and salaries of all interns working the evening shift.

>   **OUTPUT** *STAFF. Name, Salary*
>   **SELECT** *STAFF. Duty*='INTERN' **AND** *Shift*='E'

A path in the data base that is composed of more than one bead is given in Query 3.  It is implicitly assumed that if two entity sets are related directly (i.e., via one relationship set as from *HOSPITAL* to *WARD*), that path is taken.  Otherwise, the path must be given explicitly.  The beads that are specified are separated by '/'.

**Q3.**  List the names of the patients in hospital 22.

>   **OUTPUT** *PATIENT. Name*
>   **SELECT** *HOSPITAL. Hospital code*='22'/
>          *WARD*

Since there are several paths from the *HOSPITAL* entity set to the *PATIENT* entity set, the path to be used must be specified explicitly (*WARD*).  Note that *PATIENT* does not need to be specified, since there is a direct path from *WARD* to *PATIENT*.

Query 4 shows that the path between two entities need not be specified in CABLE if it is unique.

**Q4.**  List the names of those patients whose diagnosis is cardiac arrest.

>   **OUTPUT** *PATIENT. Name*
>   **SELECT** *Diagnosis type*='CARDIAC ARREST'

The path to be used in Query 4 can be inferred by the system. A fairly complex retrieval showing several beads in a query is given in Query 5.

**Q5.** List the name and specialty of those doctors that are treating patients who have tests being performed by lab 86 and who are in hospital 22.

> **OUTPUT** *DOCTOR. Name, Specialty*
> **SELECT** *HOSPITAL. Hospital code* = '22' /
>     *LAB. Lab#* = '86' /
>     *PATIENT*

Note that because of the nature of the schema for the medical data base, there is more than one way to answer this query. Also, for each strategy more than one path is possible. In the preceding example, just enough context was given to specify the path uniquely.

Entity sets and relationship sets can be traversed more than once using chains. Query 6 demonstrates this capability.

**Q6.** List the names of those doctors that are consulting on the same patients as doctor 607.

> **OUTPUT** *DOCTOR. Name*
> **SELECT** *DOCTOR/ PATIENT/ DOCTOR. Doctor#* = '607'

It is possible to test two chains to determine those entities that have some property in common or lack a common property. Query 7 illustrates this capability.

**Q7.** List those patients who use their hospital's labs.

> **OUTPUT** *PATIENT. Name*
> **SELECT** *LAB. Name/ TEST/ PATIENT* =
>     *LAB. Name/ HOSPITAL/ WARD/ PATIENT*

Besides being able to associate entities implicitly via relationships between them, CABLE can also associate entities explicitly (i.e., via a joinlike capability). This capability is necessary to associate two entities by value when they are not related explicitly. It can also be used between entities that are already related. The keyword **LINK** is used to signal an explicit association as shown by Query 8.

**Q8.** List the names of those people that are hospital staff and also patients.

**OUTPUT** *STAFF. Name*
**SELECT LINK** *STAFF. Name* = *PATIENT. Name*

Commands for inserting, deleting, and updating entities and relationships are not discussed for CABLE. The form of these commands can be similar to those discussed for the DBTG-network specification operations or those available in a general network language such as LSL [Tsichritzis, 1976] or NUL [Deheneffe and Hennebert, 1976].

## 8.5 CONCLUDING REMARKS

Entity-relationship data models are an outgrowth of the process of designing data bases. They are intended to satisfy two requirements of the data base design process. First, they should be general enough and semantically rich enough to express the structures and constraints of the real-world situation. Second, they should not be so far removed from commercial DBMSs that their schemas are unimplementable.

Entity-relationship data models, in particular the ER data model or some variant of it, are gaining acceptance as appropriate data models for systems analysis and design [Chen, 1980]. They appear to be adequate for expressing systems analysis and design requirements vis-à-vis data base design. At the same time, they can be used by the analyst to communicate with the users during the analysis and design process.

## EXERCISES

**8.1** Suppose that we drop the functional restriction from data structure diagram links and the restriction of not allowing recursive links from a record type to itself. How would these extended data structure diagrams differ from the ERDs of the ER data model?

**8.2** How would you represent an *ISA* relationship type in the ER data model?

**8.3** Outline a predicate calculus constraint facility suitable for the ER data model.

**8.4** Express constraints **C1**, **C3**, **C4**, **C5**, and **C6** for the medical data base in terms of the constraint facility outlined in Exercise 8.4.

**8.5** Outline a navigational language for the ER data model. It should be record-at-a-time oriented and suitable for use with COBOL as a host language.

**8.6** Consider the ER data model and the RM/T data model. Outline how the two data models are similar and/or different.

**8.7** Consider the ternary relationship sets among *SUPPLIER*, *PART*, and *PROJECT* shown below. For each ERD, explain the semantics of the relationship set in terms of extensions of the ERD. State any assumptions required for the interpretation of the relationship set.

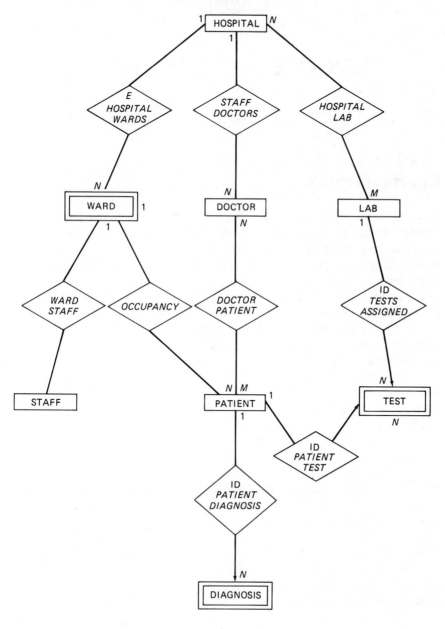

# Chapter 9

# BINARY DATA MODELS

## 9.1 INTRODUCTION

A binary data model is any graph data model in which the nodes represent simple, single attributes and the arcs represent binary relationship types between two attributes. As discussed in Chapter 2, the nodes can represent either sets or extended sets. The arcs can represent either an aggregation of two attributes of an entity type or an aggregation of two entity types into a relationship type. The exact meaning of an arc depends on the interpretation of the two nodes it connects. N-ary aggregations of attributes and entity types can also be represented by using internal nodes in a similar manner as discussed in Chapter 3 for representing functional dependencies.

The simple generic structure of a binary data model is intuitively appealing. It has attracted much attention and served as a basis for many proposed data models [Abrial, 1974; Deheneffe et al., 1974; Hainaut and Lecharlier, 1974; Senko 1975, 1976; Bracchi et al., 1976]. The data models differ in notation and sometimes in substance. For instance, Senko's data model is a multilevel data model. It attempts to model several aspects of data base management, from the user's external view to the physical access paths. Bracchi et al.'s data model is designed to be a candidate data model for the conceptual schema as proposed by the ANSI/X3/SPARC study group [Tsichritzis and Klug, 1978]. Abrial's data model incorporates powerful semantic properties and draws heavily from ideas in artificial intelligence and programming languages.

The graph structure of binary data models can be considered as a dual of the table structure of relational data models. Relational data models have received the most attention as table data models. Binary data models have received the most attention as graph data models. Many claims have been formulated as to the superiority of one over the other for data modeling. However, each approach has its strengths and weaknesses. Neither is intrinsically simpler or more powerful. Relational data models, as outlined in Chapter 5, are elegant in their simplicity, but very limited semantically. Binary data models can represent complex relationships concisely, but are not very user oriented.

Both data models are based on a few, fairly simple structures that provide an adequate basis for the specification of further data modeling facilities. However, both of them lose their simplicity and economy of concept when enhanced with more complicated data modeling facilities. As a matter of fact, the additional semantic constructs added to tables or graphs are as important as the original structures themselves. The basis of comparison, therefore, should not be on whether relations or graphs are simpler or more natural. Instead, one should consider the constructs that need to be added to tables and graphs to enable them to model more adequately complex situations.

The basic structures, constraints, and operations of a binary data model are rather simple and have been already outlined to a large extent in Chapters 2, 3, and 4. Therefore, in this chapter we discuss instead the more elaborate data modeling mechanisms which are needed to enhance binary data models. To focus our discussion, we concentrate mainly on the features of one of the first proposed binary data models, Abrial's semantic binary data model [Abrial, 1974]. This particular data model has many semantic-oriented structures which are very useful in data modeling. As we will see, the semantic binary data model can be considered as a bridge between other data models and semantic network data models discussed in Chapter 10.

## 9.2 STRUCTURES

The semantic binary data model is a graph data model of nodes and arcs. A node represents a classification of data instances into a type called a *category* (i.e., a classification generalization). An arc represents a binary relationship type between categories and is called a *binary relation*. A graph that abides by these structuring rules is called a *type graph* and represents the intension of a semantic binary data base. Figure 9.2—1 shows an example of a type graph consisting of two categories and a binary relation between them structured according to the semantic binary data model.

In the semantic binary data model the two directions of a binary relation are named uniquely, as shown in Figure 9.2—1. Each name, called an *access function*, corresponds to a binary relation followed in one

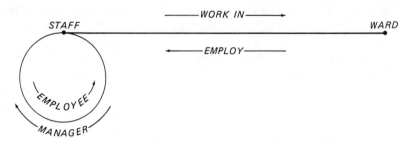

**Fig. 9.2−1** Type graph of categories and binary relations.

direction. For example, going from *WARD* to *STAFF* we have an access function labeled *EMPLOY*. The semantics of the relationship type are that *WARD*s *EMPLOY STAFF*. In the other direction the access function is *WORK IN* (i.e., *STAFF WORK IN WARD*s).

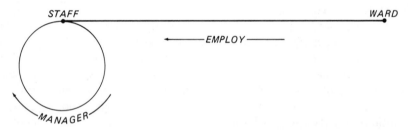

**Fig. 9.2−2** Unidirectional access function.

The semantic binary data model defines access functions for both directions of a binary relation. Some binary data models specify access functions in one direction, only as in Figure 9.2−2. The opposite direction access function in that case can be defined as **INVERSE**(*WORK IN*), or it may be undefined if not represented in the schema.

The two directions of a binary relation can also be defined using one generic name, as in Figure 9.2−3. In this case there is a difficulty when a

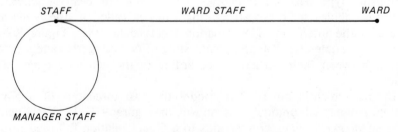

**Fig. 9.2−3** Generic binary relations.

binary relation is defined between the same category (e.g., the *MANAGER STAFF* binary relation from *STAFF* to *STAFF*). The difficulty in establishing the proper direction of the relationship type is similar to the difficulties relating to the concept of recursive DBTG-set types.

Because the semantic binary data model defines the two directions of an access function independently (Figure 9.2—1), they need to be declared explicitly as inverses of each other (e.g., *WORK IN* = **INVERSE**(*EMPLOY*)). In this way the data model knows that the two access functions are part of the same binary relation. It should be noted that access functions in the semantic binary data model are not really functions in the mathematical sense of the word. As we will see, their application can yield more than one value. Other versions of the binary data model have been proposed where the access functions do correspond to single-value functions [Kerschberg and Pacheco, 1975].

The extension of a semantic, binary type graph consists of objects and connections between objects. An *object* is an instance of a category (e.g., specific wards and staff). Objects are of two kinds: *abstract objects* and *concrete objects*. The difference between abstract and concrete objects is similar to the notion of domain extension (abstract object) and attribute extension (concrete object), as discussed in Chapter 2. That is, abstract objects exist once and for all, whereas concrete objects enter and leave the description of the world represented by the data model. For instance, the number 345 always exists as an abstract object within the domain NUMBER. The concrete object John Smith of type *PERSON* may or may not currently exist in the data base. All categories in the semantic binary data model are specified as being either abstract or concrete.

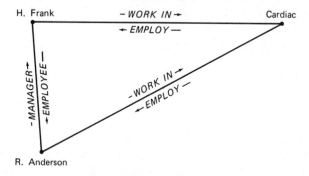

**Fig. 9.2—4** Extension of type graph.

Objects are related by *connections* between them. A connection is an instance of a binary relation. Each connection is labeled in both directions with the name of the associated access function. For instance, the connection between a *STAFF* object and a *WARD* object can be labeled

*EMPLOY* in one direction and *WORK IN* in the other direction (Figure 9.2—4). Thus, the connection can be followed in either direction, albeit with different names.

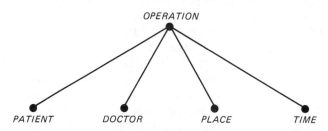

**Fig. 9.2—5** Representing a quartary relationship type.

Relationship types between more then two categories are represented by generating new categories. For instance, the category *OPERATION* can represent a quartary relationship type among the categories *PATIENT*, *DOCTOR*, *PLACE*, and *TIME* as in Figure 9.2—5. An *OPERATION* object is present to encode the nonbinary relationship type among *PATIENT*, *DOCTOR*, *PLACE*, and *TIME*. In this way, *n*-ary relationship types can be handled through the binary relations of the data model. There have been suggestions to separate this type of category into a third type of object (i.e., internal objects [Bracchi et al., 1976]). However, in many cases it is hard to distinguish whether a category has an independent existence or plays only an internal, dummy role. For instance, an operation can be considered an independent event, or it can be considered a dummy object whose purpose is to bring patients and doctors together in certain places at certain times. We will not separate internal objects into a separate category, but will handle them as concrete objects.

To create a category in the semantic binary data model, the operator

*STAFF* = **CATEGORY**

is used. This statement will generate a new category (type of object) with external name *STAFF*.

To create a binary relation in the semantic binary data model, one specifies the name of the relation, the access functions, and the categories of objects that are related. The following statement generates a binary relation with external name *WARD STAFF* connecting the categories *STAFF* and *WARD* with access function *WORK IN* from *STAFF* to *WARD* and *EMPLOY* from *WARD* to *STAFF*.

*WARD STAFF* = **RELATION**(*STAFF, WARD, WORK IN, EMPLOY*)

In the original definition of the semantic binary data model, a name for a binary relation is optional. That is, a binary relation can be defined without any associated name. If there is only one binary relation between two object types, it does not need a name. However, in what follows, for referential purposes, we usually specify a name for a binary relation.

## 9.3 CONSTRAINTS

In the semantic binary data model, constraints can be defined that specify the permissible values for the objects in a category. This type of constraint is handled very easily by defining an appropriate category of abstract objects as the domain of another category. For instance, consider telephones as concrete objects. The values of telephone numbers for telephones are obtained by connecting them to the *PHONE NUMBER* category of abstract objects consisting of seven-digit integer numbers. In this way telephone numbers are constrained to correspond to seven-digit numbers.

Constraints can be specified for the cardinality of access functions. Access functions in the semantic binary data model are multivalued functions. That is, they are functions to the powerset of the objects in the category of their range. However, we may want to specify, for example, that each person has only one social security number or at most two jobs. These constraints are specified by augmenting the definition of a binary relation with cardinality constraints. The cardinality constraints are specified by the **AFN** operator, which gives the minimum and maximum cardinality of the subsets of the powerset which the access function has as its range. For instance, the specification of the binary relation *WARD STAFF* between *STAFF* and *WARD* (Figure 9.2−1) can be augmented using the operator **AFN** as follows:

$$WARD\ STAFF = \mathbf{RELATION}(STAFF,\ WARD,\ WORK\ IN = \mathbf{AFN}(1,1),$$
$$EMPLOY = \mathbf{AFN}(0,\ \infty))$$

In this way, the cardinality of the range of an access function can be defined explicitly in a manner similar to that outlined in Chapter 3.

The example binary relation *WARD STAFF* represents the case of a binary relation that is a true single-valued function from *STAFF* to *WARD*. This property is indicated by the cardinality constraints **AFN**(1,1) of the access function *WORK IN*. The specification **AFN**(1,1) means that for each staff there is exactly one ward in which that staff member works (total functional mapping from *STAFF* to *WARD*). In the opposite direction, a ward can employ no staff or an unbounded number of staff (unrestricted mapping).

There are many other cases of special interest. For instance,

*MARRIAGE* = **RELATION** (*PERSON, PERSON, SPOUSE* = **AFN** (0, 1),
   *SPOUSE* = **AFN** (0, 1))

means that each person can have one spouse or no spouse (partial functional mapping in both directions). The binary relation

*DOCTOR PATIENT* = **RELATION** (*DOCTOR, PATIENT*,
   *PATIENTS OF DOCTOR* = **AFN** (0, ∞),
   *PATIENTS DOCTOR* = **AFN** (1, ∞))

means that a doctor can have no patients or many patients, whereas each patient must have at least one doctor (total functional mapping from *PATIENT* to *DOCTOR*). Finally,

*SPECIALIZATION* = **RELATION** (*DOCTOR, SPECIALTY*,
   *SPECIALTY OF DOCTOR* = **AFN** (1, 1),
   *DOCTORS SPECIALTY* = **AFN** (0, 1))

means that every doctor has exactly one area of specialty, but there may be specialties for which there are currently no doctors (i.e., an open position).

Another form of constraint indicates that two access functions are inverses of each other. This implies that each connection is established in both directions. For instance, we can specify that

*SPECIALTY OF DOCTOR* = **INVERSE** (*DOCTORS SPECIALTY*)

which will guarantee that the two access functions are two directions of the same binary relation. This constraint is specified implicitly when the two access functions are defined within the same binary relation definition. In addition, this facility provides the flexibility of defining an access function $f$ in only one direction and then using **INVERSE** ($f$) as the name of the access function in the opposite direction.

A special case of cardinality occurs when one of the categories has only one object. Consider, for instance, the category *HAIR*, which has the sole object "bald." The state of someone's hair can be described using a binary relation between the category *PERSON* and the category *HAIR*. This binary relation is of the form

*HAIRINESS* = **RELATION** (*PERSON, HAIR, HAIR STATE* = **AFN** (0, 1),
   *BALD PERSON* = **AFN** (0, ∞))

This binary relation distinguishes persons as having hair or being bald. A special operator **PROPERTY** can be introduced for these cases. This example can then be specified as

$$HAIRINESS = \textbf{PROPERTY} (PERSON, \ HAIR(0, \ \infty))$$

which says that a person either does or does not have hair. Note that this statement is just a shorthand notation for the previous binary relation.

Many more types of constraints can be specified by the semantic binary data model. Most of them, however, are specified via operations. This approach corresponds to a slightly different view of constraints than has been considered so far. Constraints have been described mostly in a declarative way as properties which should be true in any data base state. Operations are specified without any regard to constraints. If an operation tries to violate a constraint, the operation is left undefined. In this manner operations and constraints can be specified independently. Their only relationship is that they are applicable to the same data base.

In another approach the constraints themselves can be specified as part of the operations. That is, the definition of an operation includes whatever constraints the operation is supposed to verify and enforce. When an operation is performed, its associated constraints are checked. If a constraint is violated, the operation can fail or the user can specify explicitly what action should be taken. The constraints can be local in that they apply only to the objects the operation explicitly specifies. On the other hand, they can be global, applying to other objects not explicitly specified by the operation. In this latter case, the operations correspond more closely to data base procedures as discussed in Chapter 4.

To illustrate the two approaches, consider the constraint that each person is married to at most one person. This constraint can be specified as a cardinality constraint of the *MARRIAGE* binary relation. Alternatively, it can be specified as an integral part of an operation *MARRIAGE* that connects two *PERSON* objects according to the binary relation. That is, determining that a person is not married becomes an integral part of the operation of getting married (i.e., of connecting two *PERSON* objects). In the first case the constraint is declared explicitly in the schema as a property of the binary relation. In the second case it is encoded in the operation that connects two *PERSON* objects according to the binary relation. The semantic binary data model provides a nice vehicle for studying constraints as part of operations. In the next section we elaborate on this approach to handling constraints.

## 9.4 OPERATIONS

In Section 9.2 we introduced schema operations that allowed us to define new categories of objects and binary relations between categories. At the instance level, the semantic binary data model provides operations for manipulating objects in a category (e.g., introducing a new object) and for manipulating connections between objects (e.g., relating an object in one category to an object in another category). In addition, one can define operations that take a more general form and affect many objects in many categories according to a program. This last type of operation is very general and can be used to specify data base procedures in the semantic binary data model.

Suppose that we define a category *PERSON* by the definition operation

*PERSON* = **CATEGORY**

The **CATEGORY** operator will create a new category, but without any objects in it. To populate the category with objects, we use the insert operation

**GENERATE** *PERSON*

The effect of the **GENERATE** operator is to create a new person with an internal name that is guaranteed to be unique. This internal name corresponds to an external key as defined in Chapter 3 and is used to uniquely distinguish objects in a category, but it is not directly accessible to the user. The user, however, can specify an external *synonym* (i.e., a key) that is in direct correspondence with the internal name. This synonym is defined by the insert operation

John = **GENERATE** *PERSON*

Again, the **GENERATE** operator will create a new person with a unique internal name. However, the name John can be used by the user from now on to refer to the newly created object. In addition, the DBMS guarantees that the synonym John is unique among external names of objects of the *PERSON* category. If another person already has the external name John, the operation cannot be executed.

Sometimes we would like to create and refer to an object, but not to assign it a permanent external synonym. In this case the data model allows us to use a temporary external synonym to refer to an object. The idea is somewhat similar to that of using a variable name to refer to a storage location rather than the actual value of the storage location. The temporary external synonym is discarded as soon as the user becomes inactive (i.e., the temporary external synonym is retained only during the execution of a program). However, the object that was created and referred to by the temporary external synonym continues to exist. The temporary external synonym is referred to as a *nickname* and is associated with an object by the symbol ← rather than = as follows:

*X* ← **GENERATE** *PERSON*

This operation creates a new *PERSON* object whose nickname is *X*. The object nicknamed *X* can be related to other uniquely specified objects. For instance, consider a new person that is created with nickname *X* and then related with the binary relation

*MARRIAGE* = **RELATION** (*PERSON, PERSON,*
   *SPOUSE* = **AFN** (0, 1), *SPOUSE* = **AFN** (0, 1))

to the person whose external name is John. The newly created *PERSON* object has no external name in this case and therefore cannot be referred to directly after the execution of the program that refers to it by the nickname *X* is finished. However, it can be referred to in the future as the spouse of John because of the connection between itself and John.

To illustrate the difference between the internal name of an object, an external synonym for that object, and a separate category *NAME*, consider the following example.

*PERSON* = **CATEGORY**
*NAME* = **CATEGORY**
**RELATION** = (*PERSON, NAME, NAME OF PERSON* = **AFN** (1, 1),
   *PERSON WITH NAME* = **AFN** (0, 1))

Suppose that we specify

John = **GENERATE** *PERSON*

In this case a *PERSON* object will be generated which can be referred to by the external name John. Suppose that we specify

*X* ← **GENERATE** *PERSON*
John = **GENERATE** *NAME*

and that we connect the *NAME* object whose external name is John to the *PERSON* object referred to by the nickname *X*. In this case, John is not the external name of the *PERSON* object. Rather, it is the value of an attribute of the *PERSON* object, namely the value of its *Name* attribute.

The difference between these two examples affects the way in which we change information in the data base. Suppose that John wants to change his name to Jack in real life. In the first case, we have to eliminate the *PERSON* object referred to by the external name John and create another *PERSON* object with external name Jack. During this process, we have to retain outside the data base the knowledge that Jack is in fact John. In the second case the name of the person can be changed from John to Jack without eliminating the *PERSON* object. We merely change the connection between the *PERSON* object and the *NAME* object to which it is connected.

To remove objects from a category the delete operation

**KILL** *PERSON* John

is used. This operation deletes the object that can be referred to by the external name John. The **KILL** operator can take as an argument a more complicated expression which uniquely identifies John. The argument can also be a nickname.

The delete operation has a very interesting side effect if the cardinality of an access function does not allow the deletion because of its lower bound. In most data models the deletion operation would be unsuccessful. For instance, in the binary relation

$$CAR\ OWNER = \textbf{RELATION}(PERSON,\ CAR,\ OWN = \textbf{AFN}(0,\ \infty),$$
$$OWNER = \textbf{AFN}(1,1))$$

every car has an owner according to the cardinality of the access function *OWNER*. The deletion of a car's sole owner should not be allowed. In the semantic binary data model, however, we are allowed to use *nulls*. The deletion of a car's owner will result in connecting the car to an *unknown* owner. That is, the car still has an owner, but we do not know who she is. The semantic binary data model does not consider this situation as a violation of the cardinality of the access function.

The **CONNECT** operator connects two objects according to a specific binary relation. The objects to be connected can be referred to by their external names, by their nicknames, or by using access functions on external names and nicknames. For instance, we can specify that a particular car $X$ is related to a person $Y$ according to the *CAR OWNER* relation by specifying either

$OWNER(X)$ **CONNECT** $Y$

or

$OWN(Y)$ **CONNECT** $X$

Regardless of the direction in which the connection is established, the effect is to make it available in both directions. That is, establishing a connection by the operation

$f(X)$ **CONNECT** $Y$

has as a side effect that it also establishes the connection specified by the operation

**INVERSE** $f(Y)$ **CONNECT** $X$

The **DISCONNECT** operator specifies that two objects are no longer related. For instance, we can disconnect a car $X$ from its owner $Y$ by the operation

$OWNER(X)$ **DISCONNECT** $Y$

In this case the cardinality of the access function for $OWNER = \mathbf{AFN}((roman1, 1)$ will connect $X$ to an *unknown* object in *PERSON* rather than leave it unconnected. That is, the car will have an unknown owner rather than no owner. To illustrate the difference consider the binary relation between persons and dogs defined by

**RELATION**$(PERSON, DOG, OWN = \mathbf{AFN}(0,0), OWNER = \mathbf{AFN}(0,1))$

In this case a dog is allowed to exist with no owner at all. The operation

$OWNER(X)$ **DISCONNECT** $Y$

will disconnect (connect to nothing) dog $X$ from owner $Y$. The owner of $X$, thus, will not be *unknown*; it will be *nothing*.

In many cases we do not want to connect or disconnect objects, but to change the connections. This operation is denoted by the operator $\leftarrow$. For example, to change a car's owner from $Y$ to a new owner $Z$, we specify

$OWNER(X) \leftarrow Z$

This operation is equivalent to the operation

$OWNER(X)$ **DISCONNECT** $Y$

for each owner of $X$ followed indivisibly by the operation

$OWNER(X)$ **CONNECT** $Z$

It should be noted that the operator $f(X)$ **CONNECT** $Y$ or $f(X)$ **DISCONNECT** $Y$ does not imply any application of the access function $f$. That is, it does not specify "from $X$ follow $f$ and then ...." Rather, it specifies "**(DIS)CONNECT** $X$ and $Y$ according to $f$." As such, it is more of the form **OPERATION**$(f, X, Y)$.

Access functions can be nested in the same operation. For instance, we can denote that the owner of car $X$ is the same as the owner of car $W$ by specifying

$OWN(OWNER(W))$ **CONNECT** $X$

This operation says "connect according to the $OWN$ access function the owner of $W$ to $X$." Using nesting we can specify that a connection should be erased no matter where it connects. Thus, to remove the connection it is not necessary to know to what other objects an object is connected. For example,

$OWNER(X)$ **DISCONNECT** $OWNER(X)$

is equivalent to

$OWN(OWNER(X)$ **DISCONNECT** $X$

Both of these operations will disconnect all the owners of car $X$ (i.e., connect $X$ to *unknown*).

Up to this point we have outlined operations that insert/delete objects and that connect/disconnect objects. With these operations, one can create objects and structure them into a network according to the defined binary relations. The querying capabilities in the model are provided by testing whether an object is present in a category or by testing whether two objects are connected. The first of these operations is provided by the operator **IS**. For example, the operation

$X$ **IS** *PERSON*

determines whether the object $X$ is an object of the category *PERSON*.

Connectedness is tested for by the **TEST** operator. The operation

$Y$ **TEST** *OWNER X*

determines whether $X$ is related to $Y$ via the $OWNER$ binary relation. The outcome of both of these preceding operations is either true or false.

The preceding operation determines only whether $Y$ is *one of* the owners of $X$. $X$ may have other owners if the cardinality of the $OWNER$ access function allows it. In the case that the cardinality has been declared as **AFN**(1,1), a different operator $=$ can test for uniqueness in addition to connectedness. For example, in the binary relation *CAR OWNER* we can test whether $Y$ is the unique owner of $X$ by the operation

$Y = OWNER(X)$

As a special use of uniqueness testing, we can determine whether an object is not connected to anything or is connected to an unknown object using the operations $OWNER(X) = $ *nothing* and $OWNER(X) = $ *unknown*, respectively. Here the first operation implies a quantification. If the owner of $X$ is disconnected, there exists no object $Y$ in the *PERSON* category to which $X$ is connected.

All queries to a data base are formulated as conjectures which can be either true or false. The success or failure of a conjecture provides the answer to a query. This form of data manipulation is different from the operations we have seen in the data models discussed in Chapters 5 to 8. In these data models, data are isolated using selection and then they are accessed. In the semantic binary data model, at least the way we have discussed it up to now, there is no notion of access. Information is put in the data base by creating objects and connections. Information is obtained from the data base by testing for the presence of objects and connections.

There should be some question as to whether merely testing objects for certain properties is an adequate facility to formulate sophisticated queries and perform complex processing on the data. In the semantic binary data model, more sophisticated data model operations can be provided by extending the capabilities of conjectures. One way in which the power of conjectures can be extended is to allow the use of Boolean operators such as AND, OR, and NOT in formulating conjectures. In this way, conjectures can be specified as

$OWNER(X) = Y$ **OR** $OWNER(X) = $ *unknown*

Quantifiers can also be introduced that apply to members of a set of objects. The quantifiers $\forall$ (for all) and $\exists$ (there exists) can be used. The range of the quantifiers is a set of properly defined objects. Consider, for example, the binary relations

**RELATION**(*PERSON, PERSON, PARENT* = **AFN**(2,2),
   *CHILD* = **AFN**(0, ∞))
**RELATION**(*PERSON, SEX, SEX OF PERSON* = **AFN**(1,1),
   *PERSON OF SEX* = **AFN**(0, ∞))

between parents and children and persons and sex. The operation

$\exists\, Y\leftarrow CHILD(X)$   $(SEX(Y) = $ Male$)$

will test whether $X$ has a boy child. The operation

$\forall\, Y\leftarrow CHILD(X)$   $(SEX(Y) = $ Male$)$

will test whether all the children of $X$ are boys.

By introducing sets of objects and the set operations union, intersection, and complement instead of quantification, the same conjectures can be expressed with set operations rather than quantification. For instance

$$- ((CHILD(X) \cap PERSON \ OF \ SEX(\text{Male})) = nothing)$$

will test whether $X$ has a boy child.

Quantifiers, set operations, and other mathematical constructs can all be superseded by introducing the notion of a program as an integral part of the semantic binary data model. Formally, a category of abstract objects called *programs* can be defined. Programs consist of a list of statements and appropriate control structures (e.g., looping) that are evaluated as a unit[1]. Objects are manipulated directly by programs by allowing them to use an object's internal name (not ordinarily accessible) and access functions.

Programs can be used to customize operations for each category. A program that replaces a default operator can be associated with a particular category or binary relation. For instance, a user-defined program can be invoked each time a new object is to be generated in the category *CAR*. The program can produce side effects for this category above and beyond that of the default **GENERATE** operator. One such side effect might be to associate a car with an unknown person as owner since a car cannot exist without an owner. Another side effect can be constraint checking. Consider, for example, the operation *SPOUSE(X)* **CONNECT** *Y*. The default **CONNECT** operator for this particular binary relation can be replaced by a program which checks that both $X$ and $Y$ are not connected via the *MARRIAGE* binary relation to anybody else before establishing the connection. If a default operator is not overridden by a program, the default operator will be invoked. This facility of default specification is very important and it is not present in most data models. In most data models only default operators are allowed.

As an example of specifying operations through programs, consider the definition of the binary relation *GRANDPARENT* using the binary relation *PARENT* [Abrial, 1974].

**RELATION**(*PERSON, PERSON, PARENT* = **AFN**(2, 2),
   *CHILD* = **AFN**(0, ∞))

**RELATION**(*PERSON, PERSON, GRANDPARENT* = **AFN**(4, 4),
   *GRANDCHILD* = **AFN**(0, ∞))

---

[1] We will not elaborate on the exact syntax of programs in the semantic binary data model.

```
ACCESSOR (GRANDPARENT) ← PROGRAM (X)
    FOR  Y← PARENT(X)
        FOR  Z← PARENT(Y)
            RESUME (Z)
            UP 1
    END
    UP 1
END
```

The **FOR** statement will iterate on all objects connected to $X$ or $Y$ according to the *PARENT* binary relation. The notation **UP** 1 will end the execution of the loop and pop up to the next iteration. The **RESUME** statement returns, as the result of the program, the indicated value(s). In this example the accessor function *GRANDPARENT* has been defined to have a special relationship with the accessor function *PARENT*. This definition ensures that the *PARENT* and *GRANDPARENT* access functions are compatible. Moreover, it defines the binary relation *GRANDPARENT* as a non-information-bearing relationship type based solely on the definition of *PARENT*.

By introducing programs that replace default operators and associating them with categories or binary relations, we in essence provide a facility for specification of data base procedures as outlined in Chapter 4. These data base procedures can be used for all the different purposes outlined in Chapter 4. They can be integrity triggers, virtual fields, DBA procedures, and so on. We have the full generality of a programming language inside the data model to specify complicated data-dependent operations which cannot be anticipated beforehand. We have, in fact, a specification facility for abstract data types as discussed in Chapter 4 since programs are not general operators applying the same way to every category or binary relation, but are defined specifically for each category and binary relation.

Associated with a program is a category of concrete objects called *processes*. Programs and processes are related in that each process corresponds to the execution of a program. Processes complete with either success or failure.

Independent of programs and processes, the notion of *context* can also be introduced. The idea of context is a generalization of the idea of a data base view and is used in a similar way in the semantic binary data model as in programming languages. A data base view is usually only a restructuring of the data base. In addition, a context defines the effect of the operators on that part of the data base contained in the context.

Contexts and processes are related in that each process creates and operates within a context. Contexts enable users to have a personal view of the data base which may be different from the general view. It allows the effects of operations to be partly visible since they are performed with respect to a context. For instance, if an object is deleted with respect to a context, it is not rendered completely invisible. It is only masked out in that context, whereas it continues to exist in other contexts. An object is completely dead only when it is deleted with respect to the global context.

The concepts of programs, processes, and contexts and how they relate are notions in programming languages and operating systems and we will not elaborate on them further. In the semantic binary data model, programs, processes, and contexts are used to enhance considerably the descriptive abilities of the data model.

## 9.5 CONCLUDING REMARKS

To test the power of the semantic binary data model, Abrial uses it to describe itself. This seems like a superfluous academic exercise. It has, however, some advantages. First, if a data model has adequate descriptive power, it should be able to specify some of its own peculiar constructs. Second, a small subset of the data model can be used to describe a much larger subset. In this way, properties of the data model can be verified for the subset and then propagated to the full data model. Third, changes in the the data model can be rigorously specified by using the data model itself. Finally, if a data model can be used as a metamodel to describe itself, it can also be used as a metamodel to describe other data models.

This last use of data models is rather important. It is very confusing to argue about relative merits of data models. The confusion is due partly to the fact that data models are defined rather loosely. Hence, their concepts cannot be completely understood in a single framework. Using a precise metamodel to describe different data models provides a common framework for understanding and comparing data models. For instance, if all data models were specified using the predicate calculus, it would be much easier to pinpoint their differences.

Using the semantic binary data model as a metamodel we can define a category of categories. The categories are related to each other with the generic access functions representing access functions. Programs are related to access functions and categories by the following binary relations:

$$R_1 = \textbf{RELATION}(CATEGORY,\ PROGRAM,\ GENERATOR = \textbf{AFN}(0,1),$$
$$CATGENERATED = \textbf{AFN}(0,\ \infty))$$

$R_1$ specifies that each category can be related to at most one program that defines the insertion operation for objects in the category.

$$R_2 = \textbf{RELATION}(CATEGORY,\ PROGRAM,\ KILLER = \textbf{AFN}(0,1),$$
$$CATKILLED = \textbf{AFN}(0,\ \infty))$$

$R_2$ specifies that each category can be related to at most one program that defines the deletion operation for objects in the category.

$R_3$ = **RELATION**(*CATEGORY, PROGRAM, RECOGNIZER* = **AFN**(0,1),
        *CATRECOGNIZED* = **AFN**(0, ∞))

$R_3$ specifies that each category can be related to at most one program that defines the testing operation for determining whether an object belongs to the category.

$R_4$ = **RELATION**(*ACCESS FUNCTION, PROGRAM,*
        *CONNECTOR* = **AFN**(0,1), *FUNCTION CONNECTED* = **AFN**(0, ∞))

$R_4$ specifies that each access function can be related to at most one program that defines the connect operation for connecting objects according to the access function.

$R_5$ = **RELATION**(*ACCESS FUNCTION, PROGRAM,*
        *DISCONNECTOR* = **AFN**(0,1),
        *FUNCTION DISCONNECTED* = **AFN**(0, ∞))

$R_5$ specifies that each access function can be related to at most one program that defines the disconnect operation for disconnecting objects according to the access function.

$R_6$ = **RELATION**(*ACCESS FUNCTION, PROGRAM,*
        *ACCESSOR* = **AFN**(0,1), *FUNCTION ACCESSED* = **AFN**(0, ∞))

$R_6$ specifies that each access function can be related to at most one program that defines the side effects of that access function.

$R_7$ = **RELATION**(*ACCESS FUNCTION, PROGRAM,*
        *TESTER* = **AFN**(0,1), *FUNCTION TESTED* = **AFN**(0, ∞))

Finally, $R_7$ specifies that each access function can be related to at most one program that defines the side effects of testing connections according to that access function.

Note that the cardinality **AFN**(0,1), specified for the first access function in the preceding binary relations, always allows a category or access function not to be related to a program for a certain operator. In this case, the default operator will be invoked. If, however, it is related to a program, the operator will be defined by the program. The data model can also be used to describe relationships between programs, processes, and contexts [Abrial, 1974].

The semantic binary data model that we have outlined draws heavily from ideas in programming languages and artificial intelligence. It is capable of describing abstract data types. It was chosen as representative of binary data models mainly for two reasons. First, it shows how a simple structure, like graphs, can be augmented with additional data modeling capabilities to provide a rich data model capable of describing semantically complex situations. Second, it introduces many ideas, such as context, program, and so on, which are also part of semantic network data models outlined in Chapter 10.

## EXERCISES

**9.1** How do Bracchi et al.'s binary data model, Abrial's binary data model, and Senko's binary data model relate to each other? Outline some features that are common to all of them. Outline some features unique to each.

**9.2** Suppose that the basic structure of a data model is a relation as opposed to a graph. Can you use the same constructs as in the semantic binary data model to augment a relational data model with capabilities such as **AFN** cardinality constraints and access functions?

**9.3** In what way is a category of objects together with declared programs for its operations different from a SIMULA class [Dahl and Nygaard, 1966]?

**9.4** In the semantic binary data model one can construct relationships among objects. How can one construct relationships among relationships?

**9.5** Consider constraint specification as outlined in Abrial's paper [Abrial, 1974] and Brodie's constraint language [Brodie, 1978, 1980]. Are they equivalent? Can one language specify more constraints than the other?

**9.6** Is there a need to introduce functional dependencies into the semantic binary data model? Justify your answer.

**9.7** Express the basic properties of the semantic binary data model using predicate calculus. This should include **AFN** cardinality constraints, access functions, operators, creation of objects, and so on.

**9.8** Express transitive closure in the semantic binary data model via a program.

**9.9** Programs can verify constraints on objects. Can they also enforce protection requirements? How can the users be identified in the data model?

**9.10** Outline a set of programming language features that can be used to access and manipulate objects within the semantic binary data model. The programs should be able to express quantifications on the objects in a category or those in the range of an access function. Can you do everything that quantifiers do?

**9.11** Express, using semantic binary data model programs, the standard properties of mathematical relations (e.g., reflexivity, symmetry, and transitivity).

**9.12** In what way, if any, does a nickname as introduced in this chapter differ from a currency indicator as introduced in Chapter 4?

between attributes is not related in any way to logical properties. For instance, taking two or three joins in a relational data model in order to relate some attributes may have practical or performance implications. It does not have any semantic connotations (e.g., that entities are closely or loosely related). In semantic network data models, network distance can be important. It is used to locate, through searches, closely related concepts.

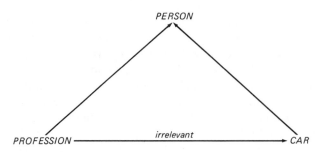

**Fig. 10.1—1** Irrelevancy arc example.

In some situations you may want to explicitly increase the semantic distance between two nodes. For instance, in Figure 10.1—1, professions relate to persons and persons relate to cars. Professions and cars are fairly close in the network, but from this it does not necessarily follow that professions relate to cars. To handle such situations some semantic network data models introduce the idea of an *irrelevancy* arc. That is, two nodes can be negatively connected as being irrelevant to each other.

A third idea introduced in semantic network data models is the idea of a *partition* [Hendrix, 1975a,b]. A partition behaves in much the same way as a context in the semantic binary data model. Only that part of a network that is relevant to the task at hand is made available. Such a facility is very important for limiting the scope of search to relevant concepts when attempting to infer facts from given facts. In most data models there is only the notion of subschema for specifying semantic context. Subschema separation is sometimes inadequate since subschemas are defined only in terms of types and not tokens. For instance, a single department and its associated employees cannot be defined as a subschema in many data models. Only the set of all departments and their employees can be specified via a subschema.

A fourth idea introduced in semantic network data models is the hierarchy of types. In Chapter 2 we introduced generalization and aggregation abstraction which define hierarchies of types. These kinds of type hierarchies, however, were introduced very early in semantic network data models as PART_OF and IS_A hierarchies [Quillian, 1968; Raphael, 1968; Winston, 1970]. Semantic networks also make a careful distinction between type-token generalization (classification) and type-type generalization which is not done in most data models. In addition, they usually specify precisely the inheritance rules for related types within the hierarchy. Hierarchy inheritance deals not only with the inheritance of attributes and their values, but also with the inheritance of permitted relationship types among types. As an example, if *EMPLOYEE* IS_A *PERSON*, it is implied that the relationship type *MARRIED TO* between *PERSON* can be inherited as a valid relationship type between *EMPLOYEE*. As such, inheritance between types is not a single connection, but a whole "cable" of connections specifying the inheritance of many properties [Brachman, 1979].

A fifth idea introduced in semantic network data models is that of *roles* [Fahlman, 1977; Hayes, 1977a,b]. The role concept for entity types was discussed in Chapter 2. The role data model introduced similar ideas for data base management systems at about the same time [Bachman and Daya, 1977]. However, the concept is used much more widely and is much more refined in semantic network data models. Roles can be applied to many data structuring concepts (e.g., entity types, attributes, and relationship types) and one can even distinguish roles of roles (e.g., a functional role such as employee versus a role filler such as person).

We have briefly discussed some of the more important data modeling concepts found in semantic network data models. There are many more concepts, each aimed at representing certain aspects of knowledge. Thus, semantic networks are very rich data models in terms of concepts. This is a mixed blessing. It certainly allows the modeling of complex situations. However, the data models become rather complicated and lack a certain economy of concepts. One of the reasons for the vast number of semantic network data models and their wide variety of concepts is that the data models are aimed at different data modeling realms from conceptual to implementational [Brachman, 1979]. Some of the data models even mix concepts from different realms. Brachman distinguishes between different realms of data modeling for semantic network data models in terms of their intended modeling goals.

One data modeling realm for which semantic network data models have been proposed, is as the implementation mechanism for a higher-level, logical representation of knowledge [Nash-Webber and Reiter, 1977]. Such an implementation-oriented realm of data modeling merely models data structures. Thus, it does not differ much from other network data models outlined in previous chapters (e.g., the DBTG-network data model).

A second data modeling realm for semantic network data models is very much related to formal mathematical logic [Schubert, 1976]. The nodes and arcs correspond to constructs of the predicate calculus. The purpose of the network is to organize information as represented in the predicate calculus in order to make access of relevant information more immediate. This realm captures, formally, logical properties of data in the same way as data base theory (see Chapter 13) uses formal logic to specify properties of data [Gallaire and Minker, 1978; Fagin, 1980].

A third realm of data modeling which is most often associated with semantic network data models is representation of word senses and cases [Fillmore, 1968]. In this realm, a small set of language-independent, conceptual modeling elements are chosen which, it is claimed, are sufficient to express knowledge in any natural language [Simmons, 1973]. The purpose of the networks in this realm is to represent natural language and the knowledge needed to understand natural language.

A still different realm of data modeling for semantic network data models is language specific [Martin, 1977]. In this type of semantic network data model, nodes and arcs correspond to constructs of a specific language (e.g., English). This type of network is again used for natural language representation and understanding.

Finally, there is a data modeling realm called the *epistemological* realm which deals with conceptual units, their structure, and their relationships without any interpretation of the conceptual units [Brachman, 1979]. The emphasis is on how nodes can be structured, what kinds of arcs are allowed between nodes, and what inheritance rules for properties are meaningful. This type of semantic network data model most closely resembles other data models discussed so far in terms of concepts for data modeling. In this realm one deals with structuring principles and conceptual units without any associated semantic interpretation or concern for their implementation. For example, a relational schema can embody an allowed relationship type between entity types without concern for what the entity types or relationship type mean or how they are implemented.

Since this last type of semantic network data model is most relevant to the topic of this book, in the rest of this chapter we concentrate on semantic network data model ideas which are concerned with this data modeling realm. The ideas presented are influenced heavily by the work carried out in the TORUS, PSN, and TAXIS projects at the University of Toronto [Roussopoulos and Mylopoulos, 1975; Roussopoulos, 1976; Levesque and Mylopoulos, 1979; Mylopoulos et al., 1976, 1980; Mylopoulos and Wong, 1980]. They illustrate how some of the concepts discussed in this section can be incorporated into semantic network data models. Details on specific semantic network data models and projects relating to them can be found in [Brachman and Smith, 1980].

## 10.2 STRUCTURES

The structures of any semantic network data model consist of a graph (network) of nodes and arcs. The way in which we distinguish between different nodes and different arcs determines the kind of semantic network data model and the data modeling realm for which it is intended. If we consider first extensional aspects of a semantic network data model, the nodes can represent *things* (instances of values or entities) and the arcs can represent *assertions* about (relationships between) things. For instance, we can have a node representing the entity "Jim" and another representing the entity "John" and an arc representing the assertion "Jim is the brother of John." Such a graph of nodes and arcs is similar to the semantic binary data model instance graph discussed in Chapter 9. The objects of the semantic binary data model correspond to the things of the semantic network data model, and the binary relations defined by the access functions correspond to the assertions.

A unit of information can be considered as either a thing or an assertion. For instance, the color "green" can be considered as a thing. It can also be considered as an assertion (i.e., a predicate) about the color of something that cannot stand on its own. The relationship "brother of" can be viewed as an assertion or as a thing in its own right for the purpose of attaching to it properties such as "it is false" or "$x$ believes it." This freedom of interpretation of an object as a thing or an assertion is similar to the problem of interpreting something as an attribute or an entity type or a relationship type as discussed in Chapter 2. However, in semantic network data models the choice is even more difficult because there are usually many more options available. One of the guidelines for choosing a representation of an information unit as a thing rather than as an assertion is if it needs to be further qualified (i.e., related to other things).

Things and assertions about them provide a very limited and rather uniform capability for expressing semantics. To provide more descriptive power, it is necessary to differentiate between different kinds of nodes and arcs. The differentiation can be based on semantic meaning independent of applications.

Nodes can be categorized according to the things they represent. One such categorization establishes four categories of nodes: concepts, events, characteristics, and values [Mylopoulos et al., 1976]. *Concepts* are constant parameters of the application we are trying to represent. They are used to specify values (e.g., John Smith, St. Mary's Hospital, etc.). *Events* correspond to actions that occur in the application being represented. For instance, the action "John hits Jim" is represented by one event node for the action "hit," and two concept nodes, one for "John" and one for "Jim" (Figure 10.2—1).

The arcs connecting event nodes and concept nodes correspond to the roles that the concepts play in an event (e.g., "John" is the agent and "Jim" is the affected in the "hit" event) (Figure 10.2−1). *Characteristics* are nodes that describe properties of a concept. They thus correspond to the natural attributes of concepts. For instance, John's weight and height are characteristics of the concept "John." Finally, *values* are nodes corresponding to domains of values that characteristics may take. For example, a characteristic node "Weight" related to "John" and to the value "150" gives John's weight as 150 (Figure 10.2−1).

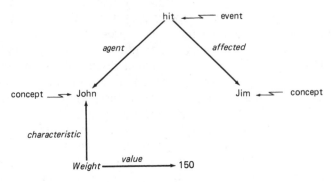

**Fig. 10.2−1** Example semantic network.

This categorization of nodes into concepts, events, characteristics, and values does not classify nodes into types, but into categories of types. Thus, individual cars and persons are both concepts represented by the concept category. There is no distinction between the type *CAR* and the type *PERSON*. This approach to data modeling has some inherent difficulties. It is not always easy to take a fact and structure it in terms of events, concepts, characteristics, and values. A fact may potentially fit into many categories, and thus it may be difficult to choose the exact category into which to place it. Because there are different types of nodes, a different interpretation of an arc is required that is dependent on the types of nodes connected. In addition, operations on nodes need to be interpreted according to the type of node.

A complementary approach for enhancing the descriptive power of semantic network data models, which can actually coexist with categorization of the nodes, is to also classify nodes into types. In addition to distinguishing nodes as concepts, events, characteristics, and values, we also distinguish between nodes that represent tokens, called *concepts*, and those that represent types, called *classes* [Levesque and Mylopoulos, 1979]. For instance, John Smith is a concept, *PERSON* is a class. A concept can be in more than one class. For instance, John Smith can be a *PERSON* and he can be a *STUDENT*. Thus, the different roles that a concept can play can be portrayed by the different classes to which a concept belongs. In other data models an entity type plays different roles by being related to different other entity types through various relationship types. For instance, John Smith plays his *PERSON* role by being related to his wife, children, and parents. He plays his *STUDENT* role by being related to his courses, teachers, and grades.

The concept-class distinction is essentially the same as the instance-type distinction made in other data models. There are, however, two important differences. First, in some semantic network data models classes and concepts are mixed in the same graph. In other data models, instances are separate from types. Types are specified in the schema, instances are placed in the data base. Second, in some semantic network data models an instance can be associated with many types. This situation is not allowed in the data models outlined in Chapters 5 to 9. An instance is declared to be of only one type.

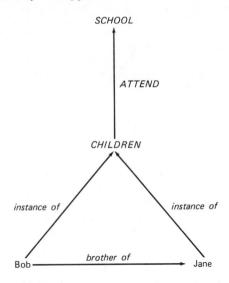

**Fig. 10.2—2** Different arcs and nodes in a semantic network.

This differentiation between concept and class nodes leads to three kinds of arcs between nodes. An arc between two concepts corresponds to an *assertion.* An arc between a concept and a class corresponds to an *instantiation.* Finally, an arc between two classes corresponds to a *binary relation* (which can itself be considered a class). Figure 10.2—2 shows an example of a semantic network illustrating the preceding discussion. Bob and Jane are concept nodes, *SCHOOL* and *CHILDREN* are class nodes. The arc *brother of* is an assertion. The two arcs relating Bob and Jane to the class *CHILDREN* are instantiation arcs. Finally, *ATTEND* is a binary relation between the classes *SCHOOL* and *CHILDREN.*

Classes can be further organized into hierarchies according to IS_A and PART_OF relationships. The IS_A and PART_OF relationships do not express types of relationships between classes, but rather give a taxonomy of classes. For instance, the relationship between *STUDENT* and *PERSON* is defined in the IS_A hierarchy as *STUDENT* IS_A *PERSON* (i.e., *STUDENT* is a subordinate class of *PERSON*) (Figure 10.2−3). On the other hand, *STUDENT* and *COURSE* are related via a binary relation between the two classes.

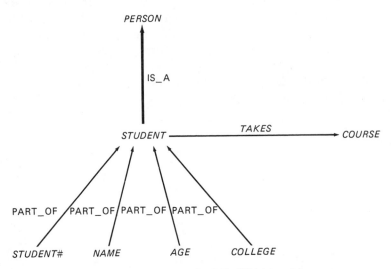

**Fig. 10.2−3** IS_A and PART_OF hierarchies.

The hierarchies of classes are used to specify inheritance of properties between classes. A class inherits all the attributes and attribute values of a higher-level class (superordinate class) in the IS_A hierarchy. At the instantiation-classification level, a concept inherits all the attributes of the classes to which it belongs.

Binary relations between classes can be thought of as classes for the purpose of structuring and property inheritance. In this way binary relations between classes can be structured in IS_A and PART_OF hierarchies and can inherit properties accordingly. For instance, given a binary relation *PERSONAL RELATIONSHIP*, we can specify that *MARRIAGE* IS_A *PERSONAL RELATIONSHIP* and that *COHABITATION* IS_A *PERSONAL RELATIONSHIP*. Suppose that the binary relation *PERSONAL RELATIONSHIP* has the property of being a one-to-one mapping between two persons. This property is then inherited by both the *MARRIAGE* and the *COHABITATION* binary relations.

Consider now the property average age of a set of persons. The property average age is an attribute not of an individual person, but of a set of persons. In this case a class *PERSON* has to be looked at as an instance which is related to another instance of the class *AVERAGE AGE*. To deal with this situation we can introduce a class that has as its instances classes. Such a class is called a *metaclass* [Levesque and Mylopoulos, 1979]. Since metaclasses are classes in themselves, they can also be placed in IS_A and PART_OF hierarchies. The top of the hierarchy can be considered as a special node called *CLASS*, which is the class of all classes.

From our discussion it should be obvious that semantic network data models can become rather complex. We can have instances, classes, and metaclasses as nodes. Assertions, instantiations, and binary relations can appear as arcs. In addition, binary relations, classes, and metaclasses are structured in IS_A and PART_OF hierarchies. The representation of the network becomes more complex when we also introduce constraints and operations within the network.

## 10.3 CONSTRAINTS

Constraints in semantic network data models are not specified separately from the structures, but are an integral part of the definition of the network. A constraint represents a fact either about a concept or about a class and is stored in the network as a fact. Most semantic network data models incorporate predicate calculus as part of the definition of the arcs between concepts and/or classes. It is, therefore, rather straightforward to introduce any meaningful constraint as a statement of the predicate calculus. Functionality of binary relations between classes can be specified using predicate calculus. For instance, the constraint "every course should be associated with at least one student" can be specified as a predicate in the predicate calculus.

Constraints in semantic network data models can be represented in many different ways. For instance, the preceding constraint also can be specified as an attendance value if *ENROLLMENT* itself became a class. In this case the attendance value should be kept above one. The same constraint can be inherited as a property of a higher-level class in an IS_A hierarchy. For instance, suppose that there is a binary relation *ATTENDANCE* between *PERSON* and *GATHERING* to which the binary relation *ENROLLMENT* is related by an IS_A relationship (i.e., *ENROLLMENT* IS_A *ATTENDANCE*). Suppose further that *ATTENDANCE* has a constraint that it has at least one *PERSON* associated with any *GATHERING*. In this case, the binary relation *ENROLLMENT* inherits this constraint from the more general binary relation *ATTENDANCE*.

The specification of constraints through inheritance rules of abstraction hierarchies is very natural. As a matter of fact, IS_A and PART_OF hierarchies are very closely related to quantification [Levesque and Mylopoulos, 1979]. The IS_A relationship expresses, in a declarative manner, the quantification that every instance of a subordinate class (e.g., *STUDENT*) has the properties of the more general class (e.g., *PERSON*). The PART_OF relationship expresses, in a declarative manner, that every instance of an aggregated class has associated with it instances of its components. In fact, both the IS_A and PART_OF binary relationships and hierarchies can be expressed as predicate calculus constraints on relations among classes.

Some types of constraints can also be expressed as properties of attributes of metaclasses. Suppose, for example, that *AVERAGE SALARY* is a class related to the metaclass *PERSON DEPARTMENT* (i.e., the class whose instances are collections of persons in departments). The constraint "the average salary in a department should not exceed $20,000" can be expressed as a property of the instances of the class *AVERAGE SALARY* related to the instances of the metaclass *PERSON DEPARTMENT*.

Constraints in semantic network data models are handled very naturally as facts in a semantic network related to other facts to which they apply. Constraints can be inherited just like any other property. In this way they can be handled in the same ways as other data in a semantic network.

## 10.4 OPERATIONS

Since structurally a semantic network data model is very similar to a binary data model, the operations can be very similar. We describe the operations for a specific semantic network data model as outlined in Sections 10.2 and 10.3, namely PSN [Levesque and Mylopoulos, 1979]. The operations in a semantic network data model decompose into operations on classes and operations on binary relations.

There are four basic operations associated with classes and their instances. The first operation creates an instance within a class. The same operation can also associate an existing instance of a class with a new class. For example, a new student can be created by introducing a new instance of the *STUDENT* class in the network, or by establishing that an existing instance of the *PERSON* class also belongs to the class *STUDENT*. The second operation destroys an instance of a class, or disassociates an instance from a class. The third operation retrieves all instances of a class. Finally, the fourth operation tests whether an instance belongs to a class.

There are also four basic operations involving binary relations. The first operation establishes a connection between two class instances. The second operation eliminates a connection between two class instances. The third operation retrieves all instances which are connected to a given instance according to a binary relation. Finally, the fourth operation tests whether a connection exists between two instances.

Operations on classes and binary relations in semantic network data model are not very different from operations in other data models. The syntax of the operations can be very similar to the operations described in Chapter 4. Although binary relations are treated as classes for the purpose of building abstraction hierarchies, this similarity does not carry over into operations. When specifying operations, concepts are treated as instances (e.g., like relational tuples or record instances) and assertions are treated as relationships (e.g., like relational joins or DBTG-set occurrences).

Unlike many other data models, operations in semantic network data models usually produce a large number of side effects as a result of the abstraction hierarchies of the network. For instance, suppose that an instance of the class *CHILD* has been declared to be related with IS_A to the class *PERSON*. Suppose further that the class *CHILD* is additionally constrained to be any person who is under 18 years old and who has a guardian. This structural information will force certain side effects as the result of some operations on the classes *CHILD* and *PERSON*. For instance, when a *CHILD* instance is created, a *PERSON* instance will be created automatically. Similarly, when a *PERSON* instance is created, a *CHILD* instance will also be created if the constraints are satisfied. This example points out that an operation for a class or binary relation can be specified in two ways. It can be invoked explicitly as an operation in the data model, or it can be invoked implicitly as a side effect of another operation because of the relationships present in the network. Side effects are not considered abnormal or undesirable as in many other data models, but are a necessary part of an operation. They, in essence, try to implement commonsense inferences that people draw automatically (e.g., that a *CHILD* is a subset of *PERSON* and so should inherit some of the properties of *PERSON*).

The operations on classes and binary relations discussed so far provide a basis for manipulating data in a semantic network data model. However, these operations are rather primitive and limited as a means of querying a network. To increase the manipulative power of these operations, we can introduce *programs* of these operations as an integral part of the description of a network. In most data models, including some semantic network data models, programs involving the allowed operations are not part of the description of the data base. The schema describes the structure and the constraints on the data base, but the programs are not described in the schema.

Programs can be considered as classes and are all instances of the metaclass *PROGRAM* [Levesque and Mylopoulos, 1979]. Invocations of programs, called *processes*, are considered instances of a particular program class. Consider, for instance, a program *ACCOUNT WITHDRAWAL* which represents a banking transaction. This program will be represented in the network as a class *ACCOUNT WITHDRAWAL*. Instances of the class will represent particular transactions of withdrawing money from an account.

Since programs are classes, they can be related using IS_A and PART_OF hierarchies. In this way inheritance rules can be specified for programs. For instance, *ACCOUNT WITHDRAWAL* may be a class which is a subordinate class of a more general *BANKING TRANSACTION* class (i.e., *ACCOUNT WITHDRAWAL* IS_A *BANKING TRANSACTION*). If the class *BANKING TRANSACTION* has the property that it is always related to the class *PERSON*, the class *ACCOUNT WITHDRAWAL* will inherit this property due to the IS_A relationship (Figure 10.4—1).

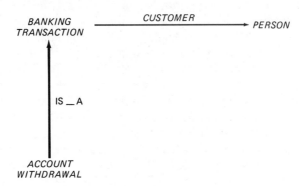

**Fig. 10.4—1** Programs and property inheritance.

Programs generally contain a prerequisite, an action, and a postrequisite part. The *prerequisite* part establishes the criterion for a valid activation of a program. The criterion can consist of checking that certain conditions are satisfied. These conditions determine whether the program should be executed. A program does not have to be invoked explicitly, but can be invoked when certain conditions are satisfied. The *action* part specifies the operations that the program is to perform. Finally, the *postrequisite* part determines whether the program ends in success or failure by checking certain specified conditions. For each case of success or failure a separate action can be performed. Programs can verify constraints as part of their prerequisites and postrequisites.

As an example, consider the processing of a bank loan application as a program. The prerequisite part can determine whether the application is a properly filled out loan application. The action part can involve a credit check and a loan rate fixing. The postrequisite part can check the availability of funds and based on this either grant or refuse the loan. Different language facilities have been proposed for the specification of such programs in a semantic network data model (e.g., TAXIS [Mylopoulos et al., 1980]).

Programs in semantic network data models are generalized procedures similar to the data base procedures discussed in Chapter 4. They are also similar to the programs in the binary data model discussed in Chapter 9, but differ from them in at least two ways. First, programs are not associated mainly with operations on objects as in binary data models. Second, programs participate in abstraction hierarchies and have inheritance properties. Programs and their properties have been studied in artificial intelligence in general, and in semantic network data models in particular, for a long time (e.g., the ACTOR facility [Hewitt, 1973]).

Semantic network data models that incorporate programs can encapsulate and model the concept of transactions in data base systems. In addition, they can relate transactions to each other and to classes. The ability to encapsulate operations on data as programs gives a data modeling capability similar to abstract data types. This feature provides a very powerful data modeling tool. At the same time this modeling power makes semantic network data models difficult to master and hard to understand.

To complete their data modeling capability, some semantic network data models introduce the notion of time. For instance, two special attributes can be associated with every class (i.e., *Insert time* and *Delete time*). In this way we can have operations which relate to time and qualifications over time. For example, we can ask for "all bank loans this year" or "old employees with high salaries" or "the age of the newest employee." Note the difference between handling time as a special attribute and as any other class. In the first case the interpretation of time is within the data model, since operations can be defined which are time relevant. In the second case the interpretation is outside the data model since operations can access time only as an attribute value and must then interpret it correctly.

## 10.5 CONCLUDING REMARKS

Semantic network data models try to represent data, categories of data, properties of categories, and operations on data within the same framework. This approach is very different from other data models. Most data models have a clear separation between data (the data base) and categories of data (the schema) and allow only operations on the data. Properties of categories, structures of categories, inheritance rules, and definition of programs are usually outside the data modeling capability of the data model. Much of the knowledge about an application is thus in the programs that operate on the data. The data model just captures the facts and some rudimentary semantic properties which can be expressed either structurally or within a small set of constraints.

Semantic network data models attempt to encode in the semantic network some of this "knowledge" in order to make the interpretation of the data easier. As a result, they have to incorporate many more data modeling tools (e.g., programs). They mix data and knowledge about the data in the semantic network. In this way the DBMS can manipulate both in a uniform way. There is no clear separation between operations on the data and operations on the schema. Both coexist in the same set of powerful data language operations.

The richness of semantic network data model structures can be used to capture semantics in many ways. The same information can be expressed in many different ways, either with identical or slightly different semantic connotations. This is the major strength (and at the same time the major weakness) of semantic network data models.

## EXERCISES

**10.1** Compare the notions of partitions as they appear in semantic network data models [Hendrix, 1975a,b, 1976] and that of context as discussed in Chapter 9 [Abrial, 1974].

**10.2** Semantic network data models define first the data and then the structures of the data. Attempt to define a relational data model starting from triplets of the form <relation, attribute, value> and giving structuring principles for the triplets.

**10.3** Semantic network data models distinguish between different categories of nodes in the semantic network. Consider the relational data model RM/T as outlined in Chapter 5. Are the RM/T categories of nodes similar to those in semantic network data models?

**10.4** Consider two semantic networks. How would you merge them to portray merging of knowledge?

**10.5** Attempt to formalize, using predicate calculus, the inheritance rules of the IS_A and PART_OF hierarchies [Mylopoulos and Wong, 1980].

**10.6** Define, formally, consistency in a semantic network.

**10.7** How can inference be introduced in semantic network data models [Gallaire and Minker, 1978]?

**10.8** Why do most data models make a clear separation between schemas and data and handle each one differently? Could the operations used for the data also be used for the schemas?

**10.9** Selection in a strongly typed data model is rather simple as outlined in Chapter 4. Selection in semantic network data models may involve a matching of a small network (frame, scenario) with a larger one [Mylopoulos et al., 1976]. How would you introduce such operations into a data language?

**10.10** Compare transactions as defined in TAXIS [Mylopoulos et al., 1980] and actors as they appear in [Hewitt, 1973].

**10.11** How would you formalize message passing between invocations of programs in semantic network data models [Mylopoulos et al., 1980]?

**10.12** How would you use the resolution principle in theorem proving to deduce facts from a semantic network data model [Gallaire and Minker, 1978]?

**10.13** Abstract data types encapsulate structures, constraints, and operations in their definition in one uniform environment. In what way are they similar to or different from semantic network data models?

**10.14** Is there a common thread among SMALLTALK objects [Goldberg and Kay, 1976], SIMULA classes [Dahl and Nygaard, 1966], actors [Hewitt, 1973], and some of the ideas in semantic network data models?

**10.15** Text traditionally is very poorly handled in data models. How can text be handled in semantic network data models [Goldstein, 1980]? How can text be handled in terms of abstract data types [Guttag and Horning, 1980]?

# Chapter 11

# INFOLOGICAL DATA MODELS

## 11.1 INTRODUCTION

One of the most important goals of data modeling is to capture the information requirements of an application in terms of structures, constraints, and operations that naturally reflect the real-world situation. That is, the information requirements should be expressed in ways that are natural to and can easily be understood by the users. The way in which most data models express information requirements often do not correspond to the way people would have naturally perceived the information represented in the data base. Their perception of the information may be shaped by the way they are forced to view it by the data model rather than the way they would view it naturally.

It can be argued that most data models employ artificial constructs for expressing information requirements. While they provide a set of general data modeling facilities which can be used to specify the information requirements, the nature of the facilities impose a certain viewpoint concerning how data should be structured, constrained, and operated on. Thus, although hopefully the schema can be understood by people, especially people trained in data modeling, there are no assurances that it will reflect the information in a natural way. This situation arises because of the need eventually to represent the data model constructs in terms of computer constructs. Most data models represent data as relations, record types, and so on, because these constructs are amenable to computerization. The emphasis on the eventual mapping to a computer representation causes data models to represent information in rather artificial and sometimes unnatural ways.

If, however, a data model is geared mainly for capturing the information requirements of an application, it is important that the data model exhibit a certain naturalness of description so that people can understand the different design alternatives and discuss them thoroughly. The role of the data model, then, is not so much to abstract the properties of a future data base, but to serve as a communication medium, a notation, for people. To meet this objective, the data model should be people oriented rather than computer oriented. It should try to represent information in ways similar to the ways in which people perceive information. It is important, therefore, to know how people, viewed as information processors, describe the real world in natural terms. It cannot be claimed that people, in their natural conversations and thought processes, understand information only as tables or graphs. In fact, the natural representation seems to be dialogue or text in natural language.

At first glance, this last observation does not appear to help at all in designing a data model since computers are still very limited in their comprehension of natural language. Consider, however, just the elementary objects of natural language which cannot be further decomposed without loss of meaning (e.g., sentences). The structure of sentences is clearly a fully general structure which can describe a data base relation or a hierarchy. It can also represent information in other ways which are meaningful and natural to people. A data model whose constructs are based on the way people perceive and communicate through sentences ensures that the structure imposed by the data model will not conflict with the natural structure as perceived by the human user.

A consequence of the emphasis on people-oriented data modeling concepts is that the mapping of an application from its real-world representation to its computer representation in a data base be composed of two separate mappings. The first mapping maps the real world into some basic human concepts that describe the application in a way natural for people. This user-oriented description is called the *infological realm* of data modeling. The second mapping maps the basic infological concepts into a corresponding computer representation called the *datalogical realm* of data modeling.

The infological realm is entirely independent of the physical attributes of the storage devices ultimately used. In fact, the final storage device might well be human, rather than computer, memory. Similarly, the datalogical realm is independent of the attributes of the real world. The data models discussed in Chapters 5 to 10 emphasized primarily the datalogical realm of data modeling. That is, although the data models dealt with user-oriented, abstract characteristics of data, they nevertheless also incorporated some computer-oriented implementation characteristics.

In this chapter we focus on the infological realm of data modeling. The concepts of the infological realm, datalogical realm, and the mapping between them were first introduced by Langefors [Langefors, 1963, 1969,

1974, 1975, 1977, 1980] and have been studied extensively in Sweden [Bubenko et al., 1971; Sundgren, 1974, 1975]. Many other researchers throughout the world have worked on data models oriented to capturing information requirements [Chen, 1976; Kahn, 1976, 1978; Teichroew and Hershey, 1977; Biller and Neuhold, 1978; Smith and Smith, 1978; Yao et al., 1978; Lindencrona-Ohlin, 1979; Lundeberg et al., 1979a,b, 1981; Bubenko, 1980]. However, the work in Sweden in general, and by Langefors and his co-researchers in particular, has been much more extensive and comprehensive, and for this reason, this chapter draws mainly from the latter work.

An infological data model is concerned, in a very formal sense, with representing the structure of data as they exist in the real world. There are other, fully general data models, which have been used for this purpose. The first, and most widely used, is natural language, such as English. The main objection to using natural language as an infological data model, besides the obvious difficulties with computer processing of natural language, is the ambiguity inherent in natural language. The early philosophers found natural language to be unsuitable for this reason, and as a result they proposed the use of formal logic, such as predicate calculus, to resolve this difficulty. However, in any representation of the real world, time is an essential ingredient and predicate calculus lacks temporal reference. The infological data model, which we will outline, treats data formally in the manner of the predicate calculus, yet also introduces time as an essential data modeling idea.

## 11.2 STRUCTURES

In the real world, there are objects, which may be entities or phenomena, about which we wish to gather information. Information about the real world involves, of necessity, percepts (i.e., our sensual experience of the real world). Each percept usually is compound, involving many interrelated facts. A fact that is atomic is called an *elementary fact*. For instance, the sentence "Nick and Maria got married yesterday and moved to California immediately" is a compound fact. It is composed of the two elementary facts "Nick and Maria got married yesterday" and "Nick and Maria moved to California yesterday."

In our representation of the real world (i.e., the infological realm of data modeling) we should be able to faithfully represent our percepts. Let us accept, as a thesis, that, in order to represent our percepts, it suffices to faithfully represent elementary facts. However, in the real world there is no representation mechanism associated with elementary facts. The only representation of them appears in the infological realm. The real world is as it is; the representation of the real world is necessary for us to understand it.

To find out how best to represent elementary facts, we can be guided by the way human beings represent them in their own environment. People describe elementary facts in their natural language in terms of an object (or a tuple of objects), a property of an object (or relationship among the objects), and a time of occurrence. In our example elementary fact "Nick and Maria got married yesterday," "Nick" and "Maria" refer to the objects, "got married" refers to a relationship between the objects, and "yesterday" refers to the time of occurrence of this elementary fact. We should therefore represent facts by structures consisting of objects, properties or relationships, and time.

An *object* in an infological data model is loosely defined as something we are interested in representing. Objects cannot be precisely defined since the interpretation of what constitutes an object is a matter of judgment (see entity-attribute Chapter 2) [Sundgren, 1975]. Each one of us looks at the world and gathers information according to our frame of reference. An object for one person may not qualify as an object for another person. The second person may not even be aware of an object's existence because it is not within his frame of reference.

The existence of an object is related to the birth, death, and change of the object. It is very hard to give guidelines for determining these basic aspects of an object's life. Objects are born when people become interested in them. They die when people stop being interested in them. They change when they are sufficiently different that people perceive them as different objects. For instance, nuclear particles existed in the real world even before physicists discovered them. However, they became objects (of interest) only when physicists knew enough about them to identify them and discuss them. On the other hand, if a new discovery shows that a certain particle does not exist in the real world, it will still be an object as long as people wish to represent it.

Objects can be atomic or compound. An *atomic object* is any object that cannot be decomposed further into other objects. *Compound objects* consist of sets of objects, tuples of objects, or constellations[1]. Applying this definition recursively we can obtain an arbitrary structure of objects and facts that can be treated as a compound object. For example, we can treat the fact "Nick and Maria got married yesterday" as an object and use this object in the definition of another fact "Bill attended their marriage."

Usually the information that people want to represent about objects is either that an object has a property or that a group of objects are related by some relationship. Again, a property cannot be defined formally except as an assertion that people may want to make about an object. In the

---

[1.] A constellation will be defined shortly. At this point it can be considered as a formal representation of a fact.

same way a relationship is an assertion that people may want to make about a set of objects.

Although properties and relationships cannot be defined precisely, we still can formulate rules by which properties and relationships can be combined to generate other properties and relationships. We present some examples to illustrate the point. The conjunction of two properties also can be a property. For instance, if "to be tall" is a property, and "to be strong" is a property, then "to be tall" and "to be strong" is a property. Properties can be combined and inherited via relationships. For example, "to be tall" and "to have a tall father" is a property obtained from a combination of properties and the "father of" relationship. As a final example, rules can be given for generating relationships from other relationships. For instance, if "to be married" is a relationship, "not to be married" is also a relationship.

If the rules for generating properties are formally defined, we can talk about fundamental properties and derived properties. A *fundamental property* cannot be generated from a set of other fundamental properties. The set of fundamental properties provides, in essence, a minimal cover of the properties of interest. From this set of fundamental properties, *derived properties* can be generated via the generation rules. In the same way we can start with a set of fundamental relationships and generate from them all the derived relationships via the formal generation rules.

In an infological data model, an object can exist independent of any property or relationship pertaining to it. However, in many data models, the existence of an object relates to a (set of) key attribute(s) which should not be null. An object in such a data model does not exist without a value for its key. For example, if employee number is the key of an employee object, then the employee does not exist unless he or she has an employee number. It is advantageous not to tie the existence of an object to a particular property or relationship. In this way all properties and relationships can change without affecting the existence of the object. It can be argued that the only properties that should be associated with the existence of an object are its time of birth and time of death (i.e., the time we become interested and the time we cease to be interested in the object).

This last observation brings us naturally to the concept of time as an important aspect of any fact[1]. Treating time formally in a data model enhances the data model's capabilities. By introducing time in an infological data model we can retain information about properties or

---

[1] Time can be thought of as a point of time or as an interval of time. For instance, the statement "he was born in 1943" makes sense in terms of yearly intervals for time. The statement "he was born on May 29, 1943" makes sense in terms of daily intervals of time. Finally, the statement "he was there before me" makes sense in terms of treating time as a point.

relationships that are no longer valid. For instance, suppose that $A$ worked for company $X$ at time $t$ but now she works for company $Y$. The statement "$A$ works for $X$" is not valid but "$A$ worked for $X$ at $t$" is perfectly valid. The reason that most other data models do not deal with time is that they are relatively closer to the datalogical realm. As such, they avoid treating time to eliminate any difficulties in the implementation of their constructs in terms of real-life computers[1].

Using the basic concepts of objects, properties, relationships, and time for structuring, we can represent facts. As we combine these basic concepts we will derive concepts present in other data models. Whenever possible we will establish the correspondence between constructs as they appear in the infological data model and as they were outlined in Chapters 1 to 10.

An elementary fact was loosely defined before as an object (or tuple of objects), a property of an object (or relationship between objects), and time. We can now formally define a representation for an elementary fact as a triple $(x, y, z)$, where $x$ is a tuple of objects $o_1, ..., o_n$, $y$ is a property of or a relationship among these objects, and $z$ is time. This basic structure for the representation of an elementary fact is called an *elementary constellation*.

The case where $x$ is an atomic object $o$ and $y$ is a property is called an *elementary constellation of property type*. This construct can represent the situation in other data models where a particular attribute takes a particular value at a particular time. For instance, consider the property "blue eyes" of a person. Establishing that a particular person has "blue eyes" at a certain time is an elementary constellation of property type. An important difference between this basic unit of information and an attribute instance in other data models is the explicit mention of time.

The case where $x$ is a tuple of objects $o_1, ..., o_n$ and $y$ is a relationship is called an *elementary constellation of relation type*. This corresponds to a relational tuple with the addition of time.

Objects can be compound consisting of sets of objects, tuples of objects, or constellations. The recursive definition of constellation allows facts to be structured in many different ways. The resulting structure can be visualized as a very complicated graph that connects many different objects, properties, and/or relationships at different times. An infological data model constellation is similar (at least visually) to a star constellation where the nodes are objects, properties, relationships, and time rather than stars, planets, and so on.

Constellations can portray situations that are hard to handle with

---

[1] One wonders why data models avoid treating time separately and not like any other attribute. This may be yet another shortcoming which is there mainly for historical reasons ready to be challenged with the freedom that new technology gives us.

conventional data models. For instance, a property associated with a relationship between objects can be handled very easily with a constellation. In most data models a relationship between atomic objects cannot have any associated properties. Only objects can have properties (attributes). For instance, if we want the relationship type *MARRIAGE* between two entity types to have an attribute, we need to view the relationship type as an entity type.

An infological data model is the epitome of a loosely typed data model. Anything of interest can be an object in the data model and any relationship or property at a certain time can be defined as a fact. There is no a priori definition of types of objects, properties, or relationships to which all facts have to conform. There is no a priori defined schema. However, types of objects can be defined, if they are needed, by appropriately grouping objects and their properties.

An *object group* $O(p)$ related to a property $p$ is defined as all objects that can potentially (regardless of time) have property $p$. For instance, consider the property "of age 35." The object group of this property is all people who have the property $p$ at any time. The people who have the property at time $t$ $(O_t(p))$ is a subset of $O(p)$ called a *time slice* of the object group. For instance, $in_{1980}$("of age 35") are those people who are 35 in the year 1980. It should be obvious that the union of all possible time slices of an object group is the object group.

The concept of an attribute is generic in most data models. That is, it is considered so basic that it cannot be formally defined. In an infological data model, an attribute is not a generic concept, but is a concept derived from the concepts of object, property, relationship, and time. It is defined as a set of properties $A = \{p_i\}$ for an object group $O(p)$ such that at any time $t$, each object $x$ in $O_t(p)$ is contained in at least one $O_t(p_i)$ for some $p_i$. The properties $p_i$ are the values of the attribute $A$ of the object group $O(p)$.

Consider as an example the object group $O(p)$ of people that is defined by the property $p$ "being employed." Suppose that we define an employee as someone who has the property $(p_i = $"working for company $i$"$)$. Consider an object $x$ that is a member of $O_t(p)$ at time $t$ (i.e., a person employed at time $t$). The person $x$ will also necessarily belong to some, at least one, $O_t(p_i)$ (i.e., the person $x$ will be working for at least one company at time $t$). The property "working for company $i$" give us the values of the attribute *Employer*. The attribute *Employer* is defined as the set of properties $p_i = $"working for company $i$." The definition of attribute allows multiple values (i.e., a repeating group). A single-valued attribute can be defined by requiring that $x$ belong to exactly one $O_t(p_i)$. Hence, it has only one value $p_i$ at any point of time $t$.

We can now define types which are similar to the data types present in other data models. To arrive at these definitions we abstract out the concept of time.

An object group $O$, whose objects can potentially have a given property $p$ at different times, and an attribute $A$ define a pair $(O, A)$ called an *attribute elementary constellation type*. An attribute elementary constellation type corresponds to an attribute in more traditional data models. The properties $p_i$ that define $A$ are the values of $A$ that an object in $O$ can possibly take at any time (i.e., the domain of $A$). At any time $t$ the set of objects $O$ and their values correspond to the extension of the attribute $A$ in more traditional data models (e.g., a column in a table data model). An instance of an elementary constellation of property type $(o, p, t)$ corresponds to an attribute elementary constellation type $(O, A)$ if $o \in O$ and $p \in A$.

A tuple of object groups $(O_1, ..., O_n)$ and an $n$-ary object relationship $R$ define a pair $((O_1, ..., O_n), R)$ called a *relational elementary constellation type*. A relational elementary constellation type corresponds to the definition of a relation in a relational data model. An instance of an elementary constellation of relation type $((o_1, ..., o_n), r, t)$ corresponds to a relational elementary constellation type $((O_1, ..., O_n), R)$ if $o_1 \in O_1, ..., o_n \in O_n$ and $r = R$.

Using these definitions we can make the usual distinction between types and instances of data. There are, however, some important differences between these concepts as defined in an infological data model and in other data models. First, the concepts of attribute, relationship type, and so on, are not generic in an infological data model, but are defined in terms of more basic concepts. Second, the types are not given first, but can be constructed from relevant instances (i.e., the data model is loosely typed). Third, there is a concept of time explicitly defined in an infological data model. Finally, an infological data model makes a clear distinction between an object and a reference to that object. We will elaborate on this last point.

In most data models an object is identified by a property (e.g., the value of a key). Earlier in this section, we argued against identifying an object in this way. Subsequently, in all our discussion of objects, properties, relationships, and time we dealt with them directly. However, to represent them, we need references (i.e., names) by which we can refer to them. Our subsequent discussion will be mainly in terms of objects, but the same arguments can be made for properties, relationships, and time (collectively referred to as infological items).

A reference can be explicit, referring directly to an object, or it can be implicit, referring indirectly to an object through other objects. For instance, "Mary" is an explicit reference to an object, whereas "George's wife" is an implicit reference. A reference can be unique if it refers to a single object. Alternatively, a reference can be ambiguous if its target is more than one object (e.g., an object group). For instance, "Mary" may be an ambiguous reference if there are many people with that name within the context in which this reference is used. A reference can be typed according to the kind of infological item to which it refers. For instance, object, property, relation, and time references reference objects, properties, relations, and time, respectively.

The concept of a reference to an infological item is different from the actual infological item to which it refers and different also from whatever real-world object the infological item represents. It makes a difference, for instance, if we pass to somebody an object or a reference to the object. The same reference can lead to different infological items, depending on the context of the reference. For instance, the name *MARRIED* can refer to a property of an object or a relationship between two objects. At the same time the same infological item can be referred to with more than one reference. For instance, "Mary" and "George's wife" may refer to the same object. This distinction of a reference to an object versus the actual object has been present in programming languages for a long time (e.g., call by reference versus call by value).

Traditional data models avoid the separation of objects and references to objects in several ways. First of all, they place every object within a certain type (e.g., an entity type). Properties of the entity type are defined by its attribute values. An entity itself is identified by a conjunction of properties (i.e., a key). Relationships between entities are only permitted according to the relationship types defined in a schema. Each relationship instance is identified by the entities that participate in it. Finally, all attributes, entity types, and relationship types are uniquely named in a schema. Under these conditions there is almost no need for distinguishing objects from object names. We say almost because there are problems.

One problem is that occasionally we need to have temporal names for references to objects. Many data models solve this problem by using currency indicators. A currency indicator and its value serve as a temporal reference to an object. Another far more serious problem arises when there is a need for a change in the identifying property of an object. Consider, for instance, names as unique identifiers for persons. Suppose that someone wants to change her name from "Smith" to "Jones." Many data models will insist that a new object be created with name "Jones" and subsequently the object "Smith" should be deleted. However, the information that Jones is in fact Smith will no longer be in the data base. To circumvent these problems we introduce artificial properties as unique identifiers (e.g., social security number). Although these artificial properties serve as references for identifying objects, they are limited in many ways. They behave like global variables and thus do not have any concept of context. As a result, they do not offer a flexible environment in which to refer to objects by using many references to the same object, or in which to bind a reference to different objects at different times.

References to infological items can be used to represent constellations rather than the infological items themselves. This representation of a constellation is referred to as a message. A (*complete*) *elementary message* is a triple $(x, y, z)$, where $x$ is a tuple of unique object references, $y$ is a unique property or relationship reference, and $z$ is a time reference. An elementary message refers to a unique elementary constellation of either property type or relation type. An elementary message is considered incomplete if one of its references is not unique (i.e., the object reference of the message refers to more than one object). An incomplete message can be regarded as a query. For example, (*PERSONS, p, t*) can be regarded as the query "What persons have property referred to by $p$ at a time referred to by $t$?" Similar messages can be grouped into types in the same way that constellations were grouped into types. For instance, an *attribute message type* is a pair $(x, y)$, where $x$ is an object group reference and $y$ is an attribute reference. One should note the difference between a constellation type and a message type. In the first case we deal with the objects themselves, in the second case with references to the objects[1].

One immediate (and common) objection to the concept of an elementary message is that people rarely employ messages which are atomic. It is an unfortunate fact that human beings often describe the real world with obviously compound messages. To allow nonatomic messages, the concept of a pseudo-elementary message is introduced. A *pseudo-elementary message* is considered by the user to be atomic, but in fact may be divisible into many elementary messages. The system breaks the compound messages into their component elementary messages. However, this process of breaking compound messages into elementary messages can create interpretation problems unless there is a unique way to break them into elementary messages [Sundgren, 1975].

We now turn to the mapping of the infological realm to the datalogical realm. The infological realm is a conceptual, nonphysical description of the real world. We can naturally view elementary messages as data, but we must first physically represent them. This is the function of the mapping onto the datalogical realm.

An elementary message in the infological realm is represented by an *elementary record* in the datalogical realm. A collection of elementary records of the same type forms an *elementary file*. An elementary file can also be considered as the physical realization of an elementary message type. Elementary records can be amalgamated to form *compound records*.

---

[1] As an analogy to the representation of the real world by messages employing references rather than constellations employing the actual infological items, we can say that the real world is like the stars in the sky. The stars are there, but our understanding of them is limited by what we see. We visualize them as constellations (sic!) and represent them by charts using names that refer to things within them.

Compound records are physical realizations of compound messages. This notation is used for any mapping onto a physical realization. One aesthetic constraint on the mapping is that elementary records closely resemble the structure of elementary messages, as well as satisfying the restriction of the system architecture involved. The mapping is itself defined in terms of elementary messages, which are in this case represented by *meta-elementary records*. In this way the mapping from the infological realm to the datalogical realm can be represented by the description capabilities of an infological data model.

Sundgren has expanded on the datalogical realm described by Langefors. Sundgren discusses the possibility of allowing the data base to have inferencing power by deduction. This allows the concept of *virtual elementary records*, which are deducible by the system although not physically stored. He calls the set of physically present messages the *nucleus* [Sundgren, 1975]. From the nucleus messages can be deduced which are not represented. Sometimes these deducible messages are stored redundantly in the nucleus. Those deducible messages which are not stored in the nucleus are called *virtual messages*. There are also *unknown messages*, which are messages that can be meaningful, but represent facts not yet stated. Finally, there are *forgotten messages*, which are not present now in the nucleus, but had been there previously.

We can relate this representation for the datalogical realm with the data models discussed in Part 2. For instance, in a relational data model the nucleus corresponds to the current tuples of the defined relations. Virtual messages correspond to the tuples in the derived relations using, for instance, the relational algebra. Any unknown messages are not considered, or rather they are considered as false. Finally, forgotten messages do not exist since the data base retains only the most current tuples. Although a relational data model retains only certain parts of the data retained by an infological data model, some of the other data may actually exist as part of the checkpoints and journals of the system. However, as such they are not part of the data base and hence not formally represented by the data model.

## 11.3 CONSTRAINTS

An infological data model allows the representation of syntactic constraints. A syntactic constraint defines the set of constellations that potentially can be valid. All elementary messages that can possibly be specified correspond to these valid constellations. The set of syntactic constraints enables us to limit messages to have some desired properties or to conform to a type. This is important because the data model itself is not strongly typed. If we need types of infological items, we need to specify that by limiting the allowable messages. For instance, consider an input message to the system which says that a patient in a hospital has four wheels. The property of having four wheels is not a possibly valid property for a patient. In an infological data model we can specify syntactic constraints that eliminate this type of message.

Among all the possible messages that correspond to valid constellations, some of the messages are specified as being true. These true messages in turn specify true constellations. However, the mapping from messages to constellations is not straightforward, but depends on context. A message has to be de-referenced and associated with the proper, valid constellation before we have any increment of knowledge in the data base. This point is very critical for an infological data model. Namely, no piece of information means anything unless it is specified within a certain context. This requirement tries to mirror people's behavior. People can only understand something if it is specified within a particular (and alas sometimes very complicated) context. The concept of context greatly complicates the specification of constraints. A message can map into more than one constellation, depending on the context. In this way a message can be true in one context and false in another.

In most data models there is a notion of consistency. It is assumed that a fact and its negation should not be allowed to be specified within the data base. It is also assumed that if a fact is not specified, it should be considered false. This notion is called the closed-world assumption [Reiter, 1978]. Under this assumption, constraints attempt to delineate general categories of facts which are false and should not be allowed to be specified. For instance, the constraint "nobody should make more money than their manager" specifies a general category of facts which are not allowed (i.e., employees with higher salaries than their managers). In addition, sometimes the constraints try to enforce some consistency checks on what can be specified. The constraint "one cannot be married and single" specifies a certain consistency requirement stemming from the knowledge that married is equivalent to not single.

On the other hand, in an infological data model constraints divide facts into three categories: true, meaningful, and false. This flexibility in constraint specification introduces many complications. Because time is associated with every constellation, two constellations that negate each other can still be specified, provided that the times are different. For instance, Nick can be single today and married tomorrow and both facts can coexist in the data base. Since each message is specified with respect to a context, for two different contexts the same message can be mapped to different constellations. For instance, Nick can be considered married in the context of a civil wedding, but single in the context of a religious wedding. Again, both facts can be specified in an infological data model. In addition, the concept of infological distance between messages allows a user to specify messages that are not true, but are "close" to being true.

To explain the difference between regular data model constraints and those in an infological data model, we use as an analogy the difference between opinion and truth. In most data models, any message has a universal truth or falsehood. Only true messages are allowed in the data base. In addition, if a message is not stored, it is false. All the checks on messages are made at the time the message is input. If this approach sounds very dogmatic, it is and is perhaps one of the reasons for the difficulty in specifying constraints (i.e., the checks on true messages). On the other hand, in an infological data model any message can be stated, provided that it potentially can be valid. A message thus corresponds to an opinion. However, this opinion can only be understood in a certain context. Hence it may always be true given the right context. A message, even if it proves to be wrong eventually, can still be stated as an opinion.

An infological data model allows a user to specify one or more *filters* which enforce constraints during the interpretation of the constellations. In this way, information can be interpreted within a context and the user can be protected by the filters from seeing inconsistent or untrue information. This is a very different approach to constraint handling than in most other data models. In other data models, constraints are supposed to prevent the user from entering wrong or inconsistent information. In an infological data model wrong or inconsistent information can still be allowed and mapped as a valid constellation within a context. The user can be protected from some of this wrong or inconsistent information by the filters he or she defines for the interpretations.

In an infological data model, the data base filters are used as an all-purpose facility for enforcing constraints. Any sort of constraint can be enforced by simply specifying a new data base filter. For example, the data base filters can be used to implement security and privacy constraints. They are even supposed to regenerate the data base and cleanse it during idle times. Although an infological data model defines the concept of a data base filter, it does not specify its ultimate form in an implementation. This is consistent with the stated view of an infological data model that minimal specifications allow the implementor to make design decisions for performance reasons.

## 11.4 OPERATIONS

The most basic operation in an infological data model is the ability to enter a new elementary message. This operation requires that there be a mechanism for interpreting an elementary message as an elementary constellation and mapping it into an elementary record. The general framework of the data model allows all update, insert, and delete operations to be specified as new elementary messages. An insert is, by definition, the addition of a message which adds an elementary record to the nucleus. A delete operation is the addition of a message which specifies that the appropriate record is deleted. Finally, an update operation is the addition of a message which specifies that the appropriate record is changed.

Consider as an example the elementary message "Nick is married to Maria on Saturday." This message can be considered as an addition (insertion) of a fact. If the system currently knows that Nick is single, it can be considered as a deletion of the message "Nick is single." On the other hand, if the system currently knows that Nick is married to Vivian, it can be considered as an update of the message "Nick is married to Vivian."

Query operations can be specified as incomplete messages. For instance, "people working on project $A$ in June" has a unique time reference and a unique property reference, but an ambiguous object reference. This message represents in essence the query "Who was working on project $A$ in June?"

A more appropriate data language can be specified for the infological data model [Sundgren, 1975]. The queries take a simple form called $\alpha\beta$ queries. Certain attributes called the $\alpha$ attributes are specified with search values for the properties. Other attributes, called the $\beta$ attributes, are sought. For instance, consider the query "List names and addresses of people who are married and have salary greater than $30,000." The $\alpha$ attributes are "marital status" and "salary" with specified values "married" and "greater than $30,000." The $\beta$ attributes are "names" and "addresses." The specification of $\alpha\beta$ queries is, in fact, very similar to many other high-level data languages that express selection according to contents and request values of associated attributes.

More general queries which do not conform to the pattern of $\alpha\beta$ queries are called $\alpha\beta\gamma$ queries. These queries can be broken down using some well defined rules given by a theory of hierarchical query decomposition called box theory [Sundgren, 1975]. For instance, the query "list names and telephone numbers of people by department" is an $\alpha\beta\gamma$ query. It can be decomposed into a series of $\alpha\beta$ queries, one for each department.

In order to have an inferencing capability, there must be a means to represent things which are dynamic. This capability is provided by an *elementary process*. An elementary process provides the capability of creating new elementary messages from given elementary messages. An elementary process is defined by a set of preconditions and a set of actions. If the elementary messages representing the preconditions are found, elementary messages representing the actions are added to the data base. The specification of elementary processes is a very powerful tool because it can specify data base procedures. For instance, the age of a person can be calculated from their birthdate by an elementary process. This represents an implementation of a virtual message or a virtual attribute as defined in Chapter 4.

In addition to the elementary processes, there are implied operations performed on the data which are triggered automatically as a result of specified properties or relationships. Messages, for instance, can be related by a precedence relation. That is, in some cases, the existence of one elementary message presupposes the existence of some others. Consider as an example a message $e_1$ which entails another message $e_2$. This implies that if $e_1$ becomes present, $e_2$ would become present. For instance, if $e_1$ is a message that informs us that "John is a manager this year," this message implies the message $e_2$, "John is an employee this year."

## 11.5 CONCLUDING REMARKS

An infological data model has as its goal the capture and representation of information in a way that is most natural for people to understand. It draws heavily from analogies with natural language, but stops short of allowing it. It can be considered a very terse version of natural language which states just the facts in a clear way.

In terms of structures, an infological data model allows the specification of any simple fact. The elementary concepts used to represent a fact can be combined to give more strict types of objects similar to those in strictly typed data models (e.g., attributes, relations, etc.). The data model separates reference to an object from the object itself and introduces the concept of context for the interpretation of a message. Using this framework, very general structures of data can be constructed which can be referenced and interpreted in many different ways. Finally, it introduces the concept of time explicitly everywhere in the data model.

In terms of constraints an infological data model allows the specification of many different constraints. It has some very general mechanisms, such as the elementary process, which can generate any side effect, and the data base filter, which can enforce any constraint in a user view. It also views integrity as a property relevant for all operations, not associated only with insertion and update. At idle time or as the result of an operation, data base filters and elementary processes which try to clean the data base can be triggered. Finally, integrity of the data base is defined according to a context. This capability enables someone to have a personal set of constraints which are enforced for their view, but are not applicable to the overall view of the data base.

All operations in the data model can be specified as elementary messages and elementary processes. The basic operations can be combined into more general query facilities. The elementary processes provide the ability to specify data base procedures. Finally, the data model allows the manipulation of meta-information. That is, operations can be issued on messages which describe the schema. Using these operations the schema can be modified.

The infological data model is extremely general. It incorporates many ideas that have been proposed independently in other data models. Although the data model is specified in detail, the exact implementation is left to the implementor. Langefors concluded that the closest data model to an infological data model is a relational data model [Langefors, 1980]. In particular, a relational data model can be viewed as a special case of an infological data model. Although this opinion is valid, we feel that an infological data model is closer to other semantic-oriented data models. For instance, it is very close to both the semantic binary data model and semantic network data models discussed in Chapters 9 and 10.

## EXERCISES

**11.1** Consider the different data modeling realms in the DIAM data model [Senko, 1975, 1976] and the ANSI/X3/SPARC framework [Tsichritzis and Klug, 1978]. How do these realms correspond to the infological and datalogical realms?

**11.2** Why is the concept of time abstracted out of most data models? Would a feature such as Petri nets be helpful for handling time in data modeling?

**11.3** Most data models do not handle time in any special way. They allow attributes to take time values, but these attributes are treated in a similar manner as other attributes. Discuss the merits of handling time this way and the disadvantages if any. What additional capabilities does a data model with a separate time construct give you?

**11.4** Most DBMSs incorporate a time-stamping mechanism which is very useful for synchronization, locking, backout, recovery, and so on. How is a time-stamping mechanism related to the introduction of time in a data model?

**11.5** Outline a set of generating rules $G_p$ for specifying properties of objects. Consider a set of properties $P$. Outline an algorithm which given $P$ produces a nonredundant cover for $P$. How would you define a notion of completeness for the rules $G_p$? Is your set of rules $G_p$ complete under your definition?

**11.6** An attribute can be considered as a set of related properties. In this way we can derive the concept of attribute from the concept of property. Given the concept of attribute as we have seen it in many data models, do you still need a concept of property? Justify your answer.

**11.7** Outline a set of generating rules $G_r$ for specifying relationships between objects. Consider a set of relationships $R$. Outline an algorithm which given $R$ produces a nonredundant cover for $R$. Is your cover necessarily minimal? Are your set of generating rules in any way related to the relational algebra? Can you define a concept of completeness for your generating rules?

**11.8** In an infological data model there is an explicit concept of reference. In some data models an object's name is defined as the value of its primary key. In other data models there is a concept of external key (e.g., a data base key). Discuss the relative merits of each approach. Draw parallels between this situation and global variables in programming languages. Can you establish a case against unique global identifiers as in [Wulf and Shaw, 1973]?

**11.9** Take a letter and try to identify the elementary messages associated with it. Do the same for a telegram. Did you find any difficulties or ambiguities in the specification of the messages?

**11.10** Show that a collection of elementary messages can generate all information structures.

**11.11** Consider $\alpha\beta\gamma$ queries as described by Sundgren. The $\alpha\beta\gamma$ queries can be decomposed into $\alpha\beta$ queries using the box theory [Sundgren, 1975]. Can you establish a parallel between this operation and decomposition of relational queries [Wong and Youssefi, 1976; Youssefi, 1978; Chiu, 1979]?

# Part 4

# USING DATA MODELS

A data model is only as good as it is useful to people in thinking about, organizing, and using data. In Parts 1, 2, and 3, we examined data models in terms of their properties. These properties allow us to think about, organize, and use data in different ways. That is, they provide us with the tools for modeling data. As in most situations, the problem at hand determines the tools required to attack it. Since different data models provide us with different data modeling tools, their usefulness depends on the problem to which they are applied. In Part 4, we examine three aspects of data modeling — schema design, schema analysis and DBMS mappings — and the specific properties of data models that are required to handle each aspect.

# Chapter 12

# SCHEMA DESIGN

## 12.1 DATA MODEL EVALUATION AND SELECTION

In data modeling, there are usually many levels and viewpoints of data and information that we would like to represent. For example, we can look at data modeling from the user's viewpoint or from the computer system's viewpoint. In the first case, we specify the information needs of the users. Intuitive approaches to data modeling which enhance understanding are very important. In the second case we design systems that achieve the information requirements. Formal and rigorous approaches to data modeling are important so that the information requirements can be translated eventually into computer-oriented programs and data structures.

Different names have been used to differentiate between these two data modeling levels. We will use the names *infological* and *datalogical* realm as discussed in Chapter 11 [Langefors, 1974, 1977; Sundgren, 1974, 1975, 1978]. There are other proposals which distinguish levels of data description and data base schemas. For instance, in both the ANSI/X3/SPARC and the DDLC framework, three levels are perceived, which, following ANSI/X3/SPARC terminology, are the external, conceptual, and internal levels [CODASYL, 1978; Tsichritzis and Klug, 1978].

Depending on the data modeling realm, there is a clear distinction as to the purpose of the schema specified according to a data model. It can be only for the purpose of design to aid human understanding (i.e., it belongs to the infological realm). Alternatively, it can be geared mainly for computer processing (i.e., it belongs to the datalogical realm). We will call an *enterprise description* a description of information requirements which is used mainly for infological purposes. It is not tied to a DBMS except through human intervention. A *data base description*, on the other hand, is for datalogical purposes and is accessible to and used by a DBMS.

People used to hold the opinion that perhaps there was one data model (a super data model) that, if we found it, would solve all our data modeling problems. Thus, there has been a good deal of controversy about what is a "good" or what is the "best" data model. Some of the debate has concerned the relative advantages of relational and network data models [Rustin, 1974]. This debate is similar to stating and arguing the relative merits of programming languages [Dijkstra, 1965]. It is very difficult to argue persuasively that one data model is best uniformly. Each data model has advantages, depending on who is doing the schema design and the realm in which one is working. This is also true in other fields of science. For instance, although Einstein's theory is more universal, Newton's theory is still adequate to design and build bridges.

Similarly, in data modeling, because of the different orientation of the infological and datalogical realms, it should be clear that the same data model will not necessarily be useful for both realms. In one case, the objects and their properties are used to represent information that is oriented for use by people. In the other case, they are used to represent data that are oriented for computer processing. Some data models have been conceived for, and are clearly intended to be used at, a particular level. For a given situation one may want one data model for the infological realm and one or more different data models for the datalogical realm. With today's technology it is perhaps realistic to have two data models, one for the infological realm and one for the datalogical realm. These choices are not totally independent since one data model (infological) will have to be mapped to the other (datalogical) [Senko, 1976; Langefors, 1977].

Although many different data models have been discussed in previous chapters, the choice one has from among commercial systems is somewhat limited. Basically, only three data models — hierarchical, network, and relational — are available in commercial systems. One might think that this would make the selection of a data model easier. It is true that for the datalogical realm our choices are restricted to the three commercially available approaches. For the infological realm, however, we are practically free to choose from among all available data models. How, then, do we select appropriate data models for each realm?

For the infological realm, people use data models to abstract and understand concepts about data and information. Thus, a data model is useful in this realm when people use it to develop insights that they could not develop without the data model. In addition, we want the data model to be able to capture all the semantics of the data. The data model is used here mainly to document the information requirements and to provide a means of communicating these requirements to users and implementors. Since the data model does not need to be implemented on a computer, it can provide very flexible data modeling capabilities.

For the datalogical realm, we want to put the right facilities with the right users and environment. We do not want to give users a data model they find difficult to understand or a data language that is difficult to use. Therefore, to select a data model for this realm, we should go back to the people using the data model and ask them how they like it. Unfortunately, there is no great population of users with experience in different data models, and extensive experiments have not been performed.

Often the choice of a data model for the datalogical realm is predicated on DBMS success. Thus, it is often the case that users choose a DBMS rather than a data model. However, a good data model does not necessarily imply a successful DBMS based on it. Although a DBMS's evaluation can be based on success [Datamation, 1980], one cannot extrapolate from this that the system's success is related primarily to its inherent data model. The data model comes along as part of the DBMS and users are stuck with it whether they like it or not. When one chooses a DBMS one usually makes a life-long commitment. It is very hard to change to another DBMS (i.e., data model). If change is to come, it will probably have to be evolutionary rather than revolutionary. This evolution may be accomplished when DBMSs evolve to permit multiple data model interfaces.

If system success cannot be used as the measure of a data model's inherent quality, we should look in other directions. Some research has been done on evaluating different DBMSs and their related facilities such as data model and data language [Gould and Ascher, 1975; Reisner et al., 1975; Thomas and Gould, 1975; Reisner, 1977, 1981; Lochovsky, 1978; Shneiderman, 1978; Welty and Stemple, 1981]. This research concerns human factors studies of DBMSs and DBMS facilities. The thrust of the research is to provide some objective criteria for evaluating and selecting between different DBMS facilities. Since the choice of a data model at the datalogical level greatly affects the usefulness of the schema design for the users, we will summarize some of the results of this research.

One of the major issues in selecting a data model involves its complexity or conversely its simplicity. It is felt that the less complex a data model is, the easier it is for people to understand and use it properly. For example, the simplicity argument is cited extensively by proponents of relational data models as an advantage of relational data models over hierarchical and network data models [Codd and Date, 1974].

We can distinguish two kinds of data model complexity: structure complexity and constraint complexity. In both cases relational data models are less complex than hierarchical or network data models.

However, the lack of complexity may be a disadvantage as there are no mechanisms to guide the user in interpretation of the data. Both hierarchical and network data models provide structural complexity in terms of links. Studies have found that these links, when expressed pictorially, allow users to remember the structures and relationships of a schema [Kuhn and Shneiderman, 1978]. Lack of structural complexity in relational data models appears to result in a reduced ability to recall the relationships among the data.

Constraint complexity also appears to guide the user in interpreting the semantics of the data base. As an example, lack of constraints in relational data models allows meaningless relationships (joins) to be formed. Severe inherent constraints, such as in hierarchical data models, limit the data modeling capability and may force unnatural organizations of data. Explicit constraints appear to be desirable, as they provide more flexibility in constraint specification than inherent constraints.

Another issue in selecting a data model concerns matching the structure of the data to the data modeling capabilities of the data model. For example, if the data are naturally hierarchical, a hierarchical data model may be the best choice for the application [Brosey and Shneiderman, 1978]. Such a matching may also be desirable to minimize retraining of users and to accommodate current data collection and entry. If users are already familiar with a data organization, their hostility (inertia) to change may be reduced by selecting an appropriate data model. Reorganization of data collection and entry facilities to accommodate a new data model may not be trivial.

Although the current data organization may indicate a certain data model, the operations performed on the data may not be totally compatible with the indicated choice. For example, one study found that a hierarchical data model naturally leads to navigation up and down data base trees. However, when users are required to navigate across data base trees, they encounter difficulty in expressing their navigation [Lochovsky, 1978].

The ability to partition the data into subschemas or views may be an important consideration. In addition, the ability eventually to provide very different views of the data may be desired. Thus the mappability of the data model into other data models may be important[1]. This requirement is in line with our earlier stated belief that change to data models will be evolutionary rather than revolutionary. The ability to evolve into an ANSI/X3/SPARC framework may be important.

Finally, the terminology used in a data model can affect the associations that users make between the data model concepts and already familiar concepts. Bad terminology can lead to incorrect use of the data

---

[1]. Mappings between data models are discussed in Chapter 14.

model concepts. The syntactic/semantic relationship of the data model should be clear and not open to several interpretations. One study found that users can effectively use the major types of data structures (e.g., lists) provided that the associations are consistent with preexisting semantic information [Durding et al., 1977].

The choice of a data model can be greatly influenced by the data language available with the data model. Data languages have traditionally been navigational. This resulted from the need to interface with record-at-a-time-oriented host programming languages. However, specification data languages are now available with some DBMSs and the trend seems to be in this direction.

Navigation data languages allow a lot of flexibility in specifying how data are to be retrieved. This flexibility may be undesirable for novice users, but more experienced users may require it. Specification data languages may be easier to use for novice users, but they may be harder to debug since a lot of information is packed into one or two statements [Lochovsky, 1978]. From work done so far the indication seems to be that a range of data languages is required for different types of users. Perhaps one data language with several levels in which the users are able to go back and forth between levels as needs change is the desired goal [Reisner, 1977].

The characteristics of the interface provided to users is an important issue. We can examine this interface in terms of how requests are formed by the user and presented to the system, how replies are presented to the user, and the dynamics of the interactions between the user and the system. Different interfaces, such as keyword, menu selection, fill-in-the-blank, and parametric interfaces, have different characteristics. The characteristics of the interface should be tailored to the type of users and the tasks they are performing [Lochovsky and Tsichritzis, 1981].

An interesting data language issue is that of natural language versus artificial languages. It has long been argued that if we could only provide natural language interfaces, the services of a DBMS could be made readily available to everyone. The main stumbling block so far has been the tremendous amount of software required to extract the exact meaning out of natural language queries. Some tentative steps in this direction have been taken [Codd, 1974; Codd et al., 1978]. However, these systems require a substantial amount of clarification dialogue and there is no guarantee that the system will ever get the query exactly right.

Studies have shown that natural language is perhaps not the best data language [Hill, 1972; Montgomery, 1972; Shneiderman, 1978]. It appears that natural language users sometimes make unreasonable requests from a data base. Natural language seems to allow too much freedom in query formulation. Artificial languages tend to guide users in the process of question asking and result in fewer unanswerable queries [Shneiderman, 1978].

Based on the issues discussed in this section, appropriate data models can be chosen for each data modeling realm. After we select some data model(s) we are ready to proceed with the schema design. In subsequent sections, schema design is discussed in terms of a stepwise, iterative process of specification and refinement [Sundgren, 1978; Tsichritzis and Lochovsky, 1978; Lum et al., 1979; Teorey and Fry, 1980]. The first two steps comprise the infological realm of schema design. The first and most important step is to determine the information requirements for the different areas of the organization involved in the schema design. In the second step, these requirements are expressed as an enterprise description. The next two steps comprise the datalogical realm of schema design. The third step is to obtain a data base description which more rigorously defines the data base structures and constraints, and satisfies the information requirements. The fourth step is to check the schema for performance requirements of the prospective users.

The data are modeled initially and administered thereafter by people in certain roles [Weldon, 1981]. The ANSI/X3/SPARC report makes a distinction between the enterprise administrator, the data base administrator, and the application administrator [Tsichritzis and Klug, 1978]. The *enterprise administrator* specifies the enterprise description (conceptual schema). The *data base administrator* is concerned with specifying the physical aspects of the data base description (internal schema). Finally, the *application administrators* provide the multiple views (external schemas) for the various application areas within an organization.

These positions are *roles* as opposed to *individuals.* The same individual may function in different roles and one role may involve several individuals simultaneously. In addition, the functions of the different administrators may be combined in some organizations.

Each administrator is responsible for providing a particular view of the necessary data, the relevant relationships among the data, the rules and controls pertinent to their use, and the mappings between this view and other views. Each administrator role uses tools and techniques as provided by data models for the successful description and operation of the data base [Chen and Yao, 1977; Fry and Teorey, 1978]. In the rest of this chapter, we concentrate on the use of data modeling tools for the abstraction and representation of the data of an organization.

## 12.2 REQUIREMENTS ANALYSIS

The requirements analysis step consists of a high-level analysis of the operation of an organization. Its purpose is to:

1. Gain familiarity with the area of the organization to be modeled.
2. Determine the information requirements of the organization without regard to constraints other than the way in which the organization does business.
3. Represent these requirements via some formal modeling technique.

To gain familiarity with the organizational area(s), one tries to understand the organization in terms of its goals and the strategies it uses to achieve these goals. To determine the information requirements, one collects metadata about the data and processes in the organization. These metadata provide much of the input to the other steps in the schema design process. Finally, one uses data modeling techniques to represent the information requirements formally.

Requirements analysis is effected by studying the documents of the organization and by a series of interviews within the different areas of the organization involved in the schema design. By asking appropriate questions, the information requirements of each area and an outline of the organization's overall information requirements are ascertained. This process is iterative. Normally, several interviews will be required within each area to clarify the needs and to resolve seemingly conflicting or contradictory requirements. As well, it is necessary to obtain the users' approval of the results of the requirements analysis.

Information requirements are collected from users at all levels in the organization [Lucas, 1981]. In most organizations one can identify at least three levels of the organization that provide metadata: top management, middle management, and operations management. The type of metadata obtained and the techniques used to obtain it differ among these three levels. Interviews are used at each level to clarify written documents and to obtain information requirements that are not explicitly documented.

From top management one obtains information on the goals and objectives of the organization, strategies and methods for managing the implementation of the strategies, probable changes in the organization's operations, and current as well as future changes in the operating policies of the organization. Middle management provides information for the refinement of the scope of the analysis effort. It provides more detailed policies and constraints, distinguishes between control and business operations, and provides data about required response times, reliability, security, and privacy. Finally, operations management provide more specific information, such as names, sizes, number of occurrences, integrity constraints, reliability, security and privacy of data. They also provide information on data usage, volume, frequency of occurrence of transactions, priority of transactions, sequencing with other transactions, and performance constraints [Lum et al., 1979].

Communication with and feedback from the users are crucial to the success of the requirements analysis step. Appropriate models for representing information requirements and flows must be chosen carefully so that the user can understand them and comment on them [Taggart and Tharp, 1977]. For representing information flows, models, such as data flow diagrams, can be used [DeMarco, 1979; Gane and Sarson, 1979]. For representing information requirements, which is our main concern here, any of the data models discussed in previous chapters can be used; however, some may be better than others depending on the intended audience.

It is rather difficult to arrive directly at a completely formal representation of the information requirements. Moreover, feedback from the users implies understanding of the description of the information requirements by unsophisticated users. The description cannot, therefore, be initially in terms of a very complicated and difficult-to-understand data model. It is important to have a data model in mind, however, while representing the information requirements. This will help focus the discussion and point to specific questions that should be asked. In addition, it will make later representation in a formal data model easier. It is not important that the data model used correspond directly to the data model available in a DBMS. The main purpose of this step is to understand the user's needs. Subsequent steps of the schema design process can transform these needs to schemas according to a data model.

One approach to requirements analysis produces as an outcome of this step a business model [Arlow, 1980; Melli, 1980; Walker, 1981]. A *business model* details *how* the organization operates and *what* is required to support the operation. The how and what aspects of an organization can be represented in terms of the functions of the organization and the data classes that support these functions. In addition, a matrix showing which functions use which data classes can be produced.

A *function* in an organization is an essential activity or decision required to manage the resources and operations of the organization (i.e., a process or procedure). Functions in an organization are identified by:

1. Examining statements of purpose of a task or an organizational area.
2. Examining work programs in an organizational area.
3. Identifying products or services provided by an organizational area and determining what functions are needed to produce such products or services.

Examples of functions within an organization might be activities such as marketing, production, and accounting. The functions of an organization define the activities that the organization performs to meet its goals.

A *data class* in an organization is an aggregation of data (attributes) that is required by a function or is produced by it. Data classes in an organization are identified by examining the data required or produced by a function. Examples of data classes in an organization might be data about sales, inventory, and customers.

To illustrate this and subsequent steps in the schema design process, we will examine the operation of an insurance company [Tsichritzis and Lochovsky, 1978]. Such an organization is quite complex, consisting of many departments concerned with both internal and external operations. To keep the size and complexity of the example within manageable bounds, we consider only a very small part of the total organization. Specifically, we consider that part of the organization concerned with handling data directly related to the processing of individual life insurance policies. In our example, this function is performed by three departments: Underwriting and Issue, Agency, and Insurance Administration. The Underwriting and Issue department handles data related to the issuance of policies. The Agency department keeps data on the company's insurance agents. Finally, the Insurance Administration department looks after the financial and policyholder service aspects of insurance policies.

For each department we identify the functions and data classes of interest to that department. In our example, Underwriting and Issue is interested in writing policies, Agency is interested in writing policies and paying agents, and Insurance Administration is interested in administering policies, paying agents, and billing clients for various charges. To perform these functions, Underwriting and Issue requires data on policies and clients, Agency requires data on policies, clients, agents, and commissions, and Insurance Administration requires data on policies, clients, commissions, and financial aspects of policies.

| Functions | Data Classes | | | | |
|---|---|---|---|---|---|
|  | Policy | Client | Agent | Financial | Commission |
| Write policies | X | X | | | |
| Pay agents | X | X | X | | X |
| Bill clients | X | X | | X | |
| Administer policies | X | X | | | |

Fig. 12.2—1 Functions and data classes for insurance company example.

Once we have identified the functions and data classes for each department, we check that the definitions are consistent, nonredundant, and clear. We then can obtain a list of functions, data classes, and their definition as well as a matrix showing which functions use which data classes. Such a matrix for our example is shown in Figure 12.2—1. The generation of the data dictionary which documents the functions, data classes, and their interrelationships can be initiated at this point [BCS, 1977; Lomax, 1978; Curtice, 1981; Weldon, 1981]. The data dictionary contains descriptions of the metadata of the organization.  As such, it is useful in all steps of the schema design process.

## 12.3 ENTERPRISE DESCRIPTION

In the first phase of the enterprise description step, all the entity types of interest to each organizational area, the relationship types between them, and the constraints are identified [Chen and Yao, 1977].  This results in a view of the schema for each organizational area.  These views are then integrated to form an enterprise description which describes the entire schema [Navathe and Schkolnick, 1978; Baldissera et al., 1979; Ceri et al., 1981].  The entity-relationship data model will be used for our discussion of the enterprise description.  This description is used mainly for communication between the users and the schema designers.  It should be informal enough to be understandable by nonprogrammers.  There is no need for the enterprise description to have the same data model as the target DBMS.

Entity types are extracted from the data classes identified during the requirements analysis step.  Some of the information required to extract entity types will have been gathered during the requirements analysis step. Additional information may need to be obtained by further interviews with the users.  This will also be the case for subsequent phases of the enterprise description step.

To help identify the entity types, some questions to ask are:

1.  What are the entity types described by each data class?
2.  What is the appropriate name(s) for each entity type?
3.  What is the meaning (semantics) of each entity type?
4.  What attributes are of interest for each entity type?
5.  What is the appropriate name(s) for each attribute?
6.  What is the meaning (semantics) of each attribute?

For each entity type identified, a description of the entity type is produced and the associated data classes identified.  The description names the entity type, defines what it represents, and lists its associated attributes.  Synonyms and acronyms for an entity type (and attribute) are documented as well as any subtypes related to this entity type.  This documentation is entered into the data dictionary.

Entity type identification is an iterative process.  The description of an entity type may change many times before everyone agrees that it is right. The entity types identified for the insurance company example are shown in Figure 12.3−1.

Next, the relationship types are identified from the functions and the entity types that use a function.  To help identify relationship types between entity types, one can ask:

**Underwriting and Issue**

POLICY                    - *Policy number, Last activity, Last activity date,*
                          *Next activity, Next activity date, Social security number*
COVERAGE                  - *Coverage type, Coverage amount, Premium rate, Issue date*
CLIENT                    - *Social security number, Name, Address, Birthdate*
PRIOR COVERAGE            - *Policy number, Type, Amount, Rating*
BENEFICIARY               - *Social security number, Name, Address*
TERMINATION               - *Termination date, Reinstatement date, Termination reason*

**Agency**

AGENT                     - *Agent number, Name, Address, Area*
POLICY                    - *Policy number, Coverage type, Coverage amount, Issue date*
CLIENT                    - *Social security number, Name, Address, Birthdate*
COMMISSION                - *Type, Rate*

**Insurance Administration**

POLICY                    - *Policy number, Last activity, Last activity date, Next activity,*
                          *Next activity date*
CLIENT                    - *Social security number, Name, Address, Birthdate*
BILLING                   - *Mode, Amount, Next premium date, Name, Address*
LOANS                     - *Principal, Balance, Interest rate, Interest due date*
COMMISSION                - *Type, Rate*

**Fig. 12.3—1** Entity types and attributes for insurance company example.

1. For each function, what are the known correspondences (relationship types) between entity types associated with the function?
2. What is the appropriate name(s) for each relationship type?
3. Is the relationship type expressible in closed form using the attributes of the entity types (e.g., is policyholder true when social security number in client equals social security number in policy)?
4. What is the meaning (semantics) of each relationship type, either formally or informally in English?
5. What are the possible relationship types that are not used, but are still meaningful?
6. What combinations of relationship types make sense as separate, identifiable relationship types (e.g., client's beneficiaries)?

As for each entity type, a description of each relationship type containing its name, synonyms, acronyms, definition, and entity types related is produced. This information is again entered into the data dictionary. As for entity types, relationship types are obtained by successive refinement. The relationship types obtained from this process for the insurance company example are shown in Figure 12.3—2.

Finally, to complete the first phase of the enterprise description step, we identify the constraints on the attributes, entity types, and relationship types [Bracchi et al., 1979]. It seems better to state all constraints

**Underwriting and Issue**

| | | |
|---|---|---|
| *POLICY COVERAGE* | - | between *POLICY* and *COVERAGE* |
| *PRIOR POLICY COVERAGE* | - | between *POLICY* and *PRIOR COVERAGE* |
| *POLICY BENEFICIARY* | - | between *POLICY* and *BENEFICIARY* |
| *POLICY TERMINATION* | - | between *POLICY* and *TERMINATION* |
| *POLICYHOLDER* | - | between *CLIENT* and *POLICY* |

**Agency**

| | | |
|---|---|---|
| *POLICYHOLDER* | - | between *CLIENT* and *POLICY* |
| *POLICY COMMISSION* | - | between *POLICY* and *COMMISSION* |
| *AGENT COMMISSION* | - | between *AGENT* and *COMMISSION* |
| *CLIENT AGENT* | - | between *CLIENT* and *AGENT* |

**Insurance Administration**

| | | |
|---|---|---|
| *POLICYHOLDER* | - | between *CLIENT* and *POLICY* |
| *POLICY BILLING* | - | between *POLICY* and *BILLING* |
| *POLICY LOANS* | - | between *POLICY* and *LOANS* |
| *POLICY COMMISSION* | - | between *POLICY* and *COMMISSION* |

**Fig. 12.3—2** Relationship types for insurance company example.

explicitly rather than as inherent constraints. In this manner, constraints stand out to be subjected to user scrutiny. At the same time, they are specified in an incremental manner and it is easier to manipulate them separately and add or subtract from the specified set.

There are at least four types of constraints that can be specified:

1. Domain constraints for each attribute.
2. Functional dependency constraints among attributes and on relationship types.
3. General dependencies among attributes and among entity types.
4. Further general predicate constraints.

Constraints are identified by asking questions such as:

1. What is the domain of values for each attribute (e.g., is commission rate a percentage between 0 and 100)?
2. What are the known functional dependencies between attributes of each entity type (e.g., does type of coverage determine premium rate)?
3. What are the keys (if any) for each entity type (e.g., is policy number a key)?
4. What is the mapping property of each relationship type (e.g., one-to-one, functional, or many-to-many)?
5. What are the predicate constraints to be placed upon the data?

Some of the constraints obtained for the insurance company example are shown in Figure 12.3—3.

**Keys**

*Policy number* in *POLICY*
*Social security number* in *CLIENT*
*Policy number* in *PRIOR COVERAGE*
*Social security number* in *BENEFICIARY*
*Agent number* in *AGENT*

**Functional Dependencies**

*Coverage type, Coverage amount* → *Premium rate*
*Type* → *Rate*

**Mappings**

*(a) One-to-one*
*POLICY COVERAGE*
*POLICY BILLING*

*(b) Functional*
*PRIOR POLICY COVERAGE*        *POLICY* → *PRIOR COVERAGE*
*POLICY BENEFICIARY*           *POLICY* → *BENEFICIARY*
*POLICY LOANS*                 *POLICY* → *LOANS*
*POLICY TERMINATION*           *POLICY* → *TERMINATION*
*POLICYHOLDER*                 *CLIENT* → *POLICY*

*(c) Many-to-many*
*POLICY COMMISSION*
*AGENT COMMISSION*
*CLIENT AGENT*

**Fig. 12.3—3** Some constraints for insurance company example.

It is extremely hard to arrive at a set of constraints that represents the application and are consistent among each other and satisfiable. It is difficult to get the proper set of constraints for the application because some forms of constraints are difficult to understand and are prone to misunderstandings and errors. It is difficult to show that a set of constraints are consistent, especially if some constraints are general predicate constraints. We are led very quickly to intractable problems in theorem proving. Finally, a given set of constraints may be so stringent that the data base, which may already exist, cannot satisfy it.

It is not surprising that, for a given data base, after specification of what is considered to be a proper set of constraints, one may find that most of the existing data do not abide by the constraints. Unfortunately, most real data bases are very "dirty." That is, they contain data that do not abide by the formal constraints derived from the requirements analysis. This situation should not be considered a fault of the data base. The world is full of special cases which are not thought of when specifying constraints. The data bases accept and digest these special cases, while the constraint specification and enforcement do not.

Consider as an example the filling out of application forms which serve as input to a data base. The schema designer has a very firm idea about what people should state on the form. However, people take the liberty to specify many different values or special cases. This data will find its way into the data base since they cannot be arbitrarily stopped at data entry. The data base cannot be called "dirty"; it merely reflects the real-world situation.

The result of this phase of the enterprise description step is a list of the entity types and their attributes, the relationship types, and the constraints for each organizational area. The next phase of the enterprise description step integrates the separate views for each organizational area in one enterprise description. The enterprise description is a synthesis of the information requirements of each organizational area. While integrating the views name conflicts, redundancies, and ambiguities need to be resolved [Baldissera et al., 1979]. For example, in Figure 12.3−1, *POLICY* has several definitions. For the insurance company example this process results in the enterprise description shown in Figure 12.3−4.

Documentation of the enterprise description consists of summarizing the data obtained from the interviews in a suitable manner. It also includes retention of the universe of discourse of who uses each entity type and relationship type. The documentation and schematic of the enterprise description is presented to each organizational area for its approval. It may be necessary to iterate by negotiating with each organizational area until all organizational areas agree that the enterprise description accurately reflects their information (view) requirements.

The final phase of the enterprise description step identifies the transaction-processing requirements of the organization with respect to the enterprise description. All current and projected transactions are included. For each transaction we identify its nature (retrieval, update), its frequency, its origin (organizational area), and its purpose, together with the part(s) of the schema it affects. The enterprise description of the previous step is used as a basis for describing the transactions.

To help identify requirements for supporting transactions, some of the relevant questions to ask are:

1. What transactions are required by each organizational area?
2. What entity types, attributes, and relationship types are involved in each transaction?
3. What is a sketchy outline of each transaction in terms of the enterprise description and English or a problem specification language?
4. What kind of access is required by each transaction (e.g., retrieval, update)?
5. What is the mode of operation of each transaction (e.g., batch, on-line, etc.)?

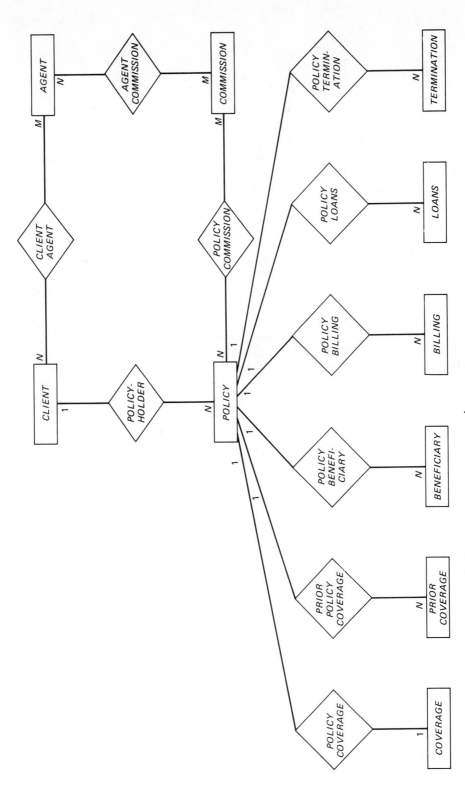

**Fig. 12.3—4** Enterprise description for insurance company example.

6.  What is the frequency of each transaction (e.g., daily, weekly)?
7.  What is the processing priority of each transaction?
8.  What is the need for concurrent update activity?
9.  What kind of pattern of data base usage do we expect (e.g., mix of transactions, when done, etc.)?
10. What reports are needed?
11. What is the format of each report?
12. What is the acceptable time frame for producing each report?
13. What security requirements are important?
14. What parts of the data base are essential for the operation of the organization?

The result of this step is a list of all transactions and their characteristics. Figure 12.3—5 contains some transactions required for the insurance company example. The list of transactions is shown to the different organizational areas and an agreement on a final list is reached together with some priorities for implementation.

TRANSACTION: List the policies held by a client.
> **Entity types**: *CLIENT, POLICY.*
> **Relationship types**: *POLICYHOLDER.*
> 1. Retrieve the *CLIENT* entity.
> 2. Retrieve a *POLICY* entity related to the *CLIENT* entity via a *POLICYHOLDER* relationship.

TRANSACTION: Perform today's policy-processing activities.
> **Entity types**: *POLICY, BILLING, LOANS.*
> **Relationship types**: *POLICY BILLING, POLICY LOANS.*
> **Description**
> 1. For each *POLICY* entity where *Next activity date* is today, do the activity indicated by *Next activity.*
> 2. Update *Last activity* and *Last activity date* in *POLICY.*
> 3. Determine the *Next activity* by finding the minimum of *Next premium date* in *BILLING* or *Interest due date* in *LOANS.*
> 4. Update *Next activity* and *Next activity date* in *POLICY.*

TRANSACTION: List a client's beneficiaries by policy.
> **Entity types**: *CLIENT, POLICY, BENEFICIARY.*
> **Relationship types**: *POLICYHOLDER, POLICY BENEFICIARY.*
> **Description**
> 1. Retrieve the *CLIENT* entity.
> 2. Retrieve all *POLICY* entities related to the *CLIENT* entity via a *POLICYHOLDER* relationship.
> 3. For each *POLICY* entity retrieved, retrieve all *BENEFICIARY* entities related to the *POLICY* entity via a *POLICY BENEFICIARY* relationship.

**Fig. 12.3—5** Some sample transactions for the insurance company example.

Although there are many data models that can be used for the enterprise description, there are not many data models that can adequately capture the transaction descriptions. Most data models are relatively rich in data structuring features. (After all, they are *data* models.) They are relatively poor in features that can describe precisely the transactions on the data. Their data languages are often rather detailed and cannot be used to convey any overall understanding of the transactions before they are programmed. Specification data languages can be very useful in this respect. They are more abstract than navigation data languages and can describe in a few simple statements some very complicated transactions. Specification data languages can be regarded as abstract languages to be used for the representation of transactions.

So far, we have not considered the existing data files and their properties. It is important to identify the information requirements of an organization as the users perceive them or would like them to be. Often, existing data files do not accurately reflect an organization's information requirements. In most cases, existing data files emerged on an ad hoc basis. They are thus often highly dependent upon specific applications (no matter how transient) and contain redundant and/or improperly defined attributes. Because of their ad hoc nature, integration of data and evolution of the files to meet changing needs is very difficult, if not impossible. Merely converting existing files to a DBMS without any analysis of current needs often defeats the whole purpose of the DBMS approach. It can result in even more costly and less effective operation than prior to conversion.

## 12.4 DATA BASE DESCRIPTION

Following agreement on an enterprise description, the next step is to transform the enterprise description into a data base description. By a *data base description*, we mean a description of the proposed schema according to the data model implicit in the target DBMS. Since existing commercial DBMSs can be grouped under three main approaches — relational, network, or hierarchical — we can illustrate the process, for the insurance company example, for each approach.

For a hierarchical DBMS, the enterprise description is transformed into a set of spanning trees (Figure 12.4—1). Entity types usually will be mapped into record types and relationship types into parent-child relationships. The transformation of the enterprise description to a hierarchical schema is by no means algorithmic or unique. The nature and type of the data base transactions will often influence the particular hierarchy chosen. For example, in some systems access to root record

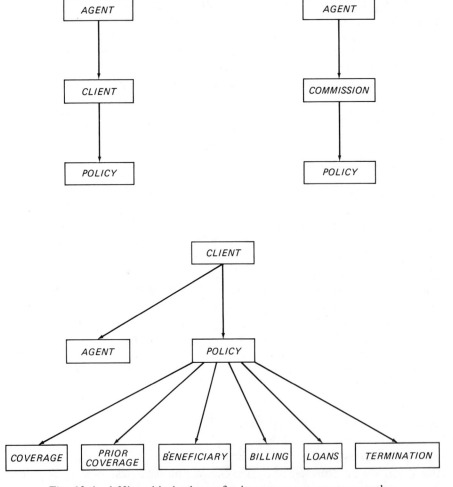

**Fig. 12.4—1** Hiearchical schema for insurance company example.

types is usually faster and more efficient than access to dependent record types. Therefore, frequently accessed record types will tend to be placed at or near the root record type of a hierarchy. Also, the exact placement of record types within the hierarchy (right or left of each other) may also be dictated by the type of transactions required. After the hierarchical schema is produced, each data base transaction is expressed in terms of this schema.

For a network DBMS, the enterprise description is transformed into a data structure diagram (Figure 12.4—2). Entity types are usually mapped into record types and relationship types into DBTG-set types. Each data base transaction is mapped into a navigation through the data structure

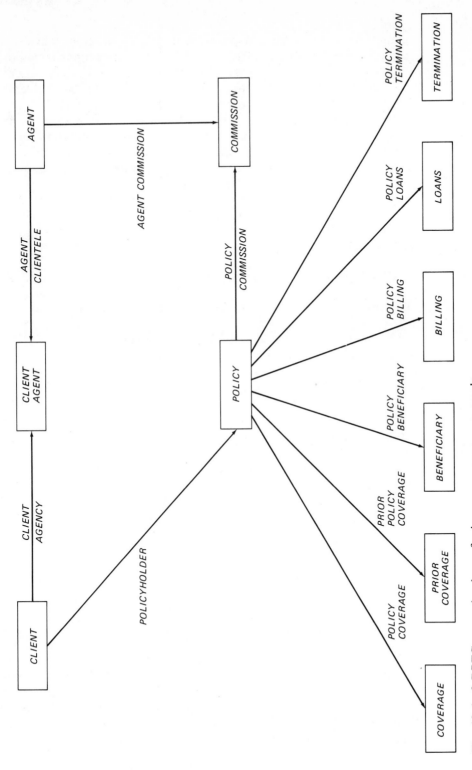

**Fig. 12.4–2** DBTG-network schema for insurance company example.

diagram. The set membership of each DBTG-set type reflects the semantic properties of each relationship type. Any restrictions imposed by a DBTG-set type must be observed and may require a transformation of the enterprise description before the mapping to DBTG-set types is performed. For example, any relationship type that is not functional must first be transformed into a (set of) functional relationship type(s). This transformation can be accomplished in two ways: duplication or the introduction of an intermediate record type as discussed in Chapter 6. In Figure 12.4—2, duplication of *COMMISSION* records is used to transform the many-to-many relationship types *POLICY COMMISSION* and *AGENT COMMISSION* into two functional relationship types. The introduction of the intermediate record type *CLIENT AGENT* is used to transform the many-to-many relationship type *CLIENT AGENT* into two functional relationship types.

*POLICY(Policy number, Last activity, Last activity date, Next activity,*
    *Next activity date)*

*COVERAGE(Policy number, Coverage type, Coverage amount, Premium rate,*
    *Issue date)*

*CLIENT(Social security number, Name, Address, Birthdate)*

*POLICYHOLDER(Social security number, Agent number)*

*BENEFICIARY(Policy number, Social security number, Name, Address)*

*PRIOR COVERAGE(Social security number, Current policy number,*
    *Prior policy number, Type, Amount, Rating)*

*BILLING(Policy number, Mode, Amount, Next premium date, Name, Address)*

*LOANS(Policy number, Principal, Balance, Interest rate, Interest due date)*

*TERMINATION(Policy number, Termination date, Reinstatement date,*
    *Termination reason)*

*AGENT(Agent number, Name, Address, Area)*

*CLIENT AGENT(Social security number, Agent number)*

*COMMISSION(Policy number, Agent number, Type, Rate)*

**Fig. 12.4—3** Relational schema for insurance company example.

For a relational DBMS, the enterprise description is transformed into a relational schema (Figure 12.4—3). Entities are mapped into base relations (relations which are permanently stored in the data base). Relationship types are mapped into base relations if they are information bearing (are not expressible as a closed-form property). Non-information-bearing relationship types can be mapped into derived relations (i.e., joins). If some non-information-bearing relationship types are used very frequently, they may be mapped into permanent joins (if the system permits them) (e.g., links and nets in System R [Boyce and Chamberlin, 1973]). Data base transactions are mapped into relational operations on the base relations.

The result of transforming the enterprise description into a data base description represents a documentation of the schema. In addition, we have a sketch of each transaction to be performed. The schema(s) and transaction sketch(es) should again be discussed with the different organizational areas in order to obtain their approval.

We have discussed data base description in purely conceptual terms. In many cases, a DBMS and an associated data model have already been selected. The DBMS choice may be predicated on hardware, economic, political, or similar considerations. In this case, the data base description effort may be directed toward generating a schema for a particular DBMS. On the other hand, as discussed here, a data base description can be done for more than one data model. It may then be agreed that one of the data models best meets the requirements of the application. In this case, the choice of data model can influence the choice of a DBMS.

The mapping from enterprise description to data base description was outlined informally as a procedure that human beings follow to obtain a schema from an abstract description. Abstraction and stepwise refinement can be used to give more discipline to this manual procedure [Smith and Smith, 1977a,b, 1978]. Alternatively, the mapping can be more automated from an abstract description to a concrete data base description [Gerritsen, 1975, 1978; Gambino and Gerritsen, 1977; Fry and Teorey, 1978; Iossiphidis, 1980; Sakai, 1980].

There is a tremendous amount of choice in the schema design regarding structuring of the data and the specification of constraints. Many different schemas can be associated with the same application. It would be nice to come up with one that is "good" and "right". "Good" usually means a schema that provides reasonable data base performance. Data base performance is a function of physical data base design and is examined briefly in the next section.

"Right" usually means that the schema reflects the real properties of the world we are trying to represent. This requirement is extremely difficult to meet because we are not dealing with a closed system. Both the real world and our perception of it change very rapidly. It is important, however, to at least attempt to reconcile the schema with our informal view of what it represents. After we introduce the schema, requirements of the real world probably will have to be bent to abide by it. It is very important, therefore, to bring the schema design under careful scrutiny so that we can validate[1] that it complies with the information requirements stated both formally and informally.

---

[1] Schema validation is not the same as schema verification. Schema verification implies a very rigorous definition of the schema which is amenable to formal treatment. Such formal treatments will be discussed in Chapter 13.

There are mainly two ways to check whether the schema satisfies our information requirements.  One way is to specify the requirements in a different, maybe more abstract data model description as outlined in this chapter.  We then reconcile the abstract description of the requirements with the schema.  There are many data models and methodologies proposed for the abstract specification of information requirements [Benci et al., 1976; Falkenberg, 1976a; Bubenko, 1977a, 1980; Chen, 1980; Lundeberg et al., 1981].  In this case, schema validation reduces to two parts.  First, the abstract description is checked to establish that it complies with real-world requirements.  The abstract description is assumed to be easier to understand and, therefore, more amenable to close inspection by users.  Second, the abstract description is mapped into the schema to verify its structures, constraints, and operations [Bubenko, 1977b; Baldissera et al., 1979].

Schema validation under this approach has two components.  The first component deals with checking that the schema specification is clear and does not contain syntactic or other obvious errors.  This step can be effected by textual analysis of the specified schema.  The second component deals with the validation of the expressions corresponding to the explicit constraints.  Finally, there is an implicit third component that deals with the implicit constraints that are the results of the first and second components.

There are many textual checks that can be effected in the schema specification [Brodie, 1978].  For instance:

1.  No syntactic errors exist.
2.  Each identifier has a unique scope.
3.  Arguments in comparability terms (e.g., joins) are compatible.
4.  Ranges and units of variables are appropriate.

Textual analysis enables us to check the schema specification for obvious errors and to check that all objects are syntactically correct and are used properly.  There are many properties, however, that textual analysis cannot check.  For instance, constraints should be formally analyzed as discussed in Chapter 13.

Another, different way to reconcile the schema in terms of real-world information requirements is to try it out experimentally.  Before the actual data base is loaded, the schema is generated on a system using small amounts of data.  The users then try the system out prior to a full implementation.  In this way, the users can identify the problems in the schema design and propose changes.  This approach can also be tried as a first step to any schema design using the existing facilities of the target system.  It is better, however, to use a design tool that has been built specifically for this purpose (e.g., CS4 [Berild and Nachmens, 1977a]).

The experimental approach enables the schema designer to capture user requirements which are very difficult to specify. In addition, it allows the user to modify the requirements and identify the real needs after contact with the facilities of the proposed system. Building prototypes before the actual product is not specific to schema design. It is accepted practice in engineering design.

The CS4 system has been used in many pilot implementations. It has been observed in these pilot implementations that the user requirements changed and grew as the users became more acquainted with computers and the system facilities [Berild and Nachmens, 1977b]. Some of the options and features that were designed in the system initially were found not to be essential. The resulting system, after the experimentation, turned out to be very different. A nice advantage of the pilot system approach is that different ideas can be tried out in an iterative manner. A good idea may turn out to be unrealistic or a mediocre idea may translate into a great success.

Schema validation is an extremely important and at the same time extremely difficult problem. It makes schema design very complex in practice. The data models and their features discussed in previous chapters provide the tools for visualizing the data. It is important to remember, however, that data models and schemas are only as good as they are useful to their users. Schema validation has exactly that goal: to make sure that the data models, structures, systems, machines, and so on, have some impact on and some benefits for the people who subsidize them in the first place (i.e., their ultimate users).

## 12.5 PHYSICAL DATA BASE DESIGN

In an ideal world, the structure of the schema captures only logical properties of the data base. It is independent of any operational characteristics. However, in a realistic situation the structure of the schema greatly influences performance issues, at least in current commercial systems. In future systems there is hope that the structure will be purely logical as represented in the enterprise description. Even in this case, however, performance considerations are important in the design of the internal schema. It seems, therefore, that both current and future architectures will require a schema analysis for performance considerations [Chen and Yao, 1977; Wiederhold, 1977; Schkolnick, 1978; Yao and DeJong, 1978; Sevcik, 1981]. As the main emphasis of this book is on the logical properties of data models, we will discuss only briefly physical data base design as it relates to schema design.

An important problem in physical data base design deals with the selection of the storage organization. Since many systems offer alternatives in storage organization, the properties of the data base and the reference patterns should be analyzed to choose storage organizations appropriately. Much research has been done on this problem, especially in file organization [Hsiao and Harary, 1970; Cardenas, 1973; Severance, 1975; Yao, 1977]. To adequately portray choices in physical data base design, one needs a detailed model of physical data base organization. Such models capture the parameters of file storage and under certain assumptions can evaluate different alternatives [Batory, 1980a,b; Batory and Gotlieb, 1980].

Another important performance issue is related to the selection and use of access paths in the system. *Access paths* are storage structures (e.g., indices) that relate contents of a logical object to its corresponding (physical) records in the data base. In selecting access paths, the problem is what access paths to maintain and how to take advantage of them [King, 1974; Schkolnick, 1975]. In using access paths, the problem is how best to make use of the access paths (e.g., in processing queries [Farley and Schuster, 1975; Kerschberg et al., 1979]).

Another important performance issue is related to the analysis of the reference patterns and the buffering characteristics of the system. Models are needed for analyzing what buffer sizes, prefetching policies and replacement algorithms to use in a DBMS [Rodriguez-Rosell, 1976; Smith, 1978; Magalhaes, 1981]. Buffer management is especially important as it relates to memory hierarchies and storage organization [Tsichritzis and Wladawsky, 1979].

Another performance characteristic deals with analyzing operations and determining the best ways to service a transaction. Most of the work in this area has been done in query optimization strategies. For instance, algorithms that utilize query decomposition for better performance have been proposed and analyzed [Wong and Youssefi, 1976; Youssefi, 1978]. This problem is especially important in distributed DBMSs [Wong, 1977; Chiu, 1979; Kerschberg et al., 1979]. Different ways of doing joins in a distributed environment have been studied at length [Blasgen and Eswaran, 1977; Yao and DeJong, 1978; Selinger et al, 1979; Bernstein and Chiu, 1981].

Performance predictors for data bases use analytical tools and simulation. Analytical tools specify a model, a set of parameters, cost functions, and some equations relating the parameters [Teorey and Das, 1976; March and Severance, 1978]. The equations are then programmed in a simulation system to estimate storage and access time performance [Senko et al., 1968; Cardenas, 1975]. There are some simulation data base performance predictors which have been designed specifically for simulation of data base behavior [Nakamura et al., 1975; DeLutis and Smith, 1976].

Data base performance is an extremely complicated issue. The choices in the data base parameters are many. Research has been done to study individual physical data base parameters. Unfortunately, the design parameters are not independent [Christodoulakis, 1981]. There is a need for a unified framework for data base performance estimations. Such an environment for design can be obtained by making the choices in a well-structured hierarchical way [Sevcik, 1981]. In this way, physical data base design can proceed according to well-accepted principles of structured design [Yourdon and Constantine, 1979].

## 12.6 USER-ORIENTED DESIGN

In this book we have concentrated mainly on data modeling tools. The application of these tools for schema design was outlined in this chapter. We feel that the application of these tools is the most important problem and perhaps will be with us for quite some time. The world needs better DBMSs. It may even need better data models. But what it really needs is better ways to use what is at hand.

The way schema design was outlined in the previous sections, it may appear that a complete methodology is at hand or at least near. This is not true and may never be true. A methodology will always be easy to outline conceptually. It will be very difficult to apply in practice. The main stumbling block is understanding what an organization does and trying to influence it to adopt another, perhaps better, operational mode.

DBMSs and any design analysis or methodology about them always have the same difficulty. The operation of the DBMS should be completely integrated with the operation of the organization to be successful. However, the introduction of a DBMS induces some changes both in the organization and the way people do their work. As such, it will always stumble on the ability of people to communicate their ideas and the natural inertia of people to accept changes. The main problems in using DBMSs and data models are people problems [Sibley, 1980].

The important consideration therefore should be to match the right facilities to the right users. It may be that DBMSs should provide a continuum of facilities and let the user choose the level at which he or she is most comfortable. Different data models, data languages, and even schemas may need to be provided for different types of users [Klug, 1981].

A major issue to consider is the criterion for classifying users. Typically, users are classified according to their frequency of interaction with a DBMS. This leads to classifications such as novice users (least frequent), casual users, computer users, and application programmers (most frequent) [Lochovsky, 1978; Shneiderman, 1978]. However, other classification criteria, such as task performed, may be equally valid. This leads to classifications such as clerks, specialists, and managers. It is not clear that one classification is better than another. Different classifications may be relevant for different situations. The important consideration is to determine what type of user the DBMS is intended for and to choose DBMS facilities accordingly.

Not surprisingly, studies have shown that inexperienced users have considerably more trouble using DBMS facilities initially than do more experienced users [Reisner et al., 1975; Lochovsky, 1978; Reisner, 1981]. Inexperienced users require facilities that can guide and help them at every step. Menu selection and table data models may be most appropriate for these users. As users gain experience in using the DBMS, they usually require greater flexibility in specifying data relationships and data base requests. Specification or navigation data languages should be available for these users. Again, probably a continuum of data languages is required with the ability to go freely back and forth between levels of language as the users' needs change. Specialized interfaces for specialized tasks are also required to minimize training time as well as errors in interaction [Lochovsky, 1980].

Given that one has to make a choice between different alternative data models and DBMSs, how does one go about this? There are several approaches [Shneiderman, 1978]. The first is introspection. One ponders the alternatives, and based on experience and intuition, one makes a choice. Much software and hardware design has proceeded in this way. Unfortunately, it is not always the best way to proceed and we usually end up living with our misjudgments and bequeathing them to our descendants [Thomas, 1977].

A second approach is to perform some field studies. One goes out and sees how things are done now, interviews users, and forms some opinions about good and bad design features. Again, however, there is no objective way to evaluate alternatives. The choice may at best prove no better than the original design and at worst prove to be worse. Asking users about their opinions of different facilities is not always a useful exercise. Users who have spent time and effort to master some system will tend not to say anything bad about it. They do not want to believe that all that time and effort was really a waste [Thomas, 1977].

The final alternative is to perform controlled experimental evaluation of different facilities. Human factors studies of DBMSs are a recent trend and only a handful of experiments have been performed [Gould and Ascher, 1975; Reisner et al., 1975; Thomas and Gould, 1975; Lochovsky, 1978; Shneiderman, 1978]. However, they provide the most objective method of evaluating and comparing different DBMS facilities. Some generalizations of results obtained so far were cited in previous sections. These results tentatively point to certain design goals and selection criterion, but many more studies need to be performed to permit concrete generalizations.

Some may question the value of such studies. They may point to the fact that any programming language, no matter how bad, can be learned eventually. Similarly, any DBMS facility can be mastered in time. Although this assertion may be true, the real issue is not the ability to just learn to use a facility, but to use it effectively and productively. The aim of human factors studies is to provide better facilities that make the life of the user easier when interacting with the facility. The machine should be the servant of the user, not vice versa!

## EXERCISES

**12.1** Create a list of desirable features in a data model. Compare some data models with respect to this list of features. Is there a data model that is remarkably superior?

**12.2** There are some natural trade-offs in any model between economy of concept (having a small number of powerful features), descriptive power (having very refined descriptive ability), and size of descriptions. Discuss these trade-offs in terms of data models.

**12.3** Propose a candidate data model for the conceptual schema facility of the ANSI/X3/SPARC framework [Benci et al., 1976; Bracchi et al., 1976; Senko, 1976; Biller and Neuhold, 1977; Nijssen, 1976, 1977; Schmid, 1977; Klug, 1978].

**12.4** Outline a data model for the internal schema facility of the ANSI/X3/SPARC framework.

**12.5** Propose a set of language extensions that will make IMS's DL/1 or the DBTG COBOL DML more palatable to casual users.

**12.6** Outline a communication facility (diagrams, forms, etc.) to permit the interchange of ideas during schema design.

**12.7** If you have been involved in the design of a schema, discuss some problems that you have encountered in practice which are not discussed in this chapter.

**12.8** How would you apply queuing network theory for analyzing the transaction patterns and queuing properties in a distributed data base?

**12.9** What would you consider the important performance parameters in physical data base design?

**12.10** Outline the trade-offs between analytic techniques and simulation in analyzing the performance of a physical data base design [Graham, 1978].

**12.11** The attorney general's office is considering a switch to a DBMS to handle scheduling of criminal court cases. Currently, this function is performed manually. You have been retained to analyze the information requirements of the application and to design a schema to represent these requirements.

An initial study of the manual system shows that it consists of three files that contain all information required to schedule criminal court cases. These files have been analyzed and the results of this analysis follow.

One file lists all the judges capable of presiding at criminal prosecutions. The judges are categorized as to their current judicial appointment (e.g., county court, district court, appeals court, supreme court, etc.). They are also classified according to their jurisdiction (e.g., town, city, township, county, etc.). Other data maintained about judges include their name, address, telephone number, and their current schedule of cases. The latter data include the case id, start date, time, court house, and expected duration (in days) of the hearing.

Another file lists all prosecutors who are capable of handling criminal prosecutions. Prosecutors are categorized according to the regional office to which they are assigned. Other data maintained about prosecutors include their name, office address, phone number, and their caseload. The caseload data include the case id, crime, defendant(s), defense lawyer(s), and the start date, time, courthouse, and expected duration (in days) of the hearing.

The final file lists all outstanding criminal prosecutions. Each prosecution case includes a description of the crime, who the defendant(s) is, who his or her lawyer(s) is (if known), and who the prosecutor and presiding judge are (if known). A case can have at most one judge and one prosecutor. A case can consist of more than one crime. Each crime can have one or more defendants. Each defendant can have one or more lawyers representing him or her. If a crime has multiple defendants, each defendant may have his or her own lawyers.

Each case is identified by a unique case id. The description of the crime(s) includes type of crime (e.g., murder, arson, etc.), when committed (date), location (city) and name of arresting officer, his or her affiliation, and date of arrest. Data on defendants include name, last known address and telephone number, birthdate, and sex. Data kept about lawyers include their name, address, and telephone number. There may be several outstanding cases against a defendant. Other data maintained about cases are the name of the presiding judge and prosecutor, and the start date, time, court house, and expected duration of the trial.

Design an enterprise description for this application using the entity-relationship data model. From the enterprise description, design hierarchical, DBTG-network, and relational schemas.

# Chapter 13

# SCHEMA ANALYSIS

## 13.1 GETTING A BETTER SCHEMA

In Chapter 12 steps were outlined for obtaining a schema. The major direction of the effort was to obtain an accurate schema, that is, a schema representing the data base application on which the transactions of the application could be serviced. The measure of "goodness" of the desired schema was rather vague. It would be nice to evaluate a schema for correctness and efficiency. It would also be nice to have algorithms to turn a schema into another "better" but "equivalent" schema. Before we can proceed with such an effort, we need to formalize what it means for the schema to be correct, what it means for the schema to be better, and under what conditions two schemas are equivalent. Such formalization will necessarily abstract the properties of the schema into properties that can be treated formally. The notion of a schema itself has to be abstracted so as to be able to talk about equivalent schemas. Care should always be exercised in understanding the limitations of the abstractions.

In any theoretical formulation, the results are only as good as the assumptions underlying the theoretical foundations. In data modeling, sometimes the assumptions are rather strong which makes the theory (often called *data base theory*) interesting but not readily applicable. However, data base theory usually provides a deeper understanding of data models, data base schemas, and their properties. Thus, it should be treated as a tool for understanding and not necessarily as a tool for design. Data base theory itself is often billed as "schema design." It always assumes, however, an initial description as a starting point. It is better, therefore, to call it schema analysis. That is, given an abstract schema, what are the desired properties it should have, and how do we transform the schema into another equivalent schema with the desired properties?

A schema consists of structures and constraints. It would be very hard to argue that a schema is better in terms of structures alone. For instance, how can one decide objectively about assembling attributes into entity types? Without taking account of constraints, the only grounds for this decision are informal semantics. Semantics can dictate that some attributes fit naturally together. However, to do any analysis we have to translate vague semantic requirements into syntactic properties that can be formally manipulated. This can be done if we capture both structures and constraints. The constraints give us the additional properties which can be used to decide about the most appropriate structure for the schema.

Constraints can be used as a guideline for deciding the schema's structure according to three directions [Beeri et al., 1978]. The first direction is *representation*. A constraint can be thought of as a property of the schema which should be true. It can also be thought of as a natural relationship between some attributes or entity types. All such natural relationships represented by constraints should be represented in the schema. These representations should be a guideline for getting a good schema. The second direction is *nonredundancy*. That is, a constraint that can be derived from the structures and other constraints already specified in a schema, should not be redundantly specified. It may be confusing to represent the same information in more than one way. The third direction is *separation*. That is, it would be nice to structure the schema in such a way that information units, as represented by constraints, are separated. In this way they do not interfere with each other.

With these three directions in mind, constraints can be used as a yardstick to evaluate and manipulate schemas. The most well understood and simple to manipulate type of constraint deals with dependencies between attributes in a schema. It is not surprising, therefore, that schema analysis deals primarily with using these dependencies and their properties to guide the evaluation of the schema.

We will start by formalizing these dependencies. The formalization is cast in terms of relational data models. There are two reasons for using relational data models as a basis for discussing these dependencies. First, historically, these dependencies were first proposed and later studied in terms of (data base) relations [Codd, 1971a, 1972a]. However, there is a second, more important reason. Relational data models have only explicit constraints. Thus, the dependencies can be studied independently (as explicit constraints) and their role in schema design and analysis can be clarified. In other data models, the dependencies inherent in the structures interfere with the explicit dependencies. Therefore, the constraints cannot be captured easily and studied independently. Nevertheless, schema analysis in terms of dependencies applies equally well to all data models. After all, all data models deal with the problem of using constraints to decide what the basic structures are: whether they use relations, record types, segment types, and so on.

## 13.2 DEPENDENCIES

The idea of a dependency as a constraint is intuitively appealing. For instance, it makes sense to say that "Your salary will depend only on your performance" or that "Your manners depend on your upbringing." Intuitively, a dependency expresses the fact that an object depends on another object. In terms of data base theory an object is either an attribute or a tuple. A dependency, therefore, can be of two kinds [Beeri, 1980]. In one case the values of some attributes solely determine the values of some other attributes. In the other case the properties of some tuples determine the properties of some other tuples. Sometimes the same dependency can be considered in either form. Consider, for instance, functional dependencies as defined in Chapter 3. The functional dependency *Name → Age* can be explained in two ways. First, the value of the attribute *Name* solely determines the value of the attribute *Age*. Second, if we have a tuple in a relation with name Smith J. and age 28, any other tuple with the same name Smith J. will have to have the same age 28.

Functional dependencies were the first type of dependency to be introduced and studied. They have, however, some important limitations. Functional dependencies not only express the constraint that *Name* determines *Age*, but it determines a unique value for *Age*. As we will see later in this section, there are other dependencies which do not insist on functionality. For instance, upbringing may not determine a unique value for manners, but it determines a range of values independent of anything else.

We formalize the notion of functional dependencies first [Bernstein, 1975, 1976; Fagin, 1977a; Beeri et al., 1978; Ullman, 1980]. In what follows we use the letters *A*, *B*, *C*, ... for single attributes, the letters *X*, *Y*, *Z*, ... for sets of attributes, and the letters *a*, *b*, *c*, ... and *x*, *y*, *z*, ... for corresponding values [Ullman, 1980]. We write *XY* to represent the union of attributes *X* and *Y*. We use the letters *R*, *S*, ... to refer to relation schemes. Each relation scheme implies a name for a relation and a collection of attributes. We represent by *r*, *s*, ... relation extensions (i.e., tables) of the relation schemes *R*, *S*, .... The purpose of introducing this notation is to be compatible with the literature. In this way the reader can proceed smoothly to the numerous papers on data base theory.

Most of our discussion assumes the existence of a *universal relation scheme U* on all the sets of attributes [Honeyman, 1980; Sciore, 1980; Ullman, 1980]. In this universal relation scheme, each attribute is uniquely named and any relation scheme we consider is a subset of the attributes of $U$. We will discuss this assumption in more detail later in this chapter.

Let $X$ and $Y$ be the attributes of a relation scheme $R$ and let $f$ be a time-varying function such that $f$ is a function from the underlying domain of $X$ to the underlying domain of $Y$ (written $f:X \to Y$). In the precise mathematical sense, $f$ is not a function because it is allowed to change over time. That is, $f$ changes as the relation extension $r$ of $R$ changes. If $f$ is thought of as a set of ordered pairs $\{(x, y) | x \in X \text{ and } y \in Y\}$, then at every point in time, for a given value of $x$ in $X$ there is at most one value of $y$ in $Y$ associated with $x$. Another way of saying the same thing is that there exists no counterexample of a relation extension $r$ of $R$ in which $X \to Y$ is not a function. To distinguish $f$ from a mathematical function, it is called a *functional dependency* (FD) [Codd 1971a, 1972a, Bernstein, 1976].

If $f:X \to Y$, then $Y$ is said to be *functionally dependent* (or simply *dependent*) on $X$, and $X$ is said to *functionally determine* (or simply *determine*) $Y$. When there is only one functional dependency $f$ from $X$ to $Y$, the notation $X \to Y$ (i.e., $X$ determines $Y$) is used as an abbreviation. $X \nrightarrow Y$ means that there is no functional dependency between $X$ and $Y$. If both $X \to Y$ and $Y \to X$ hold, at all times $X$ and $Y$ are in a one-to-one correspondence and the notation $X \longleftrightarrow Y$ is used.

Let $f:A_1, ..., A_n \to B$ and $g:A_1, ..., A_m \to B$ where $m < n$. The attributes $A_{m+1}, A_{m+2}, ..., A_n$ are extraneous in $f$ since $A_1, ..., A_m$ are sufficient to functionally determine $B$. In this case, $B$ is said to be *partially dependent* on $A_1, ..., A_n$. If for a given $f$ there is no $g$ with the foregoing property, $B$ is *fully dependent* on $A_1, ..., A_n$. That is, there are no extraneous attributes in the domain of $f$ [Bernstein, 1976].

Functional dependencies have been completely axiomatized [Armstrong, 1974, Beeri et al., 1977; Sadri and Ullman, 1980]. Consider a set of attributes $A_1, ..., A_n$ of a relation scheme $R$ and a set $\mathbf{F}$ of functional dependencies $X \to Y$ where $X$, $Y$ are subsets of the attributes $A_1, ..., A_n$. It is assumed that all functional dependencies between $A_1, ..., A_n$ are given and that they are unique. That is, there are no two different functional dependencies $X \to Y$. This assumption can be satisfied by renaming attributes until all functional dependencies are distinct.

Suppose now that all the attributes are considered together as part of this large underlying relation scheme $R$. This relation scheme supposedly contains all the relationships possible between $A_1, ..., A_n$. The functional dependencies $\mathbf{F}$ stated between $A_1, ..., A_n$ may imply some other implicit functional dependencies which can be derived from the stated functional dependencies. We say that a functional dependency $f$ is implied by $\mathbf{F}$ if $f$ is true for any relation extension $r$ of $R$ which satisfies $\mathbf{F}$. If we want to derive better, equivalent schemas or to determine if two schemas are equivalent, it is important to be able to derive all of the functional dependencies $f$. The inference rules (axioms) which can be used to derive implicit functional dependencies are [Armstrong, 1974]:

**FD1** (Reflexivity): If $Y \subseteq X$, then $X \to Y$

**FD2** (Augmentation): If $Z \subseteq W$ and $X \to Y$, then $XW \to YZ$

**FD3** (Transitivity): If $X \to Y$ and $Y \to Z$, then $X \to Z$

where $X$, $Y$, and $Z$ are subsets of the attributes $A_1, ..., A_n$.

This set of rules is sound and complete. That is, it can be used to generate all other functional dependencies which are valid based on the original set **F** of functional dependencies. In addition, any functional dependency derived by the rules is implied by **F** (i.e., it will be true when **F** is true). It is convenient to introduce additional rules which are consequences of FD1, FD2, and FD3.

**FD4** (Pseudo-transitivity): If $X \to Y$ and $YW \to Z$, then $XW \to Z$

**FD5** (Union): If $X \to Y$ and $X \to Z$, then $X \to YZ$

**FD6** (Decomposition): If $X \to YZ$, then $X \to Y$ and $X \to Z$

For a set **F** of functional dependencies, the *closure* $\mathbf{F}^+$ is the set of all functional dependencies which are implied by **F**. The closure $\mathbf{F}^+$ of a set of functional dependencies can be obtained using the rules FD1, FD2, and FD3. A procedure that generates $\mathbf{F}^+$ is the following [Osborn, 1978]:

1. $\mathbf{F} \subseteq \mathbf{F}^+$.
2. For all subsets $X$ and $Y$ of $A_1, ..., A_n$, if $Y \subseteq X$, then $X \to Y \in \mathbf{F}^+$.
3. For all subsets $X$, $Y$, and $Z$ of $A_1, ..., A_n$, if $X \to Y$, $Y \to Z \in \mathbf{F}^+$, then $X \to Z \in \mathbf{F}^+$.
4. For all subsets $X$, $Y$, and $Z$ of $A_1, ..., A_n$, if $X \to Y$, $X \to Z \in \mathbf{F}^+$ then $X \to YZ \in \mathbf{F}^+$.
5. No other functional dependencies are in $\mathbf{F}^+$.

To generate all functional dependencies in $\mathbf{F}^+$ is very time consuming [Ullman, 1980]. The reason is that usually there are very many functional dependencies in $\mathbf{F}^+$ even if **F** itself is not large.

The *closure* $X^+$ of a set of attributes $X$ is the set of attributes $Y$ such that $X \to Y$ can be derived from **F** and Armstrong's rules FD1, FD2, and FD3. $X^+$ allows us to determine whether a dependency $X \to Y$ follows from **F** according to Armstrong's rules. Computing $X^+$ is not hard. In fact, it takes time proportional to the length of all the dependencies in **F** [Ullman, 1980].

Two sets of dependencies **F** and **G** in the same relation scheme $R$ are said to *cover* each other if $\mathbf{F}^+ = \mathbf{G}^+$. Among these sets of dependencies, some of them are *nonredundant*. That is, they do not have any functional dependencies which can be derived from the rest. In addition, they do not have any redundant attributes on the left-hand side of the dependencies. A nonredundant cover can always be found from a set of functional dependencies in polynomial time [Beeri et al., 1978]. Work has been done on algorithms for obtaining nonredundant, nonredundant minimal, and "useful" covers [Bernstein, 1976; Bernstein and Beeri, 1976; Beeri et al., 1977; Lewis et al., 1977; Beeri and Bernstein, 1979; Maier et al., 1979; Luk, 1981]. This work is related to the problem of getting a "better" but equivalent set of functional dependencies from the original set of functional dependencies.

LEAGUE

| Player | Team | Coach |
|--------|--------|----------|
| Larsen | Stars | McGraw |
| Larsen | Stars | Harris |
| Nelson | Lancers | Robinson |
| Wagner | Stars | McGraw |
| Wagner | Stars | Harris |

**Fig. 13.2—1** Example multivalued dependency.

Although useful as a constraint in data modeling, the idea of functional dependency is limited in the following sense. When $A \rightarrow B$, $A$ not only determines $B$, but it determines $B$ uniquely. The uniqueness limitation can be too restrictive in some cases. Consider, for instance, the following example of a relation shown in Figure 13.2—1. In this example, the coaches depend on the team, but obviously $Team \rightarrow Coach$ is not true. In addition, team determines a set of players but $Team \rightarrow Player$ is not true. However, it is true that a team determines a set of players who are related with a set of coaches. This property of data has been formalized as the notion of *multivalued dependency* (MVD) [Fagin, 1977b]. In this particular instance there is a multivalued dependency from team to coach written $Team \rightarrow\rightarrow Coach$ (e.g., Stars $\rightarrow\rightarrow$ {McGraw, Harris} and Lancers $\rightarrow\rightarrow$ {Robinson}). The multivalued dependency says that all players depend on the team and not on the individual coaches. In addition, the coaches depend on the team and not on the individual players. A functional dependency is by definition also a multivalued dependency.

To formalize multivalued dependencies, consider a relation scheme $R(X, Y, Z)$, where $X$, $Y$, and $Z$ are sets of attributes. We say that $Y \rightarrow\rightarrow Z$ ($Y$ multivalue determines $Z$) *iff* the set $Zyx = \{z \mid (x, y, z) \in R\}$ depends only on $y$. That is, for $x_1$, $x_2$ where $x_1 \neq x_2$ the set $Zyx_1 = Zyx_2$ if they are not empty. Another way of stating the same property is that for any $x_1$, $x_2$, $y$, $z_1$, and $z_2$, if $x_1yz_1$ and $x_2yz_2$ are tuples of an extension $r$ of $R$, so are the tuples $x_1yz_2$ and $x_2yz_1$.

A way to visualize the multivalued dependency is to think of $Y$ as a pivot. Suppose that we fix a particular value $y$. For every $x$ related to $y$ the set of $z$'s is identical (Figure 13.2−2). In the *LEAGUE* relation it says pick any team. The set of players related to one particular coach is also related to any other coach of the team. Another way of saying the same thing is to state that the players are independent of the coaches, but dependent on the team. The definition is symmetric. That is, if $Y \longrightarrow\!\!\!\rightarrow Z$, then $Y \longrightarrow\!\!\!\rightarrow X$ if $R$ is partitioned into attribute sets $X$, $Y$, and $Z$. For instance, if team determines coaches, it also determines players.

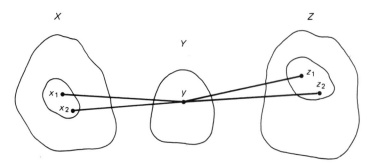

**Fig. 13.2−2** A mapping representing a multivalued dependency.

Although in the example teams determine a set of equivalence classes of both players and coaches, this is not always the case. It cannot be said in general that $Y \longrightarrow\!\!\!\rightarrow Z$ *iff* the values of $Z$ can be divided into a set of disjoint equivalence classes each of which is related to one $y$. For instance, if a player (say, a Brazilian soccer player) plays both in North America and in Brazil on two different teams, the multivalued dependency will still hold. On the other hand, if a particular coach-team-player combination is missing (because, say, the coach dislikes the player), although the players are in disjoint classes, the multivalued dependency *Team* $\longrightarrow\!\!\!\rightarrow$ *Player* will not hold. Neither will the multivalued dependency *Team* $\longrightarrow\!\!\!\rightarrow$ *Coach*.

A good way to understand multivalued dependencies is through their properties. Some of these properties are [Beeri et al., 1978; Mendelzon, 1979; Beeri, 1980]:

1.  $Y \longrightarrow\!\!\!\rightarrow Z$ if a relation $R(X, Y, Z)$ is the join of two relations $R_1(X, Y)$ and $R_2(Y, Z)$. It is obvious that in the join of $R_1$ and $R_2$, for every value of $y$ the set $R_1(X, y)$ and $R_2(y, Z)$ are related in every way.

2.  If $X$, $Y$, and $Z$ partition the attributes of a relation $R(X, Y, Z)$ and if $Y \longrightarrow\!\!\!\rightarrow Z$ then $Y \longrightarrow\!\!\!\rightarrow X$ (complementation). This property comes from the symmetric nature of multivalued dependencies. It should be pointed out, however, that complementation introduces context. That is, the property is true in the context of $R$ and may not be true in general.

3. If $X$, $Y$, and $Z$ are pairwise disjoint (not necessarily partitioned) and if $X \twoheadrightarrow Y$ and $Y \twoheadrightarrow Z$, then $X \twoheadrightarrow Z$.
4. If $X \twoheadrightarrow Y$ and $X \twoheadrightarrow Z$, then $X \twoheadrightarrow YZ$ (partitioning).
5. $X \twoheadrightarrow YZ$ does not necessarily imply that $X \twoheadrightarrow Y$ and $X \twoheadrightarrow Z$.

This last property seems counterintuitive, but it should be clear on closer examination since a multivalued dependency is context dependent. That is, to know whether $Y \twoheadrightarrow Z$ holds we should know something about the other attributes $X$ which are the complement of the attributes $YZ$ in $R$. Suppose we know that $X \twoheadrightarrow YZ$. Then the dependency $X \twoheadrightarrow Y$ may not hold because the complement of attributes has changed (i.e., it now includes $Z$). In the same way $X \twoheadrightarrow Z$ may not hold because the complement of attributes now includes $Y$. Because of this context dependency, a multivalued dependency may hold in the projection of a relation but not in the relation itself [Fagin, 1977b].

We will illustrate the idiosyncracies of multivalued dependencies through an example [Beeri, 1979]. Consider a relation scheme that relates employees $E$, projects $P$, and locations $L$. Each employee works in several projects and each project has several locations. At first glance, it may appear that $E \twoheadrightarrow P$ (each employee works on several projects independently), $P \twoheadrightarrow L$ (each project has many locations independently), and $E \twoheadrightarrow L$ (each employee goes to many locations independently). Each one of the multivalued dependencies can be nicely visualized in a relation scheme which holds only the two corresponding attributes (i.e., $P \twoheadrightarrow L$ in $R_1(P, L)$, $E \twoheadrightarrow P$ in $R_2(E, P)$, and $E \twoheadrightarrow L$ in $R_3(E, L)$).

Consider, though, the relation $R(E, P, L)$ as one relation scheme and whether the multivalued dependencies hold. The answer depends on rather sensitive semantic arguments. For instance, a worker may be associated with locations through some projects, but does not work on all projects in a location. In this case, $E \twoheadrightarrow PL$ but $E \twoheadrightarrow P$ does not hold. The multivalued dependency $E \twoheadrightarrow P$ does not truly model the intended semantics. The correct multivalued dependencies are $E \twoheadrightarrow PL$ and $P \twoheadrightarrow L$. Another possibility is that an employee is associated with a location and works on all projects in this location. In this case $E \twoheadrightarrow PL$ and $L \twoheadrightarrow P$.

Derivation rules for implied multivalued dependencies have been proposed in the same vein as Armstrong's rules for functional dependencies [Beeri et al., 1977; Mendelzon, 1979]. The inference rules are:

**MVD1** (Complementation): Let $X$, $Y$, and $Z$ be sets such that their union is $U$ and $Y \cap Z \subseteq X$, then $X \twoheadrightarrow Y$ *iff* $X \twoheadrightarrow Z$.

**MVD2** (Reflexivity): If $Y \subseteq X$, then $X \twoheadrightarrow Y$.

**MVD3** (Augmentation): If $Z \subseteq W$ and $X \twoheadrightarrow Y$, then $XW \twoheadrightarrow YZ$.

**MVD4** (Transitivity ): If $X \twoheadrightarrow Y$ and $Y \twoheadrightarrow Z$, then $X \twoheadrightarrow Z - Y$.

There are also derivation rules which apply to both functional dependencies and multivalued dependencies. These are:

**FD-MVD1**: If $X \to Y$, then $X \twoheadrightarrow Y$.

**FD-MVD2**: If $X \twoheadrightarrow Z$ and $Y \to Z'$ ($Z' \subseteq Z$), where $Y$ and $Z$ are disjoint, then $X \to Z'$.

**FD-MVD3**: If $X \twoheadrightarrow Y$ and $XY \to Z$, then $X \to Z - Y$.

Functional dependencies and multivalued dependencies are not the only dependencies which can hold between attributes of a relation scheme. Other dependencies have been formalized and investigated in the literature (e.g., join dependencies, hierarchical dependencies, and mutual dependencies [Rissanen, 1977; Delobel, 1978; Nicolas, 1978a,b; Fagin, 1979a,b; Mendelzon and Maier, 1979]). All of these dependencies can also be thought of as special cases of a general form of dependency [Fagin, 1980]. In this way a general mathematical framework for many different kinds of dependencies can be obtained which unifies the theory of dependencies. However, many of the new dependencies are hard to visualize and even harder to use during schema design and analysis [Beeri, 1979; Sciore, 1981].

Functional dependencies and other dependencies can be used to specify particular types of constraints on entity types. These constraints relate to properties of the mappings between the attributes of an entity type. These properties can be specified during schema design and used in the analysis of a schema to eliminate undesirable properties. The nature of this analysis is the topic of the next section.

## 13.3 DECOMPOSITION

Suppose that we are given a data base schema in terms of attributes, relation schemes, and dependencies. We would like to determine whether it is a "good" schema. More specifically, we would like to ensure that the schema represents adequately everything we know, or at least everything we wish to capture about the stated dependencies. We also would like to avoid any redundancies in the specification of the schema. Finally, we would hope that the schema adequately separates the different information units (i.e., clusters attributes in the right way). In the previous section we discussed dependencies extensively, especially functional dependencies. In this section we use dependencies to evaluate a schema and to transform a schema into a "better" schema. Initially, we concentrate on functional dependencies.

The original schema can be given to us in one of two ways [Fagin, 1977a]. In one case, all the attributes are given and all the functional dependencies are given. In the second case, a set of relations are given together with a set of functional dependencies between their attributes. It seems that the two cases are widely different. They are not different, however, in terms of functional dependency theory and its use. All discussion of functional dependencies so far assumes that the functional dependencies are unique on unique attributes. One of the easier ways to ensure uniqueness is to assume that all attributes are part of a large universal relation $U$. The functional dependencies are stated with respect to $U$ and the relation schemes of any schema are projections of $U$.

Under this assumption, the two cases are not radically different. In one case we are given a set $F$ of functional dependencies and, implicitly, the relation scheme $U$. We are asked to decompose $U$ to the "right" components. In the second case, we are given a decomposition $R_1, ..., R_n$ of relation schemes and a set $F$ of functional dependencies. However, this set of functional dependencies is really manipulated within the underlying relation scheme $U$ of which $R_1, ..., R_n$ are projections. We are asked to determine whether the selection of schemes $R_1, ..., R_n$ is any good. The evaluation uses exactly the same criteria as trying to obtain a good decomposition of $U$.

Before we proceed we should try to establish that decomposition itself is good. That is, why is it not a good idea to keep $U$ and all information about our universe in one relation. Many reasons have been suggested why decompositions are necessary [Codd, 1971a, 1972a]. It has been pointed out that some peculiar conditions arise when we lump attributes together which should be kept apart. These conditions are called *anomalies*. Whether they are really anomalies depends very much on the intended semantics. However, they seem to be undesirable in certain cases. We will illustrate these anomalies using the following relation scheme [Codd, 1972a].

*COMPANY(Employee#, Department#, Manager, Contract type)*

The following anomalies may arise in manipulating this relation.

1. **Update anomaly**. The change of a manager in a department necessitates a series of changes of this manager for each employee and contract type in which the department is involved. That is, a change should ripple through and cause a series of changes for the data base to be consistent. This can be thought of as an anomaly because the original change was specified in terms of a relation tuple without any considerations for its side effects.

2. **Insertion anomaly**. When the first employee is hired for a department a manager and contract type should be specified, too. This may be considered an anomaly because hiring the employee does not necessarily imply that we should make preliminary, ad hoc decisions about the department.

3.  **Deletion anomaly**. When the last employee is fired, any department information will cease to exist. This can be considered an anomaly if we would have liked to retain important, long-ranging information about the department.
4.  **Redundancy**. The contract type and the manager of a department are repeated in many tuples. This redundancy causes problems not because it is wasteful (a storage mechanism may be clever enough to eliminate it), but because redundant information should always stay consistent.

In short, the internal semantics that can be captured by functional dependencies force side effects on tuples every time there is a change in the data base extension. This situation can be avoided by decomposition. For instance, in our example, we can get rid of the anomalies by breaking the relation scheme into two relation schemes

*EMPLOYEE* (*Employee#*, *Department#* )
*DEPARTMENT* (*Department#*, *Manager*, *Contract type*)

In the decomposed schema, employees and departments are isolated and related only by specifying the department in which an employee works. This decomposition is not arbitrary. It is based on the two functional dependencies *Department#* → *Manager*, *Contract type* and *Employee#* → *Department#*. The decomposition isolated these two dependencies in separate relation schemes. As a result, they do not interfere with each other. The anomalies that were sketched informally are side effects of the dependencies. These side effects were eliminated by isolating the dependencies in different relation schemes. We now investigate the general conditions for such decompositions.

Consider a relation scheme $R$ and a set $\mathbf{F}$ of functional dependencies and the replacement of $R$ by a set of relation schemes $\rho = \{R_1, ..., R_k\}$ such that

$$\bigcup_{i=1}^{k} R_i = R$$

(i.e., all attributes of $R$ appear somewhere in the $R_i$'s). A decomposition is "good" when the schema $\rho$ is *equivalent* to $R$ and when it gets rid of some of the anomalies. For the two schemas $R$ and $\rho$ to be equivalent, we should expect [Beeri et al., 1978, 1981; Ullman, 1980]:

1.  Lossless join property.
2.  Dependency preservation.

The decomposition $\rho$ has the *lossless join property* with respect to a set of functional dependencies $\mathbf{F}$ if for every instance $r$ satisfying $\mathbf{F}$

$$r = \overset{k}{\underset{i=1}{*}} \pi_{R_i}(r)$$

Informally, the lossless join property ensures that any extension $r$ of $R$ can be recovered by the extensions of the projections of $r$ in terms of the decomposed relation schema $\{R_1, ..., R_k\}$. If we get more tuples by joining the projections than we had originally in $r$, we will lose some information. Our tuples will get "diluted" with unwanted tuples. In that case we say that the join is *lossy* and the decomposition of $R$ into $\rho$ is not lossless [Aho et al., 1979a].

Consider as an example the two relation schemes

$R_1$(*Project, Manager*)
$R_2$(*Manager, Employee#* )

with functional dependencies *Project* → *Manager* and *Employee#* → *Manager*. Suppose that we join according to *Manager* the two relations $R_1$ and $R_2$ to form $R$(*Project, Manager, Employee#* ). A problem arises because each employee will be related in $R$ not only with their projects, but with all projects in which their manager is involved. This problem can be considered as a *join anomaly* and it is referred to sometimes as the *connection trap*. The join we have obtained in this case is a "bad" or *lossy* join, since it introduces tuples that should not be there.

Consider as a different example the same two relation schemes but with functional dependencies *Manager* → *Project* and *Employee#* → *Manager*. That is, a manager manages at most one project. In this case the join that results in the relation scheme $R$(*Project, Manager, Employee#* ) will be lossless. Every employee will be associated in $R$ with exactly the projects with which he or she should be associated (i.e., the project managed by their manager). No extraneous tuples are present. Note that the join attribute *Manager* is a key in $R_1$. In fact, this property happens to be a sufficient condition for the join to be lossless. More formally, the join of $R_1$ and $R_2$ is lossless if $R_1 \cap R_2 → R_1$ or $R_1 \cap R_2 → R_2$.

Consider again the previous relation schemes but in this case the dependencies are *Manager* →→ *Project* and *Manager* →→ *Employee#*. That is, an employee works on all projects that their manager manages. In this case the join $R$(*Project, Manager, Employee#* ) of $R_1$ and $R_2$ will again be lossless. It associates every employee with all the projects that their manager manages. However, this situation is desirable since it is expressed by the multivalued dependencies. A join of $R_1$ and $R_2$ is lossless if $R_1 \cap R_2 →→ R_1 | R_2$.

A necessary and sufficient condition for a join of two relations to be lossless is that their intersection $(R_1 \cap R_2)$ determines either via functional or multivalued dependencies $R_1$ and/or $R_2$. The situation for joins of more than two relations is more complicated. There is, however, a technique for checking for lossless joins using a structure called a *tableau* [Aho et al., 1979c; Ullman, 1980]. In addition, the idea that a set of relations can be joined without any problem has been formalized as a join dependency [Rissanen, 1977; Aho et al., 1979a,b].

A decomposition is *dependency preserving* if its dependencies are preserved within the new relation schema $\rho$. Formally, this property is expressed as follows. Define the projection $F_i$ of $R_i$ as all the functional dependencies $X \rightarrow Y$ in $\mathbf{F}^+$ such that $XY \subseteq R_i$. That is, $F_i$ captures all the functional dependencies of the closure of $\mathbf{F}$ which can be captured within $R_i$. A decomposition $\rho$ preserves the set of functional dependencies $\mathbf{F}$ *iff*

$$(\bigcup_{i=1}^{k} F_i)^+ = \mathbf{F}^+$$

This property states that if we capture only the functional dependencies within the $R_i$'s, forgetting any functional dependencies that go across $R_i$'s, then we have enough functional dependencies to cover the original set.

This expectation of capturing (to generate a cover) an adequate set of functional dependencies within the relation schemes $R_i$ is rather restrictive. We sometimes refuse to deal with functional dependencies that involve attributes in different relations $R_i$. This situation is rather odd since in many data models functional mappings among entity types are handled with ease (e.g., DBTG-set types).

We have outlined a notion of equivalence of relation schemes. Using this notion we can talk about equivalent schemes that eliminate anomalies.

Anomalies in terms of our previous informal discussion seem to be caused by certain unwanted functional dependency structures. These structures can be avoided by forcing some restrictions on the allowed functional dependencies in a relation scheme. The rationale is that by avoiding these structures we eliminate anomalies [Codd, 1971a, 1972a; Fagin, 1977a]. The relation schemes that abide by the restrictions are said to be in *normal form*. There are four normal forms defined in terms of functional dependencies and one in terms of functional and multivalued dependencies [Fagin, 1977a,b]. The way that a relation scheme is turned into a normal form relation scheme is by decomposition [Codd, 1971a, 1972a; Armstrong and Delobel, 1980; Zaniolo and Melkanoff, 1981].

Before we start with a definition of normal forms, we first summarize some notation. Consider a relation scheme $R$ and a set of functional dependencies $\mathbf{F}$. A *superkey* $X$ of $R$ is a set of attributes $X$ of $R$ such that for every attribute $A$ of $R$, $X \rightarrow A$. A *key* of $R$ is a superkey which is nonredundant. That is, for every attribute $B$ of $Y$, $Y - B$ is not a superkey. An attribute of $R$ is *prime* if it participates in a key. Since a relation can have many keys, they are sometimes called *candidate keys*. A *partial dependency* occurs in $R$ if there is an attribute $A$ such that $Z \to A$, where $Z$ is a proper subset of a key $Y$. A *transitive dependency* occurs in $R$ if there is an attribute $A$ such that $X \to Y$, $Y \to A$, but $Y \not\to X$ where $X$ is a key and $Y \subset R$.

The normal forms are defined by enforcing certain properties on the relation schemes. These properties will be stated and illustrated by examples.

A relation is in *first normal form* (1NF) if every attribute is a simple attribute. That is, there are no composite attributes. Consider, for example, the relation scheme

*CARS(Model, #cylinders, Origin, Tax, Fee, Factory(Plant name, Location))*

The attribute *Factory* is obviously composite. To put a relation into 1NF we expand all composite attributes into their constituents. In our example, we obtain the relation scheme

*CARS¹(Model, #cylinders, Origin, Tax, Fee, Plant name, Location)*

This example suggests a general (and easy) algorithm to put a relation scheme into 1NF. We just expand the relation scheme by eliminating all composite attributes and replacing them with their constituent parts.

$$CARS^2$$

| Model | # cylinders | Origin | Tax | Fee |
|---|---|---|---|---|
| Rabbit | 4 | Germany | 15 | 30 |
| Mustang | 6 | USA | 0 | 45 |
| Mirafiori | 4 | Italy | 18 | 30 |
| Accord | 4 | Japan | 20 | 30 |
| Cutlass | 8 | USA | 0 | 60 |
| Mustang | 4 | Canada | 0 | 30 |
| Monaco | 6 | Canada | 0 | 45 |
| Fox | 4 | Germany | 15 | 30 |

Model, # cylinders → Origin
Model, # cylinders → Tax
Model, # cylinders → Fee
# cylinders → Fee
Origin → Tax

**Fig. 13.3−1** Example relation in 1NF.

A relation that is already in 1NF is said to be in *second normal form* (2NF) if it has no partial dependencies of nonprime attributes on keys. Consider the relation scheme, extension, and functional dependencies shown in Figure 13.3—1. For this particular relation the key is *Model, #cylinders*. However, there is a partial dependency *#cylinders → Fee* of a nonprime attribute (i.e., *Fee*) on the key *Model, #cylinders*. This partial dependency results in update, insertion, and deletion anomalies for values of the *Fee* attribute as well as redundancy of *Fee* values. To put the relation scheme into 2NF we decompose it into the two relation schemes and extensions shown in Figure 13.3—2. This example again suggests a way of putting a relation scheme into 2NF. We decompose it to get rid of partial dependencies.

*CARS* [3]

| Model | # cylinders | Origin | Tax |
|---|---|---|---|
| Rabbit | 4 | Germany | 15 |
| Mustang | 6 | USA | 0 |
| Mirafiori | 4 | Italy | 18 |
| Accord | 4 | Japan | 20 |
| Cutlass | 8 | USA | 0 |
| Mustang | 4 | Canada | 0 |
| Monaco | 6 | Canada | 0 |
| Fox | 4 | Germany | 15 |

*LICENSING*

| # cylinders | Fee |
|---|---|
| 4 | 30 |
| 6 | 45 |
| 8 | 60 |

**Fig. 13.3—2** Example relations in 2NF.

A relation is in *third normal form* (3NF) if it is in 2NF and it has no transitive dependencies of nonprime attributes on keys. In Figure 13.3—2, *CARS* [3] is in 2NF but has the transitive dependency (from Figure 13.3—1) *Model, #cylinders → Origin → Tax*, where *Tax ↛ Model, #cylinders* and *Origin ↛ Model, #cylinders*. This transitive dependency results in update, insertion, and deletion anomalies for values of the *Tax* attribute as well as redundancy of *Tax* values. To get rid of this transitive dependency we again decompose the relation scheme into the two relation schemes and extensions shown in Figure 13.3—3. This example again suggests a way of turning a relation scheme into 3NF. We decompose the relation scheme to break the transitive dependencies.

2NF and 3NF are very specific in isolating properties of nonprime attributes. There is a normal form that treats all attributes, prime and nonprime, the same way. Moreover, it is the strongest property we may want to enforce in terms of functional dependencies.

$CARS^4$

| Model | # cylinders | Origin |
|-------|-------------|--------|
| Rabbit | 4 | Germany |
| Mustang | 6 | USA |
| Mirafiori | 4 | Italy |
| Accord | 4 | Japan |
| Cutlass | 8 | USA |
| Mustang | 4 | Canada |
| Monaco | 6 | Canada |
| Fox | 4 | Germany |

TAXATION

| Origin | Tax |
|--------|-----|
| Germany | 15 |
| USA | 0 |
| Italy | 18 |
| Japan | 20 |
| Canada | 0 |

**Fig. 13.3—3** Example relations in 3NF.

A relation is in *Boyce-Codd normal form* (BCNF) if for all nontrivial functional dependencies $X \to Y$ in R, X is a superkey. A trivial functional dependency is $X \to X'$, where $X' \subseteq X$. BCNF in essence says that all functional dependencies of a relation are the result of keys. It can easily be shown that if a 1NF relation is in BCNF, then it is also in 2NF and 3NF. The property that all functional dependencies are the result of keys eliminates both partial and transitive dependencies.

Consider the relation scheme $CARS^4$ in Figure 13.3—3 but with the additional functional dependency *Origin* → *# cylinders*[1]. The relation is in 3NF because the only nonprime attribute is *Origin*. *Origin* is neither partially nor transitively dependent on the key *Model, # cylinders*. However, the prime attribute *# cylinders* is transitively dependent on the key (i.e., *Model, # cylinders* → *Origin* → *# cylinders*). 3NF does not worry about prime attributes. BCNF does, and this relation is not in BCNF. The functional dependency *Origin* → *# cylinders* is not part of a key. To put our example relation into BCNF, we again decompose it into two relation schemes

$CARS^5$(*Model, # cylinders*)
*ENGINE SIZE*(*# cylinders, Origin*)

Each one of the resulting relations is now in BCNF. Notice, however,

---

[1] Note that this functional dependency is not satisfied by the example relation extension.

that one of the dependencies (i.e., *Model, # cylinders → Origin*) is not expressed within the relation schemes. It can only be formulated in between relations. Hence, the decomposition is not dependency preserving. If we consider only functional dependencies which are within relations, this particular functional dependency is lost. As a matter of fact, close inspection reveals that any relation which has the functional dependency *Model, # cylinders → Origin* will necessarily have the functional dependency *Origin → # cylinders* and the resulting relation is not in BCNF. We see, therefore, an example where we cannot obtain a decomposition that is both BCNF and dependency preserving. We discuss these interplays between desired properties for decompositions in the next section.

All normal forms up to this point have been formulated with respect to functional dependencies. There is also a normal form that considers multivalued dependencies. A relation is in *fourth normal form* (4NF) if all the nontrivial multivalued dependencies are due to keys. A trivial multivalued dependency is $X \rightarrow\rightarrow Y$, $Y \rightarrow\rightarrow X$ in $R(X, Y)$. This property can be expressed as: if $X \rightarrow\rightarrow Y$ is nontrivial, then $X \rightarrow\rightarrow A$ for every attribute $A$ in $R$. Since functional dependencies are also multivalued dependencies, if a relation is in 4NF, it is in BCNF and hence in 3NF.

Consider as an example the relation scheme *CARS* [4] in Figure 13.3−3 but with a set of multivalued dependencies $Model \rightarrow\rightarrow \# cylinders$ and $Model \rightarrow\rightarrow Origin$. That is, each model has many countries of origin independent of number of cylinders and each model comes in various numbers of cylinders but independent of origin. The key of the relation scheme is *Model, # cylinders, Origin*. There are no functional dependencies, hence the relation scheme is trivially in BCNF. However, the multivalued dependencies are not the result of a key, since *Model* is not a key. Therefore, the relation scheme is not in 4NF. The relation can be put into 4NF by decomposing it into the two relation schemes

*CARS* [6] *(Model, # cylinders)*
*ENGINE SIZE (Model, Origin)*

Our discussion so far suggests the following approach for obtaining a normal form schema. Consider a relational schema consisting of a set of relation schemes $\rho = \{R_1, ..., R_n\}$ and dependencies **F** within them. We check each relation $R_i$ to see whether it is in the desired normal form. If it is not, we attempt to decompose it further to get it into normal form.

There are two criticisms associated with such an *analytic* approach [Fagin, 1977a]. First, an original design for a schema is assumed to be present. The analytic approach improves that design. The original design is assumed to have some nice properties (e.g., no interrelation dependencies). This assumption of a good starting schema is not always easy to fulfill. Second, the analytic approach only splits relation schemes. It does not combine relations schemes which may both get rid of unwanted dependencies and improve the schema. Thus, the analytic approach will miss those schemas, which can be obtained by other analysis methods, which are both in normal form and "better".

In a different approach, called the *synthetic* approach, the attributes and functional dependencies are assumed given [Bernstein, 1976; Bernstein and Beeri, 1976; Fagin, 1977a]. The result of the normalization is a schema that incorporates the attributes and the functional dependencies and is in third normal form. The dependencies in the synthetic approach are not given in the context of a particular relation. The dependencies are considered the primitive objects, not relations, and are supposed to exist independently of relations. However, the implicit assumption is that all the attributes and dependencies are expressed in terms of the universal relation $U$.

To illustrate this normalization process, consider as an example the following universal relation [Fagin, 1977a]:

$R$ (*Project, Part, Supplier, Location, Cost, Employee, Manager, Salary, Hiredate*)

The dependencies are

*Supplier, Part* $\rightarrow$ *Cost*
*Project* $\rightarrow$ *Manager*
*Employee* $\rightarrow$ *Salary, Hiredate*
*Supplier* $\rightarrow\!\!\rightarrow$ *Location*
*Project* $\rightarrow\!\!\rightarrow$ *Employee, Salary, Hiredate.*

The multivalued dependency *Project* $\rightarrow\!\!\rightarrow$ *Employee does not* hold. *Salary* and *Hiredate* are needed together with *Employee* for the last multivalued dependency to hold.

The normalization can proceed by following a simple rule. If $X \rightarrow Y$ or $X \rightarrow\!\!\rightarrow Y$ in $R(X, Y, Z)$, then $R$ can be decomposed into $R_1(X, Y)$ and $R_2(X, Z)$ without any problems. The original $R$ is the natural join of $R_1$ and $R_2$.

On the basis of the first functional dependency we decompose $R$ into

$R_1$(*Supplier, Part, Cost*)
$R_2$(*Supplier, Part, Project, Location, Employee, Manager, Salary, Hiredate*)

$R_1$ is in 4NF, but $R_2$ obviously is not. We concentrate on $R_2$. A dependency of $R$ is present in $R_2$ provided that all the attributes in the dependency are present in $R_2$. Hence the multivalued dependency *Project* $\rightarrow\!\!\rightarrow$ *Employee, Salary, Hiredate* is present in $R_2$. We use it to follow our simple rule and get

$R_3$(*Project, Employee, Salary, Hiredate*)
$R_4$(*Project, Supplier, Part, Location, Manager*)

Using *Employee* → *Salary, Hiredate* the relation scheme $R_3$ can be decomposed into the 4NF relation schemes

$R_5$(*Employee, Salary, Hiredate*)
$R_6$(*Employee, Project*)

The relation scheme $R_4$ can be decomposed into

$R_7$(*Project, Manager*)
$R_8$(*Project, Supplier, Part, Location*)

Finally, $R_8$ can be decomposed using *Supplier* → *Location* into

$R_9$(*Supplier, Location*)
$R_{10}$(*Supplier, Project, Part*)

We are finally left with the relation schemes

$R_1$(*Supplier, Part, Cost*)
$R_5$(*Employee, Salary, Hiredate*)
$R_6$(*Employee, Project*)
$R_7$(*Project, Manager*)
$R_9$(*Supplier, Location*)
$R_{10}$(*Supplier, Project, Part*)

It should be apparent that the synthetic decomposition could be followed in a different manner. The synthetic decomposition approach proceeds from one big relation scheme. As a result it has many options, unlike the analytic decomposition, which starts with a specific relational schema. Given the same initial set of attributes and dependencies, the resulting schema would be different depending on which decomposition method is used.

## 13.4 DECOMPOSITION EVALUATION

At this point we summarize the discussion of the previous sections and evaluate the suggested methodology for obtaining an "equivalent" and "better" schema. First, we proposed as a yardstick for equivalence the properties of lossless join and dependency preservation in the decomposed schema. Second, we proposed a series of normal forms which are supposed to eliminate anomalies. Both of these ideas rely heavily on the notion of a universal relation which relates all attributes and expresses uniquely all dependencies. We will evaluate each idea separately and then see how they work together.

To begin with, the main reason for decomposition and normal forms was to eliminate anomalies. In our treatment, anomalies were sketched and then normal forms were proposed to eliminate them. To be persuasive about the efficacy of this approach, we define more rigorously what an anomaly is and hopefully show that normal forms eliminate them.

Anomalies can be defined formally as giving rise to side effects. It has been proven that BCNF, at least in terms of a single relation, eliminates anomalies [Bernstein and Goodman, 1980]. Changes in a BCNF relation are local and do not propagate to an unpredictable number of tuples. We can be reasonably sure, therefore, that normal forms are a good approach within a single relation.

When we have a relational schema $\rho = \{R_1, ..., R_k\}$, the picture changes radically since our methodology is based on the fact that $R_1, ..., R_k$ are projections of a universal instance $U$. If all the $R_i$'s are in BCNF, a change in $R_i$ does not produce anomalies within $R_i$. However, problems may appear due to the interrelation of $R_i$'s through the universal relation $U$.

One problem is that we have to be assured that a change in a tuple of $R_i$ will get us to another data base extension which is a projection of $U$ onto the $R_i$'s. To determine this we need to check the data base, which is a very time consuming task. It has been proven to be NP-complete with respect to the size of the data base [Honeyman et al., 1980]. If the change does not get us to a data base extension which has a universal relation instance, we have a problem. The system can refuse the update, but this action is very hard to explain to the user, who thinks he is making only a local change in $R_i$. If the update does go through, we need to introduce side effects to remedy the situation and arrive at a universal relation-compatible data base extension [Bernstein and Goodman, 1980]. These side effects, however, defeat the basic philosophy of BCNF (i.e., localized changes). It is, therefore, sad but true that if we obtain a decomposition $\rho = \{R_1, ..., R_k\}$ where each $R_i$ is in BCNF, we still may have considerable problems.

Multivalued dependencies pose different problems for schema analysis. Using multivalued dependencies, we can arrive at decompositions which are 4NF [Fagin, 1977b; Beeri, 1979]. However, the multivalued dependencies depend on context and thus are very hard to visualize and to get right in the first place [Beeri, 1979; Sciore, 1981]. We can very easily capture the wrong multivalued dependencies according to our informal semantics, in which case our decomposition may be wrong.

A reasonable approach to solve this dilemma is to bring human intervention to bear on the problem by providing a good framework for data base administrators to check the results of a decomposition. One way that this objective can be achieved is by constructing a relation extension where only the given dependencies are true and all other dependencies are false. What we hope for is that a schema designer can check such relation extensions, which embody all the dependencies, and pinpoint the trouble spots[1].

A different problem relates to the definition of "equivalence." The notion of equivalence based on dependency preservation and lossless joins is rather strong. Intuitively, it seems to make sense for a dependency to be across relation schemes. Most data models not only permit it, but they encourage it by having special constructs for such dependencies (e.g., DBTG-sets and hierarchical parent-child relationships). It is not, therefore, a question of semantics, but a case of the limitations of our theory.

Consider the desirability of a lossless join. In most cases getting a "better" schema implies decomposition (i.e., normal forms). The requirement of losslessness after decomposition seems to be counterintuitive. After all, there should be some trade-offs in decomposition; you gain something, but you lose something. There should be some reason for keeping a relation scheme together rather than decomposing it. There is an obvious consideration for efficiency of access, but it does not count in our abstract framework.

The lossless join property is actually a deterrent against ill-advised decompositions. When we decompose, the only way we can relate separated facts is through joins. A join, however, is rather indiscriminate in the way it relates tuples. All tuples get related every which way provided that the join attributes match. There may be unwanted combinations which appear in the join, giving rise to connections traps (join anomalies). To handle the situation we have to make sure that unwanted combinations never occur. One way to do this is by limiting the combinations (e.g., we always join with a key). Alternatively, we can say that the combinations are not unwanted, but on the contrary they are desirable. This is exactly what a join dependency gives us[2]. It allows us to take meaningful joins by specifying that the combinations arising from the join make sense.

There is a reason to question the validity of the ideas (i.e., lossless join, dependency preservation, normal forms, and the universal relation) underlying data base theory. Regardless of practice, all of them taken together do not work well even in theory. It can be proven that BCNF decompositions cannot always be obtained which have the dependency-preserving property[3] [Beeri and Bernstein, 1979]. In addition, the requirement of the universal relation instance defeats the purpose of

---

[1] Such a relation extension is usually called an Armstrong relation [Armstrong, 1974; Beeri et al., 1980].

[2] In two relations, a join dependency is exactly a multivalued dependency.

[3] Fortunately, 3NF decompositions can always be obtained which are join lossless and dependency preserving.

BCNF [Bernstein and Goodman, 1980]. Finally, checking the universal relation assumption is itself a very time consuming (hopeless) test which is unacceptable in any practical sense and most data bases violate it.

The main difficulties with data base theory as it relates to decomposition arise because of the universal relation assumption. At the same time the universal relation assumption supports the whole theoretical framework for decomposition. We have, therefore, a paradox. The theory does not seem to hold without the universal relation assumption. At the same time, the universal relation assumption is unrealistic both on semantic and pragmatic grounds.

Before we proceed, let us recall the exact definition of the universal relation assumption. Let $R$ be a universal relation and $\rho = \{R_1, ..., R_k\}$ (where $R = \bigcup_{i=1}^{k} R_i$) be a decomposition of $R$. For any instance $\{r_1, ..., r_k\}$ of $\rho$ there exists an instance $r$ of $R$ such that $pi_{R_i}(r) = r_i \forall i = 1, ..., k$. The assumption can be viewed as a guideline for decomposition. That is, decompositions $\rho$ are good if changes in the $R_i$'s can easily be checked or proven to satisfy the universal relation assumption.

The reason for making the assumption was to guarantee uniqueness of dependencies and to obtain inference rules for dependencies. In this way, we can check all dependencies for consistency by checking them against the universal relation instance. But before we can do this, there should exist a universal relation instance. Therefore, we need the universal relation assumption. But by making this assumption we defeat the whole purpose of the theory (i.e., getting a better schema). The ways out of this seeming impasse are many, but they have not been clearly mapped.

One of the approaches suggests establishing well-defined side effects to guarantee the universal relation assumption [Bernstein and Goodman, 1980]. In fact, the semantics of operations are modified to fit the universal relation assumption. In another approach, the notion of data base consistency is changed to accommodate incomplete information (nulls) in the universal relation instance. This approach necessitates a whole theory of dependencies where the null value is not treated as just another value but is given special semantics [Lien, 1979; Biskup, 1980; Honeyman, 1980; Maier, 1980; Vassiliou, 1980a,b; Sagiv, 1981]. A third approach can try to obtain the special cases of such schemas or decompositions where the universal relation assumption is easy to check. Finally, it seems that the definition of operations on relations has to be more closely examined. The operations retrieve, insert, delete, and update on tuples seem to be natural when no constraints are given. In the presence of constraints such operations may be highly unnatural because, although they seem innocent, they imply very many side effects. Trying to eliminate side effects by structural restrictions such as decompositions may seem to be worthwhile. However, some of these side effects are not only useful, but are semantically meaningful. They may be defined more easily dynamically in terms of operations than statically in terms of the schema [Sevcik and Furtado, 1978; Furtado et al., 1979].

Relations in a decomposed schema should correspond to entity types and relationships types. If they correspond to entity types, all dependencies should be the result of keys. After all, a key identifies uniquely an entity. The rest of the attributes are characteristics of the entity type and they should have no dependencies between themselves. It follows therefore that relations corresponding to entity types should be in BCNF. Establishing relationships between entities should be done in one of three ways. If we want to relate each entity of type $E_i$ with many entities of type $E_k$, we should propagate the key of $E_i$ to $E_k$. In this way the join on the relations representing the entity types will involve the key of $E_i$, it will be lossless, and it will correspond to the desired relationship. If it makes sense that all combinations should be allowed between $E_i$ and $E_k$ according to a value of an attribute, we should permit the join. In this case there is a join dependency between $E_i$ and $E_k$ which will make the join lossless. Finally, if we want to build an arbitrary relationship type between $E_i$ and $E_k$, we should not do it by joining. Instead, we should introduce a separate relation which has as attributes the keys of $E_i$ and $E_k$. This relation gives us the desired relationships in the exact way we want it.

## 13.5 CONCLUDING REMARKS

In this chapter different approaches were discussed which will yield, under certain conditions, a better schema. The discussion was rather theoretical and conceptual. There are, however, some pragmatic issues which should not be disregarded.

The first issue deals with obtaining the dependencies. In realistic situations it may be very hard to obtain an accurate set of dependencies. The situation is especially critical with respect to more complicated dependencies. The second problem deals with the assumptions of the theory. We already elaborated on the difficulties caused by the universal relation assumption. The difficulties are especially critical because the theory has not yet been unified completely. As a result different assumptions and definitions support different results [Beeri et al., 1978]. The third problem deals with the algorithms to test properties. Many of these algorithms have been proven to be NP-complete, which limits their applicability in practice [Beeri and Bernstein, 1979]. The final issue deals with verification of constraints in practice. Many of the schema analysis techniques depend on the ability to look at constraints as always being true for an allowable data base extension. At the same time, the mechanisms to verify these constraints are rather inefficient on today's hardware and software architectures. For example, to the best of our knowledge there is no system available today that guarantees even functional dependencies, outside of those that are the result of keys.

With so many limitations, it is worth wondering exactly what data base theory gives us. In fact, it provides us with some useful insights about data and data modeling. First, it guides us to avoid functional dependencies which are outside of keys within relations. Second, it pinpoints the difficulties with using joins indiscriminately. Finally, it ties together many data modeling ideas in a data model independent way.

Data base theory is not a panacea. The results it offers can be used for better design and they can be incorporated into schema design and analysis tools. However, care should be taken about what the underlying assumptions imply and what the derived results mean.

## EXERCISES

**13.1** Propose an algorithm to obtain all the candidate keys in a relational schema given the functional dependencies. Can you design an algorithm that finds the keys in time dependent only on the number of keys?

**13.2** Suppose that you have more than one different functional dependency between two sets of attributes. You can distinguish between them by naming them uniquely. Propose an algorithm that reduces a schema with labeled functional dependencies to a schema with unlabeled functional dependencies and perhaps more nodes. What semantic role do the additional nodes play?

**13.3** To what extent can theorem-proving techniques be used to verify predicate calculus constraints specified in the schema?

**13.4** Consider the following rules for deriving multivalued dependencies.

**MVD5** (Pseudo-transitivity): If $X \longrightarrow\!\!\!\!\rightarrow Y$ and $YW \longrightarrow\!\!\!\!\rightarrow Z$, then $XW \longrightarrow\!\!\!\!\rightarrow Z - YW$.

**MVD6** (Union): If $X \longrightarrow\!\!\!\!\rightarrow Y_1$ and $X \longrightarrow\!\!\!\!\rightarrow Y_2$, then $X \longrightarrow\!\!\!\!\rightarrow Y_1 Y_2$.

**MVD7** (Decomposition): If $X \longrightarrow\!\!\!\!\rightarrow Y_1$ and $X \longrightarrow\!\!\!\!\rightarrow Y_2$, then $X \longrightarrow\!\!\!\!\rightarrow Y_1 \bigcup Y_2$, $X \longrightarrow\!\!\!\!\rightarrow Y_1 - Y_2$, and $X \longrightarrow\!\!\!\!\rightarrow Y_2 - Y_1$.

Show that these rules can be derived from MVD1, MVD2, MVD3, and MVD4.

**13.5** The complementation rule for multivalued dependencies (MVD1) is rather bothersome since it introduces context. Try to obtain a set of inference rules for multivalued dependencies which do not require complementation. What can you show about the set of multivalued dependencies derived in this manner?

**13.6** Consider a decomposition $\rho = \{R_1, ..., R_k\}$. Outline an algorithm that determines whether the decomposition is dependency preserving.

**13.7** Consider a relation schema $\rho = \{R_1, ..., R_k\}$, where each relation $R_i$ is in BCNF. Further, the only joins allowed are in terms of keys. Prove that in this case all joins are lossless.

**13.8** Outline a data structure that can be used to enforce a key as a constraint in a relation. Can this data structure also be used to enforce arbitrary functional dependencies?

**13.9** Consider a DBTG-network schema. Suppose that we translate the record types into relations by introducing an external key (tuple identifier) for the relation schemes. For every DBTG-set type, we propagate the owner record type tuple identifier into the member record type as an attribute. Show that in the resulting relational schema every relation will be in BCNF and all joins will be lossless. Note that it is assumed that only joins on external keys are allowed since only these joins capture the relationships between record types in the DBTG-network schema.

**13.10** Design a schema based on a description of entity types and relationships types using the entity-relationship data model. From this schema, construct a relational schema by translating entity types and relationship types according to the three ways discussed in Section 3.4. Prove that your relational schema is "good" according to data base theory.

**13.11** Suppose that we are given the three relation schemes $CAR$(*Registration#, Owner, Price*), $PERSON$(*Name, Occupation, Salary*), and $HOUSE$(*Address, Owner, Price*). We would like to investigate whether people with high salaries own expensive cars and houses. To obtain the answer we join the three relations according to the person's name (i.e., $CAR.Owner = PERSON.Name$ **AND** $PERSON.Name = HOUSE.Owner$). Will these joins give us the desired result, and why?

**13.12** Consider two relation schemes $R_1$ and $R_2$. We say that $R_1$ and $R_2$ have the common intersection property if for every extension $r_1$ of $R_1$ and $r_2$ of $R_2$, $\pi_{R_1 \cap R_2}(r_1) = \pi_{R_1 \cap R_2}(r_2)$. Show that for a decomposition $\rho = \{R_1, ..., R_k\}$ to abide by the universal instance assumption (i.e., be join consistent), it should have at least the common intersection property between the relation schemes $R_i$. Is the common intersection property realistic in practice? How would you check the property?

**13.13** Show that the common intersection property is not a sufficient condition for the universal relation assumption.

**13.14** One of the main reasons for the universal relation assumption was that attributes and dependencies were uniquely identified. How can this requirement be satisfied without making the assumption that there exists a universal relation instance for every data base instance?

# Chapter 14

# DBMS MAPPINGS

## 14.1 INTRODUCTION

Although most data models have been proposed independently of one another, we saw in Part 1 that some basic underlying concepts relate them. Thus it should be possible to determine equivalence relationships and equivalence preserving mappings between data models. This problem is theoretically interesting for the consolidation of data models [Borkin, 1978, 1980; Lien, 1980]. It is also of practical importance since many large organizations have many different data bases and DBMSs which have to coexist. It may be desirable to provide a global interface to all of these diverse data bases. Such a facility requires a method of presenting a global schema to the user for issuing global operations and then translating these global operations into a series of equivalent local operations in equivalent local schemas [Taylor et al., 1979].

When mapping between (not necessarily distinct) data models, there are at least four aspects that we may want to consider in the mapping process: structures, constraints, operations, and data bases. If we want the two schemas to be equivalent, structures and constraints must be considered together in the mapping process. That is, the two schemas should represent equivalent structures and constraints. Thus, we are left with three independent coordinates of a mapping: structures and constraints (henceforth referred to as the data model), operations, and data bases.

Each of these mapping coordinates can be independently one of two cases. A mapping can be either within the same data model or between two different data models. Operations may or may not be included in the mapping. Finally, the mapping can be constructive or nonconstructive. A *constructive* mapping is one in which a data base (instance) according to one schema is mapped to another data base (instance) according to another schema. In a nonconstructive mapping the target data base may exist, but it is not obtained through the mapping. The different combinations of these three mapping coordinates leads to eight distinct mapping problems of differing degrees of complexity. We outline each mapping problem briefly in the remainder of this section.

Consider the nonconstructive mapping of a source schema $S_s$ to a target schema $S_t$. If an $S_s$ data base exists, the resulting $S_t$ data base is virtual and is never actually constructed. If $S_s$ and $S_t$ are based on the same data model and operations are not mapped, we have a *schema restructuring mapping*. Such a mapping occurs, for instance, when we take a relational schema with its functional dependencies and transform it to another relational schema with the same functional dependencies during schema analysis [Navathe, 1976, 1977, 1980a]. If operations on the $S_t$ schema are mapped to the $S_s$ data base, we have a *view mapping* [Chamberlin et al., 1975]. Such a mapping is required, for instance, when we want to provide different subschemas of a schema to different users.

If the mapping is nonconstructive and $S_s$ and $S_t$ are according to different data models, the mapping problem becomes more complicated. If operations are not mapped from $S_t$ to $S_s$, we have a *schema translation mapping*. This problem arises during schema design when we express the requirements of an application according to one data model and then implement it according to another data model. If operations are mapped, we have an *operation transform mapping* as defined in the ANSI/X3/SPARC report [Tsichritzis and Klug, 1978]. This latter mapping is usually specified as: given $S_s$ according to data model $\mathbf{M}_s$ find a schema $S_t$ according to data model $\mathbf{M}_t$ which can be used to operate on the data base associated with $S_s$. That is, every data base of $S_s$ can be viewed as a data base according to $S_t$. The operation transform mapping problem arises, for example, when relational views are mapped to a hierarchical or network schema [Klug and Tsichritzis, 1977; Zaniolo, 1979a,b; Vassiliou and Lochovsky, 1980; Klug, 1981].

Consider now a constructive mapping between two different schemas $S_s$ and $S_t$, both based on the same data model. That is, we would like to map a data base according to $S_s$ to another (actual) data base according to $S_t$. If operations are not included, we have a *data base reorganization mapping*. To handle this mapping problem, we need an algorithm to obtain the $S_t$ data base from the $S_s$ data base [Fry and Jervis, 1974; Navathe and Merten, 1974]. This mapping problem incorporates the schema restructuring mapping since the $S_t$ schema must be mapped somehow from the $S_s$ schema. If we also consider operations in the mapping, we have a situation where we have several different schemas and their associated data bases all according to the same data model. In this case we need to construct a global schema that encompasses all the different schemas. Then we need to be able to map any operations against this global schema to appropriate operations on different underlying schemas. As this mapping problem appears in homogeneous distributed data bases [Rothnie et al., 1980], we call it a *homogeneous distributed system mapping.*

Suppose that the mapping is constructive and $S_s$ and $S_t$ are according to different data models $\mathbf{M}_s$ and $\mathbf{M}_t$. If operations are not included, we have a *data base translation mapping.* For instance, we may want to map a hierarchical data base to a relational data base [Shu et al., 1977]. The problem is usually posed as: given $S_s$ according to $\mathbf{M}_s$ and a data base associated with it, obtain $S_t$ and the associated data base according to $\mathbf{M}_t$. If operations are also included, we have a *data base cooperation mapping.* This mapping problem arises in heterogeneous distributed data bases [Adiba and Delobel, 1977].

| $S_s, S_t$ same data models | $S_s \rightarrow S_t$ constructive | Operations included | Mapping problem |
|---|---|---|---|
| YES | NO | NO | SCHEMA RESTRUCTURING |
| NO | NO | NO | SCHEMA TRANSLATION |
| YES | YES | NO | DATA BASE REORGANIZATION |
| NO | YES | NO | DATA BASE TRANSLATION |
| YES | NO | YES | VIEW |
| NO | NO | YES | OPERATION TRANSFORM |
| YES | YES | YES | HOMOGENEOUS DISTRIBUTED SYSTEMS |
| NO | YES | YES | DATA BASE COOPERATION |

**Fig. 14.1—1** DBMS mappings.

Figure 14.1—1 summarizes the different mapping problems discussed in this section. In the rest of this chapter we discuss three mapping problems in more detail. The first concerns the problem of schema translation which contains, as a special case, schema restructuring. This problem is concerned with mapping structures and constraints of one schema into another schema. Second, we discuss the preceding problem when operations are included (i.e., operation transform mappings). Finally, we discuss data base translation which also encompasses data base reorganization (i.e., the constructive mapping of one data base to another). The problems of homogeneous distributed systems and data base cooperation can be dealt with by a synthesis of the techniques used to deal with the preceding mapping problems. Needless to say, these last two problems are very complex and there is still much research needed to solve them completely.

## 14.2 STRUCTURE AND CONSTRAINT MAPPINGS

In Part 1 we defined the basic structures of data models as being derived from sets and relations. Since most data models can be defined in terms of these concepts, it would appear to be relatively easy to specify structure mappings between data models. The difficulties in the mapping process are introduced when we also consider constraints [Borkin, 1978]. Some data models have many inherent constraints, some only a few, and others none at all. When we try to map between data models with different degrees of inherent constraints, many problems arise. Even when the data models are the same, constraint mappings can still cause problems since the constraints that applied to the original structures may apply differently or not at all to the new structures. We investigate the issues related to structure and constraint mappings in this section.

In structure and constraint mappings we want to map the structures and constraints of a source schema $S_s$ to a target schema $S_t$. We are concerned at this point only with mapping schemas, not with mapping operations or data bases. However, the schema mappings should allow the possibility of mapping operations and data bases. Depending on whether or not the two schemas are according to the same data model, we have either a schema restructuring mapping (same data model) or a schema translation mapping (different data models).

As pointed out already, we can, in fact, consider the problem of mapping structures and constraints as two separate problems: mapping structures and mapping constraints. If we map only the structures of schema $S_s$ to another schema $S_t$, then for every data base in $S_s$ we can have a (virtual) corresponding $S_t$ data base. However, every (virtual) data base derivable from $S_t$ will not be necessarily a valid $S_s$ data base. Schema $S_s$ may have some constraints specified for it that are enforced in an $S_s$ data base. These constraints also are enforced implicitly when viewing the $S_s$ data base via the $S_t$ schema. However, the $S_t$ schema, because it is "constraint free," may potentially allow (virtual) data bases that do not preserve the constraints in the $S_s$ schema. Note that mapping problems only arise when we perform operations on $S_t$ and attempt to reflect these operations, correctly, on the $S_s$ data base (see Section 14.3) or when we map the $S_s$ data base to an $S_t$ data base and then perform operations on the $S_t$ data base (see Section 14.4). Since we will eventually want to map operations and/or data bases, schema mappings that do not preserve constraints are not very desirable.

The schema restructuring problem cannot be solved in general, but must be considered on a data model by data model basis. For relational data models, schema restructuring has a simple form since relational data models separate structure from constraint specification, allowing each to be handled more or less independently. Thus, for the structure part, given a source schema $S_s$ we can specify the structure of a target schema $S_t$ by means of relational algebra or calculus expressions involving the structures of $S_s$. That is, for every relation $R_t$ of $S_t$ of degree $n$, we associate an expression $f(R_s)$ having $n$ free variables and involving relations of and/or predicates on $S_s$. Every relation name in $S_t$ must appear on the left side of exactly one expression $f(R_s)$. The right side of each expression $f(R_s)$ is a formula defined on $S_s$. Hence, an expression $f(R_s)$ is like a defining equation for the relations of $S_t$. This definition of mappings covers, in essence, relational data base structure mappings.

To include constraints in the mapping, it is necessary to obtain from the constraints of $S_s$ the corresponding constraints of $S_t$. For functional dependency constraints, for instance, it is necessary to obtain, from a set of functional dependencies associated with $S_s$, the corresponding set of functional dependencies for each relation $R_t$ in $S_t$ that is defined from $S_s$ through an expression $f(R_s)$.

As an example of the mapping process, suppose that $S_s$ is specified by the following relations and constraints (functional dependencies):

$$S_s: R(A, B), S(C, D), A \to B, C \to D$$

If the structure part of $S_t$ is defined as

$$S_t: T = R \underset{A=C}{*} S$$

then the corresponding constraint for $S_t$ is the functional dependency $A \to BD$.

Intuitively, for the two schemas $S_s$ and $S_t$ to be equivalent, the mapping should be reversible [Lien, 1980]. That is, having derived $S_t$ from $S_s$, it should be possible to derive $S_s$ from $S_t$. For the relational schema restructuring mapping process we have defined, this may not always be the case as the following example (due to E. F. Codd) illustrates. Suppose that $S_s$ and $S_t$ are specified as

$$S_s: R(A, B, C), AB \to C, C \to B$$
$$S_t: S = \pi_{A, C}(R), T = \pi_{B, C}(R), C \to B$$

In $S_t$, only the functional dependency $C \to B$ can apply, since $A$, $B$, and $C$ do not appear together in one relation. Because of the functional dependency $C \to B$, the join of $S$ and $T$ on $C$ is lossless. Therefore, if we join $S$ and $T$ we get back $R$, but we have lost the ability to calculate (and to enforce) the functional dependency $AB \to C$.

Extensive work has been done on relational schema restructuring [Navathe, 1976, 1980a; Navathe and Fry, 1976; Klug, 1978, 1980; Dayal, 1979; Spyratos, 1980]. For instance, given a source schema $S_s$ and its functional dependencies, Klug gives mapping rules for deriving the structures and constraints of a target schema $S_t$ [Klug, 1978, 1980]. These rules are shown to be sound and complete when certain restrictions are placed on the mapping expressions $f(R_s)$. These restrictions deal with the order of application of relational algebra operators and the removal of the set difference operator from the mapping expressions.

Work has also been done on schema restructuring in other data models. For instance, consider hierarchical schema restructuring [Dale and Dale, 1976, 1977; Dale and Yurkanan, 1977]. Three hierarchical schema transformations called catenation, lifting, and shifting are identified that preserve query homomorphism.

A *catenation* transformation involves moving a subtree from under one record type and placing it under another record type. An example of a catenation transformation is shown in Figure 14.2−1.

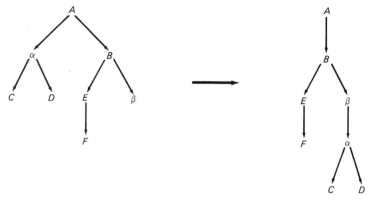

**Fig. 14.2−1** Hierarchical schema catenation transformation (reprinted by permission from Proc. Int. Conf. Very Large Data Bases © 1977 IEEE, Inc.).

A *lifting* transformation involves the rearrangement of a hierarchically adjacent pair of record types such that the parent-child relationship is reversed. The exact effect of the transformation on the schema depends on whether or not one or both of the adjacent record types have more than one child record type (i.e., are branching) or do not have more than one child record type (i.e., are not branching). Four cases arise and are summarized in Figure 14.2−2, where $\alpha$ and $\beta$ are the adjacent record types.

A *shifting* transformation involves a rearrangement of a triple of record types $\alpha$, $\beta$, and $\Omega$ such that if

1. $\alpha$ is the parent of $\beta$, and
2. $\alpha$ is an ancestor of $\Omega$, and
3. $\beta$ is not an ancestor of $\Omega$,

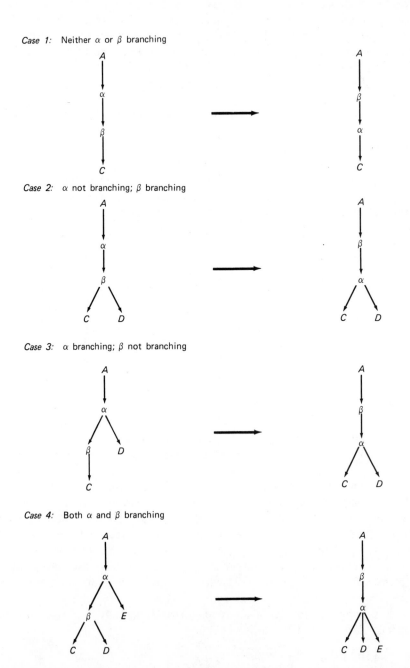

**Fig. 14.2−2** Hierarchical schema lifting transformation (reprinted by permission from Proc. ACM SIGMOD © 1977 ACM, Inc.).

then $\beta$ or any descendant of $\beta$ may be removed as a child of $\alpha$ and made a child of $\Omega$. Again, four cases arise and are summarized in Figure 14.2–3.

Using the preceding transformations, three classes of hierarchical schema restructurings that preserve query homomorphism are specification of subschemas, ancestor schemas, and descendant schemas. A subschema is a restructuring in which some record types may be masked out after catenation, lifting, and shifting transformations. An ancestor schema is one that contains all the original record types. As well, every hierarchical path in the resulting schema and data base is a subset of a hierarchical path in the original schema and data base. Finally, a descendant schema contains all the original record types and every hierarchical path is a superset of a hierarchical path in the original schema.

When the source schema $S_s$ and the target schema $S_t$ are according to different data models, we have a schema translation mapping problem. One solution to this mapping problem consists of developing a mapping algorithm between a specific pair of data models. Most often, this problem is stated as the derivation of mappings among relational, network, and/or hierarchical schemas [Kalinichenko, 1976, 1978; Zaniolo, 1979a,b; Lien, 1980, 1981; Navathe, 1980b; Vassiliou and Lochovsky, 1980]. Another approach is to use a mapping data model as an intermediary representation between any pair of data models. In this way it is necessary to map only between the mapping data model and any other data model rather than between every pair of data models [Senko, 1976; Klug, 1978, 1980, 1981; Pelagatti et al., 1978; Katz, 1980].

Very little formalism exists in the area of specification of schema translation mappings. Much of the work usually consists of the specification of ad hoc mappings between pairs of data models. Since these schema translations are most often specified among relational, network, and hierarchical data models, we explore next the nature of these mappings.

Let us consider first the mapping between relational and network data models. Suppose that the underlying data base and schema are network and that we wish to derive an equivalent relational schema. The exact details of the mapping will depend on the specific network DBMS (which is one of the reasons that schema translation is so complex). However, some characteristics of a network schema that need to be considered in the mapping and mapped to appropriate relational structures and/or constraints are [Zaniolo, 1979a,b]:

1. Record types and data items
2. Links
3. Set membership
4. Record keys (or lack thereof)
5. Uniqueness of member records in DBTG-sets

*Case 1:*  β and Ω are both terminal

*Case 2:*  β is branching and Ω is terminal

*Case 3:*  β is terminal and Ω is branching

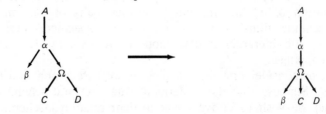

*Case 4:*  Both β and Ω are branching

**Fig. 14.2–3** Hierarchical schema shifting transformation (reprinted by permission from Proc. ACM SIGMOD © 1977 ACM, Inc.).

The need to map these inherent and explicit constraints of a network schema gives rise to several mapping problems.

One problem is that every relation in the relational schema requires a unique key. However, not every record type in a network schema need have a key. If we map record types to relations, which intuitively makes sense, we may have an identification problem for some relations. Therefore, we need a way to assign or construct a unique key for each record type in the network schema. One approach is to use a data base key (external key), but this makes visible in the relations a system controlled attribute [Vassiliou and Lochovsky, 1980]. Another approach is to construct a unique key for each record type from specified record keys by propagating data items along links [Zaniolo, 1979a,b; Navathe, 1980b].

Another mapping problem is the representation of links and set membership options in the relational schema. The representation requires the specification of explicit constraints in the relational schema, possibly the introduction of additional relations, and the presence of null values in the (virtual or actual) relational data base. One of the basic constraints introduced by links and set membership options is the *foreign-key constraint* [Smith and Smith, 1977a; Zaniolo, 1979a,b; Vassiliou and Lochovsky, 1980].

### Foreign-Key Constraint

If a key $X$ of relation $R_i$ is also an attribute combination of relation $R_j$ [denoted $FK(R_i)$ in $R_j$], then at all times every $X$-value appearing in $R_j$ must also appear in $R_i$.

For reference purposes we denote this constraint between relations $R_i$ and $R_j$ as $FC_{ij}$. A modified version of this constraint allows for the possibility of the $X$-value in $R_j$ to be null. We denote this constraint between relations $R_i$ and $R_j$ as $NFC_{ij}$.

To illustrate some of the complexities of schema translation, we will outline a possible mapping from a network schema to a relational schema [Vassiliou and Lochovsky, 1980].

### Network-to-Relational Schema Translation

1.  For each record type $N_i$ define a relation $R_i$ such that:
    (a)  $R_i$ contains one attribute for each data item of $N_i$.
    (b)  If $N_i$ has a key, the key of $R_i$ is equal to the key of $N_i$; otherwise, the key of $R_i$ is equal to the data base key of $N_i$, which appears as an explicit attribute of $R_i$.
2.  For each link $L_{ij}$, with owner record type $N_i$ and member record type $N_j$, define relational constraints and change the existing relations such that:
    (a)  The key of $N_i$ appears as a foreign key of $R_j$.

(b) One of the following sets of constraints applies, depending on the type of set membership ($R_i$ and $R_j$ are the relations corresponding to $N_i$ and $N_j$, respectively).

### Fixed Automatic

Add $FC_{ij}$

Explicit consequences:

- If we insert an $R_j$ tuple, the $r_i$ tuple with key value $FK(R_i)$ in $R_j$ must exist or the insertion is not allowed.
- If we delete an $R_i$ tuple, we must also delete all $R_j$ tuples where the value of $FK(R_i)$ in $R_j$ is equal to the key value of the $R_i$ tuple.
- If we update an $R_j$ tuple, the value of $FK(R_i)$ in $R_j$ cannot be changed.

### Fixed Manual

Add $NFC_{ij}$

Explicit consequences:

- If we delete an $R_i$ tuple, we must also delete all $R_j$ tuples where the value of $FK(R_i)$ in $R_j$ is equal to the key value of the $R_i$ tuple.
- If we update an $R_j$ tuple, the value of $FK(R_i)$ in $R_j$ cannot be changed unless it is null.

### Mandatory Automatic

Add $FC_{ij}$

Explicit consequences:

- If we insert an $R_j$ tuple, the $R_i$ tuple with key value $FK(R_i)$ in $R_j$ must exist or the insertion is not allowed.
- If we delete an $R_i$ tuple, we must also delete all $R_j$ tuples where the value of $FK(R_i)$ in $R_j$ is equal to the key value of the $R_i$ tuple.

### Mandatory Manual

Add $NFC_{ij}$

Explicit consequences:

- If we delete an $R_i$ tuple, we must also delete all $R_j$ tuples where the value of $FK(R_i)$ in $R_j$ is equal to the key value of the $R_i$ tuple.
- If we update an $R_j$ tuple, the value of $FK(R_i)$ in $R_j$ cannot be changed to null.

### Optional Automatic

Add $NFC_{ij}$

Explicit consequences:

- If we insert an $R_j$ tuple, the value of $FK(R_i)$ in $R_j$ cannot be null.
- If we delete an $R_i$ tuple, we must change all $R_j$ tuples such that the value of $FK(R_i)$ in $R_j$ becomes null.

### Optional Manual

Add $NFC_{ij}$

Explicit consequences:

- If we delete an $R_i$ tuple, we must change all $R_j$ tuples such that the value of $FK(R_i)$ in $R_j$ becomes null.

The preceding mapping introduces explicit constraints that are not functional or multivalued dependencies. It is possible to obtain a mapping that results in a relational schema that contains only relations and multivalued dependencies (that allow null values). For such a mapping to be realized, the network schema must be loop-free and the links must be fixed-automatic [Lien, 1980].

If the underlying data base and schema are relational and we wish to derive an equivalent network schema, the problem is more complex [Borkin, 1978]. First, we need to assume that all attributes in the relational schema are named uniquely (i.e., that there is an underlying universal relation scheme). We also need to be able to identify the foreign keys of a relation uniquely. The foreign keys will represent functional relationship types which can be mapped into network links. The identification of many-to-many relationship types is more difficult. If we assume that many-to-many relationship types are represented by separate relations the primary key of which consists of the foreign key of the relations involved in the many-to-many relationship type, the problem is somewhat simplified. However, in general, this assumption will not be valid.

### Relational-to-Network Schema Translation

Given a relational schema $\rho = \{R_1, R_2, ..., R_n\}$, the primary key of each relation and the assumption that functional relationship types are represented by foreign keys and many-to-many relationship types by separate "relationship" relations.

1. Using the primary keys, identify all "relationship" relations. Call this set of relations $\alpha$.
2. For each relation $R_i$ in $\rho - \alpha$:
   (a) Form a record type $N_i$ with record key equal to the primary key of $R_i$. The relation name becomes the record-type name and the relation attributes become the record-type data items.
   (b) For each subset of attributes (excluding the primary key) in $R_i$, if

it is a primary key of some other relation in $\rho - \alpha$ (i.e., is a foreign key in $R_i$) add a link $L_{ji}$ between the record type $N_i$ corresponding to $R_i$ and the record type $N_j$ corresponding to the relation $R_j$ in which the foreign key is the primary key. $N_i$ becomes the member record type and $N_j$ becomes the owner record type. Delete the foreign-key attributes for $R_j$ from $N_i$. Generate a unique name for the link $L_{ji}$. Determine the set membership for the link.

3.  For each relation $R_i$ in $\alpha$:
    (a) Form a record type $N_i$ as in step 2(a).
    (b) Add one link between the $N_i$ record type corresponding to $R_i$ and each of the $n$ other record types involved in the relationship type as determined from the foreign keys in $R_i$. Note that these $n$ other record types will already exist, having been constructed from $\rho - \alpha$. Usually, $n$ will be two, although higher-order relationship types are possible. The $n$ record types are owner record types in the links added, while the $R_i$ record type is the common member record type. The foreign keys in the $R_i$ record type can be deleted. Generate unique names for the links added. Determine the set membership of each link.

The preceding mapping procedure only outlines the mapping process and leaves many details unspecified. This is because, in general, the mapping requires additional information. We need to know that we can identify all foreign keys uniquely. This may be a problem if keys with multiple attributes are present, subsets of which are themselves keys. The determination of the correct set membership for each link is not possible unless we are given some additional constraints on foreign keys, such as in the network-to-relational mapping procedure.

In general, the relational-to-network schema translation problem is quite difficult given only the underlying relations and the functional dependencies. If the relational schema has certain properties dealing with the keys of the relations, it is possible to construct a loop-free network schema that is exactly equivalent to the relational schema [Lien, 1980]. All the links in such a network schema have fixed-automatic set membership.

Mappings between hierarchical and relational schemas are similar to those between network and relational schemas. If the underlying data base and schema are hierarchical and we wish to derive a relational schema, a "normalization" of the hierarchy will produce the relational schema [Codd, 1970]. In this case the foreign-key constraint is introduced for each parent-child relationship if we assume an IMS-like hierarchical data model.

In the other direction, a hierarchical schema can be generated by a procedure similar to that outlined for the relational-to-network schema translation. In this case the set membership problem is not an issue at the schema level since all parent-child relationships are total mappings. However, the (virtual) hierarchical data base may contain "dangling" children if null values are allowed for foreign keys in the underlying relations. We also need to map many-to-many relationship types into hierarchical structures. Techniques for doing this were outlined in Chapter 7. In general, several definition trees will result from the mapping. A formal procedure for deriving hierarchical schemas from relational schemas using functional dependencies, multivalued dependencies, and decomposition trees is outlined in [Lien, 1981].

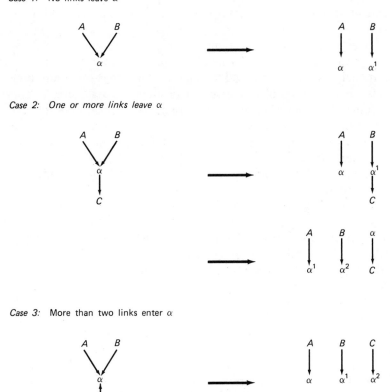

**Fig. 14.2—4** Mapping network structures to hierarchical structures.

Mappings between network and hierarchical schemas are fairly simple. If the underlying data base and schema are network, we are faced with the problem of deriving a set of spanning trees that "cover" the network schema. The type of network structure that causes problems in the mapping is that where a member record type has two or more owner record types. Several methods for mapping these structures can be applied, depending on whether the member record type is or is not itself an owner record type. Some possible mappings are shown in Figure 14.2−4.

The set membership of each link must also be mapped. Fixed-automatic membership can be mapped directly. Other types of set membership may also be mappable via mechanisms such as logical relationships in IMS.

If the underlying data base and schema are hierarchical, we already have a valid network schema. However, the hierarchical schema may contain redundant structures (e.g., as result from the network to hierarchical mappings). Thus, it may be possible to "merge" such redundant structures. We also need to generate link names for each link in the network schema.

Rather than specify mappings between every pair of data models, mappings can be defined in terms of a mapping data model. This mapping data model can then be used to specify mappings between other data models. An example of a mapping data model is a relational data model with functional dependencies and foreign-key constraints [Klug, 1978, 1980]. Since a relational data model completely separates structures from constraints, it is possible to specify as explicit constraints in a relational data model the different constraints that other data models may have. Other data models can be used as mapping data models provided that they can capture the structures and constraints of several data models. For instance, the DIAM [Senko, 1976], extended set theory [Sibley and Hardgrave, 1977], binary [Pelagatti et al., 1978] and a variation of the entity-relationship [Katz, 1980] data models have been proposed as possible candidates for a mapping data model.

It should be clear that schema restructuring and schema translation mappings are complicated, especially if we want to capture constraints. Some formalisms for specifying schema restructuring mappings exist, especially for relational schemas [Navathe, 1976, 1980a; Klug, 1978, 1980]. Little formalism exists for specifying schema translations. Many schema translations are intuitive and ad hoc [Navathe, 1980b; Vassiliou and Lochovsky, 1980], although some formalisms are emerging [Klug, 1978, 1980; Biller, 1979; Borkin, 1980; Lien, 1980].

## 14.3 OPERATION MAPPINGS

In Part 1 operations were restricted by two very important limitations. First, since most operations follow a strict sequence of selection followed by an action, a small part of the data base is isolated as a result of an operation. This part of the data base is then transformed into a (possibly) different part. Some of the data values are allowed to change as a result of an operation. These values are often clustered logically within an entity type or set of connected entity types. Thus as a result of most operations, the data base state changes only slightly and in a very localized way. Second, although an operation maps a particular data base state to possibly a different data base state, both of the data base states conform strictly to the specified schema. That is, the result of an operation is a data base state which is within the same data model and within the same schema as the data base state preceding the operation.

The dynamics of mappings under these restrictions are limited and thus easily understood. To understand an operation one needs to understand its effect on only a small part of the schema and data base and concentrate on only a few data values. This simplicity of context is perhaps the main reason that data languages conform to the preceding restrictions. However, other mappings whose dynamics are far more complex can be defined and are needed in data modeling. For example, it may be necessary to have a data base operation that maps all or part of a data base into another, different schema or even to a different data model. Such an operation cannot be explained adequately solely by the framework discussed in Part 1. The complexity and wide ranging effect of such operations makes them traditionally the hardest to handle in data modeling.

In the preceding section we established some correspondences between structures and constraints of data models. We did not deal with operations or data base extensions except to argue that operations and data bases should be mappable according to the new schema. In this section we look at the problem of mapping operations on the new schema to the data base according to the original schema. That is, given a source schema $S_s$, a data base according to $S_s$ and a target schema $S_t$ that is obtained by a schema restructuring or schema translation of $S_s$, we would like to map operations on $S_t$ to equivalent operations on $S_s$. When $S_s$ and $S_t$ are according to the same data model, we have a view mapping; otherwise, we have an operation transform mapping.

Since we are interested in performing operations on $S_t$, we need to be able to materialize, if only virtually, a data base according to $S_t$ from the $S_s$ data base. As defined in Chapter 1, the schema of $S_s$ together with a data base extension is called a data base state for $S_s$ ($DBS_s$). Similarly, the schema of $S_t$ together with its virtual data base extension is called a data base state for $S_t$ ($DBS_t$). The mapping that materializes an $S_t$ data base state from an $S_s$ data base state is called a *state mapping* [Klug, 1978].

A state mapping from $S_s$ to $S_t$ is always a total function if the two schemas are equivalent. However, an operation mapping from $S_t$ to $S_s$

can be a much more complicated partial function. That is, given $DBS_s$ and an operation $q$ on $DBS_t$, we may get a series of operations $q_n \circ ... \circ q_s$ on $DBS_s$ which performs the operations specified on $S_t$. This possibility is expressed by the commutative diagram in Figure 14.3—1.

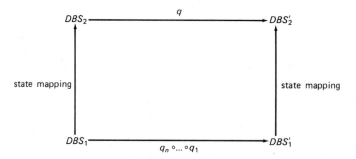

**Fig. 14.3—1** Operations mapping.

The state mapping is total because any data base state of $S_s$ should have meaning with respect to $S_t$. In the ANSI/X3/SPARC architecture, for instance, any conceptual schema data base state can be viewed as an external schema data base state. The mapping of operations is partial because an operation according to $S_t$ can violate a constraint on $S_s$. The operation mapping also cannot be expected to be one to one since an operation on $S_t$ may require a series of operations on $S_s$ or vice versa. For instance, a delete on data base states of $S_t$ according to a hierarchical data model based on $S_s$ according to a relational data model will require a series of delete operations on data base states of $S_s$.

Because of the partial nature of operation mappings, an update on $S_t$ may not map to a unique update on $S_s$ [Chamberlin et al., 1975; Paolini and Pelagatti, 1977; Todd, 1977; Dayal and Bernstein, 1978]. Note that queries can always be mapped since they correspond, in essence, to state mappings (i.e., deriving a part of the data base state for the query according to $S_t$ from $S_s$). Update operations, on the other hand, try to map a data base state of $S_t$ to an equivalent $S_s$ data base state.

When $S_s$ and $S_t$ are according to the same data model, we have a view mapping. Most of the work on view mappings has been done with relational data models. Therefore, we will discuss the problem in this context. As an example of the view mapping problem, consider a relational schema consisting of the two relations shown in Figure 14.3—2 [Klug, 1978]. We can define a view *EMPVIEW* on these relations by the SQL statement

EMPLOYEE

| Name | Address | Dept |
|------|---------|------|
| Smith | 15  Bloor | Paint |
| Jones | 25  King | Toy |
| Carter | 171 Yonge | Paint |

(a)

DEPARTMENT

| Name | Location | Manager |
|------|----------|---------|
| Paint | King | Miles |
| Toy | Queen | Quin |
| Pipe | King | Miles |

(b)

**Fig. 14.3−2** Example relational schema.

EMPVIEW ←
    **SELECT** EMPLOYEE.Name, Address, Manager
    **FROM** EMPLOYEE, DEPARTMENT
    **WHERE** EMPLOYEE.Dept = DEPARTMENT.Name

For the particular extensions of the EMPLOYEE and DEPARTMENT relations given in Figure 14.3−2, this view would appear (if materialized) as shown in Figure 14.3−3.

EMPVIEW

| Name | Address | Manager |
|------|---------|---------|
| Smith | 15  Bloor | Miles |
| Jones | 25  King | Quin |
| Carter | 171 Yonge | Miles |

**Fig. 14.3−3** View EMPVIEW of relations in Figure 14.3−2.

Now suppose that a user wanted to get an answer to the query "Who is the manager of Smith?" If the user were querying the relations EMPLOYEE and DEPARTMENT, a natural way to write the query in SQL would be

ANSWER ←
    **SELECT** Manager
    **FROM** DEPARTMENT
    **WHERE** Name = **SELECT** Dept
        **FROM** EMPLOYEE
        **WHERE** Name = 'Smith'

If the user were interacting with the *EMPVIEW*, however, only a single, simple query would be needed:

> *ANSWER* ←
> **SELECT** *Manager*
> **FROM** *EMPVIEW*
> **WHERE** *Name*='Smith'

Views thus allow queries to be formulated more simply since they tailor a data base to the user's needs [Klug, 1981]. However, a number of problems arise when users are able to interact with views as if they represented the "real" data base.

If a user of *EMPVIEW* believes that each employee has only one manager (which is true in the given example), then in order for this view to be "consistent" with the user's expectations, there must be certain constraints on the underlying relations. In this example, there must be functional dependencies from *Name* to *Dept* in *EMPLOYEE* and from *Name* to *Manager* in *DEPARTMENT*. The need for these constraints is illustrated by the following example. Suppose that the functional dependency *Name*→ *Dept* in *EMPLOYEE* did not hold, and there was also a tuple <Smith,15 Bloor,Toy> in *EMPLOYEE*. Then both <Smith,15 Bloor, Miles> and <Smith,15 Bloor,Quin> would appear in *EMPVIEW*, and this would contradict the user's expectations since Smith appears with both Miles and Quin. A similar problem would arise if *DEPARTMENT* violated the *Name*→ *Manager* functional dependency. In general, we must be able to tell what constraints the view will have knowing the constraints of the underlying data base.

Another problem with views is how to handle updates [Chamberlin et al., 1975; Todd, 1977; Dayal and Bernstein, 1978; Klug, 1978; Spyratos, 1980]. In the preceding example, suppose that a user of *EMPVIEW* wanted to change Smith's manager from Miles to Quin. Does this mean that the update on the underlying relations should be

> **UPDATE** *EMPLOYEE*
> **SET** *Dept*='Toy'
> **WHERE** *Name*='Smith'

or does it mean that we want to

> **UPDATE** *DEPARTMENT*
> **SET** *Manager*='Quin'
> **WHERE** *Name*='Paint'?

That is, do we mean to change the department Smith works in, or do we mean to change the manager of Smith's department? The problem is partly one of real-world semantics and partly a mapping problem. In this example, there would be general agreement that the most logical interpretation of the update on *EMPVIEW* would be the update on the *Dept* attribute of *EMPLOYEE*. This opinion is predicated on an understanding of "employees," "departments," and "managers" which is application specific.

As another example, suppose that we want to insert a new tuple, <Davis, 38 Queen, Hall>, into *EMPVIEW*. How do we map this operation to the underlying relations? The insertion has the effect of inserting a new *DEPARTMENT* tuple, but we do not have a value for the department name. If the functional dependency *Name→Manager* in *DEPARTMENT* is to be enforced, the insertion cannot be allowed. It is very hard to explain to a user why this operation is not valid if he or she interacts only with the *EMPVIEW* relation.

It is generally agreed that for an update on a view to be mappable to the underlying relations, there should be [Dayal and Bernstein, 1978]:

1. No extraneous updates on the underlying relations; that is, there should be no updates performed that are not reflected in the view.
2. No side effects on views; that is, the only updates that appear in the view are those specified by the view update.
3. Preservation of semantic consistency on the underlying relations; that is, no constraints on the underlying relations are violated by a view update.
4. A unique mapping to operations on the underlying relations.

Although formal necessary and sufficient conditions for view updates to be mappable have been developed [Dayal and Bernstein, 1978], what is needed is a method for constructing views that have the desired properties. In light of this, an alternative approach to the view update problem is to define the views and operations on them so that the preceding conditions are always met [Sevcik and Furtado, 1978; Furtado et al., 1979].

When $S_s$ and $S_t$ are according to different data models, we have an operation transform mapping. Approaches to this mapping problem are similar to those for the schema translation problem. That is, direct operation mappings can be established [Zaniolo, 1979b; Vassiliou and Lochovsky, 1980], or an intermediate mapping data model can be used [Klug, 1978; Katz, 1980]. In both cases, the usual approach is to specify mappings of parameterized abstractions of the operations on each data model. However, as for schema translation, very little formalism exists for specifying these operation mappings. We outline some of the issues involved by considering operation mappings among relational, network, and hierarchical data models.

Figure 14.3—4 shows three schemas according to a relational, network, and hierarchical data model with (approximately) the same structure [Klug, 1978]. We assume that appropriate state mappings have

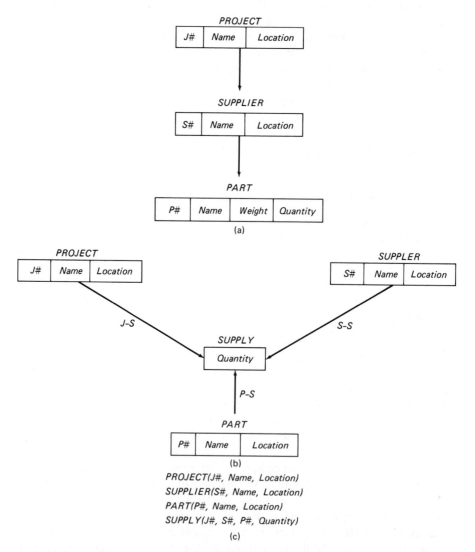

**Fig. 14.3—4** Schemas for supplier parts for three data models: (a) hierarchical; (b) DBTG-network; (c) relational.

been defined that map a data base state according to one data model into equivalent (virtual) data base states according to the other two data models.

One type of operation mapping problem is the determination of whether a query specified on one schema will give the desired result when executed on another schema. Query equivalence has been carefully studied within relational data models [Aho et al., 1979b]. In the case of queries between two different data models some difficulties may arise. For example, suppose that the underlying data base is hierarchical and we view it according to the relational schema [Figure 14.3—4(c)]. Then to map a relational query such as

**SELECT** *PROJECT.Name, PART.Name*
**FROM** *PROJECT, PART, SUPPLY*
**WHERE** *PROJECT.Location* = 'Toronto'
**AND** *SUPPLY.Supplier#* = 'S8'
**AND** *SUPPLY.Job#* = *PROJECT.Job#*
**AND** *SUPPLY.Part#* = *PART.Part#*

to the hierarchical schema requires that we be able to identify the appropriate paths to take in the hierarchical data base and that we are able to associate qualification terms in the relational query with appropriate record types in the hierarchical schema. If we have a hierarchical specification data language such as in S2K, this query might be mapped into a hierarchical query such as

**PRINT** *PROJECT Name, PART Name*
**WHERE** *PROJECT Location* **EQ** TORONTO
**AND** *SUPPLIER Supplier#* **EQ** S8

For this example, the operation mapping was quite simple and straightforward. In general, however, the mappings are quite complex, especially if conjunctive (**OR**) terms appear in the relational qualification [Vassiliou and Lochovsky, 1980].

Another type of operation mapping problem arises when we map between navigation operations and specification operations. Specification operations can be mapped into navigation operations with relative ease since we are mapping from a nonprocedural to a procedural formulation. Navigation operations are very difficult to map into specification operations or other navigation operations since navigation operations use currency indicators extensively. The state of a currency indicator in a navigation operation is difficult to capture in specification operations. This difficulty is analogous to to that of decompiling in programming languages [Katz and Wong, 1981].

Consider the following specification query, which uses the schema in Figure 14.3—4(b) and the NUL data language:

$S1 \leftarrow SUPPLIER$
    **WHERE** $S-S$ **HAS** *SUPPLY*
    **WHERE** $J-S$ **HAS** *PROJECT*
    **WHERE** *Location* = 'Toronto'
    **PRINT** $S1.Location$

This query can be expressed using an IDMS-like COBOL DML as

**FIND** *PROJECT* **RECORD WHERE** *Location* = 'Toronto'
*exit if status* $-$ *check*
*loop until no more records*
    *loop until no more records*
        **FIND NEXT** *SUPPLY* **RECORD OF** $J-S$ **SET**
        *exit loop if status* $-$ *check*
        **OBTAIN OWNER RECORD OF** $S-S$ **SET**
        *output Location of SUPPLIER if not status* $-$ *check*
    *end loop*
    **FIND NEXT DUPLICATE** *PROJECT* **RECORD**
    **WHERE** *Location* = 'Toronto'
    *exit loop if status* $-$ *check*
*end loop*

On the other hand, given the query in its navigation form, it would be very difficult, in general, to infer this query in a specification data language. Yet, if the target data model has a specification data language, and the user data model has a navigation data language, these kinds of mappings must be made. One way of achieving the mapping is by trying to infer a general pattern for a specification statement by grouping and analyzing the navigation statements. From the specification pattern we can infer the mapping to a specification statement [Katz, 1980; Katz and Wong, 1981].

Another operation mapping problem involves updates. Different data models have different side effects on modifications because of the presence of inherent and explicit constraints. For example, suppose that a *PART* record is deleted from the hierarchical schema in Figure 14.3−4(a). Should the users of the relational and network schemas see this deletion, and if so, how should they see it? Whether they see it or not depends on semantics of the application not apparent in the schemas. If it is decided that the deletion should be visible in the other schemas, there is still the question of the form the deletion should take. For example, in the network schema, the hierarchical deletion could be reflected as a deletion of a *PART* record, a deletion of a *SUPPLY* record, the deletion of both a *PART* record and a *SUPPLY* record, or a disconnection of a *SUPPLY* record from a $P-S$ DBTG-set. The operation mapping definition needs to address these problems precisely and to provide appropriate mappings.

The general problem of mappings where $S_s$ and $S_t$ are in different, arbitrary data models is very hard. It can be attacked in an ad hoc manner by trying to go between hierarchical, network, and relational data models [Vassiliou and Lochovsky, 1980]. It can also be attacked by going through a mapping data model. Such a mapping data model should be able to capture the logical description of both $S_s$ and $S_t$, all the constraints that can be specified in $S_s$ and $S_t$, and it should have a set of powerful operations to map between operations on $S_s$ and $S_t$.

There have been several proposals for such a mapping data model. Adiba et al. look at the problem where the mapping data model is Abrial's semantic binary data model [Adiba et al., 1976]. Senko uses the DIAM data model [Senko, 1976]. Paolini and Pelagatti look at the mapping of operations where the mapping data model is a binary data model [Paolini and Pelagatti, 1977]. Klug uses the relational data model with functional dependencies and foreign-key constraints and insertion, deletion, and sequences thereof as a mapping data model [Klug, 1978]. In this approach one captures $S_s$ in a relational schema $S_s^1$. The schema $S_t$ is captured again in a relational schema $S_t^1$. The mapping of $S_s$ to $S_t$ is specified as a mapping $S_s^1$ to $S_t^1$. Finally, the mapping of operations from $S_t$ to $S_s$ is specified as a mapping of operations from $S_t^1$ to $S_s^1$.

Operation mappings are easiest when $S_s$ and $S_t$ are according to the same data model. In this case the same types of operations can be applied to $S_s$ and $S_t$ and the state mappings are usually much easier. As well as the work on relational view mappings outlined in this section, there has also been some work on hierarchical view mappings [Dale and Yurkanan, 1977] and on network view mappings [Clemons, 1978, 1979; Clemons and Germano, 1979]. When $S_s$ and $S_t$ are according to different data models, the operation mapping problem is much harder. The complexity of the problem can be reduced if the data models are chosen appropriately or if a suitable mapping data model is used.

## 14.4 DATA BASE TRANSLATION

Data base translation has a different flavor from other mapping problems discussed so far. First, it is a problem where actual data base instances are mapped[1]. As such it is usually an off-line process requiring considerable resources and time. Second, the problem is very practical, as it is needed in data base conversion. Thus, it has been studied for a long time and much has been written about the problem [Fry et al., 1972a,b; Smith, 1972; Sibley and Taylor, 1973; Merten and Fry, 1974; Yamaguchi and Merten, 1974; Shoshani, 1975; Navathe and Fry, 1976; CODASYL, 1977a; Shneiderman and Thomas, 1979, 1980a,b,c; Thomas and Shneiderman, 1979, 1980].

---

[1]. The previous mapping problems dealt only with conceptual instances of target data bases which may never be materialized.

Consider two schemas $S_s$ and $S_t$ which are mappable. We are interested in mapping a data base according to the source schema $S_s$ to a data base according to the target schema $S_t$. When $S_s$ and $S_t$ are according to the same data model we have the problem of a schema restructuring, which requires a data base reorganization. When $S_s$ and $S_t$ are according to different data models, we have the more general problem of data base translation. These problems have been investigated both as conceptual problems [Navathe and Fry, 1976] and as practical problems [Shu et al., 1977].

Suppose that we want to map the data base of a source schema $S_s$ to a target schema $S_t$ (according to the same data model or different data models). To perform this mapping, we need to specify three distinct processes [CODASYL, 1977a]. One process accesses the source data (*reading*). Another process performs logical transformations on the data to place it into an internal form (*mapping*). A third process creates the target data (*writing*). We need to specify for these processes the logical description of the data, the physical description of the data (since we are dealing with real stored data), and the mapping. To describe these different aspects of the data and the mapping, we require two declarative languages and an internal form for the data.

The first declarative language, called a *stored data definition language* (SDDL), is used for describing the source and target files. It describes the logical structure of the data, the physical structure of storage devices, and the mapping from the logical to the physical structures. The SDDL is needed because of the absence of a one-to-one correspondence between the logical data structure as viewed by the user, and the physical data as they are stored in the computer [Merten and Fry, 1974]. Existing DDLs do not describe the way that data are stored in a specific hardware environment, or the hardware environment itself.

The second declarative language, called a *translation definition language* (TDL), specifies the logical relationships between the source and the target data at both the logical and physical level. The major use of the TDL is to specify the mapping that is to take place.

Finally, the internal form of the data is used for interfacing between the reading process, the mapping process, and the writing process. The internal form of data makes it possible to decompose the data base translation problem into several independent components [Fry et al., 1972b]. This decomposition is helpful in separating the reformatting process (reading and writing) from the mapping process, as well as in investigating independently each part of the problem. It also makes it possible to reduce the number of mappings from $M$ times $N$ (for $M$ input formats and $N$ output formats), to $M$ plus $N$.

The need for tools to perform data base translation is clear since ad hoc data base translation is a very expensive operation. For instance, if we have $M$ source files and $N$ target files, the total number of programs required for translation is the product of $M$ and $N$. These translation programs require machine level detail and, as a result, they involve much effort in programming [Winters and Dickey, 1976]. Some of this effort can be avoided by using a generalized data base translation system. The generalized data base translation system should be able to [Fry et al., 1972b]:

1. Handle different source and target files.
2. Provide mappings.
3. Handle several source and target files at a time (the need for merging of several files for forming a network type data structure is an example).
4. Run in different computers (at least in part) because the machine that is performing the translation may not be able to read the source data.

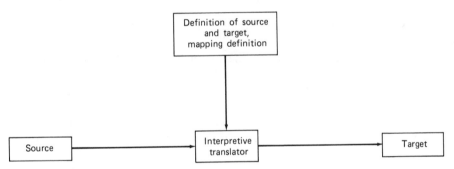

**Fig. 14.4—1** Interpretive translator approach to data base translation.

There are two major approaches to the data base translation problem [Yamaguchi and Merten, 1974]. The first is called the *interpretive translator* approach and is shown in Figure 14.4—1 [Merten and Fry, 1974; CODASYL, 1977a]. The interpretive translator accepts the two descriptions of the source and target files as well as the mapping specifications, and transforms the source file into the target file. The interpretive translator can map any source file to any target file as long as the two files can be described using the description mechanisms.

The second approach is called the *translator generator* approach and is shown in Figure 14.4—2 [Ramirez et al., 1974; Shu et al., 1977]. In this approach the translator system accepts a description of the source and the target, as well as the mapping specifications, and produces a specialized program to perform the actual mapping.

The two approaches are fundamentally different in terms of their implementation. In the first approach the translation programs are generalized, whereas in the second approach the method of constructing specialized translation programs is generalized. The distinction between

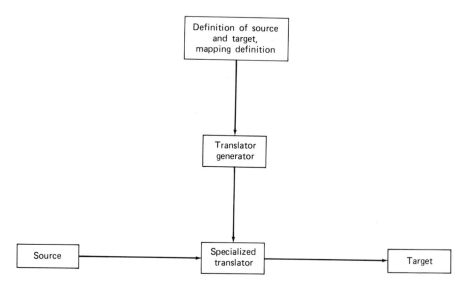

**Fig. 14.4—2** Translator generator approach to data base translation.

the two approaches is similar to the distinction between interpreters and compilers in programming languages. The translator generator is analogous to the compiler, since it accepts statements in a declarative language and produces a translation program in a procedure-oriented language (not necessarily machine language). The construction of an interpretive translator is considered to be easier than that of a translator generator.

The interpretive translator approach to data base translation will be discussed in terms of the proposal of the Stored-Data Definition and Translation Task Group (SDDTTG) of the CODASYL Systems Committee, which is shown in Figure 14.4—3 [CODASYL, 1977a]. Figure 14.4—3 shows two internal forms of data: the translator internal form (TIF), and the device internal form (DIF). It also shows the five components of the interpretive translator: the physical reader, the read process, the restructurer, the write process, and the physical writer. Input descriptions to these stages are the source and target specifications in the stored data definition language, and the restructuring specifications in the translation definition language.

The basic function of the translator internal form (TIF) is to provide a self-describing representation of the source and target data independent of the media on which the data are stored. The representation is self-describing in the sense that all the attributes of the data which are relevant for mapping are carried with the data value.

The internal representation of the data as they appear on the source or

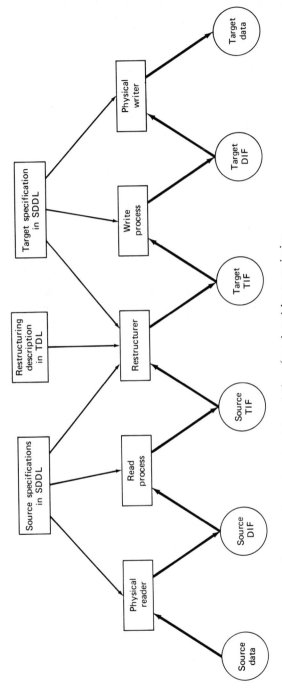

**Fig. 14.4—3** SDDTTG approach to data base translation (reprinted by permission from Inf. Syst. © 1977 Pergamon Press Ltd.).

327

target storage device is called the device internal form (DIF). The purpose of the DIF is to free the intermediate stages of the translator from hardware considerations.

The physical reader uses the description of the physical storage structure to access the source file and produce the DIF. It is assumed that the physical reader has knowledge of certain device characteristics that are not represented in the SDDL. The physical reader contains device-dependent commands and, as such, must be coded for each different device. However, by using the DIF it is possible to ensure that the intermediate components of the translator need not be concerned with device attributes not described in the SDDL. Also, since the intermediate stages need not concern themselves with the commands that access the device, the issue of when to read or write a component of the DIF can be hidden in the internal implementation of the DIF.

The physical writer is similar to the physical reader in that it uses the DIF to write the target file onto a target storage device. The physical writer also contains device-dependent commands.

The read process is used to convert the source DIF to the source TIF using the logical and physical structure descriptions. When reading source data, the read process is driven by the read specification and the physical structure description. During the read process particular paths in the physical structure are explicitly traversed. This traversal implies the need for currency indicators to point to the current position in the DIF or the TIF. It also implies a navigation language to traverse the logical structure and the physical structure.

The write process is similar to the read process. It creates the DIF of the target data. In contrast to the read process, though, the write process is driven by the write specification and the logical structure specification.

The restructurer is the central and most complex component of the translator. It has the responsibility of performing the logical translations of the data obtained from the source file so that the resulting data are structurally compatible with the target system. Its input is the source TIF, the source logical structure description, and the restructuring description. The restructuring description is a complete and precise specification of the operations to be performed in restructuring the data. The output of the restructurer is the target TIF. The transformation of the source TIF to the target TIF represents the logical restructuring specified by the user.

The translator generator approach to data base translation has been used in the implementation of some data base translation prototype systems [Ramirez et al., 1974; Bakkom and Behymer, 1975; Shu et al., 1977]. As in the case of the interpretive translator approach, two languages are used. One describes the source and target data and the other describes the mapping between source and target files [Lum et al., 1976]. Given the description for a specific application, the system produces a specialized translation program. There are two phases to the translation process: the compile time phase and the run time phase. In the compile time phase the specialized translation program is generated; in the run time phase this program is executed.

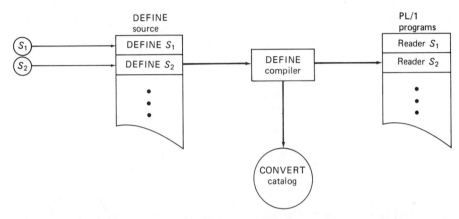

**Fig. 14.4—4** DEFINE compiler phase of XPRS (reprinted by permission from ACM Trans. Database Syst. © 1977 ACM, Inc.).

XPRS (formerly called EXPRESS) is a data base translation system which uses the translator generator approach [Shu et al., 1977]. XPRS uses two languages: DEFINE for data description and CONVERT for data restructuring [Housel et al., 1975; Shu et al., 1975; Housel and Shu, 1976]. During the compile phase the description of every source file is converted by the DEFINE compiler to a corresponding reader program as shown in Figure 14.4—4. The reader programs are used during the run time phase to convert data read by the physical reader (device-dependent program) to a system internal form. In addition, the DEFINE compiler puts information into a file called the CONVERT catalog. This catalog is used to hold common tables and statistics (e.g., descriptions of internal forms) used by various XPRS compile time and run time components.

The CONVERT compiler of the system is used for generating PL/1 procedures to do the restructuring at run time. The CONVERT compiler phase is shown in Figure 14.4—5. Each CONVERT operation in a CONVERT program is translated into a CONVERT operation procedure (COP), which is a customized PL/1 procedure. In addition, an execution schedule of these procedures is generated. The major components of the CONVERT compiler are the parser, the analyzer, and the program generator. The parser expands any nested CONVERT statements, checks the syntactic correctness of the CONVERT statements, and encodes these statements in internal table entries (i.e., in the CONVERT catalog). The analyzer next performs an "order" analysis to determine an efficient

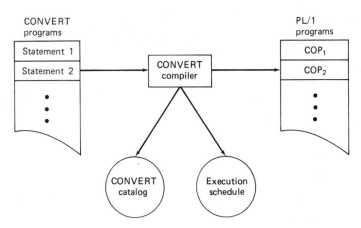

**Fig. 14.4—5** CONVERT compiler phase of XPRS (reprinted by permission from ACM Trans. Database Syst. © 1977 ACM, Inc.).

execution order. Finally, the program generator generates the restructuring procedures (COPs).

During run time, each reader program is executed in order to transform one source file into its corresponding internal form. Each COP sequentially reads its input files (in internal form) and performs the restructuring specified to produce the output.

Figure 14.4—6 gives an example of a data base translation using XPRS. The original data base contains two trees, as shown in Figure 14.4—6(a). It is necessary to create a PROJECTDEPT data base for projects located in San Jose. This data base should have the structure shown in Figure 14.4—6(b). The following CONVERT operations will accomplish the restructuring. Note that explicit reference to a record type also refers to all descendant record types when selecting data items. For example, in the **SLICE** operation, reference to the *PROJECT* record type implicitly includes all the data items of the *PROJECT* and *EQUIPMENT* record types. The data item values that are to appear in the data base according to the new schema are specified in a separate schema description [i.e., Figure 14.4—6(b)].

$T1$ = **SLICE**(*Dept#*, *Manager*, *Budget*, *PROJECT* **FROM** *DEPARTMENT*)
$T2$ = **SORT**($T1$ **BY** *Proj#*, *Dept#*)
$T3$ = **GRAFT**($T2$ **ONTO** *PROJECTS*
      **WHERE** $T2$.*Proj#* = *PROJECTS*.*Proj#*)
$T4$ = **SELECT**(**FROM** $T3$ **WHERE** *Location* = 'San Jose')
*PROJECTDEPT* = **CONSOLIDATE**($T4$)

In the translator generator approach to data base translation, the user is able to modify the generated specialized programs to improve efficiency. Automatic global and local analysis also can be performed for the

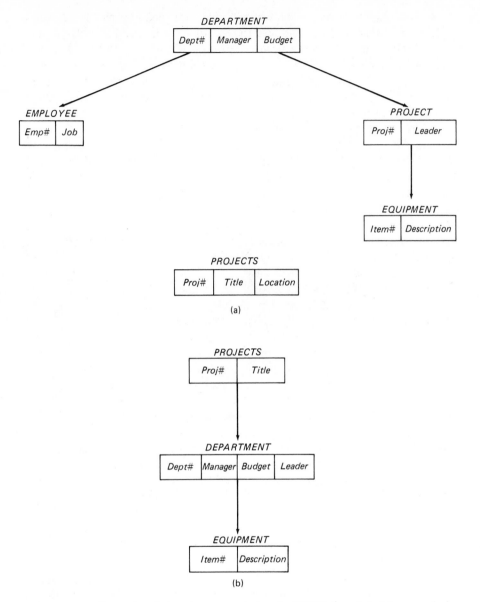

**Fig. 14.4—6** Example of data base translation in XPRS (reprinted by permission from ACM Trans. Database Syst. © 1977 ACM, Inc.).

generation of efficient programs. For example, to improve efficiency, the COPs may be run concurrently. To minimize I/O activity, pipelining of operations, which permits the use of shared input buffers, can be used [Housel, 1979].

A third approach to the data base translation mapping problem, called the *logical level* approach, proposes the elimination of storage and physical considerations and the descriptive languages [Shoshani, 1975]. Instead, the existing capabilities of the DBMS are used to access the source and the target data. The conversion process requires five steps and three languages (Figure 14.4−7). The common data description language (CDDL) describes only logical properties of data bases, the common data translation language (CDTL) expresses logical restructuring functions, and the common data format language (CDFL) specifies the source and the target formats. In the first step the source data base is accessed using the query capabilities of the source DBMS and an intermediate, usually sequential, file is generated. Next, the intermediate file is reformatted and the standard representation of data according to the logical structure of the source data base is produced. In the third step, the logical restructuring is performed to produce the standard form of the target data. Then the standard target data are reformatted to a form acceptable to the target DBMS. Finally, the target data base is generated using the target DBMS. The main objective of this approach is to make data base restructuring easy for the user. The user is not obliged to specify storage level and physical level details for the data base translation process.

The most important aspect of data base translation is the restructuring phase. To do this effectively, one requires a good internal representation for the data. Since the internal representation acts as an intermediary between the source and target data, it must be able to capture the logical and physical structure of both of them. Various data models have been used or proposed for the internal representation of the data.

Relational data models as a vehicle for the internal form have been investigated [Navathe and Merten, 1974]. Although a relational data model provides generality and machine independence, its use for describing the internal form of data poses some problems. If the relational data model is used to maintain hierarchical relationships, the primary keys should be propagated from the parent to the subordinate relations. The translator has to identify the hierarchically related groups and process them with respect to the propagation of keys. If a network structure has to be translated, the relational data model does not provide an unambiguous way of specifying the named relationships. Although there could be multiple ways of breaking up networks and of representing the relationships, an automated approach to the reduction of networks into a good set of relations is not obvious.

The hierarchical data model has also been used as a vehicle for the internal form of data [Shoshani, 1975; Shu et al., 1977]. Its limited data modeling capabilities, though, restrict the set of structures that can be described. For example, network data bases have to be broken up and processed by parts.

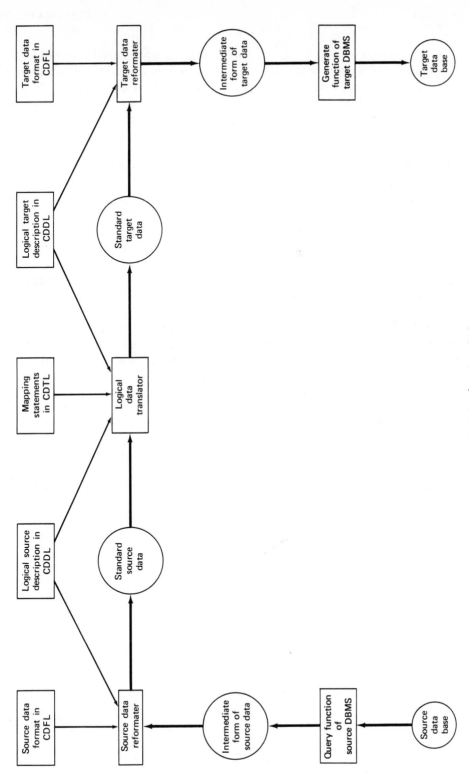

**Fig. 14.4—7** Logical level approach to data base translation (reprinted by permission from Proc. ACM SIGMOD © 1975 ACM, Inc.).

Another candidate for the internal form is the DBTG-network data model. However, this data model has not been used for the internal representation of data bases. One reason is that it does not make a clear separation between logical structures and the way that these structures are implemented. Another reason is that a complete set of restructuring operations is very difficult to specify for a network structure [Swartwout, 1977].

The Relational Interface Model (RIM), which has been used in the implementation of the Michigan Data Translator [Swartwout, 1977], is a synthesis of the salient features of the hierarchical, network, and relational data models. In the RIM, relations are expressed in first normal form. Record types of the DBTG-network data model are mapped to relations and data items to domains in the RIM. For the mapping to be possible, each record type should have a primary key. If this is not the case (e.g., intermediate record types), the keys of the owner record instances that own them must be known to the system by the set membership relationships. Set membership in the RIM is established by storing with the member record, copies of the primary keys of the appropriate owner records. These copies form a collection of special purpose data items, called set significant items. Set significant items must be declared by the user. Although it is fairly general, the RIM is not adequate for representing certain network constructs.

A very powerful data model for describing the internal form of the data is proposed by SDDTTG [CODASYL, 1977a]. The data model is an extension of the DIAM data model [Senko et al., 1973]. The data model uses elements, groups, collection relations, and aggregate relations as its primitives. Elements are the elementary structural units. Groups are relationships of elements only. Collection relations are homogeneous gathering mechanisms over elements, groups, collections, or aggregates. Aggregate relations are nonhomogenous gathering mechanisms over elements, groups, collections, and aggregates.

The SDDTTG internal data model is very powerful. There are two questions concerning its use. The first is that the person who will specify the mapping between the source and the target structures must be very knowledgable. The complexity of the mapping may not be trivial. The second question concerns the use of this data model for specifying restructuring. The SDDTTG does not provide a restructuring language for this data model. Since one of the major objectives of data base translation is to achieve restructuring, and since restructuring is considered one of the most difficult tasks of the translator system, the usefulness of an internal data model depends heavily on its ability to easily and completely specify and implement restructuring operations.

To summarize, data base translation research is essentially of three kinds. First, proposals have been made for data models and languages for the specification of the logical and physical structures and the restructuring process (e.g., ADMIRE [Navathe, 1977], DEFINE and CONVERT [Shu et al., 1977], and TDL [Merten and Fry, 1974]). Second, requirements and methodologies for data base translation have been investigated (e.g., the Michigan Data Base Translation project [Fry and Jervis, 1974; Yamaguchi and Merten, 1974; Navathe and Fry, 1976]). Third, systems for data base translation have been implemented (e.g., XPRS [Shu et al., 1977]).

To simplify the data base translation problem, most prototype systems impose restrictions on some aspect of the mapping process. For example, most systems do not consider the physical level of the translation[1]. As a consequence, these prototypes require a complete rewriting of the read process for different hardware characteristics. In addition, the structure of the source is usually restricted to hierarchical data bases. A network data base first has to be separated into hierarchical portions, which are then processed separately. With the exception of XPRS, these systems cannot handle more than one input file at a time. With respect to restructuring, in most cases only hierarchical restructuring operations are considered.

The area of data base translation is very important and has many things in common with research in the area of mappings between different levels of a data base [Senko, 1976; Klug and Tsichritzis, 1977; Tsichritzis and Klug, 1978]. When operations are also mapped, as is the case in the multilevel architectures, the problem becomes much more complicated. The problem of the development of an internal translation data model is parallel to the problem of the development of a conceptual level data model.

## 14.5 CONCLUDING REMARKS

Structure and constraint mappings, operation mappings, and data base translation have many potential applications and are extremely important in practice. For instance, many computer terminals today contain microprocessors that provide new functions for the terminal user and that simplify old functions. It will soon be economical for users to have terminals with very powerful processing and storage capabilities. These terminals could contain their own mapping processors. This concept is, in a sense, the dual of the concept of multimodel, multiview support [Klug, 1981]. In the latter case, one DBMS provides many different interfaces to many different users; in the former case, one user is provided with one interface to many different DBMSs. The user has a logical data base terminal which has the same data language irrespective of the DBMS to which it is connected. For example, suppose that a user prefers a

---

[1] The Honeywell file translator is an exception [Bakkom and Behymer, 1975].

relational, nonprocedural interface and that the DBMSs that he or she needs to use are CODASYL- and IMS-based. One of the mapping functions of the data base terminal can be to map the network and hierarchical schemas into a relational one. This mapping approach is extremely important for using external data bases in office and home information systems. In such systems, the users need simple, uniform interfaces. However, the data bases that they access are potentially in different computer systems outside their control [Lochovsky and Tsichritzis, 1981].

A second important application of structure, constraint, and operation mappings is in the area of distributed data bases. Distributed data base systems combine the features of computer networks and of DBMSs. A distributed data base provides, on the one hand, an integrated collection of data. On the other hand, it is composed of distinct, semiautonomous parts or nodes. Nodes of the computer network contain computer systems, and these may be hosts for some or all of the components of a DBMS. To integrate the description and manipulation of the distributed data, mappings may be needed. Distributed data base systems are subject to the same mapping problems already mentioned, as well as to additional problems arising from the distribution of the data. Since all needed data may not be at one site, a query must be mapped to a set of subqueries, each of which can be processed at a single node, possibly receiving intermediate results of other subqueries from other nodes [Wong, 1977; Epstein et al., 1978; Youssefi, 1978; Bernstein and Chiu, 1981].

The mapping problems of distributed systems become very complex when they are composed of heterogeneous DBMSs. We then have the general problem of different data models, the need for constructive mappings, and the need to map operations. Translation of data bases between nodes may be needed. Another approach may be to translate entire queries (programs) and ship them to the appropriate nodes. The need to map constraints is a very real problem in this situation. In addition, the optimization of the translation is very difficult [Bernstein and Chiu, 1981]. Apart from its practical implications, research in DBMS mappings is also needed to unify data models into a common framework with rigorous equivalence correspondences between their facilities [Borkin, 1978, 1980; Lien, 1980].

## EXERCISES

**14.1** Consider a graph data model $M_1$ with simple nodes and a table data model $M_2$. Outline completely the structure mappings between a schema in $M_1$ and a schema in $M_2$ for the same data base.

**14.2** Consider a set of functional dependencies relating single attributes. Construct a graph representing these dependencies.

(a) Outline an algorithm for obtaining a set of relations from the graph which internally have these dependencies. Can you devise an algorithm which will guarantee that the relations are in 3NF? (Does obtaining the closure of or cover for the functional dependencies help?)

(b) Outline an algorithm for obtaining a data structure diagram in which the record types correspond to 3NF relations.

(c) Can you generalize your algorithms to the case where the functional dependencies have more than one attribute on the left side?

**14.3** Consider a hierarchical data model constraint like the declaration of a hierarchical key. How would you express this constraint in a relational schema using (a) functional dependencies and (b) predicate calculus?

**14.4** Consider a relational data model and a constraint specification language such as the predicate calculus or some other constraint language (e.g., Beta [Brodie, 1978]). Can you capture completely all the structures and constraints of other data models as presented in this book using this framework? Outline an algorithm for some data model mappings to illustrate your argument.

**14.5** Consider the record types related by one DBTG-set type. Outline an algorithm which takes an extension of the two record types and the DBTG-set type and produces a relational extension that captures both the records and the connections between them.

**14.6** Consider a completely connected binary data model schema having only simple unordered sets as nodes. Outline an algorithm that produces one relation from any extension of the schema.

**14.7** Suppose that we would like to show equivalence between a graph data model such as the DBTG-network data model and a relational data model. The notion of equivalence should incorporate constraints. Propose a suitable abstraction of a graph data model and a relational data model that facilitates the mapping between them [Borkin, 1980; Lien, 1980].

**14.8** Consider a relation scheme $R(A_1, ..., A_n)$. Outline an algorithm that maps an extension of the relation scheme to an extension of a binary data model having $A_1, ..., A_n$ as nodes. Are $A_1, ..., A_n$ sets or ordered sets in the graph data model? Suppose there are some functional dependencies or multivalued dependencies present in $R$. How would you incorporate them into your mapping?

**14.9** Outline two algorithms as in Exercises 14.6 and 14.8 which are inverses of each other. That is, for any extension of a relation *R*, it gets mapped into an extension of a graph data model by applying the algorithm of Exercise 14.8 and back to the same extension of R by applying the algorithm of Exercise 14.6. Can you formally prove that these two algorithms are inverses of each other?

**14.10** Consider a hierarchical schema and a relational schema with functional dependencies which capture the same structures and constraints. Outline an algorithm that maps a relational query to a navigation on the data base trees. (*Hint*: Define a relational query inductively in terms of relational operators. Show the navigation for each operator and how you would combine the navigation.)

**14.11** Consider a hierarchical schema and a relational view based on it. How would a hierarchical insert, delete, or update be mirrored in the relational view? How would a relational insert, delete, or update be mapped into hierarchical operations? (*Note*: You may use null values provided that you explain carefully why they are needed and how they are used.)

**14.12** Consider the problem of Exercise 14.10 for a network schema instead of a hierarchical schema.

**14.13** Consider a hierarchical schema and a relational view based on it. We can define operations such as insert, delete, and update on the relational schema in relational terms. They will translate, as in Exercise 14.11, into a rather "unnatural" series of hierarchical operations. As a result, another user viewing the hierarchical schema will see an "unnatural" hierarchical operation. Alternatively, we can modify the relational operations so as to produce "natural" hierarchical operations. In this case, however, the relational user would have to deal with "unnatural" relational operations. Which approach is better, and why? Discuss the relative advantages not only in terms of hierarchical and relational schemas, but for any two data models $M_1$ and $M_2$. Can you outline some practical situation where one or the other approach will definitely be superior?

**14.14** Suppose that you had to translate operations between different data models. One way of doing it is to go through an *interface schema*. The interface schema plays a role similar to the ANSI/X3/SPARC conceptual schema. It serves as an intermediary for translating operations between the source schema $S_s$ and the target schema $S_t$. What data model is appropriate for this interface schema? Should it have a data language? Is a data model that is appropriate for a conceptual schema also appropriate for an interface schema? Try your data model suggestion by obtaining the structure, constraint, and operation mappings between two common data models such as the hierarchical and DBTG-network data models.

**14.15** One way of providing cooperation in a heterogeneous distributed data base is to have a facility to query the global data base which is separate and mappable to the facilities in individual nodes [Adiba and Delobel, 1977]. The global facility implies a *global schema* which is according to a different data model than the data model at the individual nodes. What data model is appropriate for this global schema? Compare the idea of this global schema with the interface schema discussed in Exercise 14.14 and the conceptual schema of ANSI/X3/SPARC.

# APPENDIX

This example application is used in Parts 2 and 3 to illustrate various concepts in the different data models described. The example represents certain information on some aspects of the operation of a hospital. It is a scaled-down version of a real application [Lam, 1974]. Although the example is mostly self-explanatory, to ensure uniformity of interpretation we present a short description of it. The entity types, their related attributes and the relationship types are shown in Figure A—1.

| Entity type | Attributes |
|---|---|
| HOSPITAL | Hospital code, Name, Address, Phone#, # of beds |
| WARD | Ward code, Name, # of beds |
| STAFF | Employee#, Name, Duty, Shift, Salary |
| DOCTOR | Doctor#, Name, Specialty |
| PATIENT | Registration#, Bed#, Name, Address, Birthdate, Sex, SSN |
| DIAGNOSIS | Diagnosis code, Diagnosis type, Complications, Precautionary info |
| LAB | Lab#, Name, Address, Phone# |
| TEST | Test code, Date ordered, Time ordered, Specimen/order#, Status |

| Relationship type | Entity types | Mapping |
|---|---|---|
| HOSPITAL WARD | HOSPITAL, WARD | functional $HOSPITAL \rightarrow WARD$ |
| STAFF DOCTORS | HOSPITAL, DOCTOR | functional $HOSPITAL \rightarrow DOCTOR$ |
| HOSPITAL LAB | HOSPITAL, LAB | many-to-many |
| WARD STAFF | WARD, STAFF | functional $WARD \rightarrow STAFF$ |
| OCCUPANCY | WARD, PATIENT | functional $WARD \rightarrow PATIENT$ |
| DOCTOR PATIENT | DOCTOR, PATIENT | many-to-many |
| PATIENT TEST | PATIENT, TEST | functional $PATIENT \rightarrow TEST$ |
| PATIENT DIAGNOSIS | PATIENT, DIAGNOSIS | functional $PATIENT \rightarrow DIAGNOSIS$ |
| TEST ASSIGNED | LAB, TEST | functional $LAB \rightarrow TEST$ |

**Fig. A—1** Entity types, attributes, and relationship types for medical data base example.

The *HOSPITAL* entity type describes certain aspects of a hospital— identifying code, name, address, phone number, and number of beds in the hospital. It is related to the *WARD*, *DOCTOR*, and *LAB* entity types. The functional relationship type *HOSPITAL WARD* between *HOSPITAL* and

*WARD* specifies the wards of a hospital. The functional relationship type *STAFF DOCTORS* between *HOSPITAL* and *DOCTOR* identifies those doctors that are on staff at the hospital. Finally, the many-to-many relationship type *HOSPITAL LAB* between *HOSPITAL* and *LAB* specifies those labs that have outstanding orders for tests on patients in the hospital.

The *WARD* entity type describes certain aspects of a ward in a hospital—identifying code, name, and number of beds in the ward. It is related to the *HOSPITAL, STAFF,* and *PATIENT* entity types. The functional relationship type *HOSPITAL WARD* between *WARD* and *HOSPITAL* specifies that a ward can be located in at most one hospital and that a hospital can have several wards. The functional relationship type *WARD STAFF* between *WARD* and *STAFF* identifies the employees that work in the ward. The functional relationship type *OCCUPANCY* between *WARD* and *PATIENT* specifies those patients that occupy a bed in a certain ward.

The *STAFF* entity type describes aspects of employees in a ward— employee number, name, duty (intern, nurse, etc.), shift (morning, afternoon, etc.), and salary. It is related to the *WARD* entity type by the functional relationship type *WARD STAFF*, which specifies the ward in which an employee works.

The *DOCTOR* entity type describes characteristics of doctors on staff at a hospital—doctor number, name, and area of specialization. It is related to the *HOSPITAL* and *PATIENT* entity types. The functional relationship type *STAFF DOCTORS* between *DOCTOR* and *HOSPITAL* specifies that a doctor may be on staff at, at most, one hospital. The many-to-many relationship type *DOCTOR PATIENT* between *DOCTOR* and *PATIENT* indicates those patients that a doctor is actively treating.

The *PATIENT* entity type describes characteristics of hospital patients—registration number, bed number in the ward, name, address, birthdate, sex, and social security number. It is related to the *WARD, DOCTOR, TEST,* and *DIAGNOSIS* entity types. The functional relationship type *OCCUPANCY* between *PATIENT* and *WARD* specifies the ward to which a patient has been assigned. The many-to-many relationship type *DOCTOR PATIENT* between *PATIENT* and *DOCTOR* indicates a patient's attending doctor(s). A patient may have several attending doctors (e.g., if several doctors are consulting on one case or if different doctors are treating different illnesses). The functional relationship type *PATIENT TEST* between *PATIENT* and *TEST* specifies those medical tests that have been ordered for a patient. Finally, the functional relationship type *PATIENT DIAGNOSIS* between *PATIENT* and *DIAGNOSIS* specifies the medical diagnosis(ses) reached for the patient. Several diagnoses are possible if there are multiple illnesses.

The *DIAGNOSIS* entity type describes characteristics about a patient's medical diagnosis—identifying code, statement of the diagnosis, any complications uncovered, and any precautionary information, such as drug reactions. It is related to the *PATIENT* entity type by the functional relationship type *PATIENT DIAGNOSIS*, which identifies the patient for which the diagnosis has been performed.

The *LAB* entity type describes certain aspects of medical laboratories—lab number, name, address, and phone number. It is related to the *HOSPITAL* and *TEST* entity types. The many-to-many relationship type *HOSPITAL LAB* between *LAB* and *HOSPITAL* specifies the hospitals for which a lab is doing work. A lab may be doing work for several hospitals and a hospital may use several different labs. The functional relationship type *TESTS ASSIGNED* between *LAB* and *TEST* specifies the medical tests to be performed by the lab.

Finally, the *TEST* entity type describes aspects of medical tests—identifying code, type of test, date ordered, time ordered, specimen/order number, and the current status of the test. It is related to the *LAB* and the *PATIENT* entity types. The functional relationship type *TESTS ASSIGNED* between *TEST* and *LAB* specifies the lab that has been assigned to do the test. The functional relationship type *PATIENT TEST* between *TEST* and *PATIENT* identifies the patient for which the test has been ordered.

**C1:**  The value of *Time ordered* for a test must be between 0 and 24.

**C2:**  The sum of the beds in all the wards must equal the total number of beds in the hospital.

**C3:**  *Sex* is one of 'M' or 'F'.

**C4:**  Social security number (*SSN*) is unique within the data base.

**C5:**  A bed number can be assigned to only one patient within a ward.

**C6:**  The number of patients in each ward must be less than or equal to the number of beds in each ward.

**C7:**  Keys: *Hospital code, Ward code, Doctor#, Lab#, Registration#*.

**C8:**  Every *DIAGNOSIS* entity corresponds to some *PATIENT* entity (existence constraint).

**Fig. A—2** Constraints on medical data base example.

There are also several constraints that apply to the example application. Some of these are summarized in Figure A—2.

# REFERENCES

The following abbreviations are used:

ACM        Association For Computing Machinery
AFIPS      American Federation of Information Processing Societies
CODASYL    Conference on Data Systems Languages
IFIP       International Federation for Information Processing
NCC        National Computer Conference
SIAM       Society for Industrial and Applied Mathematics
SIGART     Special Interest Group on Artificial Intelligence
SIGFIDET   Special Interest Group on File Description and Translation
SIGMOD     Special Interest Group on Management of Data (formerly SIGFIDET)
SIGPLAN    Special Interest Group on Programming Languages

Abrial, J. R. [1974]. "Data semantics," in *Data Base Management* (Klimbie, J. W., and Koffeman, K. L., eds.), pp. 1-59. North-Holland, Amsterdam.

Adiba, M., and Delobel, C. [1977]. "The problem of the cooperation between different D.B.M.S.," in *Architecture and Models in Data Base Management Systems* (Nijssen, G. M., ed.), pp. 165-186. North-Holland, Amsterdam.

Adiba, M., Delobel, C., and Leonard, M. [1976]. "A unified approach for modelling data in logical data base design," in *Modelling in Data Base Management Systems* (Nijssen, G. M., ed.), pp. 311-338. North-Holland, Amsterdam.

Aho, A. V., Beeri, C., and Ullman, J. D. [1979a]. "The theory of joins in relational databases," *ACM Trans. Database Syst.* 4, pp. 297-314.

Aho, A. V., Sagiv, Y., and Ullman, J. D. [1979b]. "Equivalences among relational expressions," *SIAM J. Comput.* 8, pp. 218-246.

Aho, A. V., Sagiv, Y., and Ullman, J. D. [1979c]. "Efficient optimization of a class of relational expressions," *ACM Trans. Database Syst.* 4, pp. 435-454.

ANSI [1981]. *ANSI X3H2 Data Definition Language dpANS draft.* ANSI/X3 Secretariat, Washington, DC.

Arlow, B. E. [1980]. "Conceptual data modeling and S2K database design," *The ASTUTE Conf. Proc. for Fall 1980*, pp. 64-96.

Armstrong, W. W. [1974]. "Dependency structures of data base relationships," *Proc. IFIP Congr. 74*, pp. 580-583. North-Holland, Amsterdam.

Armstrong, W. W., and Delobel, C. [1980]. "Decompositions and functional dependencies in relations," *ACM Trans. Database Syst.* 5, pp. 404-430.

Astrahan, M. M., et al. [1976]. "System R: Relational approach to database management," *ACM Trans. Database Syst.* **1**, pp. 97-137.

Bachman, C. W. [1969]. "Data structure diagrams," *Data Base* **1** (2), pp. 4-10.

Bachman, C. W. [1977]. "Why restrict the data modelling capability of CODASYL data structure sets?," *Proc. AFIPS NCC* **44**, pp. 69-75.

Bachman, C. W., and Daya, M. [1977]. "The role concept in data models," *Proc. 3rd Int. Conf. Very Large Data Bases*, pp. 464-476.

Bachman, C. W., and Williams, S. B. [1964]. "A general purpose programming system for random access memories," *Proc. AFIPS Fall Joint Comput. Conf.* **26**, pp. 411-422.

Badal, D. Z., and Popek, G. J. [1979]. "Cost performance analysis of semantic integrity validation methods," *Proc. ACM SIGMOD*, pp. 109-115.

Bakkom, D. E., and Behymer, J. A. [1975]. "Implementation of a prototype generalized file translator," *Proc. ACM SIGMOD*, pp. 99-110.

Baldissera, C., Ceri, S., Pelagatti, G., and Bracchi, G. [1979]. "Interactive specification and formal verification of user's views in data base design," *Proc. 5th Int. Conf. Very Large Data Bases*, pp. 262-272.

Batory, D. S. [1980a]. *Optimal File Designs and Reorganization Points.* Tech. Rep. CSRG-110, Comput. Syst. Res. Group, Univ. of Toronto, Toronto.

Batory, D. S. [1980b]. *An Analytic Model of Physical Databases.* Ph.D. thesis, Dep. of Comput. Sci., Univ. of Toronto, Toronto.

Batory, D. S., and Gotlieb, C. C. [1980]. *A Unifying Model of Physical Databases.* Tech. Rep. CSRG-109, Comput. Syst. Res. Group, Univ. of Toronto, Toronto.

BCS [1977]. "The British Computer Society data dictionary systems working party report," *ACM SIGMOD Record* **9** (4), pp. 2-24.

Beeri, C. [1979]. *On the Role of Data Dependencies in the Construction of Relational Database Schemas.* Tech. Rep. 43, Dep. of Comput. Sci., The Hebrew Univ. of Jerusalem, Jerusalem, Israel.

Beeri, C. [1980]. "On the membership problem for functional and multivalued dependencies in relational databases," *ACM Trans. Database Syst.* **5**, pp. 241-259.

Beeri, C., and Bernstein, P. A. [1979]. "Computational problems related to the design of normal form relational schemas," *ACM Trans. Database Syst.* **4**, pp. 30-59.

Beeri, C., Fagin, R., and Howard, J. H. [1977]. "A complete axiomatization for functional and multivalued dependencies in database relations," *Proc. ACM SIGMOD*, pp. 47-61.

Beeri, C., Bernstein, P. A., and Goodman, N., [1978]. "A sophisticate's introduction to database normalization theory," *Proc. 4th Int. Conf. Very Large Data Bases*, pp. 113-124.

Beeri, C., Dowd, M., Fagin, R., and Statman, R. [1980]. *On the Structure of Armstrong Relations for Functional Dependencies.* Tech. Rep. RJ2901, IBM Res. Lab., San Jose, CA.

Beeri, C., Mendelzon, A. O., Sagiv, Y., and Ullman, J. D. [1981]. "Equivalence of relational database schemes," *SIAM J. Comput.* **10**, pp. 352-370.

Benci, E., Bodart, F., Bogaert, H., and Cabanes, A. [1976]. "Concepts for the design of a conceptual schema," in *Modelling in Data Base Management Systems* (Nijssen, G. M., ed.), pp. 181-200. North-Holland, Amsterdam.

Benneworth, R., Bishop, C., Turnbull, C., Holman, W., and Monette, E. [1981]. "The implementation of GERM, an entity relationship data base management system," *Proc. 7th Int. Conf. Very Large Data Bases.*

Berild, S., and Nachmens, S. [1977a]. "CS4 — A tool for database design by infological simulation," *Proc. 3rd Int. Conf. Very Large Data Bases*, pp. 533-544.

Berild, S., and Nachmens, S. [1977b]. "Some practical applications of CS4 — A DBMS for associative databases," in *Architecture and Models in Data Base Management Systems* (Nijssen, G. M., ed.), pp. 213-235. North-Holland, Amsterdam.

Bernstein, P. A. [1975]. *Normalization and Functional Dependencies in the Relational Data Base Model.* Ph.D. thesis, Dep. of Comput. Sci., Univ. of Toronto, Toronto.

Bernstein, P. A. [1976]. "Synthesizing third normal form relations from functional dependencies," *ACM Trans. Database Syst.* **1**, pp. 277-298.

Bernstein, P. A., and Beeri, C. [1976]. *An Algorithmic Approach to Normalization of Relational Database Schemas.* Tech. Rep. CSRG-73, Comput. Syst. Res. Group, Univ. of Toronto, Toronto.

Bernstein, P. A., and Chiu, D. W. [1981]. "Using semi-joins to solve relational queries," *J. ACM* **28**, pp. 25-40.

Bernstein, P. A., and Goodman, N. [1979]. *The Theory of Semi-joins.* Tech. Rep. CCA-27-79, Comput. Corp. of America, Cambridge, MA.

Bernstein, P. A., and Goodman, N. [1980]. "What does Boyce-Codd normal form do?," *Proc. 6th Int. Conf. Very Large Data Bases*, pp. 245-259.

Bernstein, P. A., Blaustein, B. T., and Clarke, E. M. [1980]. "Fast maintenance of semantic integrity assertions using redundant aggregate data," *Proc. 6th Int. Conf. Very Large Data Bases*, pp. 126-136.

Biller, H. [1979]. "On the equivalence of data base schemas — A semantic approach to data translation," *Inf. Syst.* **4**, pp. 35-47.

Biller, H., and Neuhold, E. J. [1977]. "Concepts for the conceptual schema," in *Architecture and Models in Data Base Management Systems* (Nijssen, G. M., ed.), pp. 1-30. North-Holland, Amsterdam.

Biller, H., and Neuhold, E. J. [1978]. "Semantics of data bases: The semantics of data models," *Inf. Syst.* **3**, pp. 11-30.

Biskup, J. [1980]. *On Existential and Universal Null Values and Maybe-Tuples in Database Relations.* Lehrstuhl fur Angewandte Mathematik Insbesondere Informatik, Aachen (unpublished manuscript).

Bjørner, D., Codd, E. F., Deckert, K. L., and Traiger, I. L. [1973]. *The Gamma Zero N-ary Relational Data Base Interface: Specification of Objects and Operations.* Tech. Rep. RJ1200, IBM Res. Lab., San Jose, CA.

Blasgen, M. W., and Eswaran, K. P. [1977]. "Storage and access in relational data bases," *IBM Syst. J.* **16**, pp. 363-377.

Blasgen, M. W., et al. [1981]. "System R: An architectural overview," *IBM Syst. J.* **20**, pp. 41-62.

Bleier, R. E. [1967]. "Treating hierarchical data structures in the SDC time-shared data management system (TDMS)," *Proc. ACM Natl. Conf.*, pp. 41-49.

Borkin, S. A. [1978]. "Data model equivalence," *Proc. 4th Int. Conf. Very Large Data Bases*, pp. 526-534.

Borkin, S. A. [1980]. *Data Models: A Semantic Approach for Database Systems.* MIT Press, Cambridge, MA.

Boyce, R. F., and Chamberlin, D. D. [1973]. *Using a Structured English Query Language as a Data Definition Facility.* Tech. Rep. RJ1318, IBM Res. Lab., San Jose, CA.

Bracchi, G., Paolini, P., and Pelagatti, G. [1976]. "Binary logical associations in data modelling," in *Modelling in Data Base Management Systems* (Nijssen, G. M., ed.), pp. 125-148. North-Holland, Amsterdam.

Bracchi, G., Furtado, A. L., and Pelagatti, G. [1979]. "Constraint specification in evolutionary data base design," in *Formal Models and Practical Tools for Information System Design* (Schneider, H.-J., ed.), pp. 149-165. North-Holland, Amsterdam.

Brachman, R. J. [1979]. "On the epistemological status of semantic networks," in *Associative Networks* (Findler, N., ed.), pp. 3-50. Academic Press, New York.

Brachman, R. J., and Smith, B. C. [1980]. "Special issue on knowledge representation," *SIGART Newsletter* No. 70.

Brodie, M. L. [1978]. *Specification and Verification of Data Base Semantic Integrity.* Ph.D. thesis, Dep. of Comput. Sci., Univ. of Toronto, Toronto.

Brodie, M. L. [1980]. "The application of data types to database semantic integrity," *Inf. Syst.* **5**, pp. 287-296.

Brodie, M. L., and Zilles, S. N. (eds.) [1981]. "Proceedings of the workshop on data abstraction, databases and conceptual modelling," *ACM SIGMOD Record* **11**(2). ACM Order No. 474800.

Brosey, M., and Shneiderman, B. [1978]. "Two experimental comparisons of relational and hierarchical database models," *Int. J. Man—Machine Stud.* **10**, pp. 625-637.

Bubenko, J. A., Jr. [1977a]. "IAM: An inferential abstract modeling approach to design of conceptual schemas," *Proc. ACM SIGMOD*, pp. 62-74.

Bubenko, J. A., Jr. [1977b]. "Validity and verification aspects of information modeling," *Proc. 3rd Int. Conf. Very Large Data Bases*, pp. 556-565.

Bubenko, J. A., Jr. [1980]. "Information modeling in the context of system development," *Proc. IFIP Congr. 80*, pp. 395-411.

Bubenko, J. A., Jr., Langefors, B., and Solvberg, A. (eds.) [1971]. *Computer-Aided Information Systems Analysis and Design.* Studentlitteratur, Lund, Sweden.

Burroughs [1975]. *B6700/B7700 DMS II* publications: *Data and Structure Definition Language (DASDL) Reference Manual,* 5001084; *Host Language Interface Reference Manual,* 5001092. Burroughs Corp., Detroit, MI.

Cardenas, A. F. [1973]. "Evaluation and selection of file organizations — A model and a system," *Commun. ACM* **16**, pp. 540-548.

Cardenas, A. F. [1975]. "Analysis and performance of inverted data base structures," *Commun. ACM* **18**, pp. 253-263.

Cardenas, A. F. [1979]. *Data Base Management Systems.* Allyn and Bacon, Boston.

Ceri, S., Pelagatti, G., and Bracchi, G. [1981]. "Structured methodology for designing static and dynamic aspects of data base applications," *Inf. Syst.* **6**, pp. 31-45.

Chamberlin, D. D. [1976]. "Relational data-base management systems," *ACM Comput. Surv.* **8**, pp. 43-66.

Chamberlin, D. D., and Boyce, R. F. [1974]. "SEQUEL: A structured English query language," *Proc. ACM SIGMOD,* pp. 249-264.

Chamberlin, D. D., Gray, J. N., and Traiger, I. L. [1975]. "Views, authorization and locking in a relational data base system," *Proc. AFIPS NCC* **44**, pp. 425-430.

Chamberlin, D. D., et al. [1976]. "SEQUEL 2: A unified approach to data definition, manipulation, and control," *IBM J. Res. Dev.* **20**, pp. 560-575.

Chen, P. P. [1976]. "The entity-relationship model: Toward a unified view of data," *ACM Trans. Database Syst.* **1**, pp. 9-36.

Chen, P. P. [1977]. "The entity-relationship model: A basis for the enterprise view of data," *Proc. AFIPS NCC* **46**, pp. 77-84.

Chen, P. P. (ed.) [1980]. *Entity-Relationship Approach to Systems Analysis and Design.* North-Holland, Amsterdam.

Chen, P. P., and Yao, S. B. [1977]. "Design and performance tools for data base systems," *Proc. 3rd Int. Conf. Very Large Data Bases,* pp. 3-15.

Childs, D. L. [1968]. "Feasibility of a set-theoretic data structure — A general structure based on a reconstituted definition of relation," *Proc. IFIP Congr. 68,* pp. 162-172. North-Holland, Amsterdam.

Childs, D. L. [1974]. *Extended Set Theory, A Foundation for the Design, Implementation and Operation of Information Systems.* STIS Corp., Ann Arbor, MI.

Childs, D. L. [1977]. "Extended set theory — A general model for very large, distributed, backend information systems," *Proc. 3rd Int. Conf. Very Large Data Bases,* pp. 28-46.

Chiu, D. W. [1979]. *Optimal Query Interpretation for Distributed Databases.* Ph.D. thesis, Div. of Appl. Sci., Harvard Univ.

Christodoulakis, S. [1981]. *Estimating Selectivities in Data Base Systems.* Ph.D. thesis, Dep. of Comput. Sci., Univ. of Toronto, Toronto.

Church, A. [1956]. *An Introduction to Mathematical Logic I.* Princeton Univ. Press, Princeton, NJ.

Cincom [1974]. *Total/7* publications: *Application Programming Reference Manual*, P02-1321-2; *Data Base Administration Reference Manual*, P02-1322-2. Cincom Systems, Inc., Cincinnati, OH.

Clemons, E. K. [1978]. "An external schema facility to support data base update," in *Databases: Improving Usability and Responsiveness* (Shneiderman, B., ed.), pp. 371-398. Academic Press, New York.

Clemons, E. K. [1979]. "An external schema facility for CODASYL 1978," *Proc. 5th Int. Conf. Very Large Data Bases*, pp. 119-128.

Clemons, E. K., and Germano, F., Jr. [1979]. *An Experimental Implementation of an External Schema Facility for CODASYL.* Decision Sci. Working Paper 79-03-02, Univ. of Pennsylvania, Philadelphia, PA.

CODASYL [1971]. *CODASYL Data Base Task Group Report.* Conf. on Data Syst. Languages, ACM, New York.

CODASYL [1973]. *CODASYL Data Description Language Journal of Development.* National Bureau of Standards Handbook 113, U.S. Government Printing Office, (SD Catalog No. C13.6/2:113), Washington, DC.

CODASYL [1976]. *CODASYL COBOL Journal of Development.* Material Data Management Branch, Dep. of Supply and Services, Ottawa.

CODASYL [1977a]. "Stored-data description and data translation: A model and language," The Stored-Data Definition and Translation Task Group of the CODASYL Systems Committee report. *Inf. Syst.* **2**, pp. 95-148.

CODASYL [1977b]. *CODASYL FORTRAN Data Base Facility Journal of Development.* Material Data Management Branch, Dep. of Supply and Services, Ottawa.

CODASYL [1978]. *CODASYL Data Description Language Journal of Development.* Material Data Management Branch, Dep. of Supply and Services, Ottawa.

Codd, E. F. [1970]. "A relational model of data for large shared data banks," *Commun. ACM* **13**, pp. 377-387.

Codd, E. F. [1971a]. "Normalized data base structure: A brief tutorial," *Proc. ACM SIGFIDET Workshop on Data Description, Access and Control*, pp. 1-17.

Codd, E. F. [1971b]. "A data base sublanguage founded on the relational calculus," *Proc. ACM SIGFIDET Workshop on Data Description, Access and Control*, pp. 35-68.

Codd, E. F. [1972a]. "Further normalization of the data base relational model," in *Data Base Systems, Courant Comput. Sci. Symp. 6th* (Rustin, R., ed.), pp. 33-64. Prentice-Hall, Englewood Cliffs, NJ.

Codd, E. F. [1972b]. "Relational completeness of data base sublanguages," in *Data Base Systems, Courant Comput. Sci. Symp. 6th* (Rustin, R., ed.), pp. 65-98. Prentice-Hall, Englewood Cliffs, NJ.

Codd, E. F. [1974]. "Seven steps to RENDEZVOUS with the casual user," in *Data Base Management* (Klimbie, J. W., and Koffeman, K. L., eds.), pp. 179-199. North-Holland, Amsterdam.

Codd, E. F. [1979]. "Extending the database relational model to capture more meaning," *ACM Trans. Database Syst.* **4**, pp. 397-434.

Codd, E. F., and Date, C. J. [1974]. "Interactive support for non-programmers: The relational and network approaches," *Proc. ACM SIGMOD, Data Models: Data-Structure-Set versus Relational* (Rustin, R., ed.), pp. 11-41. ACM, New York.

Codd, E. F., Arnold, R. S., Cadiou, J.-M., Chang, C. L., and Roussopoulos, N. [1978]. *RENDEZVOUS Version 1: An Experimental English-language Query Formulation System for Casual Users of Relational Data Bases.* Tech. Rep. RJ2144, IBM Res. Lab., San Jose, CA.

Cullinane [1975]. *Integrated Database Management System (IDMS)*, publications: *Data Definition Languages, Utilities and GCI Reference Guide*, release 3.1; *Data Manipulation Language Programmer's Reference Guide*, release 3.1. Cullinane Corp., Boston.

Curtice, R. [1981]. "Data dictionaries: an assessment of current practice and problems," *Proc. 7th Int. Conf. Very Large Data Bases.*

Czarnik, B., Schuster, S. A., and Tsichritzis, D. C. [1975]. "ZETA: A relational data base management system," *Proc. ACM Pacific 75*, pp. 21-25.

Dahl, O.-J., and Nygaard, K. [1966]. "SIMULA — An ALGOL-based simulation language," *Commun. ACM 9*, pp. 671-678.

Dale, A. G., and Dale, N. B. [1976]. "Schema and occurrence structure transformations in hierarchical systems," *Proc. ACM SIGMOD*, pp. 157-168.

Dale, A. G., and Dale, N. B. [1977]. "Main schema-external schema interaction in hierarchically organized data bases," *Proc. ACM SIGMOD*, pp. 102-110.

Dale, A. G., and Yurkanan, C. V. [1977]. "A processing interface for multiple external schema access to a data base management system," *Proc. 3rd Int. Conf. Very Large Data Bases*, pp. 318-325.

Datamation [1980]. "Evaluating off-the-shelf packages," *Datamation* **26**(12), p. 84-.

Date, C. J. [1981]. *An Introduction to Database Systems*, 3rd ed. Addison-Wesley, Reading, MA.

Dayal, U. [1979]. *Schema Mapping Problems in Database Systems.* Ph.D. thesis, Div. of Appl. Sci., Harvard Univ.

Dayal, U., and Bernstein, P. A. [1978]. "On the updatability of relational views," *Proc. 4th Int. Conf. Very Large Data Bases*, pp. 368-377.

Deheneffe, C., and Hennebert, H. [1976]. "NUL: A navigational user's language for a network structured data base," *Proc. ACM SIGMOD*, pp. 135-142.

Deheneffe, C., Hennebert, H., and Paulus, W. [1974]. "Relational model for a data base," *Proc. IFIP Congr. 74*, pp. 1022-1025. North-Holland, Amsterdam.

Deliyanni, A., and Kowalski, R. A. [1979]. "Logic and semantic networks," *Commun. ACM 22*, pp. 184-192.

Delobel, C. [1978]. "Normalization and hierarchical dependencies in the relational data model," *ACM Trans. Database Syst.* **3**, pp. 201-222.

DeLutis, T. G., and Smith, J. D. [1976]. *IPSS/DBMS: A Simulator for Modeling Data Base Management Systems.* Dep. of Comput. and Inf. Sci., The Ohio State Univ., Columbus, OH.

DeMarco, T. [1979]. *Structured Analysis and System Specification.* Prentice-Hall, Englewood Cliffs, NJ.

Denny, G. H. [1977]. *An Introduction to SQL, A Structured Query Language.* Tech. Rep. RA93(28099), IBM Res. Lab., San Jose, CA.

Dijkstra, E. W. [1965]. "Programming considered as a human activity," *Proc. IFIP Congr. 65,* pp. 213-217. North-Holland, Amsterdam.

Dijkstra, E. W. [1972]. "Notes on structured programming," in *Structured Programming* (Dahl, O.-J., Dijkstra, E. W., and Hoare, C. A.R., eds.), pp. 1-82. Academic Press, New York.

Dodd, G. G. [1966]. "APL — A language for associative data handling in PL/1," *Proc. AFIPS Fall Joint Comput. Conf.* **29**, pp. 667-684.

Durding, B. M., Becker, C. A., and Gould, J. D. [1977]. "Data organization," *Hum. Fac.* **19**, pp. 1-14.

Earnest, C. P. [1975]. "Selection and higher level structures in networks," in *Data Base Description* (Douque, B. C., and Nijssen, G. M., eds.), pp. 215-236. North-Holland, Amsterdam.

Edwards, P. (ed.) [1967]. "Models and analogy in science," in *The Encylopedia of Philosophy* **5**, pp. 354-359. The Macmillan Company and The Free Press, New York.

El-Masri, R., and Wiederhold, G. [1979]. *Properties of Relationships and their Representation.* Comput. Sci. Dep., Stanford Univ., Stanford, CA.

Enderton, H. [1972]. *A Mathematical Introduction to Logic.* Academic Press, New York.

Epstein, R., Stonebraker, M. R., and Wong, E. [1978]. "Distributed query processing in a relational data base system," *Proc. ACM SIGMOD,* pp. 169-180.

Eswaran, K. P. [1976]. *Specifications, Implementations and Interaction of a Trigger Subsystem in an Integrated Database System.* Tech. Rep. RJ1820, IBM Res. Lab., San Jose, CA.

Eswaran, K. P., and Chamberlin, D. D. [1975]. "Functional specifications of a subsystem for data base integrity," *Proc. 1st Int. Conf. Very Large Data Bases,* pp. 48-68.

Everest, G. C. [1977]. *Data Base Management: Objectives, System Functions, and Administration.* McGraw-Hill, New York.

Everett, G. D., Dissly, C. W., and Hardgrave, W. T. [1971]. *Remote File Management System (RFMS) Users Manual.* TRM-16, Computation Ctr., Univ. of Texas at Austin, Austin, TX.

Fagin, R. [1977a]. "The decomposition versus the synthetic approach to relational database design," *Proc. 3rd Int. Conf. Very Large Data Bases,* pp. 441-446.

Fagin, R. [1977b]. "Multivalued dependencies and a new normal form for relational databases," *ACM Trans. Database Syst.* **2**, pp. 262-278.

Fagin, R. [1979a]. "Normal forms and relational database operators," *Proc. ACM SIGMOD,* pp. 153-160.

Fagin, R. [1979b]. *A Normal Form for Relational Databases that is Based on Domains and Keys.* Tech. Rep. RJ2520, IBM Res. Lab., San Jose, CA.

Fagin, R. [1980]. "Horn clauses and data dependencies," *Proc. 12th ACM Symp. on Theory of Comput.*, pp. 123-134.

Fahlman, S. E. [1977]. *A System for Representing and Using Real-World Knowledge.* Ph.D. thesis, Artificial Intelligence Lab., MIT.

Falkenberg, E. [1976a]. "Concepts for modelling information," in *Modelling in Data Base Management Systems* (Nijssen, G. M., ed.), pp. 95-110. North-Holland, Amsterdam.

Falkenberg, E. [1976b]. "Significations: The key to unify data base management." *Inf. Syst.* 2, pp. 19-28.

Farley, G. H., and Schuster, S. A. [1975]. *Query Execution and Index Selection for Relational Data Bases.* Tech. Rep. CSRG-53, Comput. Syst. Res. Group, Univ. of Toronto, Toronto.

Fillmore, C. J. [1968]. "The case for case," in *Universals in Linguistic Theory* (Bach, E., and Harms, R., eds.), pp. 1-88. Holt, Rinehart and Winston, New York.

Findler, N. (ed.) [1979]. *Associative Networks.* Academic Press, New York.

Fraenkel, A. A., Bar-Hillel, Y., and Levy, A. [1973]. *Foundations of Set Theory.* North-Holland, Amsterdam.

Fry, J. P., and Jervis, D. W. [1974]. "Towards a formulation and definition of data reorganization," *Proc. ACM SIGMOD*, pp. 83-100.

Fry, J. P., and Sibley, E. H. [1976]. "The evolution of database management systems," *ACM Comput. Surv.* 8, pp. 7-42.

Fry, J. P., and Teorey, T. J. [1978]. "Design and performance tools for improving database usability and responsiveness," in *Databases: Improving Usability and Responsiveness* (Shneiderman, B., ed.), pp. 151-189. Academic Press, New York.

Fry, J. P., Frank, R. L., and Hershey, E. A., III [1972a]. "A developmental model for data translation," *Proc. ACM SIGFIDET Workshop on Data Description, Access and Control*, pp. 77-105.

Fry, J. P., Smith, D. C. P., and Taylor, R. W. [1972b]. "An approach to stored data definition and translation," *Proc. ACM SIGFIDET Workshop on Data Description, Access and Control*, pp. 13-55.

Furtado, A. L., Sevcik, K. C., and dos Santos, C. S. [1979]. "Permitting updates through views of data bases," *Inf. Syst.* 4, pp. 269-283.

Furtado, A. L., dos Santos, C. S., and de Castilho, J. M. V. [1981]. "Dynamic modelling of a simple existence constraint," *Inf. Syst.* 6, pp. 73-80.

Gallaire, H., and Minker, J. (eds.) [1978]. *Logic and Data Bases.* Plenum Press, New York.

Gambino, T. J., and Gerritsen, R. [1977]. "A database design decision support system," *Proc. 3rd Int. Conf. Very Large Data Bases*, pp. 534-544.

Gane, C., and Sarson, T. [1979]. *Structured Systems Analysis: Tools and Techniques.* Prentice-Hall, Englewood Cliffs, NJ.

Gerritsen, R. [1975]. "A preliminary system for the design of DBTG data structures," *Commun. ACM* **18**, pp. 551-557.

Gerritsen, R. [1978]. "Tools for the automation of database design," *Proc. NYU Symp. on Database Design*, pp. 91-97.

Goldberg, A., and Kay, A. (eds.) [1976]. *Smalltalk-72 Instruction Manual.* Tech. Rep. SSL-76-6, Xerox Palo Alto Res. Ctr., Palo Alto, CA.

Goldstein, I. [1980]. *PIE: A Network-based Personal Information Environment.* Xerox Palo Alto Res. Ctr., Palo Alto, CA.

Gould, J. D., and Ascher, R. [1975]. *Use of an IQF-like Query Language by Non-programmers.* Tech. Rep. RC5279, IBM T. J. Watson Res. Ctr., Yorktown Heights, NY.

Graham, G. S. [1978]. "Queueing network models of computer system performance," *ACM Comput. Surv.* **10**, pp. 219-224.

Guttag, J. V. [1975]. *The Specification and Application to Programming of Abstract Data Types.* Ph.D. thesis, Dep. of Comput. Sci., Univ. of Toronto, Toronto.

Guttag, J. V., and Horning, J. J. [1980]. "Formal specification as a design tool," *Proc. Seventh ACM Symp. on Principles of Programming Languages*, pp. 251-261.

Hainaut, J. L., and Lecharlier, B. [1974]. "An extensible semantic model of data base and its data language," *Proc. IFIP Congr. 74*, pp. 1026-1030. North-Holland, Amsterdam.

Hall, P., Owlett, J., and Todd, S. J. P. [1976]. "Relations and entities," in *Modelling in Data Base Management Systems* (Nijssen, G. M., ed.), pp. 201-220. North-Holland, Amsterdam.

Hammer, M. M. [1976]. "Data abstractions for data bases," *Proc. Conf. on Data: Abstraction, Definition and Structure, ACM FDT* **8**(2), pp. 58-59.

Hammer, M. M., and McLeod, D. J. [1975]. "Semantic integrity in a relational data base system," *Proc. 1st Int. Conf. Very Large Data Bases*, pp. 25-47.

Harary, F. [1969]. *Graph Theory.* Addison-Wesley, Reading, MA.

Hardgrave, W. T. [1972]. *Theoretical Aspects of Boolean Operations on Tree Structures and Implications for Generalized Data Management.* TSN-26, Computation Ctr., Univ. of Texas at Austin, Austin, TX.

Hardgrave, W. T. [1981]. "Positional set notation," in *Advances in Database Management 2.* Heyden and Son, New York.

Haseman, W. D., and Whinston, A. B. [1977]. *Introduction to Data Management.* Richard D. Irwin, Homewood, IL.

Hawryszkiewycz, I. T. [1980]. "Alternate implementations of the conceptual schema," *Inf. Syst.* **5**, pp. 203-217.

Hayes, P. J. [1977a]. *Some Association-Based Techniques for Lexical Disambiguation by Machine.* Tech. Rep. 25, Dep. of Comput. Sci., Univ. of Rochester, Rochester, NY.

Hayes, P. J. [1977b]. "On semantic nets, frames and associations," *Proc. 5th Int. Joint Conf. on Artificial Intelligence*, pp. 99-107.

Held, G. D., Stonebraker, M. R., and Wong, E. [1975]. "INGRES — A relational data base system," *Proc. AFIPS NCC* **44**, pp. 409-416.

Hendrix, G. G. [1975a]. *Partitioned Networks for the Mathematical Modeling of Natural Language Semantics.* Tech. Rep. NL-28, Dep. of Comput. Sci., Univ. of Texas at Austin, Austin, TX.

Hendrix, G. G. [1975b]. "Expanding the utility of semantic networks through partitioning," *Proc. 4th Int. Joint Conf. on Artificial Intelligence*, pp. 115-121.

Hendrix, G. G. [1976]. "The representation of semantic knowledge," in *Speech Understanding Research: Final Technical Report* (Walker, D. E., ed.), Chapter 5. Stanford Res. Inst., Menlo Park, CA.

Hendrix, G. G. [1977]. "Some general comments on semantic networks," *Proc. 5th Int. Joint Conf. on Artificial Intelligence*, pp. 984-985.

Hewitt, C. [1973]. "A universal ACTOR formalism for artificial intelligence," *Proc. 3rd Int. Joint Conf. on Artificial Intelligence*, pp. 235-245.

Hill, I. D. [1972]. "Wouldn't it be nice if we could write computer programs in ordinary English — or would it?" *Honeywell Comput. J.* **6**, pp. 76-83.

Hoare, C. A. R. [1972]. "Notes on data structuring," in *Structured Programming* (Dahl, O.-J., Dijkstra, E. W., and Hoare, C. A. R., eds.), pp. 83-174. Academic Press, New York.

Honeyman, P. [1980]. *Functional Dependencies and the Universal Instance Property in the Relational Model of Database Systems.* Ph.D. thesis, Dep. of Electrical Eng. and Comput. Sci., Princeton Univ., Princeton, NJ.

Honeyman, P., Ladner, R. E., and Yannakakis, M. [1980]. "Testing the universal instance assumption," *Inf. Processing Letters* **10**, pp. 14-19.

Honeywell [1975]. *Integrated Data Store/II (IDS/II)* publications: *IDS/II Programmer Reference Manual*, DE09; *IDS/II Data Base Administration Guide*, DE10; *Interactive IDS/II Reference Manual*, DE11; *UFAS (United File Access System)*, DC89; *I/O Supervisor*, DD82; *File Management Supervisor*, DD45. Honeywell Information Systems, Waltham, MA.

Housel, B. C. [1979]. "Pipelining: A technique for implementing data restructurers," *ACM Trans. Database Syst.* **4**, pp. 470-492.

Housel, B. C., and Shu, N. C. [1976]. "A high-level data manipulation language for hierarchical data structures," *Proc. Conf. on Data: Abstraction, Definition and Structure, ACM FDT* **8**(2), pp. 155-169.

Housel, B. C., Smith, D. C. P., Shu, N. C., and Lum, V. Y. [1975]. "DEFINE — A nonprocedural language for defining information easily," *Proc. ACM Pacific 75*, pp. 62-70.

Hsiao, D. K., and Harary, F. [1970]. "A formal system for information retrieval from files," *Commun. ACM* **13**, pp. 67-73.

Hsiao, D. K., and Kannan, K. [1977]. "The architecture of a data base computer — A summary," *Proc. 3rd Workshop on Comput. Architecture for Non-numeric Processing*, pp. 31-34.

IBM [1975]. *Information Management System/Virtual Storage (IMS/VS)* publications: *General Information Manual*, GH20-1260-3; *System/Application Design Guide*, SH20-9025-2; *Application Programming Reference Manual*,

SH20-9026-2; *System Programming Reference Manual*, SH20-9027-2; *Operator's Reference Manual*, SH20-9028-1; *Utilities Reference Manual*, SH20-9030-2. IBM Corp., White Plains, NY.

Iossiphidis, J. [1980]. "A translator to convert the DDL of ERM to the DDL of System 2000," in *Entity-Relationship Approach to Systems Analysis and Design* (Chen, P.P., ed.), pp. 477-504. North-Holland, Amsterdam.

Kahn, B. K. [1976]. "A method for describing information required by the database design process," *Proc. ACM SIGMOD*, pp. 53-64.

Kahn, B. K. [1978]. "A structured logical database design methodology," *Proc. NYU Symp. on Database Design*, pp. 15-24.

Kalinichenko, L. A. [1976]. "Relational-network data structure mapping," in *Modelling in Data Base Management Systems* (Nijssen, G. M., ed.), pp. 303-309. North-Holland, Amsterdam.

Kalinichenko, L. A. [1978]. "Data model transformation method based on axiomatic data model extension," *Proc. 4th Int. Conf. Very Large Data Bases*, pp. 549-555.

Katz, R. H. [1980]. *Database Design and Translation for Multiple Data Models*. Ph.D. thesis, Memo. No. UCB/ERL M80/24, Electronics Res. Lab., College of Eng., Univ. of Calif., Berkeley, CA.

Katz, R. H., and Wong, E. [1981]. "Decompiling CODASYL DML into relational queries," *ACM Trans. Database Syst.*, (in press).

Kent, W. [1976]. *Describing Information (Not Data, Reality?)*. Tech. Rep. 03.012, IBM General Products Div., Palo Alto, CA.

Kent, W. [1978]. *Data and Reality*. North-Holland, Amsterdam.

Kent, W. [1979]. "Limitations of record-oriented information models," *ACM Trans. Database Syst.* **4**, pp. 107-131.

Kerschberg, L., and Pacheco, J. E. S. [1975]. *A Functional Data Base Model*. Monograph Series in Comput. Sci. and Comput. Appl. Dep. de Informatica, Pontificia Univ. Catolica do Rio de Janeiro, Brazil.

Kerschberg, L., Klug, A., and Tsichritzis, D. C. [1976]. "A taxonomy of data models," in *Systems for Large Data Bases* (Lockemann, P. C., and Neuhold, E.J., eds.), pp. 43-64. North-Holland, Amsterdam.

Kerschberg, L., Ting, P. D., and Yao, S. B. [1979]. *Optimal Distributed Query Processing*. Bell Labs, Holmdel, NJ (submitted to *ACM Trans. Database Syst.*).

King, W. F. [1974]. *On the Selection of Indices for a File*. Tech. Rep. RJ1341, IBM Res. Lab., San Jose, CA.

Klug, A. [1978]. *Theory of Database Mappings*. Ph.D. thesis, Dep. of Comput. Sci., Univ. of Toronto, Toronto.

Klug, A. [1980]. "Calculating constraints on relational expressions," *ACM Trans. Database Syst.* **5**, pp. 260-290.

Klug, A. [1981]. *Multiple View, Multiple Data Model Support in the CHEOPS Database Management System*. Tech. Rep. 418, Comput. Sci. Dep., Univ. of Wisconsin-Madison, Madison, WI.

Klug, A., and Tsichritzis, D. C. [1977]. "Multiple view support within the ANSI/SPARC framework," *Proc. 3rd Int. Conf. Very Large Data Bases*, pp. 477-488.

Knuth, D. E. [1968]. *The Art of Computer Programming 1, Fundamental Algorithms.* Addison-Wesley, Reading, MA.

Kornatowski, J. [1979]. *The MRS User's Manual.* Comput. Syst. Res. Group, Univ. of Toronto, Toronto.

Kowalski, R. A. [1974]. "Predicate logic as programming language," *Proc. IFIP Congr. 74*, pp. 569-574. North-Holland, Amsterdam.

Kowalski, R. A. [1979]. "Algorithm=logic+control," *Commun. ACM* **22**, pp. 424-436.

Kroenke, D. [1977]. *Database Processing: Fundamentals, Modeling, Applications.* Science Research Associates, Palo Alto, CA.

Kuhn, M., and Shneiderman, B. [1978]. *Two Experimental Comparisons of Relational and Hierarchical Database Models.* Tech. Rep. 31, Dep. of Inf. Syst. Management, Univ. of Maryland, College Park, MD.

Kuratowski, K., and Mostowski, A. [1975]. *Set Theory.* North-Holland, Amsterdam.

Lam, L. H. [1974]. *Comparison of Three Logical Views of Data in Hospital Information Systems.* M.Sc. thesis, Dep. of Comput. Sci., Univ. of Toronto, Toronto.

Lampson, B. W., Horning, J. J., London, R. L., Mitchell, J. G., and Popek, G. J. [1977]. "Report on the programming language Euclid," *ACM SIGPLAN Notices* **12** (2), pp. 1-79.

Langefors, B. [1963]. "Some approaches to the theory of information systems," *BIT* **3**, pp. 229-254.

Langefors, B. [1969]. "Management information system design," *IAG Quart.* **2** (4), pp. 7-17.

Langefors, B. [1974]. "Information systems," *Proc. IFIP Congr. 74*, pp. 937-945. North-Holland, Amsterdam.

Langefors, B. [1975]. "Control structure and formalized information analysis in an organization," in *Information Systems and Organizational Structure* (Grochla, E., and Szyperski, N., eds.), pp. 311-322. Walter de Gruyter, New York.

Langefors, B. [1977]. "Information systems theory," *Inf. Syst.* **2**, pp. 207-219.

Langefors, B. [1980]. "Infological models and information user views," *Inf. Syst.* **5**, pp. 17-32.

Levesque, H. J. [1981]. *Incompleteness in Knowledge Bases.* Ph.D. thesis, Dep. of Comput. Sci., Univ. of Toronto, Toronto.

Levesque, H. J., and Mylopoulos, J. [1979]. "A procedural semantics for semantic networks," in *Associative Networks* (Findler, N., ed.), pp. 93-120. Academic Press, New York.

Lewis, E. A., Sekino, L. C., and Ting, P. D. [1977]. "A canonical representation for the relational schema and logical data independence," *Proc. COMPSAC 77, IEEE Comput. Software and Appl. Conf.*, pp. 276-280.

Lien, Y. E. [1979]. "Multivalued dependencies with null values in relational data bases," *Proc. 5th Int. Conf. Very Large Data Bases*, pp. 61-74.

Lien, Y. E. [1980]. *On the Equivalence of Database Models*. Database Res. Rep. 3, Bell Labs, Holmdel, NJ.

Lien, Y. E. [1981]. "Hierarchical schemata for relational databases," *ACM Trans. Database Syst.* **6**, pp. 48-69.

Lindencrona-Ohlin, E. [1979]. *A Study On Conceptual Data Modeling*. Ph.D. thesis, Dep. of Comput. Sci., Chalmers Univ. of Technology, Gothenburg, Sweden.

Liskov, B. H., and Zilles, S. N. [1974]. "Programming with abstract data types," *Proc. Symp. on Very High Level Languages, SIGPLAN Notices* **9**(4), pp. 50-59.

Liskov, B. H., and Zilles, S. N. [1975]. "Specification techniques for data abstractions," *Proc. Int. Conf. on Reliable Software, ACM SIGPLAN Notices* **10**(6), pp. 72-87.

Lochovsky, F. H. [1978]. *Data Base Management System User Performance*. Ph.D. thesis, Dep. of Comput. Sci., Univ. of Toronto, Toronto.

Lochovsky, F. H. [1980]. "Human factors issues in office information systems," *Proc. Int. Congr. Applied Syst. Res. and Cybernetics*, Acapulco, Mexico.

Lochovsky, F. H., and Tsichritzis, D. C. [1981]. *Interactive Query Languages for External Data Bases*. Dep. of Communications, Ottawa.

Lockemann, P. C., Mayr, H. C., Weil, W. H., and Wohlleber, W. H. [1979]. "Data abstractions for database systems," *ACM Trans. Database Syst.* **4**, pp. 60-75.

Lomax, J. D. [1978]. *Data Dictionary Systems*. NCC Publications, London, England.

Lowenthal, E. I. [1971]. *A Functional Approach to the Design of Storage Structures for Generalized Data Management Systems*. Ph.D. thesis, Dep. of Comput. Sci., Univ. of Texas at Austin, Austin, TX.

Lucas, H. J., Jr. [1981]. *The Analysis, Design, and Implementation of Information Systems*. McGraw-Hill, New York.

Luk, W. S. [1981]. "On data dependency structures of relational databases," *Inf. Syst.* **6**, pp. 23-29.

Lum, V. Y., Shu, N. C., and Housel, B. C. [1976]. "A general methodology for data conversion and restructuring," *IBM J. Res. Dev.* **20**, pp. 483-497.

Lum, V. Y., et al. [1979]. "1978 New Orleans data base design workshop report," *Proc. 5th Int. Conf. Very Large Data Bases*, pp. 328-350.

Lundeberg, M., Goldkuhl, G., and Nilsson, A. [1979a]. "A systematic approach to information systems development — I. Introduction," *Inf. Syst.* **4**, pp. 1-12.

Lundeberg, M., Goldkuhl, G., and Nilsson, A. [1979b]. "A systematic approach to information systems development — II. Problem and data oriented methodology," *Inf. Syst.* **4**, pp. 93-118.

Lundeberg, M., Goldkuhl, G., and Nilsson, A. [1981]. *Information Systems Development — A Systematic Approach*. Prentice-Hall, Englewood Cliffs, NJ.

Magalhaes, G. [1981]. *Improving the Performance of Data Base Systems.* Ph.D. thesis, Dep. of Comput. Sci., Univ. of Toronto, Toronto.

Maier, D. [1980]. "Discarding the universal instance assumption: Preliminary results," *XP1 Workshop on Relational Database Theory*, Stony Brook, NY.

Maier, D., Mendelzon, A. O., and Sagiv, Y. [1979]. "Testing implications of data dependencies," *ACM Trans. Database Syst.* **4**, pp. 455-469.

Manola, F. [1977]. "The CODASYL data description language: Status and activities, April 1976," in *The ANSI/SPARC DBMS Model* (Jardine, D.A., ed.), pp. 101-129. North-Holland, Amsterdam.

Manola, F. [1978]. "A review of the 1978 CODASYL database specifications," *Proc. 4th Int. Conf. Very Large Data Bases*, pp. 232-242.

March, S. T., and Severance, D. G. [1978]. "A mathematical modeling approach to the automatic selection of database designs," *Proc. ACM SIGMOD*, pp. 52-65.

Martin, J. T. [1975]. *Computer Data-Base Organization.* Prentice-Hall, Englewood Cliffs, NJ.

Martin, W. A. [1977]. "OWL," *Proc. 5th Int. Joint Conf. on Artificial Intelligence*, pp. 985-987.

McDonald, N., and Stonebraker, M. R. [1975]. "CUPID — The friendly query language," *Proc. ACM Pacific 75*, pp. 127-131.

McGee, W. C. [1977]. "The information management system IMS/VS," *IBM Syst. J.* **16**, pp. 84-168.

Melli, L. [1980]. *Conceptual Data Model Methodology.* Internal Rep., Ontario Hydro, Toronto.

Mendelson, E. [1979]. *Introduction to Mathematical Logic*, 2nd ed. D. Van Nostrand, New York.

Mendelzon, A. O. [1979]. "On axiomatizing multivalued dependencies in relational databases," *J. ACM* **26**, pp. 37-44.

Mendelzon, A. O., and Maier, D. [1979]. "Generalized mutual dependencies and the decomposition of database relations," *Proc. 5th Int. Conf. Very Large Data Bases*, pp. 75-82.

Merten, A. G., and Fry, J. P. [1974]. "A data description language approach to file translation," *Proc. ACM SIGMOD*, pp. 191-205.

Metaxides, A. [1975]. "'Information bearing' and 'non-information bearing' sets," in *Data Base Description* (Douque, B. C., and Nijssen, G. M., eds.), pp. 363-368. North-Holland, Amsterdam.

Mills, H. D. [1973]. "On the development of large reliable programs," *IEEE Symp. on Comput. Software Reliability*, pp. 155-159.

Montgomery, C. A. [1972]. "Is natural language an unnatural query language?" *Proc. ACM Natl. Conf.*, pp. 1075-1078.

MRI [1974]. *System 2000* publications: *Reference Manual; Immediate Access Feature; Procedural Language Feature — COBOL; Procedural Language Feature — FORTRAN; Procedural Language Feature — PL/1; Report Writer Feature; Diagnostic Messages.* MRI Systems Corp., Austin, TX.

Mylopoulos, J., and Wong, H. K. T. [1980]. "Some features of the TAXIS data model," *Proc. 6th Int. Conf. Very Large Data Bases*, pp. 399-410.

Mylopoulos, J., Borgida, A., Cohen, P., Roussopoulos, N., Tsotsos, J., and Wong, H. K. T. [1976]. "TORUS: A step towards bridging the gap between data bases and the casual user," *Inf. Syst.* 2, pp. 71-77.

Mylopoulos, J., Bernstein, P. A., and Wong, H. K. T. [1980]. "A language facility for designing database-intensive applications," *ACM Trans. Database Syst.* 5, pp. 185-207.

Nakamura, F., Yoshida, I., and Kondo, H. [1975]. "A simulation model for data base system performance evaluation," *Proc. AFIPS NCC* 44, pp.459-465.

Nash-Webber, B., and Reiter, R. [1977]. "Anaphora and logical form: On formal meaning representations for natural language," *Proc. 5th Int. Joint Conf. on Artificial Intelligence*, pp. 121-131.

Navathe, S. B. [1976]. *A Methodology for Generalized Database Restructuring.* Ph.D. thesis, Grad. School of Bus. Admin., Univ. of Michigan, Ann Arbor, MI.

Navathe, S. B. [1977]. *ADMIRE: A Data Model to Incorporate Restructuring Effectively.* Grad. School of Bus., New York Univ., New York.

Navathe, S. B. [1980a]. "Schema analysis for database restructuring," *ACM Trans. Database Syst.* 5, pp. 157-184.

Navathe, S. B. [1980b]. "An intuitive approach to normalize network structured data," *Proc. 6th Int. Conf. Very Large Data Bases*, pp. 350-358.

Navathe, S. B., and Fry, J. P. [1976]. "Restructuring for large databases: Three levels of abstraction," *ACM Trans. Database Syst.* 1, pp. 138-158.

Navathe, S. B., and Merten, A. G. [1974]. "Investigation into the application of the relational model to data translation," *Proc. ACM SIGMOD*, pp. 123-138.

Navathe, S. B., and Schkolnick, M. [1978]. "View representation in logical data base design," *Proc. ACM SIGMOD*, pp. 144-156.

Nicolas, J. M. [1978a]. "First order logic formalization for functional, multivalued and mutual dependencies," *Proc. ACM SIGMOD*, pp. 40-51.

Nicolas, J. M. [1978b]. "Mutual dependencies and some results on undecomposable relations," *Proc. 4th Int. Conf. Very Large Data Bases*, pp. 360-367.

Nijssen, G. M. [1975]. "Set and CODASYL set or coset," in *Data Base Description* (Douque, B. C., and Nijssen, G. M., eds.), pp. 1-70. North-Holland, Amsterdam.

Nijssen, G. M. [1976]. "A gross architecture for the next generation database management systems," in *Modelling in Data Base Management Systems* (Nijssen, G. M., ed.), pp. 1-24. North-Holland, Amsterdam.

Nijssen, G. M. [1977]. "Current issues in conceptual schema," in *Architecture and Models in Data Base Management Systems* (Nijssen, G. M., ed.), pp. 31-65. North-Holland, Amsterdam.

Olle, T. W. [1974]. "Data definition spectrum and procedurality spectrum in data base management systems," in *Data Base Management* (Klimbie, J. W., and Koffeman, K. L., eds.), pp. 289-293. North-Holland, Amsterdam.

Olle, T. W. [1979]. *Equivalence of Alternative Conceptual Schema Models.* T. William Olle Associates, Ltd., Surrey, England.

Osborn, S. L. [1978]. *Testing for Existence of a Covering Boyce-Codd Normal Form.* Comput. Sci. Dep., Univ. of Western Ontario, London.

Ozkarahan, E. A., Schuster, S. A., and Smith, K. C. [1975]. "RAP: An associative processor for data base management," *Proc. AFIPS NCC* **44**, pp. 379-387.

Paolini, P., and Pelagatti, G. [1977]. "Formal definition of mappings in a data base," *Proc. ACM SIGMOD*, pp. 40-46.

Pelagatti, G., Paolini, P., and Bracchi, G. [1978]. "Mapping external views to a common data model," *Inf. Syst.* **3**, pp. 141-151.

Philips [1974]. *Philips Host Language System (PHOLAS)* publications: *Introduction to PHOLAS*, publ. no. 5122 991 25221; *System and Operations*, publ. no. 5122 991 26071; *Schema DDL and SSL*, publ. no. 5122 991 25841; *Sub-Schema DDL and DML*, publ. no. 5122 991 25861. Philips Electrologica B.V., Amsterdam.

Pirotte, A. [1977]. "The entity-property-association model: An information oriented data base model," *Proc. Int. Comput. Symp..* North-Holland, Amsterdam.

Quillian, M. R. [1968]. "Semantic memory," in *Semantic Information Processing* (Minsky, M., ed.), pp. 227-270. MIT Press, Cambridge, MA.

Ramirez, J. A., Rin, N. A., and Prywes, N. S. [1974]. "Automatic generation of data conversion programs using a data description language," *Proc. ACM SIGMOD*, pp. 207-225.

Raphael, B. [1968]. "SIR: Semantic information retrieval," in *Semantic Information Processing* (Minsky, M., ed.), pp. 33-145. MIT Press, Cambridge, MA.

Reisner, P. [1977]. "Use of psychological experimentation as an aid to development of a query language," *IEEE Trans. Software Eng.* **3**, pp. 218-229.

Reisner, P. [1981]. "Human factors studies of database query languages: A survey and assessment," *ACM Comput. Surv.* **13**, pp. 13-31.

Reisner, P., Boyce, R. F., and Chamberlin, D. D. [1975]. "Human factors evaluation of two data base query languages — SQUARE and SEQUEL," *Proc. AFIPS NCC* **44**, pp. 447-452.

Reiter, R. [1978]. "On closed world databases," in *Logic and Data Bases* (Gallaire, H., and Minker, J., eds.), pp. 55-76. Plenum Press, New York.

Rissanen, J. [1977]. "Independent components of relations," *ACM Trans. Database Syst.* **2**, pp. 317-325.

Rodriguez-Rosell, J. [1976]. "Empirical data reference behavior in data base systems," *Comput.* **9**, pp. 9-13.

Ross, R. G. [1978]. *Data Base Systems: Design, Implementation, and Management.* Amacom, New York.

Rothnie, J. B., and Hardgrave, W. T. [1976]. *Data Model Theory: A Beginning.* Tech. Rep. 10, Dep. of Inf. Syst. Management, Univ. of Maryland, College Park, MD.

Rothnie, J. B., et al. [1980]. "Introduction to a system for distributed databases (SDD-1)," *ACM Trans. Database Syst.* **5**, pp. 1-17.

Roussopoulos, N. [1976]. *A Semantic Network Model for Data Bases.* Ph.D. thesis, Dep. of Comput. Sci., Univ. of Toronto, Toronto.

Roussopoulos, N., and Mylopoulos, J. [1975]. "Using semantic networks for data base management," *Proc. 1st Int. Conf. Very Large Data Bases*, pp. 144-172.

RSI [1980]. *Oracle* publications: *Introduction* — Version 1.5; *Users' Guide* — Version 2.2. Relational Software Inc., Menlo Park, CA.

Rustin, R. (ed.) [1974]. *Data Models: Data-Structure-Set versus Relational, Proc. ACM SIGMOD.* ACM, New York.

Sadri, F., and Ullman, J. D. [1980]. "A complete axiomatization for a large class of dependencies in relational databases," *Proc. 12th ACM Symp. on Theory of Comput.*, pp. 117-122.

Sagiv, Y. [1981]. "Can we use the universal instance assumption without using nulls?." *Proc. ACM SIGMOD*, pp. 108-120.

Sakai, H. [1980]. "A unified approach to the logical design of a hierarchical data model," in *Entity-Relationship Approach to Systems Analysis and Design* (Chen, P.P., ed.), pp. 61-74. North-Holland, Amsterdam.

Schkolnick, M. [1975]. "The optimal selection of secondary indices for files," *Inf. Syst.* **1**, pp. 141-146.

Schkolnick, M. [1978]. "Physical database design techniques," *Proc. NYU Symp. on Database Design*, pp. 99-109.

Schmid, H. A. [1977]. "An analysis of some constructs for conceptual models," in *Architecture and Models in Data Base Management Systems* (Nijssen, G. M., ed.), pp. 119-148. North-Holland, Amsterdam.

Schmid, H. A., and Swenson, J. R. [1975]. "On the semantics of the relational data model," *Proc. ACM SIGMOD*, pp. 211-223.

Schmidt, J. W. [1977]. "Some high level language constructs for data of type relation," *ACM Trans. Database Syst.* **2**, pp. 247-267.

Schmidt, J. W. [1978]. "Type concepts for database definition," in *Databases: Improving Usability and Responsiveness* (Shneiderman, B., ed.), pp. 215-244. Academic Press, New York.

Schubert, L. K. [1976]. "Extending the expressive power of semantic networks," *Artificial Intelligence* **7**, pp. 163-198.

Sciore, E. [1980]. *The Universal Instance and Database Design.* Tech. Rep. 271, Dep. of Electrical Eng. and Comput. Sci., Princeton Univ., Princeton, NJ.

Sciore, E. [1981]. "Real-world MVD's," *Proc. ACM SIGMOD*, pp. 121-132.

Selinger, P. G., Astrahan, M. M., Chamberlin, D. D., Lorie, R. A., and Price, T. G. [1979]. "Access path selection in a relational database management system," *Proc. ACM SIGMOD*, pp. 23-34.

Senko, M. E. [1975]. "Information systems: records, relations, set, entities, and things," *Inf. Syst.* **1**, pp. 3-13.

Senko, M. E. [1976]. "DIAM as a detailed example of the ANSI SPARC architecture," in *Modelling in Data Base Management Systems* (Nijssen, G. M., ed.), pp. 73-94. North-Holland, Amsterdam.

Senko, M. E. [1977]. "Data structures and data accessing in database systems past, present and future," *IBM Syst. J.* **16**, pp. 208-257.

Senko, M. E., Lum, V. Y., and Owens, P. J. [1968]. "A file organization evaluation model (FOREM)," *Proc. IFIP Congr. 68*, pp. C19-C28. North-Holland, Amsterdam.

Senko, M. E., Altman, E. B., Astrahan, M. M., and Fehder, P. L. [1973]. "Data structures and accessing in data-base systems," *IBM Syst. J.* **12**, pp. 30-93.

Sevcik, K. C. [1981]. "Data base system performance prediction using an analytical model," *Proc. 7th Int. Conf. Very Large Data Bases.*

Sevcik, K. C., and Furtado, A. L. [1978]. "Complete and compatible sets of update operations," *Proc. ICMOD 78 Conf.*, pp. 247-260.

Severance, D. G. [1975]. "A parametric model of alternative file structures," *Inf. Syst.* **1**, pp. 51-56.

Shneiderman, B. [1978]. "Improving the human factors aspect of database interactions," *ACM Trans. Database Syst.* **3**, pp. 417-439.

Shneiderman, B., and Thomas, G. [1979]. *Automatic Database System Conversion I: Data Definition and Manipulation Facilities.* Tech. Rep. 820, Dep. of Comput. Sci., Univ. of Maryland, College Park, MD.

Shneiderman, B., and Thomas, G. [1980a]. *Pure Database System Report: A Transformation Language Approach to Automatic Schema, Stored Data and Program Conversion.* Tech. Rep. 880, Dep. of Comput. Sci., Univ. of Maryland, College Park, MD.

Shneiderman, B., and Thomas, G. [1980b]. "Path expressions for complex queries and automatic database program conversion," *Proc. 6th Int. Conf. Very Large Data Bases*, pp. 33-44.

Shneiderman, B., and Thomas, G. [1980c]. *An Architecture for Automatic Relational Database System Conversion.* Tech. Rep. 969, Dep. of Comput. Sci., Univ. of Maryland, College Park, MD.

Shoshani, A. [1975]. "A logical-level approach to database conversion," *Proc. ACM SIGMOD*, pp. 112-122.

Shoshani, A. [1978]. *CABLE: A Language Based on the Entity-relationship Model.* Lawrence Berkeley Lab., Berkeley, CA.

Shu, N. C., Housel, B. C., and Lum,, V. Y. [1975]. "A high level translation definition language for data conversion," *Commun. ACM* **18**, pp. 557-567.

Shu, N. C., Housel, B. C., Taylor, R. W., Ghosh, S. P., and Lum, V. Y. [1977]. "EXPRESS: A data extraction, processing, and restructuring system," *ACM Trans. Database Syst.* **2**, pp. 134-174.

Sibley, E. H. [1980]. *Very Large Data Base Systems.* Dep. of Inf. Syst. Management, Univ. of Maryland, College Park, MD.

Sibley, E. H., and Hardgrave, W. T. [1977]. "Data model theory and positional set processing," in *Data Models and Database Systems, Proc. Joint U.S.-U.S.S.R. Seminar* (Dale, A. G., and Suvorov, B.P., eds.), pp. 5-71. Inst. for Comput. Sci. and Comput. Appl., The Univ. of Texas at Austin, Austin, TX.

Sibley, E. H., and Taylor, R. W. [1973]. "A data definition and mapping language," *Commun. ACM* **16**, pp. 750-759.

Simmons, R. F. [1973]. "Semantic networks: Their computation and use for understanding English sentences," in *Computer Models of Thought and Language* (Schank, R. C., and Colby, R. F., eds.), pp. 63-113. W. H. Freeman, San Francisco.

Smith, A. J. [1978]. "Sequentiality and prefetching in database systems," *ACM Trans. Database Syst.* **3**, pp. 223-247.

Smith, D. C. P. [1972]. "A method for data translation using the stored data definition and translation task group languages," *Proc. ACM SIGFIDET Workshop on Data Description, Access and Control*, pp. 107-127.

Smith, J. M., and Smith, D. C. P. [1977a]. "Database abstractions: Aggregation and generalization," *ACM Trans. Database Syst.* **2**, pp. 105-133.

Smith, J. M., and Smith, D. C. P. [1977b]. "Database abstractions: Aggregation," *Commun. ACM* **20**, pp. 405-413.

Smith, J. M., and Smith, D. C. P. [1977c]. *Integrated Specifications for Abstract Systems.* Tech. Rep. UUCS-77-112, Comput. Sci. Dep., Univ. of Utah, Salt Lake City, UT.

Smith, J. M., and Smith, D. C. P. [1978]. "Principles of database conceptual design," *Proc. NYU Symp. on Database Design*, pp. 35-49.

Software AG [1971]. *ADABAS* publications: *General Information Manual; Reference Manual; Utilities Manual.* Software AG, Reston, VA.

Sperry Univac [1973]. *UNIVAC 1100 Series, Data Management System (DMS 1100)* publications: *Schema Definition, Data Administrator Reference, American National Standard COBOL (Fielddata), Data Manipulation Language, Programmer Reference.* Sperry Rand Corp., Blue Bell, PA.

Spyratos, N. [1980]. "Translation structures of relational views," *Proc. 6th Int. Conf. Very Large Data Bases*, pp. 411-416.

Stonebraker, M. R. [1975]. "Implementation of integrity constraints and views by query modification," *Proc. ACM SIGMOD*, pp. 65-78.

Stonebraker, M. R., Wong, E., and Kreps, P. [1976]. "The design and implementation of INGRES," *ACM Trans. Database Syst.* **1**, pp. 189-222.

Sundgren, B. [1974]. "Conceptual foundation of the infological approach to data bases," in *Data Base Management* (Klimbie, J. W., and Koffeman, K. L., eds.), pp. 61-96. North-Holland, Amsterdam.

Sundgren, B. [1975]. *Theory of Data Bases.* Mason/Charter, New York.

Sundgren, B. [1978]. "Data base design in theory and practice: Towards an integrated methodology," *Proc. 4th Int. Conf. Very Large Data Bases*, pp. 3-16.

Swartwout, D. [1977]. "An access path specification language for restructuring network databases," *Proc. ACM SIGMOD*, pp. 88-101.

Taggart, W. M., Jr., and Tharp, M. O. [1977]. "A survey of information requirements analysis techniques," *ACM Comput. Surv.* **9**, pp. 273-290.

Taylor, R. W., and Frank, R. L. [1976]. "CODASYL data-base management systems," *ACM Comput. Surv.* **8**, pp. 67-103.

Taylor, R. W., Fry, J. P., Shneiderman, B., Smith, D. C. P., and Su, S. Y. W. [1979]. "Database program conversion: A framework for research," *Proc. 5th Int. Conf. Very Large Data Bases*, pp. 299-312.

Teichroew, D., and Hershey, E. A., III [1977]. "PSL/PSA: A computer-aided technique for structured documentation and analysis of information processing systems," *IEEE Trans. Software Eng.* 3, pp. 41-48.

Teorey, T. J., and Das, K. S. [1976]. "Application of an analytical model to evaluate storage structures," *Proc. ACM SIGMOD*, pp. 9-20.

Teorey, T. J., and Fry, J. P. [1980]. "The logical record access approach to database design," *ACM Comput. Surv.* 12, pp. 179-211.

Thomas, G., and Shneiderman, B. [1979]. *Automatic Database System Conversion II: A Transformation Language.* Tech. Rep. 821, Dep. of Comput. Sci., Univ. of Maryland, College Park, MD.

Thomas, G., and Shneiderman, B. [1980]. "Automatic database system conversion: A transformation language approach to sub-schema implementation," *Proc. COMPSAC 80, IEEE Comput. Software and Appl. Conf.*, pp. 80-88.

Thomas, J. C. [1977]. "Psychological issues in data base management," *Proc. 3rd Int. Conf. Very Large Data Bases*, pp. 165-185.

Thomas, J. C., and Gould, J. D. [1975]. "A psychological study of query by example," *Proc. AFIPS NCC* 44, pp. 439-445.

Todd, S. J. P. [1975]. *Peterlee Relational Test Vehicle PRTV, A Technical Overview.* IBM UK Scientific Centre Report UKSC-0075, Peterlee, England.

Todd, S. J. P. [1977]. "Automatic constraint maintenance and updating defined relations," *Proc. IFIP Congr.* 77, pp. 145-148. North-Holland, Amsterdam.

Tsichritzis, D. C. [1975a]. "A network framework for relational implementation," in *Data Base Description* (Douque, B. C., and Nijssen, G. M., eds.), pp. 269-282. North-Holland, Amsterdam.

Tsichritzis, D. C. [1975b]. *Features of a Conceptual Schema.* Tech. Rep. CSRG-56, Comput. Syst. Res. Group, Univ. of Toronto, Toronto.

Tsichritzis, D. C. [1976]. "LSL: A link and selector language," *Proc. ACM SIGMOD*, pp. 123-133.

Tsichritzis, D. C., and Klug, A. (eds.) [1978]. "The ANSI/X3/SPARC DBMS framework report of the study group on database management systems," *Inf. Syst.* 3, pp. 173-191.

Tsichritzis, D. C., and Lochovsky, F. H. [1976]. "Hierarchical data-base management: A survey," *ACM Comput. Surv.* 8, pp. 67-103.

Tsichritzis, D. C., and Lochovsky, F. H. [1977]. *Data Base Management Systems.* Academic Press, New York.

Tsichritzis, D. C., and Lochovsky, F. H. [1978]. "Designing the data base," *Datamation* 24(8), pp. 147-151.

Tsichritzis, D. C., and Wladawsky, I. [1979]. "Staging large data bases in memory hierarchies," in *A Panache of DBMS Ideas II* (Lochovsky, F. H., ed.), pp. 180-197. Tech. Rep. CSRG-101, Comput. Syst. Res. Group, Univ. of Toronto, Toronto.

Ullman, J. D. [1980]. *Principles of Database Systems.* Computer Science Press, Potomac, MD.

Vassiliou, Y. [1980a]. *A Formal Treatment of Imperfect Information in Database Management.* Ph.D. thesis, Dep. of Comput. Sci., Univ. of Toronto, Toronto.

Vassiliou, Y. [1980b]. "Functional dependencies and incomplete information," *Proc. 6th Int. Conf. Very Large Data Bases,* pp. 260-269.

Vassiliou, Y., and Lochovsky, F. H. [1980]. "DBMS transaction translation," *Proc. COMPSAC 80, IEEE Comput. Software and Appl. Conf.,* pp. 89-96.

Vorhaus, A., and Mills, R. [1967]. *The Time-Shared Data Management System: A New Approach to Data Management.* Tech. Memo. SP-2634, System Development Corp., Santa Monica, CA.

Walker, W. A. [1981]. "Experience in data modelling at Ontario Hydro," *Guide 52,* Atlanta.

Wasserman, A. I. [1979]. "The data management facilities of PLAIN," *Proc. ACM SIGMOD,* pp. 60-70.

Wegbreit, B. [1974]. "The treatment of data types in EL1," *Commun. ACM* **17,** pp. 251-264.

Weizenbaum, J. [1976]. *Computer Power and Human Reason.* W. H. Freeman, San Francisco.

Weldon, J.-L. [1981]. *Data Base Administration.* Plenum Press, New York.

Welty, C., and Stemple, D. W. [1981]. "Human factors comparison of a procedural and a nonprocedural query language," *ACM Trans. Database Syst.,* (in press).

Wiederhold, G. [1977]. *Database Design.* McGraw-Hill, New York.

Winston, P. H. [1970]. *Learning Structural Descriptions from Examples.* Tech. Rep. 76, Project MAC, MIT.

Winters, E. W., and Dickey, A. F. [1976]. "A business application of data translation," *Proc. ACM SIGMOD,* pp. 189-196.

Wirth, N. [1971]. "Program development by stepwise refinement," *Commun. ACM* **14,** pp. 221-227.

Wong, E. [1977]. "Retrieving dispersed data from SDD-1: A system for distributed databases," *Proc. 2nd Berkeley Workshop on Distributed Data Management and Comput. Networks,* pp. 217-235.

Wong, E., and Youssefi, K. A. A. [1976]. "Decomposition — A strategy for query processing," *ACM Trans. Database Syst.* **1,** pp. 223-241.

Wong, H. K. T., and Mylopoulos, J. [1977]. "Two views of data semantics: A survey of data models in artificial intelligence and database management," *INFOR* **15,** pp. 344-383.

Woods, W. A. [1975]. "What's in a link? Foundations for semantic networks," in *Representation and Understanding* (Bobrow, D. G., and Collins, A.M., eds.), pp. 35-82. Academic Press, New York.

Wulf, W. A., and Shaw, M. [1973]. "Global variable considered harmful," *ACM SIGPLAN Notices* **8**(2), pp. 28-34.

Yamaguchi, K., and Merten, A. G. [1974]. "Methodology for transferring programs and data," *Proc. ACM SIGMOD*, pp. 141-155.

Yao, S. B. [1977]. "An attribute based model for data base access cost analysis," *ACM Trans. Database Syst.* **2**, pp. 45-67.

Yao, S. B., and DeJong, D. [1978]. "Evaluation of database access paths," *Proc. ACM SIGMOD*, pp. 66-77.

Yao, S. B., Navathe, S. B., and Weldon, J.-L. [1978]. "An integrated approach to logical database design," *Proc. NYU Symp. on Database Design*, pp. 1-14.

Yourdon, E., and Constantine, L. L. [1979]. *Structured Design: Fundamentals of a Discipline of Computer Program and Systems Design.* Prentice-Hall, Englewood Cliffs, NJ.

Youssefi, K. A. A. [1978]. *Query Processing for a Relational Database System.* Ph.D. thesis, Memo. No. UCB/ERL M78/3, Electronics Res. Lab., College of Eng., Univ. of Calif., Berkeley, CA.

Zahle, T. U. [1978]. "SCAN — A simple record at-a-time DML for the relational data model," *Proc. ICMOD 78 Conf.*, pp. 115-126.

Zaniolo, C. [1979a]. "Design of relational views over network schemas," *Proc. ACM SIGMOD*, pp. 179-190.

Zaniolo, C. [1979b]. "Multimodel external schemas for CODASYL data base management systems," in *Data Base Architecture* (Bracchi, G., and Nijssen, G. M., eds.), pp. 157-176. North-Holland, Amsterdam.

Zaniolo, C., and Melkanoff, M. A. [1981]. "On the design of relational database schemata," *ACM Trans. Database Syst.* **6**, pp. 1-47.

Zloof, M. M. [1975a]. "Query by example," *Proc. AFIPS NCC* **44**, pp. 431-438.

Zloof, M. M. [1975b]. "Query by example: The invocation and definition of tables and forms," *Proc. 1st Int. Conf. Very Large Data Bases*, pp. 1-24.

# INDEX

366